The Global Studies Reader

Introduced and Edited by

MANFRED B. STEGER
University of Hawai'i–Mānoa

SECOND EDITION

New York   Oxford

OXFORD UNIVERSITY PRESS

Oxford University Press is a department of the University of Oxford. It furthers the University's objective of excellence in research, scholarship, and education by publishing worldwide.

Oxford   New York
Auckland   Cape Town   Dar es Salaam   Hong Kong   Karachi
Kuala Lumpur   Madrid   Melbourne   Mexico City   Nairobi
New Delhi   Shanghai   Taipei   Toronto

With offices in
Argentina   Austria   Brazil   Chile   Czech Republic   France   Greece
Guatemala   Hungary   Italy   Japan   Poland   Portugal   Singapore
South Korea   Switzerland   Thailand   Turkey   Ukraine   Vietnam

For titles covered by Section 112 of the US Higher Education
Opportunity Act, please visit www.oup.com/us/he for the
latest information about pricing and alternate formats.

Published in the United States of America by
Oxford University Press
198 Madison Avenue, New York, NY 10016
http://www.oup.com

Library of Congress Cataloging-in-Publication Data
The global studies reader / introduced and edited by Manfred B. Steger,
University of Hawai'i-Manoa.
       pages cm
   Includes index.
   ISBN 978-0-19-933846-7 (alk. paper)
 1. Globalization. I. Steger, Manfred B., 1961- , author, editor of compilation.
   JZ1318.G55894 2015
   303.48'2--dc23

                                                              2014012435

Printing number: 9 8 7 6 5 4 3 2 1

Printed in the United States of America
on acid-free paper

*To my students at the University
of Hawai'i–Mānoa and RMIT University.*

CONTENTS

PREFACE

"Globalization" rules the public discourse of the early twenty-first century as one of its most powerful buzzwords. Since the 1990s, it has been gripping the imagination of billions of people around the world who find themselves witnesses to one of the most rapid social and environmental transformations in human history. Regardless of our geographic location and occupation, most of us have by now formed some opinion about the nature of globalization and its impact on local settings. Indeed, many people hold strong views about whether today's unprecedented intensification of global interdependence should be seen as a "good" or a "bad" thing.

As someone interested in this book, you are likely to be more open to sampling some expert perspectives before coming to a firm opinion about globalization. As discussed in some detail in the introduction to this book, there are several influential views on the subject. "Globalizers," for example, consider the integration of global markets and the concurrent demise of the modern nation-state system a foregone conclusion. "Skeptics" question the extent and significance of globalization. "Modifiers" acknowledge the potent forces of globalization but doubt the alleged novelty of planetary interdependence. And finally, a dwindling number of "rejectionists" dismiss trendy globalization talk as nothing more than "globaloney." Regardless of your preliminary views, you surely stand to benefit from a close reading of crucial academic writings that define the new and rapidly growing transdisciplinary field of "global studies" dedicated to the study of globalization.

But this is where the problem starts. Where can you find such an authoritative yet accessible collection of writings produced by first-rate global studies scholars? Although thousands of academic books and journal articles on globalization have been published since the early 1990s, none have taken the explicit form of a manageable *Global Studies Reader*. The few specific "globalization readers" are rather eclectic collections, often mixing terse journalistic pieces with dense academic articles, tedious policy reports with fiery declarations of principles, and detached social-scientific treatises with engaged polemics. In addition, most of these readers tend to cram dozens of writings on all conceivable aspects of globalization into hundreds of pages of text, subdivided into a dozen sections, and headed by intricate introductions.

Fortunately, you need not look any further, for you are already holding the solution to the problem in your hands! The three basic ideas behind the creation of *The Global Studies Reader* are simple. First, it contains an accessible introduction to globalization that will give you a better understanding of what constitutes global studies—the transdisciplinary field dedicated to the study of globalization. Thus, this reader has been carefully designed to provide a representative selection of transdisciplinary writings appropriate for undergraduate students in global studies. Secondly, this book brings together in a single midsize volume some of the best pieces on the subject written by recognized scholars. Third, these twenty seminal contributions have been kept to an easily digestible length while at the same time covering the major dimensions of globalization: politics and societies; economies and technologies; cultures and histories; and spaces and environments.

Although *The Global Studies Reader* purposely contains no additional sectional introductions that might interrupt the conceptual flow of the writings, it offers at the end of each of its four parts five discussion points designed to help clarify the authors' arguments and to stimulate further conversation. You will also find suggestions for additional readings and recommended websites to guide your further research. In a way, the principles of this reader are based on the efforts of record companies to produce high-quality selections of representative songs by popular solo artists and bands that have been making music for decades. Thus, we enjoy listening to the Foo Fighters' "Greatest Hits," "The Best" of Michael Jackson, "The Very Best" of Prince, "Number 1 Hits" of the Beatles, and so on. I readily concede that choosing the "best" of anything always remains a very subjective and incomplete endeavor—in addition to being a rather contentious task. After all, at some point in our lives, haven't we all wondered why a supposed "Greatest Hits of . . ." album did not include our favorite song? Invariably, some of you will be disappointed in the inclusion or omission of a selection for that very reason. However, I trust that, in addition to finding several top-notch writings in a single collection, most of you will enjoy exploring unfamiliar pieces of striking clarity and obvious significance.

NEW TO THIS EDITION

Taking into consideration excellent feedback and suggestions from users of *Globalization, The Greatest Hits: A Global Studies Reader,* I determined to produce in this book a more accessible and teachable edition. To this end, I engaged in a wholesale rewriting and restructuring of that work. The result is a new volume that contains

- Fifteen new chapters, specifically selected for undergraduate students in introductory global studies courses and beyond (Chapters 2–3; 5–6; 8–10; 12–15; 17–20).

- Four *thematically* (rather than *chronologically*) structured parts that cover the main dimensions of globalization: Politics and Societies; Economies and Technologies; Cultures and Histories; and Spaces and Environments.
- At the end of each part, students are provided with discussion points and a Guide to Further Readings that also includes a list of recommended websites.
- Finally, and most importantly, a brand-new introduction, "What Is Global Studies?", which offers an accessible overview of the main features and perspectives of the growing transdisciplinary field of global studies.

ACKNOWLEDGMENTS

It is a pleasant duty to record my debts of gratitude. I want to thank my colleagues and friends at the University of Hawai'i–Mānoa and the Royal Melbourne Institute of Technology (RMIT University) for their steady intellectual encouragement. I appreciate the engagement of many academic colleagues from around the world who have channeled much of their enthusiasm for the study of globalization into the development of the Global Studies Consortium, a transcontinental professional organization dedicated to strengthening the new transdisciplinary field of Global Studies (http://globalstudiesconsortium.org).

I also want to express my gratitude to numerous readers, reviewers, and audiences around the world, who, for nearly two decades, have made insightful comments in response to my public lectures and publications on the subject of globalization. Reviewers include Richard Bownas, University of Northern Colorado; Roberto E. Campo, University of North Carolina–Greensboro; Dan Cassino, Fairleigh Dickinson University; Chris J. Dolan, Lebanon Valley College; Lisa Laverty, Eastern Michigan University; Amentahru Wahlrab, University of Texas at Tyler; and Sharon R. Wesoky, Allegheny College. I want to thank Jeff Berlin, my research assistant at the University of Hawai'i–Mānoa, for helping me to organize relevant materials. Jennifer Carpenter and Maegan Sherlock, my editors at Oxford University Press, have been shining examples of professionalism and competence. Finally, I want to thank my wife, Perle, for her important editorial support. Many people have contributed to improving the quality of this book; its remaining flaws are my own responsibility.

INTRODUCTION

What Is Global Studies?

We live in an unprecedented age of connectivity brought about by globalization—the latest and most intense phase in the age-old human story of expanding and multiplying social relations across world-time and world-space. The rising global imaginary is reflected in the proliferation of novel terms such as "glocalization," "globality," "globish," "creolization," "McDonaldization," "McWorld," "hybridity," "outsourcing," and so on. New technologies facilitate the movement of people, goods, services, money, ideas, and culture across political borders more easily and more quickly than ever before. Despite the growing mountain of digitalized "information" readily accessible in real time to billions around the world, globalization has unsettled people's familiar frames of reference. New sources of insecurity and disruption are reflected in a public discourse that increasingly revolves around "global problems" such as transnational terrorism, pandemics like AIDS or H1N1, the global financial crisis, the Eurozone debt crisis, the planetary climate crisis, and the food crisis in the Global South. And these are but the most prominent entries in a long list of global challenges that reach deeply into every aspect of daily life.

Responding to these global issues effectively requires the generation and implementation of new ideas that goes beyond the traditional academic framework of the twentieth century. In particular, we need to gain a better understanding of how the local has become entangled with the global in myriad ways that profoundly shape how we live our daily lives in the twenty-first century. This imperative to grasp the complex dynamics of globalization stands at the very center of new transdisciplinary efforts to reorder human knowledge and create innovate learning environments. Yet, many scholars in the social sciences and humanities have been struggling to make sense of these enormous global reconfigurations. Even after two decades of intense scholarly exploration, globalization has remained a hotly contested and surprisingly slippery concept. Academics remain divided on their assessments of the extent, impact, and direction of globalization. Still, it might be helpful to assign the voices in the ongoing academic debate to four distinct "camps" or perspectives: globalizers, rejectionists, skeptics, and modifiers. Let us examine these influential outlooks in more detail.

FOUR PERSPECTIVES ON GLOBALIZATION

Globalizers argue that globalization is a profoundly transformative set of social processes that is moving us into an entirely novel chapter of human history. While conceding that globalization is not a single monolithic process but a complex and often contradictory dynamic of simultaneous social integration and fragmentation, they insist that research clearly points to the existence of significant worldwide flows that can be appropriately subsumed under the general term "globalization." To be sure, some of the more extreme globalizers could be labeled "hyperglobalizers," for they see globalization as the main driver of nearly all of social change today. But more moderate globalizers are reluctant to embrace such sweeping generalizations and overarching "grand narratives," opting instead for less sweeping approaches designed to provide specific explanations of particular manifestations of globalization. Still, the representatives of this perspective are united in their conviction that globalization is highly significant, empirically "real," and truly global in its reach and impact.

Rejectionists contend that most of these accounts offered by globalizers are incorrect and exaggerated. They note that just about everything that can be linked to some transnational process is cited as evidence for globalization and its growing influence. Considering "globalization" a prime example of a big idea resting on slim foundations, they claim that the term could be associated with anything from the Internet to a hamburger. Suspecting that such generalizations often amount to little more than "globaloney," rejectionists dismiss the utility of "globalization" for scientific academic discourse. Charging that the term obscures more than it illuminates, they suggest breaking the concept of globalization into smaller, more manageable parts because these could be more easily linked to processes in the "real world." However, as recent empirical studies have provided more evidence for the globalizers' perspective, the number of dyed-in-the-wool rejectionists has dramatically dwindled.

The third camp consists of *skeptics* who acknowledge some forms and manifestations of globalization, but also emphasize the limited nature of current globalizing processes. Some skeptical political economists, for example, claim that the world economy is not a truly global phenomenon, but one centered on Europe, East Asia, and North America. Insisting that the majority of economic activity around the world still remains primarily national in origin and scope, they utilize data on trade, foreign direct investment, and financial flows that appear to limit increased levels of economic interaction to advanced industrial countries. Without a truly global economic system, these skeptics insist, there can be no such thing as "globalization." Hence, they argue that globalization—as conceived by most globalizers—is largely a myth.

In response, globalizers have repeatedly pointed to two major problems with the skeptics' position. First, they accuse them of setting overly high standards for the world economy to be counted as "fully globalized." Second, globalizers charge that projecting such a utopian model of a perfectly globalized economy unnecessarily polarizes the topic by pressuring people to either completely embrace or entirely reject the concept of globalization. In addition, some globalizers have noted that skeptics see globalization primarily as an economic phenomenon, portraying all other dimensions of globalization such as culture, politics, and ecology as secondary to deeper economic processes. But since globalization is truly a multidimensional phenomenon, globalizers suggest, intensifying economic relations constitutes but one of its many aspects.

Finally, *modifiers* dispute the novelty of globalization, implying that the term has been used in a historically imprecise manner. Accepting the existence of globalizing tendencies, they nonetheless insist that the world economy before the outbreak of World War I in 1914 was, in a number of important aspects, almost as integrated as the global economy of the early twenty-first century. Thus inveighing against the "unhistorical" arguments of globalizers, modifiers assert that the globalization of labor was actually much greater prior to World War I, citing that international migration declined considerably after 1918. Similar arguments come from the proponents of neo-Marxist "world-system theory" who have long suggested that the modern capitalist economy in which we live today has been "global" since its inception five centuries ago. Thus, world-system theorists seek to modify the use of the term "globalization" from signifying a relatively recent phenomenon to the idea that major globalizing tendencies have been proceeding along the continuum of "modernization" since the sixteenth century. More recently, however, some world-system scholars have acknowledged that the pace of globalization has significantly quickened in the last few decades and that this accelerated dynamic might indeed warrant a new label.

Overall, then, global studies scholars articulating these four perspectives make an important contribution to the academic debate on the subject. Globalizers draw our attention to the existence of many different manifestations of globalization. Critics belonging to the other three camps are helpful in their insistence on a more precise and empirical usage of the term. Forcing the participants in the ongoing globalization debate to offer more careful analyses, critical interventions serve as an important reminder that some aspects of globalization may neither constitute new developments nor reach to all corners of the earth. At the same time, however, critics sometimes focus too narrowly on issues of terminology and on "empirical data," which can lead to premature dismissals of the significance of cultural and ideological globalization.

The persistence of such academic divisions and disagreements notwithstanding, it is important to point out that there also has been significant agreement among many scholars to reorganize the conventional academic disciplines to better capture the multidimensional dynamic of globalization. Picking up steam over the last decade or so, these efforts to rethink current domains of knowledge have contributed to the development of the new transdisciplinary field of global studies.

GLOBAL STUDIES (GS)
AND INTERNATIONAL RELATIONS (IR)

Over the last dozen years or so, global studies (GS) has emerged as a vibrant field of academic study that cuts across conventional disciplinary boundaries and subject markers. Global studies programs, departments, and schools have sprung up in major universities around the world, including in the United States, Japan, Korea, India, China, Australia, Canada, Germany, Denmark, Poland, Russia, and the United Kingdom. In addition, many existing programs in "international studies" and "area studies" have been renamed "global studies." Demand for courses and undergraduate and postgraduate degrees in global studies has dramatically risen. Some large U.S. universities like the University of California Santa Barbara or the University of North Carolina at Chapel Hill currently enroll about eight hundred declared global studies undergraduate majors. The Division of Global Affairs at Rutgers University—Newark and RMIT University's (Melbourne, Australia) School of Global, Urban, and Social Studies, for example, serve dozens of masters and doctoral students. In addition to these successful degree-granting programs, there has been a proliferation of scholarly literature: new journals, book series, textbooks, academic conferences, and professional associations nestled under the umbrella designation of "global studies."

Containing multiple perspectives and methodological approaches, GS both draws on and departs from traditional International Relations (IR) analysis of the post—World War II period, which was largely organized around the two opposing "schools" of realism and idealism. Still, the differences between IR and GS clearly outweigh their similarities. Traditional IR tends to focus primarily on the actions of states in world politics—especially with regard to security issues—at the expense of other crucial areas such as economics and culture. Emphasizing theoretical designs and modeling, traditional IR researchers attempt to find overarching frameworks that can explain and predict power dynamics in world affairs with the ultimate objective that such theories will contribute to the prevention of large-scale wars. Since the 1980s, some IR scholars have endeavored to broaden their research agenda to incorporate analyses of international political economy and cultural aspects of relationships between states, as well as considering the growing significance of non-state actors. Over time, a good number of these researchers have joined the broader academic effort to establish GS as a new transdisciplinary field of inquiry.

Many IR scholars, however, continue to treat the state as the central unit of analysis and primary mover of world politics. By contrast, GS researchers consider the state as but one actor that spins the fluid web of today's material and ideational interdependencies together with proliferating non-state entities, nongovernmental organizations, transnational social movements, and other social and political forces "beyond the state." This multi-centric and multi-dimensional understanding of the dynamics shaping our globalizing world makes GS a field with strong "applied" interests in public policy. Thus, GS scholars eagerly seize upon issues generally excluded from international relations, for example, issues connected to gender, poverty (conceived in terms of linkages across state boundaries), the global spread and concentration of media, the impact of hyper-media, and ecology. In short, the problem-centered focus of GS encourages the forging of strong links between theory and practice—between the world of academia and political organizations (and social movements)—operating in concrete contexts outside the university. Thus, GS scholars tend to engage critically with global problems ranging from managing transnational flows of goods, people, and information to designing new forms of global governance.

At the risk of generalization, I think it is important to identify some overarching characteristics of the new field. As I see it, global studies can be organized around four connected "prisms" or "framings." Let us briefly consider these before we turn to a preview of the twenty chapters collected in *The Global Studies Reader*.

FOUR PRISMS OF GLOBAL STUDIES

First, global studies investigates social and natural phenomena through the prism of *globalization*. Understood as a multidimensional set of processes of intensifying connectivity, globalization also involves people's growing awareness of interdependence. Although the concept of "globalization" has spawned countless intellectual battles and disagreements over how to define it and which of its many dimensions should be privileged, there is little dispute over the significance of globalization processes for GS. In fact, it is no accident that the academic origins of the new field of inquiry coincide with the explosion of the keyword in both academic and public discourses in the 1990s. Like "industrialization" and other verbal nouns that end in the suffix "-ization," globalization signifies the sort of processes best captured by the idea of "development" or "unfolding" within complex but ultimately discernible patterns. Such unfolding may occur quickly or slowly (and often in geographically uneven ways), but it always corresponds to dynamic change across and within national and local boundaries. This focus on global change also reaffirms the importance of "globalization" at the heart of GS, which privileges the examination of flows, nodes, networks, movement, and shifting scales at the expense of static entities and fixed spatial arrangements. To sum up, then, the globalization prism allows for a scrutiny of countless processes that unfold toward a still unrealized (and thus indeterminate) social condition of "globality."

Second, GS relies on a *transdisciplinary framing* to the study of globalization. Challenging the Eurocentric disciplinary framework shaped by the national imaginary of the nineteenth and twentieth centuries, such forms of *trans-* and *multi*disciplinarity involve, for example, the forging of links among several disciplines such as sociology, urban studies, political science, geography, and economics. Far from merely constituting the latest fad in a rapidly globalizing higher education environment, transdisciplinarity and its corresponding mixed methodologies are steeped in ideas of diversity and interdependence. But the pursuit of such radical transdisciplinarity is no easy task for GS. In order to be effective within the still dominant academic order of largely self-contained, traditional disciplines, GS faces considerable pressures to join the dominant order as—yes—yet another separate discipline. The task, then, is for the new field to gain a foothold in the current academic landscape while at the same time working against the disciplinary separation and isolation.

Committed to projecting "the global" across the conventional disciplines, GS scholars must play at least three distinct roles: (i) *mavericks* bent on establishing global studies as a separate discipline; (ii) *insurgents* seeking to globalize established disciplines from within; and (iii) *nomads* traveling across disciplines while at the same time (re)ordering existing and new knowledge around concrete globalization research questions and projects. The nomadic role, in particular, demands from GS students to familiarize themselves with vast literatures on related subjects that are usually studied in isolation from each other. This means that one of the intellectual challenges facing the new field lies in connecting strands of knowledge in ways that do justice to the fluidity and connectivity of our globalizing world. In short, GS must be sufficiently broad (without being grandiose) to encourage the revival of "big picture" approaches yet remain specific enough to nurture small-scale projects.

Third, the *spatial* prism frames GS because dynamics of space (and time) such as "deterritorialization" and "denationalization" are the principal reason for why the term "globalization" was coined in the first place. Still, "the global" should not be imagined as a disconnected space sitting on top of vertical scales running downward to the regional, national, and local. Instead, GS scholars insist that globalization is not just about processes of deterritorialization—the transcending of traditional boundaries—but also about processes of reterritorialization, that is, inscriptions and eruptions of the global *within* the national and the local. "The local" and "the global" are not mutually exclusive endpoints on a vertical spatial scale but overlapping horizontal (cyber)spaces. Hence, the *local* is an excellent place for studying the global: global financial flows converging in Tokyo or London; the impact of globalizing ideas on localized social struggles in Seattle or Athens; or the Korean cultural manifestation of rap music "Gangnam style."

Fourth, GS examines globalization processes through a *critical* prism. This framing includes suspicion toward mainstream stories spun by corporate media; the recognition that facts are socially constructed and serve particular power interests; the decentering of the Western imagination; and an understanding of the global as a multipolar dynamic emerging from the Global South as much as from the North. GS relies on multi-centric chronologies that avoid conventional Eurocentric historical narratives, which tend to present globalization as a linear, diffusionist process starting in the West. The critical prism also informs GS's mission to advance the values of "global citizenship." The recognition of specific aspects of diverse cultures and economic practices as well as globally experienced dynamics of our increasingly interdependent world makes it easier for students to see themselves as "citizens of the world." Since pressing global problems of our time cannot be solved by even the most powerful nation-state alone, they require a new generation of professionals trained within the normative framework of global citizenship.

CHAPTER PREVIEW

As can be seen in the following preview, the first three prisms of global studies—globalization, transdisciplinarity, and spatiality—are at the very core of the twenty rich contributions that make up the twenty chapters of *The Global Studies Reader*.

The critical framing of GS, too, runs through the selections as a common challenge to today's dominant ideological vision of globalization as an inevitable market juggernaut beyond human control.

Centered on the social and political dimensions of globalization, Part I of *The Global Studies Reader* opens with an important contribution by Mary Kaldor, who has emerged as a prominent voice in the growing chorus of scholars exploring the reinvention of civil society in the context of globalization. In this reproduced first chapter of her critically acclaimed study *Global Civil Society* (2003), the British social scientist introduces and discusses five different versions of the concept of civil society and how these distinct perspectives relate to the formation of our globalizing world. Most importantly, she shows how the novel phenomenon of a "global civil society"—often also referred to as a worldwide network of social activists advocating the Left alternative of "globalization-from-below"—is linked to efforts of minimizing violence in social relations. Seen through the eyes of "alter-globalization" activists, then, the building of a global civil society is not just about the struggle to rectify economic inequities created by global capitalism, but also about finding a permanent solution to the perennial problem of war. A clear testimony to the strong impact of social movement scholars on the development of global studies, Kaldor's contribution also reflects the new insecurities of a destabilized post-9/11 world on the eve of the U.S.-led invasion of Iraq in March 2003.

In the second chapter of Part I, Ramesh Thakur and Thomas Weiss tackle one of the most hotly debated topics in global studies: "global governance." This term refers to institutional problem-solving arrangements for transnational challenges and threats that are beyond the capacity of a single state to address. Conceding that national governments and the nation-state will still have a crucial role to play for a long time to come, the authors nonetheless argue for the growing importance of international and transnational actors to facilitate robust responses to collective global problems and crises. Setting out to prove their thesis, Thakur and Weiss discuss the connection between globalization and global governance with special reference to what they call the "five gaps" opening up between concrete global problems and feeble global solutions: (1) knowledge gaps; (2) normative gaps; (3) policy gaps; (4) institutional gaps; and (5) compliance gaps. Applying their discussion of these "gaps" to two concrete examples—the 2004 Indonesia earthquake (and the resulting Indian Ocean tsunami) and the painfully slow progress of developing collective global climate change protocols—these global studies researchers make a strong case for global governance structures that would enhance our collective capacity to manage the complex interdependencies of our global age.

Most debates on globalization have revolved around its objective dynamics, especially the worldwide integration of markets aided by the information and communications revolution of the last quarter century. While its material dimension is certainly important, it would be a serious mistake to neglect globalization's subjective aspects related to the creation of new political ideas and subjectivities. In the third chapter of Part I, I argue that globalization has had a dramatic impact on political ideologies—those shared mental maps people utilize for the navigation of their complex political environments. This process is reflected in a proliferation of "neo" and "post" prefixes, which adorn todays new "isms" such as neoliberalism, neoconservatism, neo-Marxism, post-Communism, and so on. But what is actually new about political ideologies? Have we really moved "post" the grand political ideologies codified by power elites since the French Revolution? Responding to these questions, my chapter discusses at some length the crucial relationship between two "social imaginaries"—the national and the global—and the rise of new political ideologies I call "globalisms." Following my description of three major globalisms—market globalism, justice globalism, and religious globalisms— I show how they translate the rising global imaginary into concrete political programs and agendas. Potent as they are, these ideological reconfigurations at the heart of globalization neither propel the world to an inevitable endpoint nor have they dispensed with the nation-state. Hence, I speculate that the twenty-first century promises to be a transitional era in which the national and the global will rub up against each other on multiple levels and in concrete local settings, thus producing new ideological tensions and compromises.

The fourth contribution to Part I comes from Jackie Smith, a prominent analyst of today's "global justice movements." Co-authored by a dozen scholars working on related issues, the chapter extends my preceding discussion of "justice globalism" by offering a useful history of the evolution of the regional and global "World Social Forums" (WSFs). Constituting progressive ideological and organizational meeting places, these WSFs are comprised of hundreds of progressive groups and alliances dedicated to forms of globalization anchored in egalitarian values and principles. Intentionally established as "counter-forums" to the dominant neoliberal World Economic Forum convened annually in Davos, Switzerland, these alternative public spaces were designed to allow excluded and marginalized voices "to speak and act in plurality." Usually held annually in the Global South, the global WSF thus serves as an open discussion space for social activists engaged in a "new form of politics that breaks with the historical sequence of events that led to the dominance of neoliberal globalization." Smith's chapter brilliantly succeeds in compressing a wealth of empirical and historical information into a discerning analysis of today's global justice movements.

The last chapter in Part I examines the recent uprisings in North Africa and the Middle East—particularly the Jasmine Revolution in Tunisia and the January 25, 2011, uprising in Egypt. Hans Schattle analyzes the role of social media in bringing together a new generation of globally aware and technologically astute activists— and also the tactics employed by national governments to disrupt these movements in cyberspace as well as on the streets. For the Korea-based global studies scholar, the Arab uprisings illustrate the globalization of citizenship norms and values facilitated by the new global social media platforms. Although Arab citizens are reminded at every turn of events that they still remain subjects of national governments—secular or Islamist—the flow of ideas across political borders has made it easier for them to organize themselves, project their voices, and facilitate a transnational political awakening in pursuit of basic human rights and democratic citizenship. As Schattle notes, the "Arab Spring" provides an illustration of how globalization dynamics set the stage for powerful struggles for democratic citizenship.

Exploring the economic and technological aspects of globalization, Part II starts with Pietra Rivoli's engrossing account of world trade as seen from the microscopic perspective of a clothing market in the African nation of Tanzania. The American business professor introduces us to Geofrey Milonge, a local entrepreneur, who specialized in selling *mitumba*—clothing thrown away by consumers in the wealthy Global North. Most of these items involve American T-shirts which are worn by almost all of the men and boys in the nation's capital of Dar es Salaam. Tracing the long and amazing journey of these T-shirts from the place of origin to Tanzania, Rivoli illustrates how the complexity of global economic dynamics often dissolves into surprisingly simple transactions that tell us more about global inequalities than abstract mathematical equations or detached statistical tables.

Part II continues with a chapter taken from Valentine Moghadam's award-winning study, *Globalizing Women*. Drawing on global studies, social movements research, and the scholarship on women's organization, the Iranian-American sociologist and women's studies scholar examines the rise of a specific segment of "global civil society": "transnational feminist networks" (TFN). Tracing the formation and evolution of these networks in the context of a rapidly globalizing economy, she notes that female labor and women's organizations have been crucial elements of globalization in all its dimensions. One of the most surprising findings of her research is that social movements of women often project "a more radical and transformative vision of the socio-economic and political order than do many of the 'new social movements' that have been the focus of much sociological research." Confirming insights presented in this collection by both Mary Kaldor and Jackie Smith, Moghadam emphasizes that TFN are not "anti"-globalization but "alter"-globalization, for they articulate the rising global imaginary as an alternative political agenda that challenges neoliberal market globalism while at the same time advancing the cause of women's rights around the world.

Suggesting that globalization involves the worldwide extension of capitalism, Dani Rodrik's contribution to Part II nonetheless criticizes the neoliberal, deregulated version of the global economy that ended in the financial meltdown of the 2008 and the ensuing Great Recession. The Harvard economist argues that the restoration of economic health requires nothing less than the reinvention of capitalism by creating a better balance between national markets and their supporting institutions on a global level. In his view, such a more moderate vision of globalization would recognize the virtues of national diversity and centrality of national governance while at the same time providing the necessary mechanisms for global interactions. Explaining his seven "commonsense" principles for a downsized globalization framework, the chapter ends with a plea for collective action to limit the reach of global markets by the scope of mostly national governance. Thus, Rodrik's nation-state—centered plea for more moderate forms of globalization stands in stark contrast to the cosmopolitan vision of global governance presented by Thakur and Weiss in Part I of this reader.

In the next chapter, Manuel Castells analyzes the transformation of the global media industry by the ongoing revolution in information and communication technologies that deeply affect the ways people around the world feel, think, and behave. In particular, he outlines the contours of the rising "global network society"—a highly interconnected society whose social structure is made around multiple "networks" of financial markets, geopolitical forces, and media giants powered by microelectronics-based, digitally processed, and increasingly mobile communication technologies. Insisting that the speed and intensity of the current process of globalization far surpasses previous forms in earlier historical periods, the Spanish communications and urban studies scholar shows how a network-based division of labor involving work, class, and gender serves as the engine for the new global power dynamics of the twenty-first century.

In the last chapter of Part II, Shiva Vaidhyanathan examines Google's attempts to expand across the globe, including the transnational corporation's digital strategies of profiling and targeting ordinary people for commercial purposes. The media and legal scholar refers to these processes as "the Googlization of everything"—the harvesting, copying, aggregating, and ranking of information about "us." Moreover, Vaidyanathan shows how a seemingly harmless application like "Google Street View" can be made to serve a "universalization of surveillance" that has never been possible before. Making a strong case for why this generally accepted universalization of surveillance via "infrastructural imperialism" should draw our critical attention, the author points to serious political consequences of state surveillance that might endanger democratic freedoms in the name of offering new "choices" and "options" to unsuspecting citizens. Indeed, this chapter raises the timely issue of proliferating global techniques of surveillance and routine monitoring of people's daily activities by governments, which has been at the center of the recent public debates about the leaking of sensitive information by WikiLeaks operatives and NSA whistleblower Edward Snowden.

Organized around cultural and historical themes, the selections in Part III deal with the intensification and expansion of cultural flows and interactions across the world. Indeed, the volume and extent of cultural transmissions in the contemporary period have far exceeded those of earlier eras. "Culture" is concerned with the symbolic construction, articulation, and dissemination of meaning and related material practices. Given that language, communication, art, music, and images constitute major forms of symbolic expression, they assume special significance in the sphere of culture. Facilitated by the Internet, mobile phones, e-tablets, and other new digital technologies, the dominant symbolic systems of meaning of our age—such as individualism, consumerism, and democracy—circulate in the global age more freely and widely than ever before.

Fittingly, Part III starts with William H. McNeill's reflection on the historical dimensions of globalization. A pioneer of "global history"—a new branch of historical studies increasingly intertwined with Global Studies—the American historian ponders the crucial question of whether globalization should be seen as a long-term process or a new era in human affairs. Summarizing crucial milestones in the evolution of human societies, McNeill offers a seemingly paradoxical re-sponse to his overarching question: although the world has always been one inter-acting whole, the recent extension and proliferation of contemporary networks of interdependence point to a dramatic acceleration and intensification of social rela-tions and consciousness across world-time and world-space. McNeill's conclusions are symptomatic of what might be seen as a "historical turn" in global studies—the growing attention on evolving historical patterns and shifting temporal and cultural contexts. For example, recent periodization efforts have yielded much revised chro-nologies that tend to eschew conventional Eurocentric historical narratives and instead present globalization not merely as a linear, diffusionist process starting in the West in the 1970s (or the late nineteenth century, or the early sixteenth century) but as a multi-nodal, multi-directional dynamic full of unanticipated surprises, violent twists, sudden punctuations, and dramatic reversals.

Continuing in this historical vein, Nayan Chanda's contribution examines the dark side of expanding global connections by concentrating on the pivotal role of traders, preachers, soldiers, and adventurers in this process. As they spread out across the world, they also brought serious problems in their wake such as slavery and diseases. In more recent times, writers of malicious computer viruses have exploited their high-speed fiber optic connections to disrupt and destroy com-puter operations around the planet. Thus the intensifying fabric of human inter-course, trade, and communications across the world has not only resulted in all sorts of material "progress," but has also given wings to diseases, exploitation, and criminal networks.

Shifting their focus to more explicit cultural themes, sociologists Richard Giulianotti and Roland Robertson discuss in their chapter various interrelation-ships between globalization processes and "the global game" of football (soccer). At the core of their argument stands the contention that football's globalization must be understood in terms of the highly complex interplay of the local and the global, or the particular and the universal. For example, although football's global diffusion points to a worldwide convergence over the popularity of a particular sport, many societies organize, interpret, and play the game differently. In addition to assessing the possible "Americanization" of football, the authors also show how football's globalization in recent times has harbored significant "postmodern" cultural influences that are visible in the popular media coverage of the game.

Picking up on Giulianotti and Robertson's discussion of "Americanization," Lane Crothers' chapter offers a comprehensive insight into the ways that American popular culture, such as movies, music, fast food, clothing, sports, and social net-working, both shapes and is shaped by contemporary globalization. Emphasizing that understanding the impact of American popular culture on globalization dy-namics necessarily entails exploring how it crosses national and cultural boundaries, the American political scientist traces the global expansion of American franchises and brands like Coca Cola, Starbucks, and Levi Strauss blue jeans as well as the central role of social networking—especially Facebook—in the "Americanization" of cultural environments around the world. Crothers ends the chapter with an important discussion of how the globalization of American popular culture not only generates much appeal but also fuels fear and anger as people worry that their children are adopting alien values shaped by a distant power over which they have no influence.

In the final contribution to Part III, Olivier Roy argues that globalization has led to the creation of a global "religion market" populated by "consumers" who have spiritual needs to be fulfilled and who find themselves confronted with a choice of "products" that are varied and accessible in any part of the world. These religious products are standardized and they are marketed in several languages, most notably English. Discussing five applicable "market conditions"—circulation, export religions, the deterritorialization of the local, the de-ethnicization of religion, and deculturation—the French social theorist concludes that the religion market works by separating religious and cultural markers in ways that allow individuals to "choose" their favorite religion without having to worry about matching its "correct" cultural background.

Part IV of *The Global Studies Reader* explores the ways in which globalization has transformed conventional spatial relations, in the process seriously altering our natural environment. Hence, the rise of "global cities" and ecological deterioration are at the very core of the five contributions to this section.

Indeed, the early twenty-first century constitutes a period in which urban living has, for the first time in human history, supplanted rural life. This is a momentous shift. However, cities, for all their vibrancy and dynamism, face the growing challenge of providing secure and sustainable places to live. In his best-selling book on the world's growing population relegated to shantytowns, *Planet of Slums*, Mike Davis predicts that today's radically unequal and unstable urban growth has created explosive social environments in many of the Global South's sprawling mega-cities. Part IV opens with the first chapter of Davis' brilliant study. The American urban studies expert integrates a wealth of terrifying empirical data into a powerful narrative, explaining how global forces facilitate rapid urban growth in the developing world, which, "in the context of structural adjustments, currency devaluations, and state retrenchment, has been an inevitable recipe for the mass production of slums" (p. 247, this volume). Davis warns that large regions of our planet have entered into an "urban climacteric" that might be the harbinger of a future very different from the one envisioned by urban planners only a few decades ago. Rather than dominated by postmodern "cities of light" constructed of glass and steel, our cityscapes are turning into disease-ridden, environmental disaster zones, cobbled "out of crude brick, recycled plastic, cement blocks, and scrap wood" and surrounded by "pollution, excrement, and decay" (p. 248)

Continuing the discussion of the expanding urban zones around the world, Jeb Brugmann offers an eye-opening new anatomy of global cities by taking his readers on a street-level tour of our urbanized planet. Arguing that globalization has been organizing the world into an interconnected urban system that requires a new urban strategy, the Canadian city planner discusses in his chapter a number of concrete city neighborhoods in Toronto, Mumbai, Manila, Johannesburg, and other cities around the world to understand how they work as "microcosms" of the global system of cities. For Brugmann, these "urban patches" are beginning to resemble each other not only in their increasingly multiethnic composition but also in their efforts to create unique advantages in the common world City system.

In the third contribution to Part III, Luis Cabrera examines how global migrants create new spaces that might be conducive to the development of new forms of global citizenship. In his chapter, the American political theorist and former journalist presents an argument that unauthorized immigrants to such regions as Western Europe and North America are already practicing a concrete and mostly defensible form of trans-state citizenship. They are "mobile global citizens" who also engage in forms of global civil disobedience as they violate laws against unauthorized entry, which are increasingly at odds with an emerging global order grounded in universal human rights. As Cabrera shows, mass street protests across the United States, and smaller but significant actions by undocumented persons in Western Europe, add a significant publicity dimension that cuts across national borders.

Tackling the enormous challenge of global climate change, the fourth chapter of this part seeks to shed light on how the major domains of globalization—the economic, scientific/technological, cultural, and political—relate to our planet's biophysical environments. In particular, the Australian social theorists and ecologists Peter Christoff and Robyn Eckersley track the complex ways in which our different domains of globalization (and their precursors) have combined to create a looming climate and biodiversity crisis, and identify the wide-ranging transformations that are required to stem these crises. In addition, one of the many virtues of this chapter is to show in some detail how scientific, ethical, and economic discourses have all fed into a two-decade-long attempt by states to negotiate a global climate change regime to govern and manage global warming under the auspices of the United Nations.

In the final contribution of the book, Paul Gilding continues the previous chapter's discussion on the impact of the global climate crisis. Arguing that we have come to the end of an unsustainable world economy based on consumption and waste, the former head of Greenpeace International predicts that the coming decades will see loss, suffering, and conflict, but they might also bring out the best human qualities such as compassion, solidarity, resilience, and adaptability. Gilding's chapter outlines in some detail the kind of struggle that lies ahead and suggests how we can prevent an even more catastrophic warming of our planet. At the center of his prescription lies the notion of "The One-Degree War," which entails a number of dramatic measures that must be taken to limit warming to one degree centigrade above the current level. If successful, such measures like massive reduction of greenhouse gas emissions and switching to alternative energy sources would stabilize the climate and create more manageable environmental conditions for global society in the twenty-second century. Thus wrestling with what is shaping up to be the most serious challenge in the history of our species, *The Global Studies Reader* ends its discussion of ecological globalization on a hopeful note.

GUIDE TO FURTHER READING
AND ONLINE RESEARCH

I. The four perspectives on globalization can be found in the following works:

Globalizers:
- Martin Albrow, *The Global Age: State and Society Beyond Modernity*. Stanford, CA: Stanford University Press, 1997.
- David Held and Anthony McGrew, *Globalization/Antiglobalization*, 2nd ed. Cambridge: Polity Press, 2007.
- Anthony McGrew and David Held, *Globalization Theory: Approaches and Controversies*. Cambridge: Polity Press, 2007.

Rejectionists:
- Susan Strange, *The Retreat of the State: The Diffusion of Power in the World Economy*. Cambridge: Cambridge University Press, 1996.
- Linda Weiss, *The Myth of the Powerless State: Governing the Economy in a Global Era*. Ithaca, NY: Cornell University Press, 1998.
- Justin Rosenberg, *The Follies of Globalisation Theory*. London, Verso, 2000.

Skeptics:
- John Ralston Saul, *The Collapse of Globalism and the Reinvention of the World*. London: Penguin, 2005.
- Paul Hirst, Grahame Thompson, and Simon Bromley. *Globalization in Question: The International Economy and the Possibilities of Governance*, 3rd ed. Cambridge: Polity, 2009.

Modifiers:
- Christopher Chase-Dunn, *Global Formations: Structures of the World Economy*. Lanham, MD: Rowman & Littlefield, 1998.
- Andre Gunder Frank, *ReORIENT: Global Economy in the Asian Age*. Berkeley: University of California Press, 1998.
- Barry K. Gills, ed., *Globalization and the Politics of Resistance*. New York: St. Martin's Press, 2000.
- Robert Gilpin, *The Challenge of Global Capitalism: The World Economy in the 21st Century*. Princeton: Princeton University Press, 2002.
- Barry K. Gills and William R. Thompson, eds. *Globalization and Global History*. London and New York: Routledge, 2006.

An insightful history of the concept of "globaloney" and its current usages are offered in Michael Veseth, *Globaloney 2.0: The Crash of 2008 and the Future of Globalization*. Lanham, MD: Rowman and Littlefield, 2010.

II. Comprehensive anthologies related to Global Studies include:
- Richard P. Appelbaum and William I. Robinson, eds. *Critical Globalization Studies: A Reader*. New York: Routledge, 2005.

- Helmut K. Anheier and Mark Juergensmeyer, eds. *Encyclopedia of Global Studies*, 4 vols. London: Sage, 2012.
- Manfred B. Steger, Paul Battersby, and Joseph Siracusa, eds. *The Sage Handbook of Globalization*, 2 vols. London, Sage 2014.

Mark Juergensmeyer also published an excellent short online article on GS: http://global-ejournal.org/2011/05/06/what-is-global-studies-3/

For a comprehensive global studies textbook, see Patricia J. Campbell, Aran MacKinnon, and Christy R. Stevens, *An Introduction to Global Studies*. Malden, MA: Wiley-Blackwell, 2010.

III. Professional academic associations dedicated to global studies can be found on the Internet:
- The Global Studies Consortium: http://globalstudiesconsortium.org/
- The Global Studies Association: http://www.net4dem.org/mayglobal/
- Asia Association for Global Studies: http://asia-globalstudies.org/join_us

IV. Accessible general introductions to globalization include:
- Manfred B. Steger, *Globalization: A Very Short Introduction*, 3rd ed. Oxford and New York: Oxford University Press, 2013.
- Alex MacGillivray, *A Brief History of Globalization*. New York: Carroll & Graf Publishers, 2006.
- Jan Aart Scholte, *Globalization: A Critical Introduction*, 2nd ed. Houndsmill: Palgrave Macmillan, 2005.

V. There are now several excellent academic journals dedicated to the study of globalization. Some of the most influential include:
- *Globalizations*
- *Global Networks*
- *New Global Studies*
- *Journal of Critical Globalisation Studies*
- *Global Change, Peace & Security*

VI. Websites dedicated to the many dimensions of globalization include:
- Yale Global Online: http://yaleglobal.yale.edu/globalization
- Globalization 101: http://www.globalization101.org/
- Global Policy Forum: http://www.globalpolicy.org/globalization.html
- The World Social Forum: http://www.fsm2013.org/en
- Globalisation Café: http://globalisationcafe.com

These websites can guide your further research and also introduce you to films, video clips, and other useful visual materials related to globalization.

PART I

Politics and Societies

Discussion Points:

- What are some of the major differences between the "activist" and "neoliberal" versions of global civil society? Which version do you prefer and why?
- Facebook and Twitter played an important role for anti-government activists in the Arab Spring. But are those technologies necessarily positive forces for democracy, or can they also contribute to political repression? If so, how?
- The rise of the global imaginary has been reflected in the emergence of new political ideologies. In your view, which of these three "globalisms" has the greatest potential to tackle the new challenges of the twenty-first century?
- Is "global governance" a utopian dream, or can it be realized in this century? If so, what concrete forms (and institutions) might global governance take?
- Should the World Social Forum remain a neutral space for discussion, or should it become a politically involved place for progressive activists seeking to challenge the dominant forces of market globalism?

CHAPTER 1

Five Meanings of Global Civil Society

Mary Kaldor

The terms "global" and "civil society" became the new buzzwords of the 1990s. I want to suggest that the two terms are interconnected and reflect a new reality, however imperfectly understood. The reinvention of "civil society" in the 1970s and 1980s, simultaneously in Latin America and Eastern Europe, had something to do with the global context—the social, political, and economic transformations that were taking place in different parts of the world and that came to the surface after 1989. Indeed, although the term "civil society" has a long history, and its contemporary meanings draw on that history, the various ways in which it is used, I shall argue, are quite different from in the past.

What is new about the concept of civil society since 1989 is globalization. Civil society is no longer confined to the borders of the territorial state. There was always a common core of meaning in the civil society literature, which still has relevance. Civil society was associated with a rule-governed society based largely on the consent of individual citizens rather than coercion. Different definitions of civil society have reflected the different ways in which consent was generated, manufactured, nurtured, or purchased, the different rights and obligations that formed the basis of consent, and the different interpretations of this process. However, the fact that civil society was territorially bound meant that it was always contrasted with coercive rule-governed societies and with societies that lacked rules. In particular, as I shall argue, civil society within the territorial boundaries of the state was circumscribed by war.

This is what has changed. The end of the Cold War and growing global inter-connectedness have undermined the territorial distinction between "civil" and "uncivil" societies, between the "democratic" West and the "non-democratic" East and South, and have called into question the traditional centralized war-making state. And these developments, in turn, have opened up new possibilities for political emancipation as well as new risks and greater insecurity. Whether we are talking about isolated dissidents in repressive regimes, landless labourers in Central America or Asia, global campaigns against land mines or third world debt, or even religious fundamentalists and fanatic nationalists, what has changed are the opportunities for linking up with other like-minded groups in different parts of the world, and for addressing demands not just to the state but to global institutions and other states. On the one hand, global civil society is in the process of helping to constitute and being constituted by a global system of rules, underpinned by overlapping inter-governmental, governmental, and global authorities. In other words, a new form of politics, which we call civil society, is both an outcome and an agent of global interconnectedness. And on the other hand, new forms of violence, which restrict, suppress, and assault civil society, also spill over borders so that it is no longer possible to contain war or lawlessness territorially.

In the aftermath of the revolutions of 1989, the term "civil society" was taken up in widely different circles and circumstances. Yet there is no agreed definition of the term. Indeed, its ambiguity is one of its attractions. The fact that neoliberals, Islamicists, or post-Marxists use the same language provides a common platform through which ideas, projects, and policy proposals can be worked out. The debate about its meaning is part of what it is about. As John Keane suggests, the global spread of the term and the discussion about what it betokens is, in itself, a signal of an emerging global civil society.[1]

This global discussion has involved the resurrection of a body of civil society literature. The search for classic texts has provided what might be called a legitimizing narrative, which has had the advantage of conferring respectability on the term but has also often weakened our understanding of the novel aspects of the rediscovery of the term. By clothing the concept in historical garb, it is possible that the past has imposed a kind of straitjacket which obscures or even confines the more radical contemporary implications. Comaroff and Comaroff talk about the "archaeology" of civil society "usually told, layer upon layer, as a chronological epic of ideas and authors" starting with an "origin story" in the late 1700s. They argue that the term has become a "neo-modern myth: consider the extent to which a diverse body of works—some of them analytic, some pragmatic and prescriptive, some purely philosophical—have begun to tell about the genesis and genealogy of the concept, even as they argue over its interpretation, its telos, its theoretical and socio-moral virtues."[2]

The "neo-modern myth" does obscure the implications of the break with territorially bound civil society. On the other hand, agreement about the history of the concept is part of what provides a common basis for a global conversation. The civil society literature is so diverse that it allows for selectivity; the choice of texts to be studied can be used to justify one interpretation rather than another. While the debate about earlier literature can reify particular meanings that are no longer applicable, it can also serve as a way of investigating the idea, exploring the answers to questions which were faced in earlier periods as well as today, finding out what questions were different and how they were distinguished from the present situation.

This chapter is about a political idea that expresses a real phenomenon, even if the boundaries of the phenomenon vary according to different definitions, and even if the shape and direction of the phenomenon are constantly changing. The investigation of these different definitions, the study of past debates as well as the actions and arguments of the present, are a way of directly influencing the phenomenon, of contributing to a changing reality, if possible for the better.

The book to which this chapter belongs is subtitled "An Answer to War." This is because the concept of civil society has always been linked to the notion of minimizing violence in social relations, to the public use of reason as a way of managing human affairs in place of submission based on fear and insecurity, or ideology and superstition. The word "answer" does not imply that global civil society is some sort of magic formula—a solution or alternative to war. Rather, it is a way of addressing the problem of war, of debating, arguing about, discussing, and pressing for possible solutions or alternatives.

I will start by briefly recapitulating the context in which the term was "reinvented." I will then set out five different meanings of global civil society, two historical and three contemporary.

CONTEXT

Developments variously known as globalization, post-industrialism, and information society came to the surface in the aftermath of the end of the Cold War. Two aspects of these developments are of particular significance in providing a context for the evolution of the concept of global civil society.

First of all, concern about personal autonomy, self-organization, and private space became salient not only in Eastern Europe as a way of getting around the totalitarian militaristic state but also in other parts of the world where the paternalism and rigidity of the state in the post-war period was called into question. In the United States and Western Europe, these concerns had already surfaced in the 1960s and 1970s, with the emergence of movements concerned about civil rights, feminism, or the environment. Giddens and Beck emphasize the growing importance of these concerns in societies which are increasingly complex, vulnerable to manufactured risk, and where expert systems no longer hold unquestioned sway.[3] The rediscovery of the term "civil society" in Eastern Europe in the 1980s, therefore, had a resonance in other parts of the world. The term "civil society" and related terms such as "anti-politics" or "power of the powerless" seemed to offer a discourse within which to frame parallel concerns about the ability to control the circumstances in which individuals live, about substantive empowerment of citizens. Indeed, East European thinkers like Václav Havel believed their ideas were not only applicable to Eastern Europe; they were a response to what Havel called the "global technological civilization."[4] While Western elites seized upon the language as evidence for the victory of actually existing democracies, the inheritors of the so-called new social movements began to use the term to express a demand for a radical extension of democracy for political as well as economic emancipation.[5]

Even though these ideas had echoes of the eighteenth-century preoccupation with restraints on state power, it seems to me that they were responses to an entirely novel situation. It was a situation characterized by the actual experience of an overbearing state, which reached into everyday life far more widely than ever before. In the case of Eastern Europe, it was experience of arbitrary power and the extension of state activity into every sphere of social life, even, at least during the Stalinist period, private life. Elsewhere, it was both the extension of state power and the rigidity and lack of responsiveness to social, economic, and cultural change. As I shall argue, the character of the state has to be understood in terms of the heritage of war and Cold War. It was also a time of social, economic, technological, and cultural transformations in lifestyles, ranging from work (greater insecurity, greater flexibility, and greater inequality) to gender and family relations, which called into question institutional loyalties and assumptions about collective or traditional behaviour.

Secondly, growing interconnectedness and the end of the last great global interstate conflict have eroded the boundaries of civil society. It was growing interconnectedness that allowed the emergence of "islands of civic engagement" in Eastern Europe and in those Latin American countries suffering from military dictatorships. The activists of that period were able to seek international allies both at governmental and non-governmental levels and pierce through the closed societies in which they lived, even before the great advances in information and communications technology. On the one hand, the extension of transnational legal arrangements from above, for example the Helsinki Agreement of 1975, provided an instrument for opening up autonomous spaces in Eastern Europe and elsewhere. On the other hand, the inheritors of the "new" social movements, the European peace movements, and the North American human rights movements were able to link up with groups and individuals in Eastern Europe and Latin America to provide some kind of support and protection. Keck and Sikkink use the term the "boomerang effect" to describe the way civil society groups bypassed the state and appealed to transnational networks and institutions as well as foreign governments, so that their demands bounced back, as it were, on their own situation.[6] In effect, these movements and their successors made use of and contributed to global political and legal arrangements; they were an essential part of the process of constructing a framework for global governance.

The end of the Cold War has contributed to the breakdown of the sharp distinction between internal and external, what is often called in the International Relations literature the Great Divide.[7] Some argue that something like a global civil society (however this is defined) exists in the North Atlantic region but not elsewhere.[8] Hence the boundaries of civil society have merely moved outward. This could perhaps have been said to be true during the Cold War where the boundaries of the West were pushed outward to protect a North Atlantic group of nations. But, in the aftermath of the Cold War, I would suggest that something different is happening. It is no longer possible to insulate territory from anarchy and disorder. In place of vertical territorial-based forms of civil society, we are witnessing the emergence of horizontal transnational global networks, both civil and uncivil. What one might call zones of civility and zones of incivility exist side by side in the same territorial space; North Atlantic space may have more extensive zones of civility than other parts of the world, but such sharp geographic distinctions can no longer be drawn. The events of September 11 were a traumatic expression of the fact that territorial borders no longer define the zones of civility. In other words, the territorial restructuring of social, economic, and political relations has profound implications for how we think about civil society.[9]

To sum up, I want to suggest that the discussion about global civil society has to be understood in terms of what one might call deepening and widening, a move away from state-centred approaches, combining more concern with individual empowerment and personal autonomy, as well as a territorial restructuring of social and political relations in different realms.

DEFINITIONS OF GLOBAL CIVIL SOCIETY

In this section of the chapter, I propose to set out five different versions of the concept of civil society in common usage and to say something about what they imply in a global context. This is a non-exhaustive and abbreviated (but not altogether arbitrary) list. The civil society literature is much richer and more complex than this summary would suggest; the aim is to set up some basic parameters.

The first two versions are drawn from past versions of the concept; the last three are contemporary versions, with echoes of historical usage. It is not straightforward to transpose the concept of civil society into the concept of global civil society, since, as I have argued, the key to understanding what is new about contemporary meanings is precisely their global character. Yet the exercise may be illuminating, since I do believe that there is a common core of meaning and we can investigate the nature of the contemporary phenomenon by trying to understand the relevance of past meanings.

Societas Civilis

Here I am referring to what could be described as the original version of the term—civil society as a rule of law and a political community, a peaceful order based on implicit or explicit consent of individuals, a zone of "civility." Civility is defined not just as "good manners" or "polite society" but as a state of affairs where violence has been minimized as a way of organizing social relations. It is public security that creates the basis for more "civil" procedures for settling conflicts— legal arrangements, for example, or public deliberation. Most later definitions of civil society are predicated on the assumption of a rule of law and the relative absence of coercion in human affairs, at least within the boundaries of the state. Thus, it is assumed that such a *societas civilis* requires a state, with a public monopoly of legitimate violence. According to this definition, the meaning of civil society cannot be separated from the existence of a state. Civil society is distinguished not from the state but from non-civil societies—the state of nature or absolutist empires—and from war.

One of the main objections to the notion of global civil society is the absence of a world state.[10] However, it can be argued that the coming together of humanitarian and human rights law, the establishment of an international criminal court, and the expansion of international peacekeeping betoken an emerging framework of global governance, what Immanuel Kant described as a universal civil society, in the sense of a cosmopolitan rule of law, guaranteed by a combination of international treaties and institutions.

Bourgeois Society (*Bürgerliche Gesellschaft*)

For Hegel and Marx, civil society was that arena of ethical life in between the state and the family. It was a historically produced phenomenon linked to the emergence of capitalism. They drew on the insights of the Scottish enlightenment, especially Adam Smith and Adam Ferguson, who argued that the advent of commercial society created the individuals who were the necessary condition for civil society. Markets, social classes, civil law, and welfare organizations were all part of civil society. Civil society was, for the first time, contrasted with the state. For Hegel, civil society was the "achievement of the modern age." And for Marx, civil society was the "theatre of history."[11]

Transposed to a global level, civil society could be more or less equated with "globalization from below"—all those aspects of global developments below and beyond the state and international political institutions, including transnational corporations, foreign investment, migration, global culture, etc.[12]

The Activist Version

The activist perspective is probably closest to the version of civil society that emerged from the opposition in Central Europe in the 1970s and 1980s. It is sometimes described as the post-Marxist or utopian version of the concept. It is a definition that presupposes a state or rule of law, but insists not only on restraints on state power but on a redistribution of power. It is a radicalization of democracy and an extension of participation and autonomy. On this definition, civil society refers to active citizenship, to growing self-organization outside formal political circles, and expanded space in which individual citizens can influence the conditions in which they live both directly through self-organization and through political pressure.

What is important, according to this definition, at a transnational level is the existence of a global public sphere—a global space where non-instrumental communication can take place, inhabited by transnational advocacy networks like Greenpeace or Amnesty International, global social movements like the protestors in Seattle, Prague, and Genoa, international media through which their campaigns can be brought to global attention, new global "civic religions" like human rights or environmentalism.

The Neoliberal Version

In the aftermath of 1989, neoliberals claimed their victory and began to popularize the term "civil society" as what the West has, or even what the United States has. This version might be described as "laissez-faire politics", a kind of market in politics. According to this definition, civil society consists of associational life—a non-profit, voluntary "third sector"—that not only restrains state power but also actually provides a substitute for many of the functions performed by the state. Thus, charities and voluntary associations carry out functions in the field of welfare which the state can no longer afford to perform. This definition is perhaps the easiest to transpose to the global arena; it is viewed as the political or social counterpart of the process of globalization understood as economic globalization, liberalization, privatization, deregulation, and the growing mobility of capital and goods. In the absence of a global state, an army of NGOs (nongovernmental organizations) perform the functions necessary to smooth the path of economic globalization. Humanitarian NGOs provide the safety net to deal with the casualties of liberalization and privatization strategies in the economic field. Funding for democracy-building and human rights NGOs is somehow supposed to help establish a rule of law and respect for human rights. Thus critics have charged that the term is reactionary, a way of evading the responsibilities of states for welfare or security.[13]

The Postmodern Version

The postmodern definition of civil society departs from the universalism of the activist and neoliberal versions, although even this version requires one universal principle—that of tolerance.[14] Civil society is an arena of pluralism and contestation, a source of incivility as well as civility. Some postmodernists criticize the concept of civil society as Eurocentric; a product of a specific Western culture that is imposed on the rest of the world. Others suggest a reformulation so as to encompass other more communalist understandings of political culture. In particular, it is argued that classic Islamic society represented a form of civil society in the balance between religion, the bazaar, and the ruler.

For the activist version, the inhabitants of civil society can be roughly equated with civic-minded or public-spirited groups. Those active in civil society would be those concerned about public affairs and public debate. For the postmodernists, civic-minded groups are only one component of civil society. In particular, postmodernists emphasize the importance of national and religious identities as well as multiple identities as a precondition for civil society, whereas for the activists, a shared cosmopolitanism is more important. Whether or not groups advocating violence should be included is open to question.

From this perspective, it is possible to talk about global civil society in the sense of the global spread of fields of contestation. Indeed, one might talk about a plurality of global civil societies through different globally organized networks. These might include Islam, nationalist Diaspora networks, as well as human rights networks etc.

These five versions are summarized in Table 1.1. My own understanding of global civil society incorporates much of these different meanings. I do believe that both the first two versions, a rule of law and a market society, or at least the aspiration for a rule of law and for economic autonomy, are constituted by what we now tend to mean by civil society; for civil society to exist there has to be a relationship with markets, which secure economic autonomy, and the rule of law, which provides security. I also think that the various actors that inhabit contemporary versions of civil society are all part of global civil society—the social movements and the civic networks of the activist version; the charities, voluntary associations, and what I shall call the "tamed" NGOs of the neoliberal version; and the nationalist and fundamentalist groups that are included in the postmodern version.

In terms of normative considerations, however, I am closest to the activist version. All versions of civil society are both normative and descriptive. They describe a political project, i.e. a goal, and at the same time an actually existing reality, which

Table 1.1 The Five Versions of Civil Society

TYPE OF SOCIETY	TERRITORIALLY BOUNDED	GLOBAL
Societas civilis	Rule of law/Civility	Cosmopolitan order
Bürgerliche Gesellschaft	All organized social life between the state and the family	Economic, social, and cultural globalization
Activist	Social movements, civic activists	A global public sphere
Neoliberal	Charities, voluntary associations, third sector	Privatization of democracy building, humanitarianism
Postmodern	Nationalists, fundamentalists, as well as above	Plurality of global networks of contestation

may not measure up to the goal. *Societas civilis* expressed the goal of public security, of a civilized, i.e. non-violent, society. *Bürgerliche Gesellschaft* was about the
rise of market society as a condition for individual freedom, and the balance between the state and the market. For Hegel, this was the *telos* (end goal) of history;
for Marx, civil society was merely a stage towards the *telos* of communism.

The contemporary versions of civil society all have normative goals, which
can only be fully explained in the context of globalization. The neoliberal version
is about the benefits of Western, especially American, society; thus the goal is the
spread of this type of society to the rest of the world. Globalization, the spread of
global capitalism, is viewed as a positive development, the vehicle, supplemented
by global civil society, for achieving global Westernization or "the end of history."

The postmodern version has to be related to the break with modernity of
which a key component was the nation-state. Even though the postmodernists are
anti-teleological, they would see the contestation that is currently taking place on a
global scale as a way of breaking with grand narratives, teleological political projects
that were associated with states. The rise of the Internet allows for a riot of virtuality
and for a denial of the existence of something called the real.

The activist version is about political emancipation. It is about the empowerment of individuals and the extension of democracy. I will argue that war and the
threat of war always represented a limitation on democracy. Globalization offers the
possibility of overcoming that limitation and, at the same time, the global extension
of democracy has become, as a consequence of globalization, the necessary condition for political emancipation. For activists, globalization is not an unqualified
benefit. It offers possibilities for emancipation on a global scale. But in practice, it
involves growing inequality and insecurity and new forms of violence. Global civil
society, for the activists, therefore, is about "civilizing" or democratizing globalization, about the process through which groups, movements, and individuals can
demand a global rule of law, global justice, and global empowerment. Global civil
society does, of course, in my own version, include those who are opposed to globalization and those who do not see the need for regulation. Thus my version of global
civil society is based on the belief that a genuinely free conversation, a rational critical
dialogue, will favour the "civilizing" option.

CHAPTER 2

Framing Global Governance, Five Gaps

Ramesh Thakur and Thomas G. Weiss

There is no government for the world. Yet, on any given day, mail is delivered across borders; people travel from one country to another via a variety of transport modes; goods and services are freighted across land, air, sea, and cyberspace; and a whole range of other cross-border activities take place in reasonable expectation of safety and security for the people, groups, firms, and governments involved. Disruptions and threats are rare—indeed, in many instances rarer in the international domain than in many sovereign countries that should have effective and functioning governments. That is to say, international transactions are typically characterized by order, stability, and predictability. This immediately raises a puzzle: How is the world governed even in the absence of a world government in order to produce norms, codes of conduct, and regulatory, surveillance, and compliance instruments? How are values allocated quasi-authoritatively for the world, and accepted as such, without a government to rule the world?

The answer, we argue, lies in global governance. It is the sum of laws, norms, policies, and institutions that define, constitute, and mediate relations between citizens, societies, markets, and states in the international system—the wielders and objects of the exercise of international public power.

That said, at the time we write this, the world is suffering the worst financial and economic crisis since the Great Depression that began in 1929 and continued into the 1930s. The "normal" periods of calm, stability, order, and predictability are interspersed with periodic bouts of market volatility, disorder, and crisis, as well as internal, regional, transnational, and international armed conflict and warfare on the peace and security side. Where the Asian financial crisis of 1997–1998 proved the perils of crony capitalism, the 2007–2008 US subprime and financial crises showed the pitfalls of unbridled capitalism. Governments may be fallible, but markets too are imperfect. Both the Asian crisis of a decade ago and the 2008 US market collapse demonstrate the need for efficient, effective, and transparent regulatory and surveillance instruments and institutions. The state has an essential role to play. Those countries where the state has not abandoned the market to its own supposedly self-regulating devices are seemingly better placed to weather the current crisis of confidence in capitalism.

In other words, these are crises of governance in terms of the proper role of governments and market institutions as well as the appropriate balance in the relationship between them. The second and equally important point to note is that they are crises of domestic governance. The causes of the crises lie in domestic governance imperfections, and the solutions entail domestic government and market responses. The role for global governance institutions is restricted to containing the contagion. Global governance can play a facilitative and constraining role, but rarely a determinant and predominant role. The authority and capacity for the latter is vested almost exclusively in domestic public authorities.

As the number of international actors and the frequency and intensity of their interactions have grown, so has the requirement for institutionalized cooperation among them. States are, and for the foreseeable future are likely to remain, the primary actors in world affairs; and state sovereignty is the bedrock principle on which their relations are based and organized. Intergovernmental organizations help states to cooperate in the pursuit of shared goals and to manage competition and rivalry. Arising from this, the *problématique* of global governance in our times may be simply stated: the evolution of intergovernmental organizations to facilitate robust international responses lags well behind the emergence of collective problems with trans-border, especially global, dimensions. This is the true significance of the worldwide financial and banking crisis.

The *problématique* of global security governance consists of the disconnect between the distribution of authority within existing intergovernmental institutions and the international distribution of military power. Similarly, there is a "growing gap between the distribution of authority within existing international institutions and the international distribution of economic power."[1] Historically, global financial governance focused on mediating exchanges between national markets. However, capital can no longer be parsed as national or international—it has become truly global. Accordingly, apprehending the regulation of capital and the provision of economic stability demands examining the global reach of powerful actors and institutions. While not so long ago finance essentially flowed from corporations based in states with some transnational links, today it is essentially global with some local characteristics. And it is not self-governing. Instead, "stability in financial markets requires the judicious exercise of public authority."[2] Moreover, maximizing allocative efficiency for the globe cannot be the only goal of international financial and economic policy more generally. Questions of legitimacy, distributive justice, and social safety nets are as important as efficacy, currency convertibility, or capital mobility. Yet there is nothing remotely resembling an overarching authority for global financial governance to help facilitate stability or reduce the social costs of contemporary economic developments.

This chapter begins by probing the idea of global governance before parsing five "gaps" in contemporary global governance that we believe are the best way to understand the strengths and weaknesses of the UN's past, present, and future roles. We then discuss the 2004 tsunami and global climate change to illustrate how this analytical lens works when examining a specific event and an issue-area.

THE IDEA OF GLOBAL GOVERNANCE AND GLOBALIZATION

"Good governance" incorporates participation and empowerment with respect to public policies, choices, and offices; rule of law and independent judiciary to which the executive and legislative branches of government are subject along with citizens and other actors and entities; and standards of probity and incorruptibility, transparency, accountability, and responsibility. It includes also institutions in which these principles and values find ongoing expression. Good governance thus can be considered a normative definition concerned with laudable standards.

"Global governance"—which can be good, bad, or indifferent—refers to collective[3] problem-solving arrangements for challenges and threats that are beyond the capacity of a single state to address. Both formal and informal, such arrangements provide more order and stability for the world than would occur naturally. Another way to think of global governance is as purposeful systems of rules or norms with imperfections and major limitations—in a phrase, international cooperation without world government—within which states pursue their own national or regional interests and only limited and often ineffective measures to require compliance with internationally agreed rules, regulations, and decisions.

Traditionally, and this is the source of some confusion, governance has been associated with "governing," or with political authority, institutions and, ultimately, control. Governance in this sense denotes formal political institutions that both aim to coordinate and control interdependent social relations and that also possess the capacity to enforce decisions. In recent years, however, some authors have used "governance" to denote the regulation of interdependent relations in the absence of overarching political authority, such as in the international system.[4] Through informal as well as formal mechanisms and arrangements, collective interests are articulated, rights and obligations are established, and differences are mediated on the global plane.

In addition to interdependence and a growing recognition of problems that defy solutions by a single state, the other explanation for a growing interest in understanding global governance stems from the sheer growth in numbers and importance of non-state actors (civil society and market), which also are conducting themselves or combining themselves in new ways. Society has become too complex for citizens' demands to be satisfied solely by governments at national, regional, and global levels. Instead, civil society organizations play increasingly active roles in shaping norms, laws, and policies. The growing influence and power of civil society actors means that they have effectively entered the realm of policymaking. They are participants in global governance as advocates, activists, and policymakers, which in turn poses challenges of representation, accountability, and legitimacy both to governments and back to the civil society actors. In an increasingly diverse, complex, and interdependent world, solutions to collective-action problems are attainable less and less at any one level or by just state actors. Instead, we have partnerships between different actors and levels of governance, and issue-specific and contingent choices between them on other issues. With influence over policy should come responsibility for the consequences of policy.

Global governance entails multilevel and networked relations and interactions[5] in order to deal with the linkages across policy levels and domains. As the planet's most representative organization, the United Nations has unparalleled legitimacy even if it cannot displace the responsibility of local, state, and national governments; but it can and should be the locus of multilateral diplomacy and collective action to solve problems shared in common by many countries. "Good" global governance implies, not exclusive policy jurisdiction, but an optimal partnership between the state, regional, and global levels of actors, and between state, intergovernmental, and nongovernmental categories of actors.

The other concept necessary to this analysis is "globalization," a process of increased interconnectivity throughout the world. Many regard it as both a desirable and an irreversible engine of commerce that will underpin growing prosperity and a higher standard of living throughout the world. Others recoil from it as the soft underbelly of corporate imperialism that plunders and profits on the basis of unrestrained consumerism. Some observers have argued that globalization has been occurring since the earliest trade expeditions (e.g., the Silk Road); international trade, as a proportion of total production in the world economy, was about the same in the 1980s as in the last two decades of the Gold Standard (1890–1913);[6] and, despite the current obsession, the process itself is not fundamentally new. Still others have suggested that the current era of globalization is unique in the rapidity of its spread and the intensity of the interactions in real time that result.[7]

Globalization creates losers as well as winners, and entails risks as well as provides opportunities. As an International Labour Organization blue-ribbon panel noted, the problems lie not in globalization per se, but in the "deficiencies in its governance."[8] The deepening of poverty and inequality—prosperity for a few countries and people, marginalization and exclusion for many—has implications for social and political stability, again among as well as within nations. That is, for governance, both domestic and global.[9] The rapid growth of global markets has not seen the parallel development of social and economic institutions to ensure their smooth and efficient functioning; labor rights have been less assiduously protected than capital and property rights; and the global rules on trade and finance are unfair to the extent that they produce asymmetric effects on rich and poor countries.

"GAPS" IN GLOBAL GOVERNANCE

The clearest way to comprehend the relevance of using the lens of global governance is by examining what we dub the five "gaps" between concrete global problems and feeble global solutions. Knowledge, normative, policy, institutional, and compliance gaps are discussed here separately as a prelude to pulling them together in the subsequent discussion of the December 2004 tsunami and climate change.

Knowledge Gaps

The first analytical lens consists of the "knowledge gap." With or without institutions and resources, there often is little or no consensus about the nature, gravity, and magnitude of a problem, either about the empirical information or about the theoretical explanation. And there is often similar—and sometimes even more bitter—disagreement over the best remedies and solutions to these problems: Two good examples are global warming and nuclear weapons, neither of which was known when the UN Charter was signed. What is the best "mix-and-match" strategy for combating the threat of global warming, for instance, the severity and causes of which remain in political if not scientific dispute, which minimizes present disruption while also minimizing future risks and damage? Or for preventing the proliferation of nuclear weapons while also trying to encourage the elimination of existing stockpiles and avoiding their use in the meantime?[10] Can we get beyond ideology and let information, data, experience, and science guide us?

We adopt a "whole-of-cycle" approach to gaps with respect to knowledge, norms, policy, institutions, and compliance. At least partially filling the knowledge gap is essential for dealing with the other gaps in global governance—normative, policy, institutional, and compliance. If we can recognize that there is a problem and agree on its approximate dimensions, then we can take steps to solve it. A critical gap in any of the five stages can cause the entire cycle to collapse. A UN-relevant knowledge gap arises from a lack of knowledge about the existence, scale, location, causes of, or possible solutions to an international policy problem. How is knowledge of new problems and issues acquired or created? How is it transmitted to the policy community? And how do solutions get formulated and adopted? Thus, the first step in eventually addressing a problem that goes beyond the capacity of states to solve is actually to recognize its existence, to understand that there is a problem. Next, it is necessary to collect solid data that challenge the consensus about the nature of the problem, to diagnose its causes—in short, to explain the problem.

One under-appreciated comparative advantage of the United Nations is its convening capacity and mobilizing power. UN-sponsored world conferences, heads-of-government summits, and blue-ribbon commissions and panels have been used for framing issues, outlining choices, making decisions; for setting, even anticipating, the agenda; for framing the rules, including for dispute settlement; for pledging and mobilizing resources; for implementing collective decisions; and for monitoring progress and recommending midterm corrections and adjustments.[11]

Normative Gaps

Once a threat or problem has been identified and diagnosed, the next step is to help solidify a new norm of behavior. To refer to the same two examples again: in the decades since 1945, the norms of environmental protection and nuclear abstinence have become firmly established. How were the existing gaps filled? There are enormous difficulties in reaching consensus about universally acceptable norms, for example, the "emerging norm" of human rights can be (and has been) culturally deconstructed to cast doubts upon the universality of even long-agreed principles. Here again, the source of ideas to fill in normative gaps is now more likely than ever to be civil society. At the same time, the United Nations is an essential and unequalled arena in which states codify norms in the form of resolutions and declarations (soft law) as well as conventions and treaties (hard law). That is, the United Nations offers the most efficient forum for processing norms—standards of behavior—into laws—rules of behavior. Again, the notion of global governance helps us to see how, despite the absence of overarching global authority, fledgling steps take place that on occasion enhance international order and stability and consolidate what Hedley Bull called "international society" more than would otherwise occur without the world organization.[12]

Norms matter because people—citizens as well as politicians and officials—care about what others think of them. This is why approbation, and its logical corollary, shaming, can be effective in regulating social behavior.[13] It is also why the United Nations and its secretaries-general, sometimes called "secular popes," have often relied upon the bully pulpit.[14] Like Josef Stalin's characterization of the papacy—"How many divisions does the pope have?"—the power of the UN's ideas and moral voice is often underestimated. In the Ottawa Treaty banning landmines, for example, norm-generation by Western middle powers was underpinned by norm-advocacy from NGOs and reinforced by norm-promoting standard-setting by the UN Secretary-General when he endorsed the Ottawa process as the negotiating track, and the convention that resulted from it.[15]

A relatively recent effort at UN norm building was the Global Compact that grew from the 2000 Millennium Summit. Principle 10 ("Businesses should work against all forms of corruption, including extortion and bribery") attempts to answer the questions: What is corruption? Why is it wrong? What can be done about it? Adequate answers to these questions suggest that filling the normative gap requires first at least partially filling the knowledge gap; there is usually a lag because norms reflect an agreement about the state of affairs as a basis for building a consensus about the most appropriate ways to frame an issue and future action.

As a universal organization, the United Nations is an ideal forum to seek consensus about normative approaches that govern global problems and would work best with a worldwide application of a norm. The host of problems ranging from reducing acid rain to impeding money laundering to halting pandemics clearly provide instances for which universal norms and approaches are emerging.

At the same time, the UN is a maddening forum because dissent by powerful states or even coalitions of less powerful ones means either no action occurs, or agreement can be reached only on a lowest common denominator. For instance, the avoidance of meaningful action against a white-minority regime in South Africa until the 1990s reflected mainly US and British refusals, which were backed by their vetoes in the Security Council. Similarly, widespread dissent even by a minority of countries can also slow normative progress. For instance, cultural differences can complicate the emergence of norms that strike most people in most parts of the world as "no-brainers." The unholy alliance of the Vatican and Islamic fundamentalists against women's reproductive rights is a clear illustration.

As elsewhere in the story of global governance, the proliferation of actors is vital. The presence and work of civil society is essential in terms of identifying normative gaps and in proposing ways to reduce them. Examples of individuals and institutions come immediately to mind: Raphael Lemkin's efforts to coin the term "genocide" and his role in the formulation and adoption of the UN Genocide Convention; Henri Dunant and the Red Cross movement in the field of international humanitarian law; Peter Benenson and Amnesty International's pursuit of human rights; and Jody Williams and the International Campaign to Ban Landmines.

Once information has been collected and knowledge gained that a problem is serious enough to warrant attention by the international policy community, new norms in which the newly acquired knowledge is embedded need to be articulated, disseminated, and institutionalized. For example, once we know that HIV/AIDS is transmitted through unprotected promiscuous sexual activity, the norm of safe sex follows logically. Or as we gain information about the sexual activities of personnel deployed in the field in UN peace operations, the norm of no sexual contact or no paid sex between UN personnel and the local population might be articulated by the UN Secretariat.

In spite of the obvious problems of accommodating the perspectives of 192 countries, the UN provides an essential, even unique, arena to permit the expression of official views from around the planet on international norms. The crucial question is how contested norms become institutionalized both within and among states, and the interactive dynamics of the process of institutionalization at the national, regional, and global levels. International norms can be transmitted down into national politics through incorporation into domestic laws or into the policy preferences of political leaders through elite learning. It is only through state structures, through governments, that international norms can be integrated into domestic standards. Norm diffusion is not in itself, therefore, about the state withering away. Indeed, the United Nations can be considered the last bastion of sovereignty. It provides a forum that has promulgated norms with the consent of most member states with a view toward sustaining, not eroding, the prerogatives of sovereigns.

Policy Gaps

By "policy" we mean the articulated and linked set of governing principles and goals, and the agreed programs of action to implement those principles and achieve those goals. Thus, the Kyoto Protocol, the Nuclear Nonproliferation Treaty (NPT), and the Comprehensive Test Ban Treaty may be seen as examples of policies for combating the threats of global warming and nuclear weapons.

That said, is "international" policy made and implemented by international organizations, or by national authorities meeting and interacting in international organizational forums?[16] To what extent is the evident policy paralysis over Darfur the result of a policy gap on the part of the UN as opposed to weak political will among key member states?

A second set of questions arises about possible disconnects between the numbers and types of actors playing ever-expanding roles in civil, political, and economic affairs within and among nations, and the concentration of decision-making authority in intergovernmental institutions. Where, for example, are operational ideas (such as measures to counter climate change) coming from? The source of ideas to fill policy gaps is likely to be governments and intergovernmental organizations. When policy is made in the absence of institutions, it takes on an ad hoc character. Such an approach can lead to fragmented and incompatible policies that become incoherent over time.

UN policymakers are the principal political organs, the Security Council and the General Assembly, and the member states collectively. But all of these are intergovernmental forums. That is, the people making the decisions in the form of adopting resolutions that set out new governing principles, articulate goals, and authorize programs of action to achieve those goals, do so as delegates of national governments from the UN's member states. And they make these choices within the governing framework of their national foreign policies, under instructions, on all important policy issues, from their home governments. Or member states may make the policy choices directly themselves, for example at summit conferences. That being the case, it is not always clear just what might be meant by "United Nations" policy, policymaking, and policymakers.

The responsibility for implementation of most "UN policy" does not rest primarily with the United Nations itself, but devolves to member states. But even UN policy, in the form of policy resolutions and actions adopted and authorized by the Security Council and the General Assembly or summit decisions made by member states directly, may exhibit regulative, distributive, and redistributive characteristics.

Based on these considerations, we conclude that some resolutions adopted by the General Assembly are the equivalent of policy declarations, in that they articulate broad principles and goals and/or call for programs of action for the attainment of these goals. One of the clearest examples of such a resolution is General Assembly resolution 2922 of 15 November 1972 reaffirming apartheid as a crime against humanity. This policy became a staple of UN resolutions over many years until the liberation of South Africa and the replacement of the apartheid regime with an elected black majority government formed by the African National Congress with Nelson Mandela as the first president.

A second set of "UN policy" documents might be goals, plans of action, and desirable codes of conduct embedded in international treaties and conventions. Good examples include the Genocide Convention; the Universal Declaration of Human Rights; the two Covenants on Civil and Political and Social, Economic, and Cultural Rights; the NPT; and the UN Convention on the Law of the Sea.

Clearly, as new problems emerge and new norms arise, they will highlight gaps in policy that also need addressing. United Nations policy might be to promote awareness about the gravity and causes of HIV/AIDS, encourage educational campaigns by member governments, or declare zero tolerance of sexual exploitation by UN peacekeepers.

Institutional Gaps

If there is a problem that is relatively well known and/or a range of agreed-upon policy, what is the machinery that will put such a policy into effect? For example, one may have determined that democratic states are less likely to go to war and that increasing their numbers is valuable, and hence a policy could be announced to hold elections after peace has broken out in a protracted conflict. However, this has little meaning unless there also are institutions such as a local election commission along with outside observers to register voters and to arrange for poll workers, polling stations, printing of ballots, verification of rolls, and tallying of results. Often, institutional gaps can exist even when knowledge, norms, and policies are in place.

If policy is to escape the trap of being ad hoc, episodic, judgmental, and idiosyncratic, it must be housed within an institutional context. This refers to the fact that there is either no overarching global institution (or such a flimsy one as to be the equivalent) or capability to address a problem with trans-border dimensions. In such cases, even the most "powerful" institutions such as the Security Council, the World Bank, or the International Monetary Fund[17] often lack either the appropriate resources or authority or both.

We use "institution" here in two senses of the term: both formal, organizational entities as well as regimes, or recurring and stable patterns of behavior around which actor expectations converge. For example, the "coalition of the willing" and the Proliferation Security Initiative are stable patterns even though the membership is variable. It is easier to identify formal institutions that have treaties and budgets, but the messier and more informal variety are just as essential to our analysis of gaps.

Institutional gaps can refer to the fact that there may be no overarching global institution, in which case many international aspects of problem-solving may be ignored, for example, the control of nuclear weapons. Or it may be impossible to address a problem because of an institutional gap of missing key member states—e.g., the World Trade Organization (WTO) before China's entry or the League of Nations without the United States—or simply because resources are incommensurate with the magnitude of a problem.

Institutions that are most effective often are those that deal with well-known areas with well-embedded norms and consensus among member states: the UN Children's Fund (UNICEF) and the World Health Organization (WHO), to name but two. Many issues treated by such organizations are seen as having little controversial political content—there is nothing in them that impacts a state's interests, and that would therefore lead to conflict. Therefore, these issues can safely be turned over to experts for resolution.[18] Positive examples thus should figure in contemporary discussions along with laments about those that fall short, for example the late but little lamented UN Commission on Human Rights as well as its successor, the Human Rights Council. These institutions may work well because they focus on specific problems and are "functional"—that is, part of their work and part of the bureaucracy deals with narrowly defined issues and technologies.

Institutions are another example of the impact of ideas. Sixty years into the UN's history, there are very few issues that do not have some global institutions working on them. Actors in world politics can and do cooperate, and they do so more often than they engage in conflict. The problems involved in cooperation include the difficulty of coordination due to the lack of reliable information about what other actors are doing. Actors thus form institutions to mitigate such problems by sharing information, reducing transaction costs, providing incentives for concessions, providing mechanisms for dispute resolution, and establishing processes for making decisions. Institutions can facilitate such problem solving even though they do not possess coercive powers. In particular, intergovernmental institutions can increase the number of productive interactions among their member states that can in turn help build confidence and bridges for other relations. Once created, because they promise benefits in one arena of technical cooperation, organizations formed by states can sow the seeds for additional cooperation—in short, they can take on a personality and life of their own.

The less formal relationships are called "regimes" in political science. As John Ruggie has explained, "international regimes have been defined as social institutions around which actor expectations converge in a given area of international relations," which create "an intersubjective framework of meaning."[19] Regimes are important because power alone cannot predict the type of order created. Change can come from power or from social purpose (or sense of legitimacy). Just as with more formal institutions, "international regimes alter the relative costs of transactions."[20]

Compliance Gaps

The "compliance gap" may usefully be divided into implementation (including monitoring) and enforcement gaps. Recalcitrant or fragile actors may be unwilling or unable to implement agreed elements of international policy, for example a ban on commercial whaling, the acquisition of proliferation-sensitive nuclear technology and material, or the cross-border movement of terrorist material and personnel. Even if an institution exists, or a treaty is in effect, or many elements of a working regime are in place, there is often a lack of political will to rely upon or even provide resources for the previously established institutions or processes. Second, confronted with clear evidence of noncompliance by one or more members amidst them, the collective grouping may lack the strength of conviction or commonality of interests to enforce the norm. How do we monitor the implementation records of states who have signed on to Kyoto and the NPT? How do we enforce treaty obligations on signatory states (e.g., the NPT and Iran and North Korea, on the one hand, with respect to nonproliferation, and all five legally recognized nuclear powers with respect to disarmament on the other)? And on nonsignatory states (e.g., nonproliferation and India, Israel, and Pakistan)—not to mention non-state actors who lie outside the jurisdiction of any formal normative architecture?

Enforcement is a subset of compliance, especially difficult at the international level in an anarchic society of sovereign states. The past six-and-a-half decades have been the story of the never-ending search for better compliance mechanisms. While looking for better institutions, the trick has been to develop governance for the world, but not world government, for powers that rival those of domestic governments in the areas of security, justice, and general welfare—the analogues of peace and security, human rights, international trade and development, and environment and sustainability.

The cumulative challenge of filling the gaps in global governance is demonstrated by the extreme difficulty in ensuring compliance—indeed, this last gap often appears as a complete void as there is actually no way to enforce decisions, certainly not to compel them. For example, in the area of international peace and security, even though the UN Charter calls for them, there are no standing UN military forces and never have been. The UN has to beg and borrow troops, which are always on loan, and there is no functioning Military Staff Committee (called for in Charter Article 47) and never has been. Perhaps even more tellingly in terms of crisis response, the UN has no rapid reaction capability, which is not because of a lack of ideas or policy proposals—Trygve Lie's proposal was first made in 1947, and the latest proposal comes from the Brahimi report in 2000.[21] As for the crucial issue of nuclear proliferation, the compliance gap has been more than evident with Iran thumbing its nose at the International Atomic Energy Agency and the Security Council.

In the area of international trade and finance, the WTO is considered a relatively effective enforcement mechanism although it is among the youngest intergovernmental organizations. In the area of human rights, whether it is hard or soft law, there is often no enforcement capability. Although the use of ad hoc tribunals and the creation of the International Criminal Court were important institutional steps that led to some indictments and convictions, there is precious little enforcement capacity in this arena.[22] For example, there has been universally accepted knowledge about, as well as norms and institutions regarding, genocide since 1948. There is credible evidence that the general prohibition of genocide is a universally accepted norm: there is substantial agreement that it is wrong, there is even a treaty/institution prohibiting it: the Genocide Convention of 1948 (hard law), which came into effect in 1951.

In the area of environment and sustainability, the 1997 Kyoto Protocol created binding emission targets for developed countries, a system whereby they could obtain credit toward their emission targets by financing energy-efficient projects in less-developed countries (known as "joint implementation"), clean-development mechanisms, and emissions trading (trading the "right to pollute"). Backtracking began almost before the ink was dry on the signatures. As the world's climate changes at breakneck speed, there is no way to ensure that even the largely inadequate agreements on the books are respected.

A policy still needs to be implemented, and shortcomings might show up in implementation. The zero-tolerance policy toward sexual exploitation by UN soldiers has been in existence for some time, yet the problem continues.[23] Inevitably, even with full knowledge, adequate norms, and policy and operations to back them up, there will always be the problem of some individuals or groups who cheat, challenge, and defy the norms and laws of the broader society and community. This is why all societies have mechanisms in place to detect violators and outlaws, subject them to trial, and punish convicted offenders. The goal is both punishment of outlaws so justice is seen to be done, and deterrence of future violations. For these goals to be achieved the modalities and procedures for enforcing compliance with community norms and laws must be efficient, effective, and credible.

AN EVENT: THE 2004 TSUNAMI AND GAPS IN GLOBAL GOVERNANCE

The worldwide response to the 2004 Indonesian earthquake and the resulting Indian Ocean tsunami, whose death toll climbed to 280,000, provides us with global governance in microcosm—how an enormous trans-border problem can be addressed in a decentralized world. On 26 December 2004, an earthquake that registered magnitude 9.0 on the Richter scale occurred off the west coast of the Indonesian island of Sumatra. The earthquake and the resulting tsunami spread mind-boggling devastation across the Indian Ocean, affecting 12 countries, some as far away as the Horn of Africa. Public attention was transfixed by the images: waves swallowing islands and cities whole, creating scenes of apocalyptic destruction. The most frequently used adjectives to describe the tragedy were "biblical" and "nuclear."

The globalizing effect of innovations in transportation and communications were obvious. Thousands of tourists from Western developed nations and from around the region were vacationing in the area with video cameras in tow. Their homemade footage began to appear on international television news and the Internet making the scope of the disaster clear. In addition, technology also made it possible to mobilize humanitarian assistance for rescue, relief, assistance, and reconstruction almost in real time. The United Nations can deploy physically to humanitarian emergencies anywhere in the world within 24 hours, barring any political or bureaucratic hurdles—or so at least it claims.

The tsunami was an illustration, first, of the thesis that many problems are truly transnational and multinational, and that solutions to them are global in scope and require substantial resource mobilization. The location of the initial earthquake was in Indonesia, but the resulting tsunami affected the entire perimeter of the Indian Ocean. Moreover, because of the time of the year, it caught thousands of holidaying Westerners in its deathly grip as well. And emergency humanitarian aid and disaster relief assistance, medium-term reconstruction and rebuilding, as well as longer-term preventive and ameliorative measures, required a coordinated effort on a global scale by a multitude of actors across all levels of analysis, from the local to the global, governmental, intergovernmental, and nongovernmental.

The effort generated by the tsunami also illustrates the remaining gaps that we have briefly sketched: knowledge, normative, policy, institutional, and compliance. Previously, for example, there was local knowledge about tsunamis in East Asia, but there was no system to dispense it: what causes them, what the warning signs are, and what the damage could be. We still lack the capacity to predict earthquakes and so prevent the death and destruction caused by tremors directly. But predictive knowledge about tsunamis generated by earthquakes is common and reliable. One of the authors, based in Japan for nine years, is only too familiar with routine statements following any significant earthquake about whether or not to expect a tsunami and, if so, where, when, and how powerful. This knowledge has been integrated into an early warning system around the Pacific which is integrated into the UN system.

Yet the Indian Ocean had no such system in place. Public authorities were no more knowledgeable than ordinary people about the potent symptoms of tsunamis, with the result that many people rushed to see and photograph the strange sight of water being sucked out to sea by powerful currents: a telltale symptom of a tsunami made famous in Japanese paintings and prints. Nor had knowledge about natural barriers to absorb and blunt the power of tsunamis, such as mangroves which were being systematically destroyed, been integrated into disaster prevention planning schemes.

After the tsunami occurred, normatively, no one questioned that there was a responsibility to protect individuals, and that if governments could not manage the disaster and its consequences, outsiders should exert pressure and come to the rescue. The United Nations has been preaching the culture of prevention with regard to disasters, natural as well as those caused by ecologically damaging patterns of human and social activity, as much as conflicts. In his millennium report, the Secretary-General noted that the cost of natural disasters in 1998 alone had exceeded the cost of all such disasters in the 1980s.[24] But the norm of disaster prevention had not been internalized by the governments around the Indian Ocean rim.

In consequence, there was a critical policy gap. Of course, policymakers faced competing priorities: should they divert resources to coping with a once-in-a-century tsunami, or invest in preparations for dealing with more regular floods and earthquakes? Should there be a tsunami warning system in the Indian Ocean (which rarely experienced tsunamis), or would the money be better spent elsewhere? The point is not that the lower policy priority given to tsunami warning and response systems is not understandable. Rather, the point is that given the existing state of knowledge in other countries and within the UN, not to invest in adequate systems to provide early warning and response mechanisms was a conscious policy choice. How else can we explain the deaths caused by the tsunami on the African continent hours after the earthquake?

That such a warning system is in place for the Pacific points also to the critical institutional gap for the Indian Ocean. Institutionally, the UN is not the main avenue for implementation, which is still seen as the primary responsibility of states and civil society. However, the tsunami highlighted that the UN was the institution of choice when it came to coordinating the response to a disaster of such enormity. Finally, with regard to compliance gaps, both dimensions of compliance may be highlighted. The political will to provide immediate assistance and help for the longer term was instantly mobilized, especially as in some cases citizens dipped into their pocketbooks more generously than their governments which were then

shamed into increasing their pledges. But there were operational failures, or implementation gaps, with aid agencies often competing with one another, and some
also proving inadequate to the challenges. The disaster also highlighted another
major and recurring gap, namely between pledges and delivery of the promised
funds and resources. There simply is no enforcement mechanism for holding governments or other donors to their word. One of the strongest methods of enforcing
compliance seems to be the UN's moral authority to call down shame on niggardly
or non-cooperative actors, which was used to nudge Western donors to substantially increase their initial contributions.

In short, and in spite of the absence of any overarching authority or established pool of financial and relief resources, ideas and experiments that had circulated for years resulted in a "crazy quilt" of responses that impressed even the UN's
harshest critics. The UN, through its Office for the Coordination of Humanitarian
Affairs (OCHA), orchestrated the relief effort across the 12 affected countries.
OCHA's Situation Reports, posted on a daily basis, represented the information-
gathering activity of the UN on a country-by-country basis, and had such useful
information as a situation summary, requirements including a breakdown of provision by sector, agency, and dollar amount, the UN's response, and the national
response. Through the ReliefWeb Internet site, OCHA was able to inform the
world both what survivors' immediate needs were, what was being done to meet
those needs, and the help aid workers required, such as transportation and communications equipment. The relief effort showed the UN's centrality and ability to
convene and foster multi-constituency processes, and its ability to provide global
leadership, as well as earlier discussions and actual experiences in human-made as
well as natural disasters. The UN-coordinated response to the 2004 tsunami thus
was far better than one might assume without any overarching global authority.

CHAPTER 3

Political Ideologies in the Age of Globalization

Manfred B. Steger

INTRODUCTION

For some time now, political and social theorists have been struggling to make sense of the transformation of what used to be a relatively durable ideological landscape dominated by the familiar mainstays of liberalism, conservatism, and socialism. Starting with the collapse of Soviet-style communism more than two decades ago, this period of conceptual destabilization accelerated further with the rise of "globalization"—the latest and most intense phase in the age-old human story of expanding and intensifying connections across world-time and world-space.[1] Most debates on the subject have revolved around its objective dynamics, especially the worldwide integration of markets aided by the information and communication revolution of the last quarter century.

While its material dimension is certainly important, it would be a serious mistake to neglect globalization's subjective aspects related to the creation of new cosmopolitan and hybrid identities linked to the thickening of a global imaginary. However, as Roland Robertson (2009: 121) has noted, the evolution of global consciousness has often been neglected in the social sciences and humanities. And yet, the study of the rising global imaginary constitutes an important area of theoretical inquiry where students of political ideologies can make crucial contributions to our understanding of subjective globalization. After all, the thickening of public awareness of the world as an interconnected whole has had a dramatic impact on political belief systems—those shared mental maps people utilize for the navigation of their complex political environments.

But what sort of evidence is there to bolster my claim that the conventional "isms" of the last two centuries have come under full-scale attack by the forces of globalization? For starters, one might consider what I have referred to elsewhere as the "proliferation of prefixes." "Neo" and "post," in particular, have managed to attach themselves to most conventional "isms" (Steger 2008: viii).[2] As a result, one encounters with remarkable frequency in both academic writings and public discourse such curious compounds as "neoliberalism," "neoconservatism," "neofascism," "neoanarchism," "post-Marxism," "postcommunism," "postmodernism," "post-colonialism," and so on. Granted, some of these isms may not constitute full-blown *political* ideologies, but this should not detract from the fact that all major political belief systems have been afflicted by the invasion of the prefixes. This prefix phenomenon not only points to a growing sense that something "neo" has descended upon the ideological landscape of the twenty-first century, but also casts a long shadow on the contemporary relevance of conventional political idea-systems and their corresponding typologies.

What then, precisely, is new about political ideologies? Have we really moved "post" our conventional ideological landscape? Responding to these questions, this chapter reflects on why and how the forces of globalization have altered the grand political ideologies codified by social power elites since the French Revolution. In order to explain these transformations, I discuss at some length the crucial relationship between two social imaginaries—the national and the global—and political ideologies. The chapter ends with a brief survey of my own attempt to arrive at a new classification system for contemporary "globalisms." This typology is based on the disaggregation of these new ideational clusters (formed around the global) not merely into core concepts, but—perhaps more dynamically—into various sets of central ideological claims that play crucial semantic and political roles. As I have argued elsewhere in some detail, these three major globalisms—market globalism, justice globalism, and religious globalisms—represent a set of political ideas and beliefs coherent and conceptually "thick" enough to warrant the status of mature ideologies (Steger 2005).

Unfortunately, the fundamental changes affecting political belief systems triggered by the forces of globalization have not been adequately described or analysed in the pertinent literature. Well-intentioned attempts to "update" modern political belief systems by adorning them with prefixes resemble futile efforts to make sense of digital word processing by drawing on the mechanics of movable print. The failure to redraw our ideological maps appears most glaringly in leading academic textbooks where the grand ideologies of the national age—complemented by various neo-isms—continue to be presented as the dominant political belief systems of our time.[3] To grasp the novelty of today's globalisms, we must realize that large chunks of the grand ideologies of modernity—liberalism, conservatism, socialism, fascism, and communism—have been discarded, absorbed, reconfigured, synthesized, and hybridized with new core concepts such as "globalization" and "sustainability" into ideologies of genuine novelty. But before we survey the morphologies (ideational structures) of these new globalisms, let us consider the crucial relationship between political ideologies and various deep-seated "social imaginaries."

IDEOLOGIES AND SOCIAL IMAGINARIES

Modern political ideologies emerged during the American and French Revolutions as malleable political belief systems that competed with religious doctrines over what sorts of ideas and values should guide human communities. Supposedly constituting "secular" perspectives on these fundamental questions, ideologies nonetheless resembled religions in their attempts to link the various ethical, cultural, and political dimensions of society into a fairly comprehensive thought-system. Imitating their rivals' penchant to trade in truth and certainty, ideologies also relied on narratives, metaphor, and myths that persuaded, praised, condemned, cajoled, convinced, and separated the "good" from the "bad." Like religion, they thrived on human emotions, generating rage, fear, enthusiasm, love, sacrifice, and altruism. Ideologies inspired mass murder, torture, and rape in much the same way as religious doctrines have run through the gamut of human vices (Hazareesingh 1994: 13). Its pejorative connotations notwithstanding, however, ideology deserves a more balanced hearing—one that acknowledges its integrative role of providing social stability as much as its propensity to contribute to fragmentation and alienation; its ability to supply standards of normative evaluation as much as its tendency to oversimplify social complexity; its role as guide and compass for political action as much as its potential to legitimize tyranny and terror in the name of noble ideals.

Drawing on this appreciative conception of ideology that takes seriously the indispensable functions of political belief systems irrespective of their particular contents or political orientations, I define ideology as comprehensive belief systems comprised of patterned ideas and claims to truth. Codified by social elites, these shared mental maps that help people navigate their complex political environments are embraced by significant groups in society (Steger 2009b; Sargent 2008). All political belief systems are historically contingent and, therefore, must be analysed with reference to particular contexts that connect their origins and developments to specific times and spaces. Linking belief and practice, ideologies encourage people to act while simultaneously constraining their actions.

To this end, ideological codifiers—typically social elites residing in large cities—construct "truth claims" that seek to fix authoritative definitions and meanings of their core concepts. Michael Freeden refers to this crucial process as "decontestation." As he puts it, "An ideology attempts to end the inevitable contention over concepts by *decontesting* them, by removing their meanings from contest. 'This is what justice means,' announces one ideology, and 'that is what democracy entails'" (Freeden 2003: 54–5).[4] By trying to convince us that their claims are "true," ideologies produce conceptual stability, thus serving as key devices for coping with the indeterminacy of meaning. Although even successfully decontested ideas always require further explanations and justifications, their meanings are accepted by significant segments of the population with such confidence that they no longer appear to be "opinions" at all. Ultimately, these decontested core concepts (such as freedom, equality, justice, tradition, class, race, and so on) are linked to related "adjacent" concepts to form coherent ideational claims which give each ideology its unique configuration. Such ideological "morphologies" should thus be pictured as decontested truth-claims that serve as devices for decontesting meanings as well as instruments for facilitating collective decision-making. It would be a mistake to reduce ideologies to mere justifications of economic class interests or impractical metaphysical speculations. Although they frequently distort and provide legitimation for dominant power interests, ideologies also contribute to the necessary construction of identities and bonds of political belonging. Thus, they are fairly comprehensive shared mental maps that guide people through the complexity of their social environments. In short, ideologies are indispensable ideational systems that shape and direct human communities in concrete political ways.[5]

To understand the fundamental changes affecting the ideological landscape of the twenty-first century, it is necessary to grasp the connection between competing political ideologies and their overarching "social imaginary." Constituting the macro-mappings of social and political space through which we perceive, judge, and act in the world, social imaginaries are deep-seated modes of understanding that provide the most general parameters within which people imagine their communal existence. Drawing on Benedict Anderson's (1991) account of the imagined community of the nation, Charles Taylor (2004: 2, 23–6) argues that social imaginaries are neither theories nor ideologies, but implicit "background understandings" that make possible communal practices and a widely shared sense of their legitimacy. Social imaginaries offer explanations of how "we"—the members of a particular community—fit together, how things go on between us, the expectations we have of each other, and the deeper normative notions and images that underlie those expectations. These background understandings are both normative and factual in the sense of providing us with the standards of what passes as common-sense. Much in the same vein, Pierre Bourdieu (1990: 54–5) notes that the social imaginary sets the pre-reflexive framework for our daily routines and social repertoires. Structured by social dynamics that produce them while at the same time also structuring those forces, social imaginaries are products of history that "generate individual and collective practices—more history—in accordance with the schemes generated by history."

Human thought is mostly unconscious, and abstract concepts are largely metaphorical. Indeed, most of human reasoning is based on mental images that are seldom explicit; usually they are merely presupposed in everyday reasoning and debates. Thus, all social imaginaries express themselves in a series of interrelated and mutually dependent narratives, visual prototypes, metaphors, and conceptual framings. Despite their apparent intangibility, however, social imaginaries are quite "real" in the sense of enabling common practices and deep-seated communal attachments. Though capable of facilitating collective fantasies and speculative reflections, they should not be dismissed as phantasms or mental fabrications. As shared visions of self and community, social imaginaries often find expression as nameable collectivities such as "Americans" or "Hutus." Endowed with specific properties, social imaginaries acquire additional solidity through the social construction of space and the repetitive performance of their assigned qualities and characteristics. Thus feigning permanence, social imaginaries are nonetheless temporary constellations subject to constant change. Social imaginaries acquire additional solidity through the (re)construction of social space and the repetitive performance of certain communal qualities and characteristics. And yet, they are temporary constellations subject to change. At certain tipping points in history, such change can occur with lightning speed and tremendous ferocity.

The late eighteenth- and early nineteenth-century social revolutions in the Americas and Europe, for example, made visible the transformation of the "traditional social imaginary" in a dramatic way. For many generations, the conventional modes of understanding had reproduced divinely sanctioned power hierarchies in the form of tribes, clanships, trading city-states, and dynastic empires. Between 1776 and 1848, however, there arose on both sides of the Atlantic the familiar template of the "nation" now no longer referring to the king at the pinnacle of the state hierarchy, but to an abstract "general will" operating in free citizens fighting for their homeland. The political message was as clear as it was audacious: henceforth it would be "the people"—not kings, aristocrats, or clerical elites—that exercised legitimate authority in political affairs. Over time, the will of the people would replace monarchical forms of communal authority based on transcendental powers emanating from a divine realm beyond the nation. Thus, modern nationhood found its expression in the transformation of subjects into citizens who laid claim to equal membership in the nation and institutionalized their sovereignty in the modern nation-state. But who really counted as part of the people and what constituted the essence of the nation became the subject of fierce intellectual debates and material struggles. Seeking to remake the world according to the rising national imaginary, citizens exhibited a restlessness that became the hallmark of modernity. As William Connolly (1988: 2–3) observes, "Modern agencies form and reform, produce and reproduce, incorporate and reincorporate, industrialize and reindustrialize. In modernity, modernization is always under way."

Countless meanings and definitions of modernity have been put forward in the last two centuries. They extend far beyond familiar designations referring to a historical era in the West characterized by its radical rupture with the past and its ensuing temporal reorientation toward notions of infinite progress, economic growth, and enduring material prosperity. As the philosopher Juergen Habermas (1987: 7) reminds us, modernity is inextricably intertwined with an expanding "public sphere"—the incubator of modernity's tendency to "create its own normativity out of itself." Various thinkers have elaborated on the main dynamics of modernity: the separation of state and civil society; conceptions of linear time; progressive secularization; individualism; intensifying geopolitical rivalries that facilitated the formation and multiplication of nation-states; new orders of rationality and their corresponding domains of knowledge; the uneven expansion of industrial capitalism; the rapid diffusion of discursive literacy; the slow trend toward democratization; and so on. The detailed genealogy of these features need not concern us here. What we ought to consider straightaway, however, is the position of the national in the modern social imaginary.

IDEOLOGIES AND THE NATIONAL IMAGINARY

New treatments of nationality and nationalism appearing on the academic scene since the early 1980s have advanced convincing arguments in favour of a tight connection between the forces of modernity, the spread of industrial capitalism, and the elite-engineered construction of the "national community" as a cultural artifact.

As Eric Hobsbawm (1992: 14) notes, "The basic characteristic of the modern nation and everything associated with it is its modernity." Even scholars like Anthony Smith (1998: 1), who reject the modernist view that nations were simply "invented" without the significant incorporation of pre-modern ethnic ties and histories, concede that nationalism represents "a modern movement and ideology, which emerged in the latter half of the eighteenth century in Western Europe and America." Smith's definition of nationalism as an "ideological movement for the attainment and maintenance of a nation" usefully highlights the idiosyncratic ways of processing and disseminating secular ideas that emerged in the nineteenth century as a distinctive feature of modernity. As Tom Nairn (2005: 13) explains, "An ism ceased to denote just a system of general ideas (like Platonism or Thomism) and evolved into a proclaimed cause or movement—no longer a mere school but a party or societal trend." In other words, ideas acquired alluring banner headlines and truth claims that resonated with people's interests and aspirations and thus bound them to a specific political program. Having to choose sides in these proliferating battles of political ideas, like-minded individuals organized themselves into clubs, associations, movements, and political parties with the primary objective of enlisting more people to their preferred normative vision of the national.

There is, however, a downside to Smith's definition: it turns nationalism into an ideology of the same ilk as liberalism or conservatism. This begs the question of how nationalism can be both a distinct political ideology and a common source of inspiration for a variety of political belief systems. Sensing the overarching stature of the national, Benedict Anderson and other social thinkers with an anthropological bent have resisted the idea that nationalism should be seen as a distinct ideology. Instead, they refer to it as a "cultural artifact of a particular kind," that is, a relatively broad cultural system more closely related to "kinship" and "religion" than to "liberalism" or "conservatism" (Geertz 1973; Anderson 1991; Dumont 1994). Following their intuition, then, I suggest that we treat the national not as an ideology in its own right but as a crucial component of the modern social imaginary. As such, the "national imaginary" corresponds to what Benedict Anderson (1991: 6–7) has called "modern imaginings of the nation" as a limited and sovereign community of individuals whose knowledge of each other is, in most cases, not direct, but mediated in linear time through the diffusion of discursive literacy. This was made possible, in part, by the invention of printing technology embedded in nascent capitalism.

Since the national decisively coloured the modern social imaginary, we ought to treat the national not as a separate ideology but as the background to our communal existence that emerged in the Northern Hemisphere with the American and French Revolutions. The national gave the modern social imaginary its distinct flavour in the form of various factual and normative assumptions that political communities, in order to count as "legitimate," had to be nation-states (Greenfeld 2004: 40). The "national imaginary," then, refers to the taken-for-granted understanding in which the nation—plus its affiliated or to-be-affiliated state—serves the central framework of the political community.

What, then, is the precise relationship between the national and ideology? Or, to reverse the question, what is the connection between political belief systems and the national imaginary? I suggest that ideologies translate and articulate the largely pre-reflexive social imaginary in compressed form as explicit political doctrine. This means that the grand ideologies of modernity gave explicit political expression to the implicit national imaginary. To be sure, each ideology deployed and assembled its core concepts in specific and unique ways. But the elite codifiers of these ideational systems pursued their specific political goals under the common background umbrella of the national imaginary. Liberalism, conservatism, socialism, communism, and Nazism/fascism were all "nationalist" in the sense of performing the same fundamental task of translating the overarching national imaginary into concrete political doctrines, agendas, and spatial arrangements. In so doing, ideologies normalized national territories; spoke in recognized national languages; appealed to national histories; told national legends and myths or glorified a national "race." They articulated the national imaginary according to certain criteria that were said to constitute the defining essence of the community.[6]

But whatever ideologies purported the essence of the nation to be, they always developed their truth-claims by decontesting their core concepts within the national imaginary. Liberals, for example, spoke of "freedom" as applying to autonomous individuals belonging to the same national community, that is, the liberties of *French, Colombian,* or *Australian* citizens. The conservative fondness for traditional "law and order" received its highest expression in the notion of *national* security. Even the apparent "internationalism" of socialists and communists was not tantamount to what I call "globalism." First, the term "inter-*national*" betrays its reliance on the "nation" as its central conceptual category. The whole point of an ideational framework centred on the "global" is to go beyond the nation-state as the basic unit of analysis. Second, socialist internationalism achieved its concrete political formulation and manifestation only as *German* social democracy or Soviet *Russia's* "socialism in one country" or "socialism with *Chinese* characteristics." Third, even the supposed *theoretical* "global" characteristics of communism/socialism reflect their unmistaken national rootedness in the basic documents of these two political belief systems.[7]

For two centuries, then, the partisans of the major political ideologies clashed with each other over such important issues as participation, the extent of civil rights, the purposes and forms of government, the role of the state, the significance of race and ethnicity, and the scope of political obligations. Clinging to their different political visions, they hardly noticed their common embeddedness in the national imaginary. Insisting on their obvious differences, they hardly questioned their common allegiance to the overarching national imaginary. After all, the business of modern political belief systems was the formidable task of realizing their core values under the banner of the nation-state—the ceaseless task of translating the national imaginary into competing political projects.

IDEOLOGIES AND THE GLOBAL IMAGINARY

In the aftermath of the Second World War, new ideas, theories, and material practices produced in the public consciousness a similar sense of rupture with the past that had occurred at the time of the French Revolution. For example, novel technologies facilitated the speed and intensity with which these ideas and practices infiltrated the national imaginary. Images, people, and materials circulated more freely across national boundaries. This new sense of "the global" that erupted within and onto the national began to undermine the sense of normalcy and self-contained coziness associated with the modern nation-state—especially deeply engrained notions of community tied to a sovereign and clearly demarcated territory containing relatively homogenous populations (Appadurai 2006; Albrow 1997). Identities based on national membership became destabilized. During the early decades of the Cold War, the changing social imaginary led prominent thinkers in the "First World" to proclaim the "end of ideology." As evidence for their assertion, they pointed to the political-cultural consensus underpinning a common Western "community of values" and the socioeconomic welfare state compromise struck between liberalism and democratic socialism. Conversely, detractors of the end of ideology thesis seized upon the decolonization dynamics in the "Third World" as well as the rise of the counter-cultural "new social movements" in the 1960s and 1970s as evidence for their view that the familiar political belief systems were being complemented by "new ideologies" such as feminism, environmentalism, and postcolonialism.

But, as indicated by the new designations First, Second, and Third *World*, the most fundamental novelty of these "new ideologies" lay in their sensitivity toward the rising global imaginary, regardless of whether they were formulated by the forces of the "New Left" or the cohorts of the "New Right." Starting in the late 1970s, and especially after the 1991 disintegration of the Soviet Union, the neoclassical economic ideas of the New Right gained the upper hand across the globe. By the mid- 1990s, a growing chorus of global social elites was fastening onto the new buzzword "globalization" as the central metaphor for their political agenda—the creation of a single global free market and the spread of consumerist values around the world. Most importantly, they translated the rising social imaginary into largely economistic claims laced with references to globality: global trade and financial markets, worldwide flows of goods, services, and labour, transnational corporations, offshore financial centres, and so on.

But globalization was never merely a matter of increasing flows of capital and goods across national borders. Rather, it constitutes a multidimensional set of processes in which images, sound bites, metaphors, myths, symbols, and spatial arrangements of globality were just as important as economic and technological dynamics. Such heightened awareness of the compression of time and space influences the direction and material instantiations of global flows. As Roland Robertson (1992, 2009) has emphasized time and again, the compression of the world into a single place increasingly makes "the global" the frame of reference for human thought and action. Thus, globalization involves both the macro-structures of community and the micro-structures of personhood. It extends deep into the core of the self and its dispositions, facilitating the creation of new identities nurtured by the intensifying relations between the individual and the globe (Elliott and Lemert 2006: 90).

Like the conceptual earthquake that shook Europe and the Americas more than two hundred years ago, today's destabilization of the national affects the entire planet. The ideologies dominating the world today are no longer exclusively articulations of the national imaginary but reconfigured ideational systems that constitute early-stage translations of the dawning global imaginary. Although my account of this transformation emphasizes rupture, it would be foolish to deny obvious continuities. As Saskia Sassen (2008: 402) notes, the incipient process of denationalization and the ascendance of novel social formations depend in good part on capabilities shaped and developed in the national age.

THREE GLOBALISMS: TOWARD A NEW TYPOLOGY OF POLITICAL IDEOLOGIES IN THE TWENTY-FIRST CENTURY

As capitalist liberalism expanded across the globe after the fall of Soviet communism, it drew on the basic neoclassical ideas of politically engaged economists like Friedrich Hayek and Milton Friedman, who had seized upon the crisis of Keynesianism in the 1970s to pitch their ideas to rising conservative politicians in the United States and United Kingdom. Still, it represented a remarkable ideological achievement for market-globalist codifiers in the 1990s to reconfigure these ideas around the buzzword "globalization," thereby articulating the rising global imaginary in concrete political agendas and programmes. The Anglo-American framers of market globalism spoke softly and persuasively as they sought to attract people worldwide to their vision of globalization as a leaderless, inevitable juggernaut that would ultimately engulf the entire world and produce liberal democracy and material benefits for everyone.

Even after the two severe crises of the 2000s—global terrorism and the Great Recession—market globalism ("neoliberalism") has remained the dominant ideology of our global age. Although market globalists across the planet share a common belief in the power of free markets to create a better world, their doctrine comes in different hues and multiple variations. "Reaganomics," for example, is not exactly the same as "Thatcherism." Bill Clinton's brand of market globalism diverges in some respects from Tony Blair's "Third Way." And political elites in the global South (often educated at the elite universities of the North) have learned to fit the dictates of the market-globalist "Washington Consensus" to their own local contexts and political objectives. Thus, market globalism has adapted to specific environments, problems, and opportunities across the world.

The discursive preeminence of the "market," of course, harkens back to the heyday of liberalism in mid-Victorian England. And yet, market globalists no longer tie this concept exclusively to the old paradigm of self-contained national economies but refer primarily to a model of global exchanges among national actors, subnational agencies, supranational bodies, networks of non-governmental organizations (NGOs), and transnational corporations. Our globalizing world contains a multiplicity of orders networked together on multiple levels. Disaggregating nation-states struggle to come to grips with relational concepts of sovereignty while facing unprecedented challenges to their authority from both subnational and supranational collectivities.

As I have argued elsewhere in much detail, market globalism emerged in the 1990s as a comprehensive ideology extolling, among other things, the virtues of globally integrating markets (Steger 2009, 2009b). Ideationally much richer than the more familiar term "neoliberalism" suggests, market globalism discarded, absorbed, and rearranged large chunks of the grand ideologies while at the same time incorporating genuinely new ideas. The outcome was a new political belief system centred on six central ideological claims that translated the global imaginary into concrete political programmes and agendas: (1) globalization is about the liberalization and global integration of markets; (2) globalization is inevitable and irreversible; (3) nobody is in charge of globalization; (4) globalization benefits everyone; (5) globalization furthers the spread of democracy in the world; and (6) globalization requires a global war on terror.[8]

The ideological codification and public dissemination of these claims fell disproportionately to global power elites enamoured with neoliberal economics and consisting mostly of corporate managers, executives of large transnational corporations, corporate lobbyists, prominent journalists and public-relations specialists, media tycoons, cultural elites and entertainment celebrities, academics writing for large audiences, high-level state bureaucrats, and political leaders. They marshalled their considerable material and ideal resources to sell to the public the alleged benefits of the liberalization of trade and the global integration of markets: rising living standards, reduction of global poverty, economic efficiency, individual freedom and democracy, and unprecedented technological progress. Ideally, the state should only provide the legal framework for contracts, defence, and law and order. Public policy initiatives should be confined to those measures that liberate the economy from social constraints: privatization of public enterprises, deregulation instead of state control, liberalization of trade and industry, massive tax cuts, strict control of organized labor, and the reduction of public expenditures. Other models of economic organization were discredited as being "protectionist" or "socialist." Seeking to enshrine their neoliberal paradigm as the self-evident and universal order of our global era, these transnational power elites articulated the rising global imaginary along the lines of their six ideological claims.

But no single ideational system ever enjoys absolute dominance. Battered by persistent gales of political dissent, the small fissures and ever-present inconsistencies in political ideologies threaten to turn into major cracks and serious contradictions. As the 1990s drew to a close, market globalism found itself challenged on the political Left by what I call "justice globalism"—an alternative translation of the rising global imaginary propagated by the members of the "global justice movement" (GJM) who argued against "corporate globalization" (Steger, Goodman, and Wilson 2013). At the core of global justice lies the ideological claim that the liberalization and global integration of markets leads, in fact, to greater social inequalities, environmental destruction, the escalation of global conflicts and violence, the weakening of participatory forms of democracy, the proliferation of self-interest and consumerism, and the further marginalization of the powerless around the world.

Hence, the chief ideological codifiers of justice globalism—often the leading voices of progressive networks and alliances connected to the World Social Forum (WSF)—seek to accomplish two fundamental tasks. The first is ideological, reflected in concerted efforts to undermine the premises and ideological framework of the reigning market-globalist world-view by constructing and disseminating alternative articulations of the global imaginary based on the core principles of the WSF: equality, global social justice, diversity, democracy, nonviolence, solidarity, ecological sustainability, and planetary citizenship (Steger and Wilson 2012). The second is political, manifested in the attempt to realize these principles by means of mass mobilizations and non-violent direct action targeting the core structures of market globalism: international economic institutions like the WTO (World Trade Organization) and the IMF (International Monetary Fund), transnational corporations and affiliated NGOs, large industry federations and lobbies, and the "American Empire."

The justice-globalist vision is neither about reviving a moribund Marxism nor about a return to the "good old days" of 1968. Although justice globalism contains elements of Gandhian Third World liberationism and traditional European social democracy, it goes beyond these Cold War ideational clusters in several respects—most importantly in its ability to bring together a large number of New Left concerns around a more pronounced orientation toward the globe as a single, interconnected arena for political action. One example of the GJM's strong global focus is its publicity campaign to highlight the negative consequences of deregulated global capitalism on the planet's environmental health. Indeed, in the first decade of the new century, the issue of global climate change has advanced to the forefront of public discourse around the world, second only to the spectre of global terrorism and warfare.

Finally, the policy vision of justice globalism lays out in some detail by now rather familiar proposals. The programmatic core of these demands is a "global Marshall Plan"—now a fashionable buzzword that has entered the mainstream discourse as a result of the lingering 2008–2009 Great Recession—that would create more political space for people around the world to determine what kind of social arrangements they want. As Susan George (2004: chaps. 6–10), a seasoned GJM activist widely considered one of the movement's premier "idea persons" notes, "another world" has to begin with a new, worldwide Keynesian-type programme of taxation and redistribution, exactly as it took off at the national level in the now-rich countries a century or so ago. Justice globalists like George envision the necessary funds for this global regulatory framework to come from the profits of transnational corporations and financial markets—hence their worldwide campaign for the introduction of the global Tobin Tax. Other proposals include the cancellation of poor countries' debts; the closing of offshore financial centres offering tax havens for wealthy individuals and corporations; the ratification and implementation of stringent global environmental agreements; the implementation of a more equitable global development agenda; the establishment of a new world development institution financed largely by the global North and administered largely by the global South; establishment of international labour protection standards, perhaps as clauses of a profoundly reformed WTO; greater transparency and accountability provided to citizens by national governments and global economic institutions; making all governance of globalization explicitly gender sensitive; the transformation of "free trade" into "fair trade," and a binding commitment to non-violent direct action as the sole vehicle of social and political change.

Market globalism has also been challenged from the political Right by various "religious globalisms." Indeed, today we are witnessing a weakening if not a reversal of the powerful secularization dynamic of the last centuries as a result of the decline of the national. Moreover, the rising global imaginary has been creating more favourable conditions for the convergence of political and religious belief systems. It is unlikely that secularism in the West will disappear any time soon, but the religious will give it a run for its money, forcing previously unimagined forms of accommodation and compromise. In short, the rising global imaginary will continue to create fertile conditions for "religious ideologies" or "ideological religions." Consequently, we ought to treat religious ideas and beliefs as an increasingly integral part of certain global ideologies. While religious globalisms are not tied to one specific religion, Al Qaeda's form of "Islamist globalism" represents one of the most potent religious ideologies of our time.

As can be gleaned from the vast literature on "Islamism," this term has been used in many different ways by both Muslims and non-Muslims to refer to various "movements" and "ideologies" dedicated to the revival of Islam and its political realization. Related terms currently in circulation include "political Islam," "Islamic fundamentalism," "Islamist purism," and the pejorative "Islamo-fascism."[9] Although different in causes, responses, strategies, and collective identities, various forms of Islamism share the common proclivity to synthesize certain religious elements of their traditional political discourses with certain elements of modern ideologies. Indeed, Islamisms are about the politicization of religion just as much as they represent the sacralization of modern politics.

This chapter's focus on al Qaeda's Islamist globalism is neither meant to downplay the diversity of ideational currents within Islamism nor to present one particular strain as its most representative or authentic manifestation. Rather, the doctrine articulated by the likes of the late Osama bin Laden, Ayman al-Zawahiri, or the late Abu Musab al-Zarqawi has been the most prominent example of Islamist globalism. Second, its tremendous influence around the world points to the rise of new political ideologies resulting from the ongoing deterritorialization of Islam. Third, Islamist globalism constitutes the most successful ideological attempt yet to articulate the rising global imaginary around its core concepts of *umma* (Islamic community of believers in the one and only God), *jihad* (armed or unarmed "struggle" against unbelief purely for the sake of God and his *umma*), and *tawhid* (the absolute unity of God). As Bruce Lawrence notes, the bulk of Osama bin Laden's writings and public addresses emerged in the context of a "virtual world" moving from print to the Internet and from wired to wireless communication. Largely scriptural in mode, the al Qaeda leader's "messages to the world" were deliberately designed for the new global media. They appeared on video and audio tapes, websites, and hand-written letters scanned onto computer disks and delivered to Arabic-language news outlets, including the influential Qatari satellite television network al-Jazeera.[10]

Decontesting their core concepts of *umma, jihad,* and *tahwid* in potent ideological claims, bin Laden and al-Zawahiri developed a narrative predicated upon globalization's destabilization of the national imaginary. Seeing themselves as members of a global *umma,* they consciously addressed a global audience of believers and non-believers. Al Qaeda's desired Islamization of modernity has taken place in global space emancipated from the confining national or regional territoriality of "Egypt" or the "Middle East" that used to constitute the political framework of religious nationalists fighting modern secular regimes in the twentieth century. As Olivier Roy (2004: 19) observes, "The Muslim *umma* no longer has anything to do with a territorial entity. It has to be thought of in abstract and imaginary terms."

Although al Qaeda embraces the Manichean dualism of a "clash of civilizations" between its imagined global *umma* and global *kufr* ("unbelief"), its globalism transcends clear-cut civilizational fault lines. Its desire for the restoration of a transnational *umma* attests to the globalization and Westernization of the Muslim world just as much as it reflects the Islamization of the West. Constructed in the ideational interregnum between the national and the global, jihadist-globalist claims still retain potent metaphors that resonate with people's national or even tribal solidarities.[11] In its contemporary phase following the killing of bin Laden on 2 May 2011 by US Special Forces, al Qaeda's focus has remained on the global as its new leaders target both the "Near Enemy" (the new secular or moderate Islamist regimes in Iraq, Afghanistan, and other countries in the region) and the "Far Enemy" (the globalizing West). This remarkable discursive and strategic shift reflects the destabilization of the national imaginary. By the early 1990s, nationally based Islamist groups were losing steam, partly as a result of their inability to mobilize their respective communities around national concerns, and partly because they were subjected to more effective counterstrategies devised by secular-nationalist regimes.[12]

Hence, bin Laden and al-Zawahiri urged their followers to take the war against Islam's enemies globally. Al Qaeda's simple ideological imperative—rebuild a unified global *umma* through global *jihad* against global *kufr*—resonated with the dynamics of a globalizing world.[13]

For example, in a videotaped address to the American people aired around the world only a few days before the 2004 election, bin Laden managed to inject himself into a national electoral contest as the self-appointed leader of the global *umma.* Articulating the rising global imaginary as the familiar set of political claims, the al Qaeda leader appeared on the TV screens of a global audience as the world's chief critic of American democracy. As Faisal Devji notes, al Qaeda's Islamist globalism projected no national ambitions, for it was as global as the West itself, both being intertwined and even internal to each other: "This is why Bin Laden's calls for the United States to leave the Muslim world do not entail the return to a cold-war geopolitics of détente, but are conceived rather in terms of a global reciprocity on equal terms."[14]

Another videotaped message delivered by the al Qaeda leader in September 2007 unleashed further verbal broadsides against the "corrupt American political system." He linked the Bush administration's involvement in Iraq to transnational corporate interests that held "the American people" hostage to their all-out scramble for war-related profits. Moreover, bin Laden charged "the capitalist system" with seeking "to turn the entire world into a fiefdom of the major corporations under the label of 'globalization.' . . ."[15] Unsurprisingly, bin Laden's first audiotaped message to President Barack Obama in June 2009 followed the same ideological pattern. Osama bin Laden's death has done little to change the form and substance of the religious globalist message now delivered by a new generation of al Qaeda leaders.

Although some political commentators have suggested that virulent forms of national-populism embodied by the likes of Jean-Marie Le Pen or Patrick Buchanan constitute the most powerful right-wing challenge to market globalism, I contend that this designation belongs to "religious globalisms." Far from being a regionally contained "last gasp" of a backward-looking, militant offshoot of political Islam, jihadism of the al Qaeda variety still represents a potent globalism of worldwide appeal. But we must not forget that "religious globalism" comes in the plural and goes beyond this article's narrow focus on one particular Islamist variant. Other religiously inspired visions of global political community include fundamentalist Christian groups such as the Army of God and Christian Identity, Sikh movements, Falun Gong, and the Aum Shinrikyo cult in Japan. Despite their deep conservatism, and in contrast to the liberal and socialist links of market and justice globalisms, religious globalisms still also promote an alternative global vision. This is not to suggest that *all* religiously inspired visions of global community are conservative and reactionary. Indeed, most religions incorporate a sense of a global community united along religious lines, although in general this is largely informal. A key point about the religious globalist visions highlighted here, however, is that these groups desire their version of a global religious community to be all-encompassing, to be given primacy and superiority over state- and secular-based political structures and are prepared to use violent means to achieve this end goal. The vast majority of religious believers do not seek to institute their global religious community over the authority of the state, rather recognizing that it should only relate to those who share the same beliefs and should remain largely informal. Thus again, religious globalisms may be considered one variant within a family of contesting ideologies.

CONCLUDING REMARKS

Potent as they are, the dynamics of denationalization at the heart of globalization neither propel the world to an inevitable endpoint nor have these forces dispensed entirely with vast ideational and material arsenals of the nation-state. The geographical concreteness of global dynamics stares us in the face as the Cuban-Chinese restaurant around the corner or the Eurasian fusion café next door. These hybrid culinary establishments are serving us up a daily taste of a global stew that is slowly thickening but still needs plenty of stirring. The national is slowly losing its grip on people's minds, but the global has not yet ascended to the commanding heights once occupied by its predecessor. It erupts in fits and false starts, offering observers confusing spectacles of social fragmentation and integration that cut across old geographical hierarchies of scale in unpredictable patterns.[16]

As the national and the global rub up against each other in myriad settings and on multiple levels, they produce new tensions and compromises. Putting the analytic spotlight on the changing ideational structures not only yields a better understanding of current globalization dynamics, but also helps us make sense of the shifting conceptual and geographical boundaries that (re)shape individual and collective identities. Although globalization unfolds toward an uncertain future, the first attempts to translate the rising global imaginary into concrete political agendas have yielded textual evidence to point to a profoundly altered ideological landscape.

CHAPTER 4

Globalization and the Emergence of the World Social Forums

Jackie Smith, Marina Karides, Marc Becker, Dorval Brunelle,
Christopher Chase-Dunn, Donatella della Porta,
Rosalba Icaza Garza, Jeffrey S. Juris, Lorenzo Mosca,
Ellen Reese, Peter (Jay) Smith, and Rolando Vasquez

In the 1970s and 1980s, protests against the lending policies of the International Monetary Fund (IMF) emerged in the global south. By the late 1990s, tens of thousands of protesters were gathering wherever the world's political and economic elite met, raising criticisms of global economic policies and calling for more just and equitable economic policies. As the numbers of protesters grew, so did the violence with which governments responded. Governments spent millions and arrested hundreds of nonviolent protesters to ensure their meetings could take place. Italian police killed Carlo Giuliani, a twenty-three-year-old protester, at the meeting of the Group of 8 (G8) in Genoa in 2001, dramatizing for activists in the global north the brutal repression against activists that is common in the global south. The size of police mobilizations against these overwhelmingly nonviolent protests was unprecedented in Western democracies, and it signaled the declining legitimacy of the system of economic globalization promoted by the world's most powerful governments. After years of such protests against the world's most powerful economic institutions—the World Bank, the International Monetary Fund, the World Trade Organization (WTO), and the G8—a team of Latin American and French activists launched the first World Social Forum (WSF) in January 2001.

Over just a few short years, the WSF has become the largest political gathering in modern history and a major focal point of global efforts to promote an alternative vision of global integration. Mobilizing around the slogan "Another World Is Possible," the WSF began as both a protest against the annual World Economic Forum (WEF) in Davos, Switzerland, and as an effort to develop a shared vision of alternatives to the predominant, market-based model of globalization. Many see the WSF as a crucial process for the development of a global civil society that can help democratize the global political and economic order, and some would argue that it is the most important political development of our time. In this chapter we describe the political and economic conditions that gave rise to the global justice movement and the WSF.

The first WSF was held in Porto Alegre, Brazil, in late January 2001. The timing of the WSF was strategically chosen to coincide with the WEF, an annual meeting of global political and economic elites typically held in Davos, Switzerland. The WEF is a private interest group that has worked since its founding in 1971 to promote dialogue among business leaders and governments and to shape the global economy. Over the years an ever-more-impressive list of political leaders have participated in this private event, for which corporate members pay upward of $15,000 for the opportunity to schmooze with the global power elite. Civil society has been largely shut out of the process of planning an increasingly powerful global economy.

The WEF is widely criticized for providing a space where the future of the world is decided while excluding the democratic participation of most of the globe's population. French and Latin American activist groups and political organizations were among the first to protest the WEF in 1999. This eventually blossomed into the idea of a WSF that received sponsorship in Brazil from the Worker's Party, a political party that won government elections in the city of Porto Alegre, supported the principles of global economic justice, and was willing to work with social change activists to coordinate the first WSF.

This first meeting in Porto Alegre, Brazil, drew more than twice the 4,000 people organizers anticipated, and the global meeting now regularly attracts more than 150,000 registered participants. Its first attempt to move outside of Porto Alegre was in 2004 when the WSF met in Mumbai, India. After a return to Porto Alegre in 2005, it moved to Africa (Nairobi) in 2007 in an effort to expand opportunities for different activists to participate. Inspired by the call for open discussions of and organizing around visions of "another world," activists launched regional and local counterparts to the WSF around the world. This expanded opportunities for citizens to become part of the WSF process and helped sustain and energize local organizing efforts.

The WSF has become an important, but certainly not the only, focal point for the global justice movement: It is a setting where activists can meet their counterparts from other parts of the world, expand their understandings of globalization and of the interdependencies among the world's peoples, and plan joint campaigns to promote their common aims. It allows people to actively debate proposals for organizing global policy while nurturing values of tolerance, equality, and participation. And it has generated some common ideas about other visions for a better world. Unlike the WEF, the activities of the WSF are crucial to cultivating a foundation for a more democratic global economic and political order.

The WSF not only fosters networking among activists from different places, but it also plays a critical role in supporting what might be called a transnational counterpublic (Olesen 2005; cf. Fraser 1992). Democracy requires public spaces for the articulation of different interests and visions of desirable futures. If we are to have a more democratic global system, we need to enable more citizens to become active participants in global policy discussions. Without a global public sphere, there can be no plural discussion of global issues. Even the most democratic governments lack public input and accountability for actions that influence the living conditions of people in other parts of the world.

Just as the WSF serves as a foundation for a more democratic global polity, it also provides routine contact among the countless individuals and organizations working to address common grievances against global economic and political structures. This contact is essential for helping activists share analyses and coordinate strategies, but it is also indispensable as a means of reaffirming a common commitment to and vision of "another world," especially when day-to-day struggles often dampen such hope. Isolated groups lack information and creative input needed to innovate and adapt their strategies. In the face of repression, exclusion, and ignorance, this transnational solidarity helps energize those who challenge the structures of global capitalism. While many activists will never have the chance to attend the global WSF meeting, they see themselves as part of the process and know they are not alone in their struggles. Aided by the Internet and an increasingly dense web of transnational citizens' networks, the WSF and its regional and local counterparts dramatize the unity among diverse local struggles and encourage coordination among activists working at local, national, and transnational levels.

THE GLOBAL SCENE: POLITICS AND ECONOMY IN THE NEOLIBERAL ERA

Globally and nationally, the logic of the relationship between governments and corporations changed somewhere between the late 1970s and the early 1980s (McMichael 2003; Brunelle 2006). The global justice movement and the WSF challenge the economic and political restructuring initiated during this period, which is seen as increasing social inequalities, environmental degradation, and political injustices worldwide. In this section, we review how global economic restructuring taking hold in the mid-1980s undermined democracy and transformed the globe.

CHANGES IN THE WORLD'S ECONOMIC PRINCIPLES

For fifty years up until the mid-1980s the ideas of John Maynard Keynes dominated economic policymaking. The principles of Keynes, or Keynesianism, included two very important features that informed economic policies in the United States and the world in the aftermath of the Great Depression. First, government involvement in economic development was encouraged as vital to successful capitalist industrialization (Portes 1997; McMichael 2003). Government duties included providing a buffer against cyclical economic downturns and planning and developing various economic sectors (Portes 1997; McMichael 2003). Second, government was also needed to reduce the inevitable inequalities produced by capitalist development. Such redistribution and assistance would not—according to Keynesian principles—interfere with economic growth, but rather it would help foster it.

The Keynesian era and the organization of the global political economy on these principles ended in the mid-1980s and were replaced with what is widely referred to as the Washington Consensus (Williamson 1997), or neoliberalism. Former U.S. president Ronald Reagan and former U.K. prime minister Margaret Thatcher are two leading politicians responsible for ushering in the neoliberal era. Neoliberals argue that prioritizing the interest of capital is the only assurance for national economic success. Governments were required to drastically reduce their involvement with the economy, and good governance was measured by the extent to which a state could promote development through market forces. Government attempts at poverty alleviation and the reduction of social inequality were viewed as detrimental to economic growth. Neoliberal proponents view all regulations on corporate activity, such as those that protect the environment from toxic dumping or workers from unsafe and unhealthy working conditions, as a hindrance to economic growth.

Proponents of economic globalization like to argue that if governments enact policies to encourage international trade and economic growth (profits) for corporations, the benefits will automatically "trickle down" to all sectors of society. One of the claims made by those advocating a free-market model for global economic governance is that, if progress is to be achieved, *there is no alternative* (TINA) to the global expansion of capitalism. Margaret Thatcher made precisely this claim. Neoliberals have shaped the policies of global institutions like the World Bank, the International Monetary Fund, and the World Trade Organization to promote this particular vision of global economic integration. Because those adopting this model of economic development occupied positions of power within the world's richest and most powerful countries, they were able to effectively impose the neoliberal model of globalization from above. They did this through the terms of international aid and loans and through unequal trading arrangements (McMichael 2003; Peet 2003; Robinson 2004; Babb 2003).

Critics of economic globalization argue that markets alone are not able to achieve many important social goals, such as ensuring a humane standard of living for all people, protecting the natural environment, and limiting inequality. Markets sometimes aid economic growth, and they have succeeded in generating vast amounts of wealth and technological innovation, but they also have contributed to rising global inequalities. Moreover, many experts argue that the recent decades of rapid globalization have not generated economic benefits for most of the world's poor. They point to World Bank and United Nations statistics to demonstrate that, for instance, the poorest 100 countries are actually worse off economically than they were before the 1980s, and that the costs of global economic restructuring have disproportionately affected the world's poorest people (see, e.g., UNDP 2005).

POLITICAL PARTICIPATION ON A GLOBAL SCALE

Given these failures of market-oriented approaches to governing the world economy, participants in the WSF criticize the "democratic deficit" in global institutions. They argue that we need a model of global integration that allows a wider range of people—not just financial experts—to be involved in shaping decisions about how our economic and social lives are organized. Yet along with the economic principles of neoliberalism guiding the current world order is the elite strategy of *depoliticization,* or the deliberate effort to exclude civil society from political participation in global governance.

Depoliticization is driven by the belief that democracy muddles leadership and economic efficiency. This crisis of democracy is reflected in the proliferation of public protests and other forms of citizen political participation, which are seen by the neoliberals as resulting from excessive citizen participation in democracy. In other words, states and governments have been overburdened by democratic demands that increase their involvement in social and economic programs. Through the depoliticization of society, citizens and their organizations, either for profit or nonprofit, are forced through measures such as the privatization of public spaces and political repression to withdraw from a shrinking public sphere. Instead, they are encouraged to operate on their own through market forces. States and governments are not only deemed incapable of tackling issues such as homelessness, housing shortages, or environmental pollution, they are also rendered powerless. Therefore, under neoliberalism, the governance of democracies is not the sole responsibility of elected and accountable governments but, rather, of markets.

How have we come to a world stage where the problems we face are not attributed to faulty economic reasoning and corporate profiteering but to the influence of "nonexpert" citizens on economic and social policy decisions? The crisis of democracy was a diagnosis developed by political and economic elites in the 1970s, a time when the WEF was first launched. Two reports had a profound impact on how governments came to redefine their relations with their citizens and social organizations in the ensuing years. The first was a report made to the Trilateral Commission in 1975, and the second was a 1995 Commission on Global Governance report.

THE TRILATERAL COMMISSION

David Rockefeller, president of the Chase Manhattan Bank, founded the Trilateral Commission in 1973 (Sklar 1980). This initiative was prompted by three sets of events. The first and foremost event was the deterioration of relations among the three economic poles of the capitalist economy (e.g., North America—basically the United States and Canada at the time, the European Community, and Japan) after former U.S. president Nixon removed the U.S. dollar from the gold standard, changing one of the major foundations of the global economy as it was structured since the Bretton Woods Agreement of 1944.

The second event was the growing politicization of Third World nations and the process of decolonization that shattered the control of colonial empires over many regions of the globe. In particular, the Bandung Conference, a meeting in 1955 of newly independent nations that had not officially aligned themselves with either the capitalist or socialist nations, and the founding of the Organization for Solidarity with the Peoples of Africa, Asia, and Latin America (OSPAAAL) in 1966 represented to U.S. economic leaders a potential threat to the country's influence around the globe. The third event that triggered the creation of the Trilateral Commission was the growing student unrest throughout the world in the late 1960s, which was fueled in part by the social revolutions in the Third World and by the growing social opposition to the war in Vietnam.

Soon after its creation, the Trilateral Commission conducted a study to assess what they saw as the ills that were plaguing democracy. The report, *The Crisis of Democracy: Report on the Governability of Democracies to the Trilateral Commission*, provided a framework accepted by many politicians and academics to define and explain the crisis of democracy (Crozier et al. 1975). The report spells out a theory of cycles according to which increasing participation on the part of citizens in political affairs leads to social polarization. In turn, this polarization fosters distrust toward the political process, which leads to a weakening of its efficacy and efficiency, and ultimately to lower political participation. Consequently, governments should encourage political passivity so that prevailing excessive citizen democratic participation can be reduced. Instead, reliance on expertise, experience, and seniority was emphasized as the best model for effective governance.

THE COMMISSION ON GLOBAL GOVERNANCE

The context leading to the creation of the Commission on Global Governance in 1995 is quite different from the one that gave birth to the Trilateral Commission. However, some of the underlying issues are similar and can help us understand the movement toward depoliticization. Two important precursors were the end of the Cold War and the mission to chart a new course for the United Nations for its fiftieth anniversary.

The growing participation of civil society organizations in UN-sponsored conferences reflected the need for some form of global governance in an increasingly interlinked global economy. For instance, the first Earth Summit held in Stockholm in 1972, which a large number of nongovernmental organizations (NGOs) attended, gained more international prominence than had previous conferences. Running parallel to the official conference was an NGO Forum, which included a daily newspaper providing immediate and often critical coverage of negotiations inside. The summit otherwise would have been much less open to public scrutiny. The Stockholm pattern was repeated, and expanded, at subsequent UN conferences on issues such as population, food, human rights, development, and women (Rice and Ritchie 1995).

Although the first Earth Summit set a precedent for international decision-making and global participation, it was the second Earth Summit in 1992 that revealed the difficulties besetting world governance and eventually led to the Commission on Global Governance. The commission report, *Our Global Neighborhood*, acknowledged that national governments had become less and less able to deal with a growing array of global problems. It argued that the international system should be renewed for three basic reasons: to weave a tighter fabric of international norms, to expand the rule of law worldwide, and to enable citizens to exert their democratic influence on global processes (Carlsson and Ramphal 1995).To reach these goals, the commission proposed a set of "radical" recommendations, most notably the reform and expansion of the UN Security Council, the replacement of ECOSOC by an Economic Security Council (ESC), and an annual meeting of a Forum of Civil Society that would allow the people and their organizations, as part of "an international civil society," to play a larger role in addressing global concerns.

The commission report recognized that global governance operates through a complex set of venues at the world level, including the International Monetary Fund, the World Bank, the World Trade Organization, and major partners such as the then Group of 7 (G7), the Organisation for Economic Co-operation and Development (OECD), as well as regional organizations such as the European Union (EU), North American Free Trade Agreement (NAFTA), and Mercosur (the Southern Common Market).The proposed Economic Security Council was to provide a focal point for global economic and social policy, mirroring the intergovernmental structure of the UN Security Council. In one of the most profound statements of the dilemmas with respect to global governance, the report stated:

> At a global level, what model of decision-making should an emerging system of economic governance adopt? It will have to draw on lessons from regional and national levels and from business organizations where inflexible, centralized command-and-control structures have been shown to be unsustainable. Multi-layered decision-making systems are emerging that depend on consultation, consensus, and flexible "rules of the games." Intergovernmental organizations, however, still face basic questions as to who should set the rules and according to what principles.

Significantly, the report also stated that global governance cannot rest on governments or public sector activity alone, but should rely on transnational corporations—which "account for a substantial and growing slice of economic activity" (Commission on Global Governance 1995: 153).Whereas it recognized a need for civil society and NGOs to be active in global governance, the report supported the increased role of market forces and the expansion of neoliberal agents of globalization such as the WTO. In effect, it endorsed the notion that business and private enterprise should take a dominant role in global governance, while NGOs and civil society should play a subordinate role assisting governments and business in (market-oriented) development at the local level.

Like the report presented by the Trilateral Commission twenty years prior, the report of the Commission of Global Governance also fails to provide a meaningful role for civil society in global governance. In both reports, society and citizens remain a depoliticized entity. However, our analysis highlights a fundamental contradiction in the globalization program envisioned by the authors of these reports. Although both seek to remove civil society from playing a substantive role in the development of global policy, the Commission on Global Governance recognized that civil society needed to have some role if the institutions of governance were to be seen as legitimate. Without popular legitimacy, the stability of this new international order would be compromised. This tension between the desire to exclude most of the population from policymaking while also strengthening the possibilities for global governance created opportunities for challenges by those denied a voice in shaping the direction of globalization (Markoff 1999).

THE WSF: A NEW PRINCIPLE OF GLOBAL POLITICS

If we consider the increasing privatization, commercialization, and depoliticization of social life and the underlying rational mechanism of efficiency, profit, and accumulation, it appears as if the wheels of history were set in the mid-1980s on an inexorable path toward the dominance of corporations and the eradication of social equality, justice, and political freedom. Given this panorama it would have been difficult to predict the emergence of the WSF as a political body running in a radically different direction. How could we have thought the WSF was possible? Yet contrary to Thatcher's claim that there is no alternative, the WSF arose as a global force, powered by transnational social movements that would have to be reckoned with by governments and corporations. The WSF is an arena for the practice of a democratic form of globalization and a common public space where previously excluded voices can speak and act together to challenge the TINA claim.

The WSF is not simply (or even mainly) a reaction against neoliberal globalization. Instead, it grows from the work of many people throughout history working to advance a just and equitable global order (see Smith 2008). In this sense, it constitutes a new body politic, a common public space where previously excluded voices can speak and act in plurality. With the help of the ideas of noted political theorist Hannah Arendt, we propose to see the WSF not as the logical consequence of global capitalism but rather as the foundation for a new form of politics that breaks with the historical sequence of events that led to the dominance of neoliberal globalization. Arendt viewed the political as a sphere that is not ruled by processes and where the unexpected can happen.

PRECURSORS TO THE WSF

If our understanding of the WSF is to be set apart from the processes of neoliberal globalization, we need to see more concretely the unexpected events that sit at the beginning of this break in our political history. The WSF is a culmination of political actions for social justice, peace, human rights, labor rights, and ecological preservation that resist neoliberal globalization and its attempts to depoliticize the world's citizens. We identify four key factors that interacted to help set the WSF in motion. These factors include:

- Third World protests against international institutions
- Transnational networks and global mobilizations that challenged the logic of depoliticization (such as those in Seattle in 1999 and Chiapas in 1994)
- Civil society dissatisfaction with the UN system
- The rise of a transnational feminist and women's movement.

More than any other global actions or transnational networking, the Zapatista uprising in Chiapas, beginning January 1, 1994, and the anti-WTO protests in Seattle in November 1999 were perhaps the most direct precursors to the WSF. After discussing the factors just listed, we showcase these two events to highlight their roles in helping to bring about the WSF process.

Protests in the Global South

The origins of the WSF lie in the countries that have been most deeply impacted by globalization—the countries of the global south. In the 1970s and 1980s, those countries found themselves increasingly squeezed by growing international debts and decreasing prices for the goods they export. They had borrowed money from the World Bank and International Monetary Fund both to cover large-scale industrial development projects as well as to meet the rising costs of fuel during the 1970s successive oil crises. Now these loans were coming due, and they found themselves unable to service their debts while also continuing to develop their national economies and meet the needs of their citizens. Furthermore, the World Bank and IMF began attaching strict conditions to the loans they made, forcing Third World governments to cut government spending and raise interest rates in order to obtain international financing (McMichael 2003). They reasoned that these policies—though painful in the short term—would allow long-term economic growth and, more importantly, ensure that debtor countries could pay back their loans. Essentially, governments had to force their citizens to bear the brunt of the costs of the debt. In many poor countries, this led to what have been called "IMF riots," where citizens protested against the policies of global financial institutions as well as the actions of their own governments (Walton and Seddon 1994).

The IMF riots demonstrated that people in the Third World saw international institutions as a major cause of their economic hardships. Moreover, they saw that their own governments were part of the problem, as their governments were limited in their ability to pursue policies at odds with those favored by the World Bank and IMF. The people also saw that their governments held little sway in those institutions.

Transnational Networks and Global Mobilizations

Meanwhile, in the global north, or the rich Western countries, citizens were organizing around a growing number of environmental problems. Environmentalists and unionists joined forces with each other, and across nations, to contest proposed international free trade agreements, such as the North American Free Trade Agreement (NAFTA) and the Multilateral Agreement on Investment (Ayres 1998; Smith and Smythe 2001). Meanwhile, workers and their allies organized transnational campaigns against the practices of transnational corporations (see, e.g., Sikkink 1986). Northern citizens also became more interested in how the policies of their governments were affecting people elsewhere in the world. Some of this interest grew from the peace and solidarity movements of the 1970s and 1980s (Rucht 2000). The interventionist policies of Western governments encouraged transnational solidarity campaigns between northern activists and their counterparts in the Third World (Gerhards and Rucht 1992; Smith 2008).

At the same time, the United Nations was sponsoring a number of global conferences on issues such as women's rights, environmental protection, and peace that provided opportunities for citizen activists from around the world to meet, exchange stories about their work, and compare analyses of the global and local problems they faced. Aided by advances in technology and reduced costs of transnational communication and travel, these efforts generated more long-term and sustained transnational cooperation than was possible in earlier decades. Beginning in the 1970s there was a tremendous growth in the numbers of formally organized groups working across national borders to promote some kind of social or political change. Thus, between the early 1970s and the late 1990s, the number of transnationally organized social change groups rose from less than two hundred to nearly one thousand (Smith 2004). Many more transnational citizens' groups were formed around other goals, such as encouraging recreational activities and supporting religious or professional identities, among others. These groups were not only building their own memberships, but they were also forging relationships with other nongovernmental actors and with international agencies, including the United Nations. In the process, they nurtured transnational identities and a broader world culture (Boli and Thomas 1999).

NGO Dissatisfaction with UN Conferences

A third factor that fueled the idea of an alternative venue was the growing dissatisfaction among NGO participants with the mediocre results, if not setbacks, coming out of the conferences convened by the UN—especially the 1992 Conference on Environment and Development (UNCED) in Rio de Janeiro, Brazil; the 1995 Fourth World Conference on Women in Beijing; and the 1995 World Summit on Social Development in Copenhagen. For a number of NGOs that participated in these UN conferences, dissatisfaction changed into disillusionment at the five-year review (dubbed "Rio/Beijing/Copenhagen plus five") conferences aimed at assessing governments' follow-through on the commitments they made at these world conferences. Activists at the review meetings called these the "Rio [or Beijing or Copenhagen] minus five" conferences, highlighting governments' failures to fulfill their conference promises.

Besides their disappointment with the inability of UN conferences to affect the practices of governments, civil society groups that worked hard to influence the texts of the conference agreements felt that much of their efforts in the UN were futile. The real obstacle, they realized, was not the absence of multilateral agreements, but rather the structure of the UN system and the refusal of major countries to address key global issues. Moreover, they saw that many environmental and human rights agreements were being superseded by the WTO, which was formed in 1994 and which privileged international trade law over other international agreements. Agreements made in the UN were thus made irrelevant by the new global trade order, in which increasingly powerful transnational corporations held sway.

The Global Women's Movement and Feminist Participation

Women's social movement organizations throughout the world have been very effective in establishing networks to promote international responses to gender injustices and violence against women. While women's organizations continue to participate in UN-led conferences, many are also very active in the WSF. The first of the Feminist Dialogues was held in 2003 in Mumbai, India, as a follow-up to the Women's Strategy Meeting held at the 2002 WSF in Porto Alegre, Brazil, in which feminists from around the world came together to discuss their dissatisfaction with men dominating the WSF. In 2005 and 2007 the Feminist Dialogues preceded the WSF event to provide a space to consider feminist concerns, which many organizations feel are sidelined at the WSF, and to collectively influence the forum (Macdonald 2005). Nevertheless, one of the main contributions of feminist political organizations has been their promotion of the participatory processes that refuse to prioritize one issue over another.

While focusing on gender, feminist activists (especially those from the global south) emphasize the intersection of inequalities such as race, gender, nation, class, and sexuality. In addition, feminist activism challenges hierarchical organizational structures that establish formal leadership that tend to silence the voices of the majority. The history of transnational feminist organizing provided important models for fostering decentralized, respectful dialogue and cooperation that helped inform other social movements seeking to bridge national and other differences (see, e.g., Rupp 1997; Alvarez et al. 2004; Polletta 2002; Gibson-Graham 2006). In fact, the model of the "encuentro," a meeting that is organized around a collectivity of interests without hierarchy, on which the Zapatistas and later the WSF process built, emerged from transnational feminist organizing in Latin America (Sternbach et al. 1992; Smith 2008).

ZAPATISMO AND THE BATTLE OF SEATTLE

Many accounts of the 1994 Zapatistas' uprising in Chiapas, Mexico, and the so-called Battle of Seattle during the WTO ministerial meetings of December 1999 speak of their implications for global democracy and for citizens' mobilizations around the world. These two key events helped break the continuity of the processes of neoliberal globalization and, therefore, helped open the possibility for the WSF to emerge as an alternative political body (see Escobar 2004). The events of Chiapas and Seattle reflect not simply resistance to globalized capitalism, but rather they were catalysts to a new political dynamic within the global landscape.

Zapatismo

In 1994 indigenous people in Mexico took up arms to protest their governments' acceptance of the North American Free Trade Agreement. The Zapatistas quickly emerged as one of the first globally networked groups to resist economic globalization. Their struggle inspired many activists in all parts of the world to more actively resist the growing global trade regime. For many, the emergence of a global citizens' movement is credited to the appearance of the Ejercito Zapatista de

Liberación Nacional (EZLN, Zapatista National Liberation Army) on the world scene, January 1, 1994, the same day that NAFTA came into force. According to Samir Amin and others, the EZLN ushered in an era of "new radicality" fundamentally different from that which prevailed before then.

Worldwide supporters of the EZLN helped popularize some of the writings of the Zapatista leader, Subcomandante Marcos, which were becoming widely known among activists during the 1990s. When the 1999 Seattle and subsequent protests generated complaints from movement critics that "we know what you're against, but what are you *for*?" Marcos's words proved fruitful in inspiring activists to focus on the quest for alternatives. He argued that one of the main problems of economic globalization is that it does not allow other forms of economic and social organization to coexist. Its need to continually expand and conquer makes it incompatible with the desire for diversity in either nature or society. Marcos argued that we can have "one world with room for many worlds" if we can rein in the movement toward economic globalization. A tolerance for diverse forms of economic organization, a respect for local autonomy and participation in economic decisions, and a celebration of the possibilities for innovation and adaptation fostered by diversity were values that Marcos encouraged (Olesen 2005). The widespread attention to his work demonstrates the transnational resonance of his ideas (Khasnabish 2005).

Following the 1994 EZLN uprising, the Zapatistas used the Internet strategically to call on others to join their struggle for a new sort of world. Many around the world responded to their call, and they traveled to Chiapas to participate in international meetings, or "encuentros," on how to confront economic globalization. Many more organized in their local communities in support of Zapatista goals: against neoliberalism and for humanity. Marcos's analysis of the problems of economic globalization and the possibilities for popular liberation inspired the "political imaginations" of many people facing common experiences in the global neoliberal order.

The Zapatista uprising and subsequent mobilization are without doubt a cornerstone of the global justice movement. They established and disseminated a pattern of transnational mobilization that continues to inspire and inform activists throughout the world. Moreover, the writings of Marcos and the approach to organizing he promoted provided a focal point that helped bring activists together around a shared understanding of their values and organizing capacities. The networks Zapatismo inspired—including an important grassroots formation called Peoples' Global Action—provided an infrastructure of people, organizations, and ideas required for the WSF's emergence. These groups helped catalyze global resistance to the G8 and WTO during the late 1990s, including the June 1999 Global Day of Action Against Capitalism and the November 1999 protests in Seattle (Juris 2008; Notes from Nowhere 2003; Starr 2005).

The Battle of Seattle

As we have seen, the preconditions for the emergence of global justice movements included increasing capacity for globally coordinated action, a growing recognition of the limitations of the UN, the diffusion of feminist organizing principles, and resistance in the global south to international institutions. While these factors percolated in various nations at different rates in numerous social justice organizations, by 1999 the stage was set for the entrance of a new form of political participation.

Unexpectedly for many, the global justice movement seemed to explode on the scene in Seattle in 1999. Tens of thousands of college students, labor union members, educators, public health workers, unemployed workers, environmental activists, feminists, immigrants, and other concerned citizens came to protest the ministerial meetings of the World Trade Organization. The vast majority of activists engaged in peaceful protest, and some sought to nonviolently disrupt the meeting by occupying the streets surrounding the conference hall where WTO delegates were to meet. But police were unprepared for the volume of protesters, and they responded with brutality, triggering what was called "the Battle of Seattle." Although subsequent inquiries showed that the police were at fault by instigating violence against protesters and bystanders, the, mainstream media portrayed the protesters as violent and unreasonable.

A key feature of the organization behind the Seattle protest was the lack of formalized leadership. Rather than a single organization or political body representing the protesters as a single entity, smaller units referred to as affinity groups came together around shared values and identities, uniting with others to forge a common front against the meetings of the WTO. While some affinity groups blocked traffic and engaged in other acts of civil disobedience, trade unionists and other activists marched along preordained march routes and gave passionate speeches denouncing the WTO's policies before a stadium full of supporters. The actions held that day in Seattle were not directed by a single person, group, or organizing unit. Rather, they happened organically from the context of protest in which they were situated and from each organization's own traditions of protest.

Global mobilizations like the one in Seattle also present opportunities for learning about the struggles of other groups and understanding the relationship among the organizations attending. For instance, many church members who participated in the Seattle protests learned about the damaging effects of global economic policies through their interactions with other church members around the world. They marched to demand greater equity and justice for all members of their faith (and presumably other faiths as well), regardless of where they were from. Students and teachers that found their schools increasingly impoverished by cuts in public budgets see a connection between their experiences and the changes in the global economy. Unions and professional associations have also been motivated by both threats to their members' interests as well as their solidarity with their counterparts around the world.

Given this rapid growth of transnational networking, by the time of the Seattle WTO meeting many participants had already learned a great deal from each other and had cultivated skills for organizing protests at the local, national, and increasingly the transnational levels. Moreover, subsequent global mobilizations in cities such as Prague, Quebec City, Genoa, Barcelona, and Washington, D.C., continued to provide critical spaces for learning, coalition building, and action. At the same time, many activists felt global protests alone were insufficient. Rather than simply denouncing what they were against, it was also important to articulate a clear vision of what they were fighting *for*. In January 2001, the first ever WSF was organized precisely to provide a space for developing concrete alternatives to corporate globalization. Indeed, the WSF process is an important place for popular education about the injustices occurring all over the world as a result of the policies of economic globalization. At the same time, the process creates opportunities for groups to learn about and articulate economic and political alternatives and plan future mobilizations.

CONCLUSION

Protesters in Seattle and elsewhere and participants in the social forums have challenged people to ask whether the world's major economic institutions are producing the kind of world in which they want to live. The answer, activists argue, is that we cannot govern by markets. Rather, we need political institutions that can help balance competing social interests and goals. By separating trade and other economic policy decisions from other policy areas (such as human rights, public safety, or environmental protection), governments have undermined their own legitimacy and introduced untenable contradictions into international law. Social forum participants argue that the goal of reducing restrictions on international trade must not be allowed to trump other social values and goals.

Governments gain their legitimacy from popular elections and recognition by their populations as their representatives. But with globalization, governments are delegating more policy decisions to international institutions such as the WTO or the European Union. While global interdependence requires some policy coordination to ensure peace and common security, the way governments have managed international policy has created a "democratic deficit" in global institutions. Many of those protesting economic globalization argue for greater government accountability and responsiveness in both domestic and international policy arenas. As they have pursued their particular aims—such as environmental protection, human rights, and equitable development—civil society groups have found themselves uniting behind demands for a more democratic global polity. The protests against economic globalization are really wider battles about whether people and democratic institutions or technical experts and markets should govern the global system.

Understanding the WSF process as a fundamentally new form of politics challenges the visions of history that emphasize chronological chains of processes where all that happens is the logical consequence of its context and its immediate past. Although growing out of a long tradition of struggle, the process of rebellion made visible in Chiapas and Seattle has begun to fracture the historical process of neoliberal domination. The continuity of corporate globalization is now in question. By challenging the relentless progression of privatization, trade liberalization, consumption, and individuation, the rebellion has created another temporality within which the WSF is clearly situated.

CHAPTER 5

Global Media, Mobilization, and Revolution

The Arab Spring

Hans Schattle

January 2011 ushered in a momentous new year—and perhaps a new era—across the Middle East and North Africa. First the people of Tunisia ousted dictator Zine al-Abidine Ben Ali, who fled the country after twenty-three years in power, in what became known as the "Jasmine Revolution," named after the country's national flower. Just eleven days later, on January 25, in the political and cultural heart of the Arab world, Egyptians flocked to the center of Cairo to insist that Hosni Mubarak step down. The demonstrations captivated the world for seventeen days until Mubarak left the presidential palace on February after nearly thirty years in power. Equipped with online social networking tools hardly envisioned during the fall of Soviet communism twenty years earlier, citizen activists inspired by their neighbors in Tunisia and Egypt, and also linked through wall-to-wall television news coverage by Al Jazeera, took to the streets and called for political change in Yemen, Bahrain, Jordan, Syria, Algeria, and Libya. The protest movements, however, met severe government crackdowns and violence, and Libya erupted into civil war as its longtime military dictator, Colonel Muammar Gaddafi, insisted on staying in power and turned his forces against his own people in an effort to quash the revolutionaries; a larger war followed with airstrikes from the United States, Britain, and France targeting Gaddafi's forces. Gaddafi lost control of Tripoli in August and was captured, beaten, and killed by a group of rebels in October. Although the outcome remains uncertain, the "Arab Spring" has given the world fascinating lessons as to how an emerging, emboldened generation of citizen activists harnessed the new global media platforms, first to connect with each other, exchange ideas, and organize campaigns and strategies, and then to communicate to the outside world their overwhelming frustration with failed national dictators as well as their alternative political and social visions for their countries.

The Arab Spring, then, provides many illustrations of how dynamics related to globalization set the stage for powerful struggles for democratic citizenship as an amalgam of rights and responsibilities, democratic empowerment and participation, and allegiance, belonging, identity, and loyalty. As citizens called for change, they insisted that freedoms of assembly and speech—online as well as in person—are fundamental rights in the twenty-first century. The round-the-clock vigils lasting for weeks in public squares in several national capitals demonstrated what it means for citizens to empower themselves, raise their voices, and join together—men and women; young and old; Muslims, Christians, and nonbelievers, all for the sake of creating new models of democracy. The activists also made it clear that they were engaging the global platforms of communication to display their loyalty and allegiances to renewed visions for their particular countries; the revolutions in Tunisia and Egypt, for instance, were widely recognized as the collective efforts of Tunisians and Egyptians themselves.

The interplay here between global citizen activism and national public space is striking. Many of the Arab Spring's leading citizen activists saw themselves as carrying out decisive roles within an emerging transnational movement for political and social change, truly inspired by universal human rights and democratic principles. But even as they communicated their ideas and aspirations for the future across a formative global online public space, with ideas and sources of inspiration migrating quickly from country to country, the citizens across North Africa and the Middle East resolutely carried out their campaigns and struggles within national public spaces—and they often had to find ways to enlist the backing of military leaders representing the coercive authority of their respective nation-states. The exceptional events of early 2011 have yet to be resolved, and it remains unclear just what kinds of democracies might emerge in Egypt and Tunisia, and elsewhere, or whether robust democracies will emerge at all. In February 2011, Václav Havel, the Czech playwright and democracy activist turned national leader after the Velvet Revolution, noted that the new generation of protesters in the Arab world has it much harder than his generation in Central and Eastern Europe because they lack historical experiences of democracy as well as established civil society institutions that can emerge quickly as alternative powers.[1]

LEADING UP TO THE ARAB SPRING: IRAN'S GREEN REVOLUTION

We can begin by tracing the recent origins of the Arab Spring to Iran, when in June 2009 vast numbers of citizens, linked by social media platforms, organized massive protests on the streets of Tehran following the country's disputed presidential election. While Iran's official leadership ultimately did not change and the incumbent president, Mahmoud Ahmadinejad, remained in power, the election became the moment in which the world learned how citizens could use social media platforms to organize political opposition and raise their voices on the global stage to challenge the legitimacy of their national governments. This marked the first time large numbers of supporters of a defeated national candidate communicated their frustration to the rest of the world by relying heavily on text messages and posts on

Twitter and Facebook, as well as the bottom-up "webcasting" platform of YouTube. In many ways, Iran's contested presidential election illustrated the rapidly accelerating globalization of social media as a tool in political communication to empower everyday people, alongside established global news organizations, and in direct challenge to government officials seeking to mute dissent.

The 2009 presidential election took place exactly thirty years after Iran's Islamic Revolution in 1979, and the official, disputed result held that Ahmadinejad won with 63 percent of the vote. While Russia, China, and India were quick to accept the official tally and congratulate Ahmadinejad, several Western governments and international journalists raised doubts. The strongest of the three defeated challengers was Mir-Hossein Mousavi, a former prime minister who gained much support among younger voters discontented with a weak economy and an unemployment rate as high as 30 percent, and in search of widespread political reforms. His campaign color happened to be green, leading this period to be remembered as the "Green Revolution," though some also took to calling it the "Twitter Revolution." Mousavi and his supporters appealed without success for the results of the election to be canceled and a new election to be held, noting that as many as fourteen million unused ballots were missing and could have been cast fraudulently; the number of missing unused ballots amounted to 37 percent of the thirty-eight million ballots counted. Iran does not allow international election monitors, and questions about the extent of possible fraud remain.

On the other hand, the impact of social media in energizing public debate in Iran was crystal clear: even before the balloting took place on June 12, 2009, the number of text messages sent via mobile phones in Iran rocketed from the usual 60 million messages per day to more than 110 million messages per day. As more and more supporters of the challengers began communicating with each other via Facebook—including an estimated 6,600 supporters of Mousavi's Facebook page—the government blocked access to Facebook on May 23, three weeks before the election, only to restore access three days later following public outrage at home and abroad. And then, on the day of the election, mobile phone communications were suddenly interrupted and even the BBC reported that its television broadcasts were disrupted by "heavy electronic jamming." A battle emerged between Ahmadinejad's government and numerous media platforms, ranging from Western news organizations such as BBC and CNN to the nascent citizen media percolating from within, to become a powerful political movement unto itself. This rising force of citizen demonstrators in Iran was not always peaceful: even before the election authorities declared Ahmadinejad the winner, street demonstrators in Tehran set buses and cars on fire and threw rocks at police to protest what they viewed as an illegitimate victory in the making.

Once Ahmadinejad was declared the winner on June 14, supporters of Mousavi organized the strongest show of discontent since the 1979 revolution. Thousands of people marched in Tehran in search of a global audience with rallying cries (in Persian) such as "Where is my vote?" and "Death to the dictator!" Protests also took place outside Iranian embassies around the world. Iran's government wasted no time in fighting back, shutting off access to portions of the Internet for a half hour on the day after the election—and also shutting down Twitter, Facebook, and numerous text messaging services. Western journalists reported it was often difficult during this period to place calls on mobile phones, as Iranian authorities tried to stop activists from communicating with each other to organize additional protests.[2] Despite the growing obstacles and outbreaks of violence, Mousavi held a public rally in Tehran on June 15, with hundreds of thousands of his supporters—some estimated the crowd at more than one million—in what turned out to be the largest demonstration in Iran since the 1979 revolution. The very next day, Ahmadinejad followed up with a rally of his supporters, as Mousavi's supporters marched once again.

Iranian dissidents living in exile around the world were amazed, as they watched the election and its contentious aftermath, by the new wave of public protest back in their native country. Hamid Dabashi, a native of Iran and critic of Ahmadinejad who presents a weekly opposition webcast via YouTube that went "viral" during this period, told the BBC that the "absolutely extraordinary and unprecedented" postelection demonstrations happened only because of the mobilization that emerged online: "Nobody called for it except on the Internet. Cyberspace was buzzing with information that there was to be a demonstration from this square to that square."[3] Bottom-up networking, coupled with an element of coordination among some organizers at the top, seemed to carry the day. Experts in Internet censorship, meanwhile, found that Iranian government officials struggled to keep up with the activists using websites and social media platforms to communicate. According to Austin Heap, executive director of the Censorship Research Center in San Francisco: "If you look at what was going on after the election, it was very clear that they [government officials] had no solid plan in place—the way they were filtering, what they were filtering. . . . Just basic things like the speed the Internet was operating at would change day by day, week by week."[4]

The filtering operations on the part of Iran's government seemed to grow more coordinated as time passed, along with growing cases of outright interference on press freedom. Several international news organizations reported that Iranian authorities confiscated cameras and other news gathering equipment, and Al Jazeera reported that some domestic newspapers were ordered to change their editorials and news headlines. BBC correspondent Jon Leyne—forced out of Iran by the government, along with several other international journalists—said he found that both sides struggled to gain the upper hand: the government's filtering attempts were "crude and ineffective," while computer programs designed to prevent filtering were eventually blocked by government censors. Leyne also noted that cyberspace in Iran throughout the campaign season was tempered by "mood swings" that peaked in the days immediately following the election. As Leyne wrote several months later: "One morning the whole BBC website would be inaccessible, and even usually secure connections were blocked. On other days the controls would be mysteriously lifted, enabling us to use the Internet to broadcast live from our office in Tehran."[5]

When the BBC Persian website was up and running, it served as a digital public square of sorts in the unfolding drama, registering 50 million page impressions for the month of June 2009 compared with 16 million one month earlier. Its online television streaming service was requested by Internet users 8 million times in June, and citizens on the streets provided much of the content, sending in thousands of e-mail messages, videos, and photos that often described and depicted incriminating images of police brutally beating protesters. Most notably, on June 15, as protests peaked three days after the election, citizen activists sent the BBC horrifying images of university students being beaten by plainclothes militia troops who dragged them from their dormitory beds. Online forwarding also turned global public opinion sharply against Iran's sitting government, especially after 40 seconds of video footage of a young woman bleeding to death from bullet wounds believed to have been inflicted by Iranian government militia troops went viral. The video was shown repeatedly on CNN after being e-mailed via mobile phone from a man in Tehran to the Voice of America, the *Guardian* newspaper in London, and five other people in Europe with the message "Please show the world." While Iran's government denied responsibility for shooting twenty-six-year-old Neda Agha Soltan on a quiet street in Tehran, the millions of people worldwide who watched the video thought otherwise.

Since the election, the Iranian government and Iranian dissidents have continued to compete for the upper hand in cyberspace and also more widely in the public space of the global media. Iran's Revolutionary Guards have reportedly drafted many of the country's most technologically adept young people, sometimes against their will, to help the government clamp down on its domestic critics by forming a new "cyber army" that has coordinated attacks on Twitter and websites associated with political opposition movements. Computer mavens in Iran and around the world, in turn, take these new methods of online censorship and suppression as a challenge. At least in Iran, however, the government of Mahmoud Ahmadinejad remained in power even as renewed protests against his rule picked up in February 2011 on the heels of the successful revolutions in Tunisia and Egypt. Authorities in Iran responded to the protests by placing Mir-Hossein Mousavi, as well as several other leaders of the citizen groups that still make up the country's Green Movement, under house arrest.

THE ONSET OF THE ARAB SPRING: TUNISIA'S JASMINE REVOLUTION

Before the end of 2010, the small North African country of Tunisia, with a population just above ten million, had a reputation as a stable but politically stifling outpost of the Arab world. Two events in December 2010 began to set in motion dynamics for change leading to the overthrow in January 2011 of Zine al-Abidine Ben Ali, the country's president since taking power in a bloodless coup in 1987. First, there were reports that Tunisia had blocked the public from accessing the website of a Lebanese newspaper, *al-Akhbar*, which had published a formerly confidential memo, written in July 2009 by the U.S. ambassador to Tunisia, calling the country a "police state" and sharply criticizing Ben Ali and his family members. Released to news organizations by WikiLeaks, the memo by U.S. ambassador

Robert Godec was titled, "Troubled Tunisia: What Should We Do?" and stated the following:

> The problem is clear. Tunisia has been ruled by the same president for 22 years. He has no successor. And, while President Ben Ali deserves credit for continuing many of the progressive policies of President [Habib] Bourguiba,[6] he and his regime have lost touch with the Tunisian people. They tolerate no advice or criticism, whether domestic or international. Increasingly, they rely on the police for control and focus on preserving power.
>
> Corruption in the inner circle is growing. Even average Tunisians are now keenly aware of it, and the chorus of complaints is rising. Tunisians intensely dislike, even hate, first lady Leila Trabelsi and her family. In private, regime opponents mock her; even those close to the government express dismay at her reported behavior. Meanwhile, anger is growing at Tunisia's high unemployment and regional inequities. As a consequence, the risks to the regime's long-term stability are increasing.[7]

While the government tried to suppress the information, citizens within Tunisia along with their friends and family members abroad easily worked around the official censorship, which banned WikiLeaks as well as other Internet communication critical of the government. Wherever they were at any given moment, critics of the government eagerly circulated via e-mail and postings on Facebook international accounts detailing extravagant lifestyles enjoyed by Ben Ali and his family in the face of the country's low incomes and stagnant economy.

A Local Incident Sets National and Global Sparks

The unflattering picture of Tunisia's political leadership confirmed the public's negative instincts about the government, further eroding its already low credibility just days before the death of Mohamed Bouazizi, twenty-six years old, who had been selling fruits and vegetables to support his family since he was ten years old. Bouazizi, according to media reports, had been bullied on a daily basis by police officers, who frequently confiscated his unlicensed vendor's stall and his merchandise. On December 17, Bouazizi used paint thinner to set himself on fire after the governor of his hometown, Sidi Bouzid, refused to meet with him to listen to his complaints about a female town official who allegedly slapped him in the face, spat at him, took away his scales, and tossed aside his vendor's cart. He died eighteen days later at a local hospital, and his family members said chronic humiliation, not poverty, threw him over the edge. Affectionately known as "Basboosa" on the streets of Sidi Bouzid and just twenty-six years old when he died, Bouazizi was a popular figure in the inland provincial city who would regularly give away fruits and vegetables to very poor families.[8] Protesters carrying "a rock in one hand, a cell phone in the other"[9] began marching on the streets of Sidi Bouzid just hours after Bouazizi set himself on fire, with political activists calling him a martyr. As word spread of the incident, several other unemployed young people in Tunisia and across the region also began trying to take their own lives, and some actually did. While the state-controlled domestic media in Tunisia avoided covering the story until December 29, the television network Al Jazeera showed a video clip of the protest that its producers found on Facebook. This linkage, once again, between social networking platforms and global news organizations proved crucial in boosting momentum and garnering worldwide attention for the protest movement. Journalists and commentators around the world came to rely on Twitter feeds of citizens tweeting instant updates and holding online conversations directly from the center of the action. One such tweet from the crowd of six thousand outside Tunisia's interior ministry declared just hours before Ben Ali fled: "Tunis now: the chants continue 'No to Ben Ali even if we die.' "[10]

The demonstrations attracted citizens from every age group and social and professional class who were fed up with high unemployment, political corruption, police brutality, and the absence of basic political rights, such as freedom of speech and freedom of assembly. The protests quickly spread from outposts such as Sidi Bouzid into the country's larger cities, especially once activists in the country's sole labor union, UGTT, began organizing rallies and marches; the protests reached the coastal capital of Tunis on December 27. The next two weeks of clashes between protesters and police turned bloody at times, with reports of police killing at least twenty-one civilians, and protesters injuring numerous police officers. Official figures later released by the government said that seventy-eight protesters died and another ninety-four were injured during the demonstrations leading up to January 14. While official state television showed little about the uprising on the streets, Tunisian citizen activists turned to the Internet to provide updates to the rest of the world. They used video cameras on their mobile phones to record harrowing clips of fires and lootings, and the digital recording files were routinely forwarded to contacts outside the country to post on websites such as YouTube.

As the pressure to step down intensified, President Ben Ali himself visited Bouazizi, who was covered in bandages, in his hospital room on December 28; Ben Ali also promised Bouazizi's mother, at a meeting in his presidential office, to send Bouazizi to France for more extensive treatment. But it was too late for both the protester and the president—Bouazizi died on January 4, and the protests drove Ben Ali out of the country ten days later.[11] Under protection from Libya, Ben Ali flew to Saudi Arabia, with French media sources reporting that their country's president, Nicolas Sarkozy, had refused him entry after earlier seeming to stand by him in public statements. On January 28 the new leaders back in Tunis asked Interpol, the cross-border police agency, for assistance in locating Ben Ali and securing his arrest; the government later asked Saudi Arabia to extradite Ben Ali back to Tunisia. Saudi Arabia refused, even after a court in Tunisia convicted Ben Ali and his wife, Leila Trabelsi, of embezzlement in June 2011 after a six-hour trial dismissed by many critics as a hasty charade on the part of the country's new authorities. The country's prime minister, Mohamed Ghannouchi, took over as the country's president, and he then quickly transferred power to the country's parliamentary speaker after being overruled by Tunisia's constitutional court.

Prospects for a successful democratic transition in Tunisia were questionable from the start, given that many of the people who actually ran Ben Ali's police state remained politically active in Tunis. Parliamentary elections took place in October 2011 to form a temporary government, charged with the task of drafting a constitution, and the new ruling coalition elected as interim president Moncef Marzouki, a human rights activist who had been imprisoned for opposing Ben Ali and then exiled in France for many years before returning to Tunisia once Ben Ali fled. As Marzouki noted at his inaugural ceremony in December: "Other nations are watching us as a laboratory of democracy."[12] While his election was billed as a power-sharing deal between the dominant, moderate Islamist party and its smaller, secular coalition partners, about forty opposition party members of the interim assembly protested the vote, casting blank ballots and emphasizing that the prime minister, Hamadi Jebali from the Ennahda party, would hold much more power for the time being. "This was a piece of theatre," said Najib Chebbi, head of Tunisia's Progressive Democratic Party. "He has accepted a presidency which is just democratic window-dressing without any real functions."[13] The current government and its prime minister will face another round of elections once a new constitution is written.

Tunisia's Social Media Showdown

While the Ben Ali government tried to censor and obstruct the usage of social media among the citizens, the global high-tech companies themselves began to respond in ways that would give the people a shot at regaining their edge against the government authorities. As technology journalist and historian Alexis Madrigal uncovered in a fascinating account published by the *Atlantic*, staffers at Facebook's headquarters in Palo Alto, California, began to notice that something was amiss in Tunisia on Christmas Day 2010: the company began receiving reports that some political protest pages on the site were getting hacked. As recalled by Facebook's chief security officer, Joe Sullivan, it turned out to be an extraordinary cyberattack orchestrated by Tunisia's authorities: "We were getting anecdotal reports saying, 'It looks like someone logged into my account and deleted it.'"[14] As Sullivan's security team looked more closely at the data, they could not prove anything was wrong, but already citizens in Tunisia sensed interference from "Ammar 404," the nickname they had given to the country's Internet censors.

As the unrest in Tunisia increased in December and the government successfully blocked many video-sharing websites, Facebook's platform remained the one key web venue where activists managed to continue uploading videos as they shared information and made plans for their next moves.

Even activists who previously had avoided Facebook began to find the social networking tool indispensable. "It basically went from being a waste of time or procrastination tool, to my go-to source on up-to-date information," said Rim Abida, a development consultant born in Tunisia, educated at Harvard, and now living in Rio de Janeiro. "My mom is back in Tunisia on her own, and my Tunisian network on Facebook was posting the most up-to-date info on what was happening on the ground. It was stuff the major media channels weren't reporting, such as numbers to call to reach the military and what was happening when in what specific neighborhood."[15] It all amounted to a dramatic case of a global media platform leading the way in providing the most immediate local information in a moment of great turmoil.

By January 5, however, as protests in Tunisia swelled to a crescendo, Facebook's security team figured out that Internet service providers in Tunisia were running malicious software that recorded the login information of web users when they signed onto Facebook and similar social networking websites. As Madrigal explained: "The software was basically a country-level keystroke logger, with the passwords presumably being fed from the ISPs to the Ben Ali regime." At the same time as Tunisia was going through its biggest political uprising in more than twenty years, the government was stealing the passwords of the country's Facebook users so authorities could then change—or delete—Facebook accounts they considered offensive or damaging. In response, Sullivan's team at Facebook headquarters rerouted all Internet requests for Facebook coming from Tunisia to a more secure "https" server commonly used to encrypt information and keep it out of view of the Tunisian Internet service providers and their spying. More innovatively, Facebook also implemented what the company called a "roadblock" for all users in Tunisia as they logged in and out of Facebook, with users in Tunisia now required to identify their friends in photos before log-ins would be accepted; this additional layer especially sought to outmaneuver the censors and monitors. These changes to Facebook's interface in Tunisia took effect on Monday, January 10. Four days later, Ben Ali left the country.

The incident in Tunisia brought a sobering reminder that Facebook not only facilitates political activism but also creates new ways for government authorities to interfere with Internet access and entrap activists, learning their true identities and monitoring their every move in cyberspace. Facebook, in particular, has insisted that its users, activists included, use their real names rather than pseudonyms and has not put in place special measures for dissidents seeking to keep their identities hidden, even as it becomes all too obvious that online dissidents are vulnerable to being "outed" and, in extreme cases, killed by their respective governments. Madrigal wondered if Facebook would soon find it necessary to become more accommodating with activists, and his reasoning converged with the widening recognition that Facebook increasingly is filling a central role in the formation of global public space.

Clearly a battle over cyberspace continues to unfold in North Africa and the Middle East. It involves a great deal of push and pull between activists and dissidents on the one hand, authoritarian governments on the other, and global social networking sites and Internet service providers—with their offices well beyond the borders of the countries in question—monitoring the turns of events and making decisions that often amount to taking sides. The departure of Ben Ali signaled a moment for celebration in the activist ranks; online communities across North Africa and the Middle East were filled with jubilant congratulations for the activists and online conversations calling for political change in their respective countries. A YouTube user identified as Algeriansunitedl, who had previously posted videos of demonstrations in Algeria, posted a message congratulating the Tunisian people. Many Facebook users within Tunisia and beyond changed their profile images to that of the red Tunisian flag—and a Facebook group with the name "Bye Bye 3ammar 404" (a poke at the "Ammar 404" moniker that protesters in Tunisia gave to the departed regime's Internet censors) posted a message (in Arabic) that stated; "A new day and the sun rises on a Tunis without the great traitor Ben Ali. Long live Tunis, free and independent."[16]

Especially in Egypt, which leads the Arab world in its number of Facebook users, many bloggers expressed their solidarity with the activists in Tunisia and hoped for a similar turn of events at home. Indeed, if the people of Tunisia could overturn their longstanding government and force Ben Ali and his family to flee, then possibly it could also be done in Egypt where far more people live in poverty, ruled by a dictator who had held onto power even longer. The very day Ben Ali fled the country, a well-known Egyptian blogger, Bint Masreya, posted a picture of the Tunisian flag and commented (in Arabic): "Tunisia: we are proud of your people; may the same happen to us."[17] A young Egyptian woman, Gigi Ibrahim, identified on Twitter as Gsquare86, tweeted these words as Ben Ali left the country: "Goose-bumps all over. I can't believe I lived through an Arab revolution!! Thank you, Tunisia! The power of the masses is capable of toppling any dictatorship. Today was Tunisia. Tomorrow is Egypt, Jordan. LONG LIVE REVOLUTION!"[18]

EGYPT'S DEMOCRATIC UPRISING:
THE JANUARY 25 REVOLUTION

Just as the death of Mohamed Bouazizi, at the young age of twenty-six, sparked the protest movement in Tunisia, the murder of a twenty-eight-year-old businessman, Khaled Said, galvanized activists in the months leading up to the January 25 uprising in Egypt. The timing of this incident, on June 6, 2010, in the coastal city of Alexandria, coincided with the rise of social media among political and social activists in the Arab world and also by younger generations of middle-class people poised to jump into political action once the window of opportunity opened. While police in Alexandria claimed that Said had choked to death after swallowing drugs he tried to hide from officers, photos of his body told a completely different and gruesome story: missing teeth, a broken jaw, and blood coming from his head. His family members told human rights activists that two police officers had dragged Said out of an Internet café and beaten him to death after he posted a video showing a group of officers sharing the spoils from a drug bust. More than a thousand people attended Said's funeral in Alexandria and held an impromptu protest; and many other protests around the country, filled with demands that Egypt's longtime and much despised interior minister be fired, continued throughout the summer of 2010. Activists also tried to hold a street demonstration in downtown Cairo, but according to a Reuters journalist, "the gathering was swiftly dispersed after state security men beat and detained demonstrators."[19] A group of Egyptian rappers made a music video, posted on YouTube, scoffing at the official account of Said's death with a phrase (in Arabic) that resonated among Egypt's protesters: "They think the people are stupid!"[20] Following tremendous public pressure, in July 2010 the two police officers in question were charged with "illegal arrest, using physical torture and brutality." After many delays, a court in Alexandria found the officers guilty, but the public furiously rejected the seven-year prison sentences they each received in October 2011 as far too lenient, and yet another wave of street protests followed.

From Social Media to Street Protests

Such allegations of torture were hardly new in Egypt; what has changed recently across the Arab world is the ability of citizen activists to chronicle human rights abuses, spur international awareness of the problems, and mobilize in response. Another crucial moment in raising consciousness in Egypt emerged in August 2010 when a woman went on television and accused police of raping her along a deserted rural road in the Nile Delta, north of Cairo.[21] Amid the outpouring of public criticism, a veteran Egyptian human rights activist who has focused especially on the rights of women and victims of torture in the country launched a website in 2010 with a hotline to report incidents of abuse or mistreatment by police, and the advocacy group El Nadim Centre for Rehabilitation of Victims of Violence began publishing an online diary to document allegations of abuse at the hands of Egypt's authorities.[22]

The murder of Said and the images of the severe torture he suffered at the hands of police, just moments before his death, outraged Egyptians and international observers alike and prompted strong demands for Egypt's government to make fundamental changes in its police system. Amnesty International called the "shocking pictures . . . [a] rare, firsthand glimpse of the routine use of brutal force by the Egyptian security forces, who expect to operate in a climate of impunity, with no questions asked."[23] A Facebook community that started anonymously—with the title "We Are All Khaled Said"—along with its companion website quickly evolved into a clearinghouse of information about the broader iniquity of police brutality in Egypt, with numerous grotesque and detailed accounts of the Egyptian government's practices of torture that accompanied President Hosni Mubarak's thirty years in power under continual martial law. On the day after Tunisia's deposed president, Zine al-Abidine Ben Ali, fled the country, about seven thousand followers of this Facebook community held a special online event calling for action in Egypt, with this summary: "Enough of being silent. . . . We are not less than Tunisia. . . . Tens of thousands took to the streets in Tunisia and succeeded in their quest to achieve liberty. . . . We want our rights. . . . We do not want repression in Egypt. . . . We want to be free."[24]

Several underlying problems in Egypt, bearing a resemblance to the sources of discontent that had long festered in Tunisia, triggered the uprising in Egypt just two weeks after Ben Ali lost power: frustration with high unemployment and low economic opportunity for all but the elites, political corruption and repression despite three decades of empty promises from Mubarak about prospects for democracy, as well as tiresome justifications for the country's harsh policing tactics. Indeed, Tuesday, January 25, the date that mass demonstrations centered on Cairo's Tahrir Square, or Liberation Square, coincided with Police Day, a national holiday observing the massacre of Egyptian police officers by British forces in 1952.

Also similar to Tunisia's Jasmine Revolution, Facebook groups based in Egypt were key to mobilizing protesters on January 25. One group that called itself "January 25: the revolution of liberty" had close to four hundred thousand fans as of January 25 and displayed the message: "Dear people of Tunisia, the sun of the revolution will not disappear!" Another group called "Day of Revolution" claimed it recruited more than eighty thousand of its online followers across Egypt to participate in street protests. While many activists in Egypt used social media to coordinate demonstrations and round up participants, others around the world posted messages of support and words of caution: one Egyptian Twitter user in California, identified as Lobna Darwish, tweeted this advice to the protesters: "To avoid electric shocks, put on several layers of clothing, particularly wool."[25] Others posted messages on Facebook advising activists about how to react if beaten by police and how to respond if taken away by officers. And some Facebook groups became forums expressing skepticism about whether the uprising would be effective; members of one such group, called "Revolution égyptienne blanche," or "Egyptian White Revolution," voiced concerns that the protests were being manipulated by the country's opposition parties. As one Facebook user posted on this group as the January 25 uprising began: "I'm a young Egyptian woman and I don't understand what you want with this revolution, who will benefit?"[26]

Several elder Egyptian opposition figures also began using Twitter, especially after the demise of Ben Ali in Tunisia, to communicate with their followers and direct their messages toward a global audience shortly before the mass demonstrations began in Cairo. Egypt's most prominent opposition figure, Mohamed ElBaradei, a leading Mubarak opponent in exile and the former head of the International Atomic Energy Agency run under the auspices of the United Nations, posted this statement on his Twitter feed on January 13: "Tunisia: repression + absence of social justice + denial of channels for peaceful change = a ticking bomb."[27] And the leader of Egypt's opposition Al-Ghad Party, Ayman Noor, sent several tweets from his Twitter account in advance of the protests; one tweet in January 2011 read: "From Ceausescu to Ben Ali, I say to those who are frustrated, you must learn your lesson: dictatorship continues to resist; it tries to tighten its grip; but suddenly it falls in the last minute."[28]

Religious organizations in Egypt also turned to social media in reaching out to their supporters. The Facebook page of a group called "No More Silence After This Day" included quotes from the Koran and a link to an Islamic organization calling upon its members to join the protests. Across the many different points of view, #Jan25 and #Cairo quickly became the Twitter hashtags most often used in Egypt and beyond to check out the latest developments. Cutting to the heart of the matter, a Facebook page run by protesters listed their demands of Mubarak: (1) declare that neither he nor his son, Gamal, will run for president in the 2011 elections; (2) dissolve the parliament immediately and hold new elections; (3) end the emergency laws giving police seemingly unlimited powers of arrest and detention; (4) release all prisoners including protesters and those who have been in jail for years without charge or trial; (5) fire the interior minister immediately—a final demand that hearkened back to the murder the previous summer of Khaled Said.

After initially responding to the protests with excessive force, Egypt's police lost their authority as the country's military sided decisively with the protesters by making it clear that soldiers would not fire against peaceful demonstrators. This move made a mockery of the government's attempts to impose daily curfews as early as 3 p.m. and keep people off the streets by closing roads and public transportation services. Christians and Muslims as well as the rich and the poor across the country called in unison for Mubarak and his government to resign immediately and flatly rejected his initial response to the protesters, communicated in a speech to the nation on February 1, that he would stay in office until regularly scheduled elections were held in September.

Older Egyptian activists watched their younger, web-savvy counterparts with much excitement and anticipation as the protests continued. Egyptian novelist Alaa Al Aswany—the founder of an earlier political movement in Egypt that also had opposed Mubarak's presidency and the prospect of a power transfer to his son—spoke to the younger activists on January 27, two days after the uprising began, and wrote his impressions later that day: "Most of them are university students who find themselves with no hope for the future. They are unable to find work, and hence unable to marry. And they are motivated by an untameable anger and a profound sense of injustice. I will always be in awe of these revolutionaries. Everything they have said shows a sharp political awareness and a death-defying desire for freedom."[29] Likewise, Egyptian novelist Ahdaf Soueif, the best-selling author of *The Map of Love* and many other books, noted how the old and the young, as well as the secular and the devout, were strongly joined together in "solidarity in action."

The January 25 Uprising Builds Momentum

The grassroots activists who mobilized the uprising quickly gained the backing of Egypt's largest and most influential opposition group, the Muslim Brotherhood, which otherwise kept a fairly low profile as it remained officially banned in Egypt. Mubarak's security officials responded by arresting several of its leaders as well as at least five members of parliament critical of the ruling party in the days immediately following January 25. The elder statesman within Egypt's political opposition, Mohamed ElBaradei, returned to Egypt on the evening of Thursday, January 27: the very next day, he was soaked by water cannons fired by police as he billed himself as a possible successor to Mubarak, saying that he hoped to lead a peaceful transition to democracy in Egypt if he could win the backing of the country's younger generations. On Sunday, January 30—the sixth day of protests—ElBaradei spoke before thousands in Tahrir Square and called for Mubarak to step down as fighter jets flew low over Cairo. It remained to be seen if ElBaradei could unify the country's fractious opposition forces and also overcome widespread perceptions of him in Egypt as an elitist and expatriate out of touch with the country's problems after years of living abroad, first as an Egyptian diplomat and later with the United Nations.

Even as Mubarak insisted in a speech on February 1 that he would stay in power for the short term, protesters intensified their calls for him to depart immediately and for the country to draft a new constitution, remove the ruling party from power, and bring Mubarak and his associates to trial—demands that were more ambitious than what the protesters had initially called for just one week earlier. An estimated two hundred and fifty thousand men, women, and children marched on Tahrir Square to reject Mubarak's speech, escalating the public pressure for him to resign. One protester carried a cardboard sign displaying song lyrics by an Egyptian pop icon, Abdel Halim Hafez, that captured the spirit of the marchers: "And we won when the army rose and revolted, when we ignited a revolution and fire, when we fought corruption, when we liberated the country, when we realized independence, and we won, we won, we won."[30] The visual images at the protests underscored the extent to which national uprisings now often take on the qualities of global events, in the ways that protesters rely on technology and also seek to reach a worldwide audience. One popular sign carried by hundreds, if not thousands, of protesters was directed at the English-speaking world and seen again and again in news photos: "Mubarak You're Down, Just Leave!" Another protester carried a sign in French with a local adaptation of a phrase that had made a great impact a few weeks earlier on the streets of Tunis: "Dégage, Mubarak!" Mubarak did just that on Friday, February 11, when he gave up his attempt to stay in office until the country's September elections and left the presidential palace for the Red Sea resort town of Sharm el-Sheikh. He and his two sons went on trial in August 2011 on charges of "intentional murder, attempted murder of demonstrators, abuse of power to intentionally waste public funds and unlawfully profiting from public funds for them and for others."[31]

As citizens around the world watched the uprising in Egypt gain strength, a gap emerged in many countries between restrained and muted responses from national leaders and assertive calls from citizens for Mubarak to resign. This gap emerged with particular clarity in the United States, where in early February 2011 President Barack Obama continued to call for a transition to democracy in Egypt without publicly calling for Mubarak to leave office immediately. As former U.S. vice president Dick Cheney went so far as to call Mubarak "a good man, a good friend and ally to the United States,"[32] many Americans sent a different message to Egypt as protests emerged in cities from Atlanta to New Orleans to Seattle, where about two hundred people gathered at Westlake Park carrying signs saying "Step down now" and "Free Egypt." Ghada Ellithy, an Egyptian immigrant, carried a handmade paper Egyptian flag—declaring "Go Egypt"—and said she wanted to support her mother and brother in Cairo who were among the protesters at that moment in Tahrir Square. Near Detroit, a group of demonstrators carried signs bearing messages to Mubarak such as "Get Out Grandpa," and one man carried a sign showing the Egyptian and U.S. flags and the slogan: "2011 is Egypt's 1776."

The Regime Fights Back: Detainments and Darkness Online

The dual dynamic between citizen activists using global media platforms to communicate with each other and raise their voices, on the one hand, and the imposition of power by national governments on the other, emerged with great clarity in Egypt when authorities managed to cut off the country's Internet access practically in one fell swoop. It was the first time a single country suddenly went dark, so to speak, in cyberspace, and it happened as journalists from A1 Jazeera, facing the forced closure of its Cairo bureau, asked Egypt's citizens to post eyewitness accounts and videos online showing the protests in Tahrir Square so the television network could broadcast them, just as in Tunisia. In response, Egypt's authorities disrupted access to social media sites, first on Thursday, January 27, when users of Facebook and Twitter found the websites off-line; mobile phone communication and text messaging services also were patchy on this day. Then, Internet communication ceased nationwide beginning at 12:34 a.m. Cairo time on Friday, January 28, when a major Internet service provider for Egypt reported that no Internet traffic was going in or out of the country. Those who monitored the effects of the protests on the Internet in Egypt pointed out the similarities with Iran's Internet tampering in 2009 during its disputed presidential election.

Experts noted that dictatorships can block Internet access fairly easily when their governments already exert strong control over their domestic online service providers. This is typically carried out by enforcing strict licensing procedures over the companies' own fiber optic cables and other technologies that enable Internet connections to be maintained—or, alternatively, shut down. "I don't think there's a big red button—it's probably a phone call that goes out to half a dozen folks," said Craig Labovitz, chief scientist for Arbor Networks, an Internet security company based in Massachusetts.[33] Five days later, on Wednesday, February 2, Egypt's government allowed the country's Internet service providers to reverse the "kill switch" and restore service; observers noted that the speed in which service was restored once again confirmed that the shutdown had been coordinated nationally. The way Egypt's government managed to suspend Internet access so quickly—imposing a virtual blackout of online public space for almost one week— caught many analysts by surprise. As technology writer Jordan Robertson noted: "Egypt has apparently done what many technologists thought was unthinkable for any country with a major Internet economy: It unplugged itself entirely from the Internet to try and silence dissent."[34] The negative global response cut across politics and economics: Egypt's stock market fell 15 percent in the three trading sessions that followed the shutdown, and ultimately, this episode had the effect of galvanizing the dissenters, many of whom immediately demanded access to Facebook and Twitter as fundamental rights and called even more forcefully for Mubarak to step down. One activist in Egypt, Wael Ghonim, a marketing executive for global Internet and communications giant Google, gave the world this fitting quotation for the early twenty-first century: "A government that is scared from [sic] #Facebook and #Twitter should govern a city in Farmville but not a country like #Egypt."[35]

Shortly after tweeting these words on Friday, January 28, Ghonim disappeared and his tweets stopped. One of Ghonim's final tweets from January 28 sounded ominous: "Pray for #Egypt. Very worried as it seems that government is planning a war crime tomorrow against people. We are all ready to die." His whereabouts were then unknown until Sunday, February 6, when a prominent Egyptian political figure told reporters Ghonim was under arrest. The next day, police freed

Ghonim after twelve days in detention, and his release energized the protest movement as word spread that it was Ghonim who had anonymously started and moderated the Facebook page "We Are All Khaled Said" and helped to organize the January 25 protests. Speaking on Egyptian television one night after his release, on February 7, Ghonim mesmerized his country and the world when he recounted his twelve days blindfolded (but not tortured) in captivity: "I am not a hero," he told Mona A1 Shazly, the interviewer for Dream TV. "I only used the keyboard—the real heroes are the ones on the ground, those I can't name."[36] Then he became emotional as he was shown images of some of the three hundred people who had died in the uprising while he was in detention: "I want to say to every mother and every father that lost his child, I am sorry, but this is not our fault. I swear to God, this is not our fault. It is the fault of everyone who was holding on to power greedily and would not let it go."[37] He then stood up and walked out of the television studio. Outdoors in Tahrir Square, Ghonim electrified a massive crowd and urged the protesters to settle for nothing less than the departure of Mubarak. His interview instantly took the Internet by storm, as millions around the world watched videos posted on YouTube with subtitles in many different languages.

In clear hindsight, the decision of Egypt's authorities to detain Ghonim backfired massively: the sensation that followed his release gave the opposition movement an appealing young face—an intelligent activist with a compelling story to project in the global media and who seemed to share more in common with cosmopolitans than fundamentalists. Egypt's opposition movement, at a pivotal and historic moment, had now found a single person who, if not exactly a leader, could still embody for a global audience the dreams for democracy shared by the next generation of Egyptians and present a clear alternative to everything that Hosni Mubarak and his authoritarian regime had come to signify. Ghonim's release and public appearances inspired many Egyptians who had not yet joined the uprising to head outdoors and reinforce the growing crowd in Tahrir Square. "He's the most credible person in Egypt right now; he feels what we are all feeling," a twenty-five-year-old protester, Reem El-Komi, told a British journalist.[38]

A chorus of support and enthusiasm also resounded on Twitter. One person, identifying herself as Menna Gamal, tweeted the following: "My aunt called me crying after Ghonim's interview saying 'I'm going to Tahrir tomorrow! God Bless him! He made us proud!'" Another Twitter activist identified only as AngelSavant, wrote with excitement: "Ghonim just became the mayor of Tahrir Square!" And Egyptian-Canadian journalist Daliah Merzaban, posting on Twitter as Desert_Dals, turned to the Arabic phrase for "God willing" to capture Ghonim's impact: "Left breathless by Wael Ghonim. InshaAllah his sincerity & patriotism, beamed into Egypt's living rooms, will ignite this revolution #Jan25."[39] It was telling that Egyptians came to admire and, indeed, love Ghonim for his sense of *patriotism*, even as he appealed to universal values of liberty and democracy, traversed the world as an executive for Google—based in the Arab world's cosmopolitan hub of Dubai—and engaged with tremendous efficacy the online tools of twenty-first-century global activism. Married to an American, Ghonim could have become a U.S. citizen but affirmed during his television interview that he wanted to remain a citizen of Egypt. In April 2011, Ghonim told his Twitter followers that he had "decided to take a long term sabbatical from @Google & start a technology focused NGO to help fight poverty & foster education in #Egypt."[40]

CONCLUSION

The Arab Spring showed the world that the Facebook and Twitter generation of political activists mobilizing on the Internet now have the power to take down dictatorships, but it isn't yet clear if they have the staying power to build up a democracy. It also isn't yet clear what kinds of democracies might emerge or whether they will be sustainable. At the start of 2012, the prospects in Egypt and Tunisia remained highly uncertain. In the months that followed Hosni Mubarak's fall from power in Egypt, critics accused the military government that took over, at least for the short term, of the same sorts of brutal police tactics, including torturing protesters taken into custody, that had prompted the uprising against Mubarak. On October 27, just one day after the controversial verdict in the Khaled Said murder case was announced, reports surfaced that a twenty-four-year-old man, Essam Atta, had been tortured to death in his prison cell, allegedly by security officials, who then dumped his body in front of a local hospital. Atta had been serving a two-year sentence for "illegally occupying an apartment," a charge disputed by his family and friends. Dozens of Atta's supporters made their way to Tahrir Square, where they joined more than twenty thousand protesters critical of the interim military government. Among them was the mother of Khaled Said, Leila Marzouk, who told the crowd as tears streamed down her face: "Sadly, I am here today to bring in another Khaled. They cannot keep killing our youth and getting away with it. My faith is in you."[41] At end of 2011, Egypt's ruling generals were accused of ordering the firing of live ammunition against protesters who filled Tahrir Square to oppose a bid by the military to retain certain key political powers permanently, rather than transfer power to democratic rule by civilians. Police were also accused of raiding the offices of several human rights and democracy organizations in Cairo. Parliamentary elections encompassing several rounds of voting began in November and were slated to be completed by March 2012, with a presidential election expected to follow by June 2012.

Meanwhile, citizens in Tunisia no longer live in fear of the secret police, and portraits of Zine al-Abidine Ben Ali no longer are displayed alongside the country's national flag. But the country's credit rating deteriorated sharply in the aftermath of the uprising, tourism dried up amid the continued instability, and unemployed young adults were leaving the country in record numbers for Europe, with an exodus of fifteen thousand estimated in the weeks following the fall of Ben Ali. This made the immigration issue in neighboring Italy and France that much more contentious—while political leaders left behind worried openly that it would take a very long time to pull Tunisia into a more open and prosperous society. As one local mayor said of the migrants: "If I were their age, I would have emigrated. . . . It's an entire country that needs to be remade. It's not going to be one year, or two years, or three years. It's going to be an entire generation."[42]

As the Arab Spring of 2011 illustrates, the dynamics of globalization, and especially the new global social media platforms, certainly have opened the doors for citizens across the Arab world to organize themselves, project their voices, and spur a transnational political awakening in pursuit of basic rights and democratic citizenship. Globalization is leading to new flows of ideas across borders and enlarging the political, economic, and social aspirations for the next generation coming of age across the Arab world. At the same time, these citizens are reminded at every turn how they still remain subject to the power of national governments that can at least temporarily disable the tools of globalization and political opening, even if ultimately it comes at great cost, and use their coercive authority to crack down on protesters. In many important respects, the opposition activists in Tunisia and Egypt still remain an exception within the Arab world—and they, too, faced much state-induced violence. Elsewhere, especially in Syria, protesters have been overwhelmed by police brutality as they continue to demand political change.

While Tahrir Square became a true public space for liberation in Egypt, even as the opposition movement had to fight bitterly to retain a presence after Mubarak fell, in March army troops in Bahrain's capital of Manama took down the Pearl Monument that had become the landmark to the country's growing democracy movement and its gathering place in Pearl Square. With demolition diggers cutting away at the six bases of the monument until it collapsed, the dismantling served as a reminder that repressive governments can disfigure, if not destroy, public space, even as citizens discover new ways to create and cultivate that space. It is also noteworthy that many of the new citizen-activists often fuse together their sweeping moral visions for the future with strong and principled senses of national allegiance, belonging, and loyalty to their native countries, just as Wael Ghonim identified resolutely as an Egyptian.

The Arab Spring, while certainly driven by citizens from within particular countries, did not emerge in isolation from the rest of the world. On the contrary, external forces tied to globalization helped set the stage for the uprising, which in turn created ripple effects far beyond the Arab world. One notable external force turned out to be WikiLeaks. The confidential U.S. State Department cables it obtained and then released in late 2010 included misgivings about practices of torture under the Mubarak government and also indicated that if Tunisia's government and military ended up in conflict, the United States would likely support the military over the Ben Ali regime. In March 2011 the cofounder of WikiLeaks, Julian Assange, told a group of students at Cambridge University that the public release of the cables, revealing the unvarnished attitudes of U.S. diplomats toward the governments of Tunisia and Egypt, made it impossible for the United States to offer anything more than tacit support to both governments once their own people turned against them. At the same time, Assange cautioned that while the Internet does set up new ways for citizens to communicate with each other and obtain transparent information about governments and corporations, it is also "the greatest spying machine the world has ever seen" and provides governments with new ways to crack down on citizens. He argued that global news coverage broadcast on television by A1 Jazeera had much greater impact in Tunisia and Egypt than the global social media platforms of Facebook and Twitter.

Indeed, media reports indicated that Egypt's police used Facebook and Twitter in the days following the January 25 uprisings to track down protesters. And in China, news of the uprisings in North Africa and the Middle East created much excitement as the country's democracy activists tried to start a "Jasmine Revolution" of their own. Street demonstrations in at least a dozen cities in February 2011 prompted authorities to arrest numerous activists, attempt to block the word "jasmine" from local social networking sites and online chat rooms,[43] and interfere with international journalists trying to interview protesters—even assaulting and detaining correspondents from CNN and Bloomberg News in Beijing.[44] Still, the Internet has been catching on in China as a political lever. Even in remote provincial areas, such as Inner Mongolia, citizen-activists—some of them calling for the northern region's independence—have been mobilizing online, holding rallies, and confronting harsh security measures.[45] The long struggle for democracy and human rights in China and the campaign by WikiLeaks for greater global transparency and access to information from governments around the world have many striking parallels when it comes to globalization and citizenship.

GUIDE TO FURTHER READINGS
AND RECOMMENDED WEBSITES

The following books and websites will guide your global studies research projects more deeply into the political and social dimensions of globalization:

- John Baylis, Steve Smith, and Patricia Owens (eds.), *The Globalization of World Politics*, 5th ed. Oxford: Oxford University Press, 2011.
- Alison Brysk (ed.), *Globalization and Human Rights*. Berkeley, CA: University of California Press, 2002.
- Mark Mazower, *Governing the World: The History of an Idea*. New York: The Penguin Press, 2012.
- Anthony G. McGrew and David Held (eds.), *Globalization Theory: Approaches and Controversies*. Cambridge, UK: Polity Press, 2007.
- Roland Robertson, *Globalization*. London: Sage, 1992.
- Thomas Weiss, *Humanitarian Intervention: Ideas in Action*. Cambridge: Polity Press, 2007.
- YaleGlobal Online: http://yaleglobal.yale.edu/
  This magazine is a publication of the Whitney and Betty MacMillan Center for International and Area Studies at Yale. It explores the implications of the growing interconnectedness of the world by drawing on the rich intellectual resources of the Yale University community, scholars from other universities, and public- and private-sector experts from around the world.
- Global-e Global Studies Journal: http://global-ejournal.org/
  Global-e is a forum for timely commentary regarding global events, processes, and issues. Each issue features a brief essay authored by leading

scholars and practitioners, offering provocative reflections on a range of topics with the aim of stimulating discussion among the global studies community.

• Global Policy Forum (GPF): http://www.globalpolicy.org/globalization.html Global Policy Forum is an independent policy watchdog that monitors the work of the United Nations and scrutinizes global policymaking. It promotes accountability and citizen participation in decisions on peace and security, social justice and international law. GPF gathers information and circulates it through a comprehensive website, as well as through reports and newsletters. GPF plays an active role in NGO networks and other advocacy arenas. It organizes meetings and conferences and publishes original research and policy papers. GPF also analyzes deep and persistent structures of power and dissects rapidly emerging issues and crises. GPF's work challenges mainstream thinking and questions conventional wisdom. GPF seeks egalitarian, cooperative, peaceful, and sustainable solutions to the world's great problems.

PART II

Economies and Technologies

Discussion Points:

- Does the expansion of small-scale entrepreneurship like Geofrey Milonge's *mitumba* business in Dar es Salaam provide a viable way out of poverty for people in the Global South?
- How can transnational feminists use national governance to advance women's rights, social policy, and new forms of transnational solidarity?
- Does global integration of markets inevitably diminish the power of nation-states, or can there be forms of globalization that bolster the rights of nation-states to establish and uphold their own domestic economic standards and regulations?
- What roles do contemporary information and communications technologies play in creating the "global network society"?
- The "Googlization of everything" entails the harvesting, copying, aggregating, and ranking of information about and contribution made by each of us. On a personal level, are you worried about the Googlization of everything? If so, why? If not, why not?

CHAPTER 6

How Small Entrepreneurs Clothe East Africa with Old American T-Shirts

Pietra Rivoli

MITUMBA NATION

Poverty in Dar es Salaam is a languid and sultry state that has settled on the city like a heavy wash of paint. Though Tanzania is one of the poorest countries in the world, the poverty is not one of frenetic wretchedness as one finds in Calcutta or Nairobi, but is instead a peaceful way of being, a slow-moving and purposeful means of navigating life's rhythms: sleep, eat, shop, laugh, smile, sing, be poor. Poverty is the weather in Tanzania. It is just there—there when the Africans go to sleep, and there when they wake up, there every day of their very short lives. Like the weather, poverty doesn't change enough to be a topic of conversation. Poor just is.

Tanzania's socialist dream is in shambles, crumbling like the colonial buildings left by the British. Julius Nyerere, the country's post-independence leader, had a dream for Tanzania of self-reliance: After generations of bowing to slave traders and colonial masters, Tanzanians would produce their own goods, grow their own food, write their own destiny. Nyerere's vision of "Socialism with Self-Reliance" was a road map to escape the past.

Under Nyerere's leadership, Tanzania in the late 1960s was the most committed of the socialist countries of Africa, and Nyerere was a spokesperson not only for socialism but for the poorest of the poor around the world. But like many of her African neighbors, Tanzania found that the socialist road led to dead end after dead end with factories that didn't produce, workers who didn't work, and farmers who didn't farm. Throughout the 1970s, incomes were falling, investment was contracting, and the majority of Tanzanians lived below the poverty line.[1] By 1980, Tanzania had the second-lowest per-capita income in the world. The Tanzanians, who had for so long been exploited by the British, were now exploited by an ideal—an ideal that could deliver pride, and perhaps a theoretical self-reliance, but could not deliver goods, food, jobs, or medicine.[2]

Today, free market economics is supposed to be the way forward for Tanzania, but this seems like an almost surreal prescription for this dusty, peaceful place of brilliant smiles. Children under 5 in Tanzania die at approximately twenty times the rate of babies in the United States, often from diseases that vanished from the West generations ago. AIDS has eviscerated villages and families, and has brought the average life expectancy in Tanzania down to 46, lower than it was a generation ago. The majority of the country's population survives by subsistence agriculture and still lives below the poverty line, and more than 40 percent of adults cannot read. How to define and measure poverty and well-being has been a challenge for development experts for generations, but it is not a challenge at all to see that by virtually any measure—income, calories, wealth, life expectancy, access to water, or brick housing—Tanzania holds down the bottom of the graph. During the past generation, as China's per-capita income has quintupled, Tanzania's has barely budged, and in 2006 reached just $1 per day.[3] Yet, in 2008, many were pointing to Tanzania as a bright spot in Africa. The country was at peace, the economy was stable, and the political system was working.

The most stunning scenery in Tanzania is not the savannah landscape but the African women. They stand taller and prouder than women anywhere, perhaps from years of carrying bananas and flour on the tops of their heads, perhaps from years of holding the country together. The white women—European backpackers, lunching wives of diplomats, missionary aid workers—fade away in comparison, graceless and silly in the shadow of the African queens. Many of the African women in Dar es Salaam are draped in the brilliantly colored native cloth, graceful folds wrapping their strong bodies and stronger spirits. They are brilliantly colored splashes across the poverty and hardship of Tanzania.

The men are a muted background to this scenery. They work, or they sit under shade trees, not as proud, not as strong, not as busy. There are some men in Muslim skullcaps and a few in Indian dhotis, but none at all in traditional African dress. Almost all of the men and boys in Dar es Salaam wear *mitumba*—clothing thrown away by Americans and Europeans, and many are in T-shirts. Julius Nyerere would turn over in his grave at the sight of it: Used clothing from the West was among the first imports banned under his prideful policy of Socialism with Self-Reliance. What could be less self-reliant or more symbolically dependent than a nation clothed in the white world's castoffs? Yet, it is difficult to see exploitation or dependence in the human landscape clothed in mitumba. I found that most of the men on the streets of Dar es Salaam looked natty and impeccable.

In 2007, used clothing was America's third-largest export to Tanzania, and exports had increased by nearly 50 percent from 2006. Tanzania was one the largest customers for American used clothing, with competition from countries such as Angola, Mozambique, and Benin.[4] Though it would take an average Tanzanian perhaps 60 years to earn enough to buy the Lexus SUV in the Bethesda parking lot, thanks to a nimble network of global entrepreneurs, Tanzanians can dress well for very little money. In this small piece of the Tanzanian experience, the markets work just fine.

TWO FOR A PENNY

When I first visited Tanzania in 2003, the Manzese market in northern Dar es Salaam was the country's largest mitumba market. The market occupied busy Morogoro Road for more than a mile and contained hundreds of stalls. Like a suburban shopping mall, the stalls were geared to different customers. Then and now, stalls specialize in baby clothing or blue jeans, athletic wear or Dockers, or even curtains. The higher-end mitumba stalls boast this year's fashions, tastefully displayed, but the perfect Dockers in 2003 were priced at $5.00 (and in 2008 were close to $8.00), so this high-end merchandise was far out of reach for the poor and accessible only to Tanzania's upper classes. Blue jeans, too, are high-end items, and the shoppers poring over the blue jeans are discerning consumers, often with a better sense of what is *in* (how many pockets? how much flare?) than the original purchaser. The young people in Dar es Salaam are as fashion savvy as young Americans, with a flawless sense of the hip and unhip.

Georgetown student Henri Minion spent the summer of 2008 in Dar es Salaam living with a host family, and I asked him to study the role of mitumba in daily life. One of the first things that Henri noticed was that the mitumba-clad students at the University of Dar es Salaam not only were well dressed, but they blended right in, fashionwise, with the American students visiting from Washington.

The market mechanism in African mitumba markets is considerably more flexible than in an American department store. The Dockers with waist sizes in the low 30s sell for more than those with sizes in the 40s, as Tanzanians in general lack Americans' paunches. Otherwise-identical polo shirts can vary in price as well, with more popular colors and sizes commanding a premium. Prices trend up at the end of the month when many workers get paid, but drift lower during periods between paychecks.

Perhaps the most interesting pricing behavior is evident in the divide between men's and women's clothing, as both supply and demand influences lead to significant price discrimination against the men. First, because Western women buy many more new clothes than men, they throw away many more clothes as well. Ed Stubin estimates that the truckloads arriving from the Salvation Army contain between two and three times as much women's clothing as men's. Women are also more particular about the condition of their clothing, so about 90 percent of what is cast aside by women is still in good condition. Men, however, not only buy less clothing but wear it longer, so only half of the men's clothing received by the used clothing exporters is in good condition. On the supply side, the bottom line is that world supply contains perhaps seven times as much women's clothing in good condition than it does men's. African demand exacerbates this imbalance, as African women's clothing preferences exclude much of Western fashion while men clamor for the limited supply of T-shirts, khakis, and suits that are in good condition. The end result of this supply-and-demand dynamic is that in the mitumba markets, similar clothing in good condition may cost four to five times as much for men as it does for women.

I first met Geofrey Milonge in 2003 at his T-shirt stall near the center of the Manzese market. Geofrey stands tall and shiny-black, with the languid pride and gentle manner that seem to be the national traits of the Tanzanians. Geofrey arrived from the countryside in the early 1990s, hoping to escape the rural poverty of his village in the interior. Geofrey had started out on the sidewalk with just a single 50-kilo bale of clothing, which he had purchased on credit. Within a few years, Geofrey had three mitumba stalls in the Manzese market, each catering to different types of consumers. His T-shirt stall was neatly laid out, with hundreds of T-shirts lining the walls on hangers. In 2003, Geofrey was selling between ten and fifty T-shirts per day, usually for between 50 cents and $1.50. Almost all of Geofrey's T-shirts were from America.

The labels showed that most of the T-shirts were originally born in Mexico, China, or Central America, and most of the T-shirts also reveal something about their life in America. The college and professional sports team shirts (Florida Gators, Chicago Bulls) are ubiquitous, and winning teams' shirts fetch higher prices. Washington Redskins shirts move slowly, but Geofrey had earlier in the morning received $2 for a Pittsburgh Steelers shirt. U.S. sportswear logos are popular, too—Nike, Reebok, Adidas—but Geofrey's customers can easily tell the fakes (cheaper, coarser cotton) from the genuine. Middle-American suburbia hangs neatly pressed as a backdrop to the more valuable sports logos. Across the back of the stall is a Beaver Cleaver caricature of America: Weekend activities (Woods Lake Fun Run 1999), family vacations (Yellowstone National Park—Don't Feed the Bears), social conscience (Race for the Cure), and neighborhood teams (Glen Valley Youth Soccer) are some of the customers' choices.

Geofrey is very careful about where he buys from. The sellers can hide all kinds of garbage in the middle of a bale, so it pays to know your suppliers and to make sure that they know that if they give you garbage you won't be back. Geofrey prefers to buy bales that have been sorted in the United States or Europe, rather than in Africa. The U.S.-sorted bales cost a bit more, but the jewels are less likely to have been skimmed off and you get a lot less junk. In the world of mitumba, an unbroken U.S.-sorted bale is a high-end luxury good.

In her study of the second-hand clothing trade in Zambia, anthropologist Karen Hansen found the perverse manifestations of the preference for castoffs fresh from American bales.[5] In the world of mitumba, Hansen found, consumers seek out "new" clothing that is wrinkled and musty-smelling. A fresh-pressed or clean-smelling garment cannot possibly have spent weeks or months in a compressed bale in a warehouse or shipping container; therefore, it is the more wrinkled and musty clothing that is likely to be "new" from America, while the fresh-pressed and clean-smelling clothing is more likely to be "old"—that is, worn or presorted in Africa.

PANNING FOR GOLD IN TANZANIA

Mitumba dealers told me repeatedly that 90 percent of a bale's value comes from 10 percent of the items. For every GAP shirt in perfect condition that might fetch $3 there will be a dozen pieces that will be hard to unload even at 50 cents. Once the few jewels have been skimmed, the bale's market value drops dramatically.

As a result, successfully plying the mitumba trade is about keeping track of jewels. A bale consisting only of suburban activities will be a losing proposition for Geofrey. If the sports teams, GAPs, and Nike snowflakes have been pilfered, the Fun Run and family vacation T-shirts that are left will not allow him to cover his costs. In Dar es Salaam, just as in Brooklyn, the business is all about snowflakes.

Geofrey told me that when he gets the chance to skim for jewels himself, he takes it. Many importers order clothing in larger bales, say 500 or even up to 1,500 pounds, which are too large for a single dealer to purchase. In these cases, the importer or wholesaler hosts a party of sorts, to which Geofrey and his peers will try to cadge an invitation. Sometimes, the dealers will pay 1,000 to 2,000 schillings ($1 to $2) to be invited. There are refreshments and a competitive camaraderie leading up to the highlight of the party: the breaking open of the bale. The bale breaking is a highlight, because only if mitumba dealers can see the breaking with their own eyes can they be sure that the jewels have not been skimmed, and in a large bale from the United States, the chances of valuable jewels are high. The mood is festive and raucous because of the surprise to come: You just never know what the Americans will throw away, and to be invited to the party to get first crack at the jewels can mean a windfall for the week.

The wholesaler breaks the bale and the melee begins. A 1,000-pound bale might contain up to 3,000 articles of clothing, and almost every bale will contain surprises. The dealers begin a competitive rummaging and quickly pull out the jewels. Multiple mini-auctions for the jewels take place simultaneously: The spotless Nike attracts offers of $1, which quickly rise to $1.50 and then $2. The baby overalls with the tags still attached draw bids of 50 cents, then 75, and finally $1.25. A special find is to uncover a group of identical items—six matching yellow sweaters, say, or a dozen blue twill shirts—the matching clothing has a ready and profitable market as uniforms for businesses.

The mini-auctions at the bale-breaking parties are close to a perfectly competitive market. There are many buyers; there is perfect information; there is, as an economist might say, excellent price discovery. And there is good fun. The element of surprise keeps it a fun market as well as a functioning one, and the party is a treasure hunt as well as a market. The hunt for treasure does not stop with the clothing but extends to the pockets, as Americans throw away not just perfectly good clothing but perfectly good money as well—U.S. dollars, no less.

The most valuable jewels will never make it to the crowded mitumba markets. Instead, the top-of-the-line jewels hang from trees in the commercial area near the harbor, close to Dar es Salaam's handful of office towers and banks, and its second-floor walk-up stock exchange. These jewels—a perfect suit, say, or a like-new prom dress—hang like solitaires from the trees on the main boulevard, away from the pedestrian hubbub of the markets. A trader lucky enough to nab such a jewel will hire a helper to sit under the tree and guard the jewel until it is purchased, or until nightfall, whichever comes first.

The middle and upper classes often do not enter the crowds at the markets, though they too are dressed in mitumba. Just as a wealthier family might have help to shop for food, many Tanzanians also have relationships with mitumba dealers who know their size and style preferences, and keep a watch for just the right suit or dress shirt. Such personal shoppers make house and office calls when just the right jewels turn up in the bales.

When Geofrey Milonge emerges from the competitive market as a buyer, he almost immediately joins another perfectly competitive market as a seller. There are hundreds of stalls and thousands of T-shirts in Dar es Salaam, and the consumers have nothing if not choices. At the other end of the spectrum from the jewels are the dregs, the clothing that is hard to unload at any price. Most mitumba dealers have a card table or two in the middle of their stall that is piled high with clearance items that haven't sold. While the vendors' better offerings will neatly line the stall on hangers, the dregs are simply piled up, mitumba's answer to the clearance table at Wal-Mart.

In the larger mitumba markets, many stalls have a worker with a microphone who drones on in a mesmerizing chant to entice shoppers to stop. As evening approaches, the competition intensifies because the shopkeepers would much rather unload a few more garments than pack them until the next day. The voices from the microphones form a cacophony that gets louder and louder as the afternoon wears on. The stall owners like Geofrey Milonge are especially loath to pack up the clearance-table items as darkness approaches. The Swahili chants ring out as the prices for items on the clearance table drop like a sharp curve along with the sun. By the end of the day, the clothing on the clearance table that sold for a dime at noon might go for two for a penny.

For Geofrey Milonge, the day ends in a seller's competition as intense as the buyer's competition with which he started the morning. If he rests in the morning, the competition will snag the jewels, and if he rests in the evening, the competition will snag his customers. The markets at the center of Geofrey's livelihood are more flexible—and closer to a "real" market—than anything the T-shirt has experienced before. With no barriers between himself and the market, Geofrey must adjust his selling prices by men's or women's, by size, by color, by weather, and by time of day and time of month, and he must adjust his buying prices at the bale-breaking party by trying to predict who will happen by that morning, what they will want, and what they will pay.

FINDING GEOFREY

I tried to track down Geofrey in 2007 and again in 2008. In 2007, the telephone number I had did not work and Google turned up nothing. I wrote to him at the address I had written down, but the letter was returned to me months later. I asked two people who had been helpful to me in Tanzania to see whether they could track him down, but I again came up empty-handed. In 2008, I gave Georgetown student Henri Minion the mission of finding Geofrey Milonge. Henri was studying in Dar for the summer. He would have six weeks.

While I remembered the approximate location of Geofrey's T-shirt stall (and of course had Geofrey's picture), this was no help because the Manzese market had closed and had in large part been replaced by other mitumba markets throughout the city. But the mission to find Geofrey seemed to be off to a good start. I had another contact in Dar es Salaam who knew Geofrey (I will call him "Mike"—not his real name), and he quickly agreed to assist Henri. For weeks, Henri tried to connect with Mike. And for weeks, the meetings were canceled or postponed. The concept of "Tanzania Time" is often used by Western diplomats and business-people to describe life in Dar. And it was apt for Henri: Tanzania Time meant Maybe Later. Or Maybe Not.

As Henri's time in Dar es Salaam was coming to a close, it appeared that the mission to find Geofrey would be unsuccessful. When Henri last tried to connect with Mike, he learned that he was in Amsterdam. Mike promised that his secretary would call Henri, but she did not. Ever resourceful, Henri received a tip from a friend about another person who would be willing to help. He called the gentle-man, and agreed to meet at his office the next day. When Henri arrived, no one there had heard of the gentleman Henri had spoken with.

With just days left in Tanzania, Henri was not going to give up. Henri had gotten to know Elina Makanja, a freelance journalist and teaching assistant at the University of Dar es Salaam. Elina was an enthusiastic mitumba shopper, and she agreed to help. The day before Henri was to leave Tanzania, Elina found Geofrey Milonge in the market.

I thought of Henri's mission to find Geofrey a few months later, when I was chatting with Julia Hughes. We were discussing which countries might soon be competitive apparel producers for the U.S. market. "What about Sub-Saharan Africa?" I asked Julia. Julia sighed. "It's sad," she said. "It's just so hard to do business there."

Tanzania Time, or living life to a slow and unscheduled rhythm, can quickly become a charmed way of life for a visitor. For an apparel company needing to stock its shelves for the next season, however, Tanzania Time was a risk they were unwilling to bear.

Happily, in 2008, Geofrey's mitumba business was healthy and growing. Since 2003, he had opened four more stores, and now had a total of seven shops throughout Dar es Salaam. Geofrey had also become active as a wholesaler. Where a few years before he had been purchasing clothing in bales, he was now importing shipping containers from the United States and Europe and selling bales to other mitumba dealers, and he often hosted his own bale-breaking parties.

As Geofrey gained experience in international trade, he was diversifying into other goods. By late 2008 Geofrey was importing building materials such as cement, and had also invested in real estate. When I first met Geofrey, he spoke only Swahili, but in late 2008 we were corresponding by e-mail in English. He wrote to me that he had recently spent a month in London, researching prices and drumming up suppliers.

Though the global supply of used clothing is increasing, Geofrey has observed steady increases in the prices at which he sells clothing. He estimates that the prices for good-quality clothing in the markets have approximately doubled during the past five years. The increase in the price of good-quality but basic T-shirts was lower but still healthy: Geofrey said that T-shirts that had sold for $1 in 2003 were selling for about $1.50 in 2008.

Ed Stubin and Geofrey Milonge describe this global industry with remarkably similar stories. In both cases, survival depends on their skill in spotting the jewels among the snowflakes and knowing their value in the market. Both men stress that they depend on personal relationships with suppliers and personal knowledge about their customers. On both sides of the Atlantic, the snowflake imperative keeps the businesses small and nimble, in close touch with suppliers and customers. Once you stop paying attention, or take your eye off the T-shirt river, or off your customer, you're finished.

Here, at the end of the T-shirt's life, is a global industry where it pays to be the little guy, where the power equation is flipped upside down away from the multi-national corporations. Indeed, the grandfather and founder of the used clothing business in Tanzania was the victim of his own success. His far-flung empire, though built on profits from the used clothing trade, became much too big to keep track of snowflakes.

TOO BIG FOR USED BRITCHES

Mohammed Enterprises Tanzania Limited (METL) is today one of the largest private companies in Tanzania, a conglomerate involved in manufacturing, agriculture, and trade. METL manufactures soap, sweeteners, cooking oil, textiles, clothing, and bicycles, and it owns 31,000 hectares of farmland producing sisal, cashews, and dairy products. METL is also a major trading house selling sesame seeds to Japan, pigeon peas to India, cocoa to the United States, and beeswax to Europe. METL seems to operate as a completely Westernized company today, committed to market awareness, customer focus, and corporate responsibility. Even METL's rise is a Western-sounding story.

As the family story goes, Gulam Dewji, METL's chairman, got his start in the 1960s by arbitraging onions in rural Tanzania. He drove a rickety truck across the crumbling non-roads, finding villages that had extra onions and connecting them with villages that had too much squash. He had a sense of market trends and impeccable timing, and he gradually added trucks and employees. In another place and time, Gulam Dewji might have run a hedge fund, but in 1960s Tanzania, Gulam used his market-timing talents on onions. Gulam remembers that the villagers, while poor, usually had enough to eat. They did not, however, have clothing, at least not to speak of. In rural Tanzania at the time, adults were mostly in rags and children were mostly naked.

Currency controls meant that hard currency was rarely available to import clothing, and mismanagement meant that the local textile industry was poorly equipped to supply the local market. There was special official scorn—and an outright ban—on mitumba. Though it was illegal to import used clothing, much made it through the porous borders with Mozambique and Kenya. But it was a furtive and haphazard trade, an underbelly business that was lubricated by bribes to border guards in the middle of the night.

In 1985, Julius Nyerere stepped down and the mitumba trade was legalized. Gulam immediately saw the business opportunity presented by the liberalization. From his decades of traveling through the rural areas he knew that people wanted decent clothing. It was not a matter of emulating Westerners, it was instead a matter of pride: Tanzanians had no desire to look like Americans, they wanted to look like well-dressed Tanzanians. Gulam went to America and began to meet with used clothing exporters.

During the next 10 years, METL's mitumba business grew rapidly and Gulam was soon importing 4,000 tons of used clothing per month into the port at Dar es Salaam. Mitumba quickly reached not only the cities but far into the rural areas as well. A network of traders plied the backcountry as Gulam had once done with onions, and mitumba markets soon sprang up in every town.

Gulam purchased the clothing from American dealers in huge bales weighing up to 2,000 pounds apiece. Compared to the intricate sorting and mining processes that characterize the business today, the process was loose at best. Often the clothing had been sorted into just three categories: Category A contained only clothing that was in like-new condition; Category B clothing was in fairly good shape, a bit faded, perhaps, or missing a button; and Category C contained garments that were torn or stained. The bales were delivered to METL's cavernous warehouse, where they were broken up and sorted again and readied for market.

Just as Ed Stubin had once found it easier—most of the clothing he sorted was saleable at a profit—Gulam, too, found the early days to be the good old days. People in Tanzania had had so few choices and so little income that they welcomed almost everything from America. A bit of wear made little difference, especially in the countryside, as the clothing was usually a step up from the rags for the adults or the nakedness for the children. Gulam could sell almost everything that arrived in the bales from America, usually at a profit.

At the beginning, there were still many self-reliance ideologues who believed that the practice of wearing the white world's castoffs was shameful. Gradually, however, the ideologues toned down and began to dress in mitumba as well. Indeed, as Karen Hansen found in Zambia, the availability of mitumba was put forth as evidence of progress in the village. ("There is even mitumba now," residents would say, so as to point to the improved quality of life.[6])

But with widespread acceptance also came the maturing of the market and the erosion of Gulam's first-mover advantages. METL was growing and diversifying into other businesses, and the agility required to keep up with the mitumba trade was difficult to maintain. There were few barriers to entry, and it seemed that almost everyone had a friend of a friend in the United States or Europe who could begin to send over bales of clothing, so hundreds of nimble entrepreneurs emerged to buy and sell mitumba. The mitumba trade was an intensely personal business, built relationship by relationship as had happened with Gulam and his American suppliers. The relationships were needed to keep unhappy surprises in the bales to a minimum and happy surprises frequent enough to engender continued loyalty but not so frequent as to erase the black ink. The delicate balance required by the snowflake business required constant attention—attention that Gulam wanted to focus on other parts of METL's activities.

Another problem for Gulam was that customers were getting pickier. Not only had the market for Category C clothing all but disappeared, customers now wanted certain styles and certain colors at certain times. Without the time or attention to keep his ear to the ground in the marketplace, Gulam found it difficult to compete with the small entrepreneurs who spent their energies staying on top of consumer preferences. Gradually, Gulam ceded his mitumba business to smaller traders. You need to be small to do this, Gulam told me.

Partly because of his success in the mitumba trade, small was what he wasn't. But for the entrepreneurs to follow him, there were opportunities, and chances for little guys to participate in a global market.

CHAPTER 7

The Specter That Haunts the Global Economy?

The Challenge of Global Feminism

Valentine Moghadam

Male-dominated monetary, trade, and financial policies are
gender blind, resulting in serious costs to all.
                    —Doris Mpoumou, of WEDO, 2000

Vigorous global feminism is perhaps the single most effective
form of resistance to the systematic degradation of human
rights standards worldwide, which makes possible the worst
ravages of the transnational economy.
                    —Margaret Spillane, in *The Nation,* 2001

Another world is possible and women are building it!
                    —Women's caucus at the Monterrey conference, 2002

We have seen how the twin processes of global economic restructuring and
religious fundamentalisms galvanized women around the world, led to a
convergence of previously divergent perspectives, and resulted in the formation of
transnational feminist networks (TFNs). In the latter part of the 1980s, the world's
women were ready for such mobilization and forms of organization, in part due to
sociodemographic changes such as rising educational attainment and employment among women. Since then, women have formed networks and have joined
forces with other advocacy networks, civil society groups, and social movement
organizations to challenge the neoliberal corporate agenda and to advance the
cause of women's human rights. Along with other organizations and networks that
are working for an alternative globalization or are engaging with global public
policies, transnational feminist networks (TFNs) have contributed to the transnational social movement infrastructure and are helping to construct global civil
society.

Female labor and women's organizations are integral elements of globalization
in its economic, cultural, and political dimensions. The capitalist world-economy

functions by means of the deployment of labor that is waged and non-waged, formal and informal, male and female. In recent decades, the involvement of women in various kinds of labor arrangements has been striking. Capitalist accumulation is achieved through the surplus-extraction of labor, and this includes the paid and unpaid economic activities of women, whether in male-headed or female-headed households. The various forms of the deployment of female labor reflect asymmetrical gender relations and patriarchal gender ideologies. Global accumulation as the driving force of the world-system not only hinges on class and regional differences across economic zones, but it is also a gendered process, predicated upon gender differences in the spheres of production and reproduction. In an era of economic globalization, the pressure for greater competitiveness through lower labor and production costs has encouraged the demand for and supply of female labor.

However, in a reflection of the contradictions of capitalism, the incorporation of women in the global economy and in national labor forces has also served to interrogate and modify gender relations and ideologies. Women have been organizing and mobilizing against the hegemonic and particularistic aspects of globalization. Organized and mobilized women—locally, nationally, and transnationally—are raising questions about social and gender arrangements and making demands on employers, governments, patriarchal movements, and international financial institutions. Many feminist organizations have been middle-class and elite, but class lines are increasingly blurred as women professionals and women proletarians find common cause around personal, economic, and social issues, including violence against women, poverty, job security, land rights, the redistribution and socialization of domestic work, reproductive health and rights, and women's roles in decision-making.

ORGANIZATIONAL DYNAMICS, STRENGTHS, AND WEAKNESSES

Women's organizations reflect women's collective consciousness, identity, experiences, and aspirations. These are forged in labor processes, in domestic experiences, and in political struggles, and give rise to feminist organizations, women's caucuses, and participation in unions. We have seen that some feminist movements and their organizations have grown out of left-wing organizations, national liberation movements, labor movements, and other struggles. Disillusionment with male-dominated organizations and movements or the marginalization of women's movements and concerns often has been the impetus for women's organizations. But feminist networks emerge and make interventions in policy dialogues and debates on national and global levels also because women are convinced that their own, feminist perspectives have value and can make a difference.

When activists form organizations, they may build on preexisting organizations and networks of women. This pattern has been noted in the social movements and women's movements literatures. Women's organizations, and transnational feminist networks (TFNs) in particular, are not exclusivist; we have seen that they join in coalitions with unions, political parties, and other civil society organizations or advocacy networks as well as with other feminist networks. And like some other civil-society or social-movement organizations, women's organizations may face state repression and resource constraints. Limited budgets are a perennial problem, but harassment or intimidation are not unknown and are more serious.

In her study of the Women's International League for Peace and Freedom, Mary Meyer contrasts the longevity of WILPF (founded in 1915) with other women's peace groups which, while often quite radical, disavowed formal organization or dissolved following specific antimilitarist campaigns. She attributes this longevity to the WILPF founders' determination to "institutionalize the international women's peace movement . . . through an organizational structure that combined both main-streaming and disengaging political strategies."[1] Like WILPF, contemporary TFNs engage with international organizations and public policy issues while also taking a radical and at times utopian stance on the social order.

Formal organizations, however, have their tensions. Like other types of women's organizations, TFNs face issues of centralization, decentralization, institutional-ization, professionalization, as well as charismatic leadership. Professionalization is a double-edged sword, as Network Women in Development in Europe (WIDE) discovered and as critics of Women's Environment and Development Organiza-tions (WEDO) maintain. Some activists feel that WEDO's New York office has been too central, that there is a one-way relationship with the contacts in develop-ing countries, and that its lobbying work overwhelms other worthwhile objectives, such as fostering or supporting grassroots women's organizations. The difficulties of effecting change in the global economy to establish gender justice and economic justice have led some feminists to question the strategy of participating in interna-tional conferences and lobbying delegates. One WEDO board member remarked: "International meetings are too distracting. There's no time to take care of your housekeeping. It's the same people who go the UN meetings all the time. It's a complex, labor-intensive, technical process." The focus, rather, should be on support for grassroots women's organizations and for the building of the movement. The WEDO board member continued: "There's been a little tension within the board regarding advocacy versus movement. Bella was clear; she wanted advocacy and not grassroots work. Now there's recognition of the importance of being more organi-cally connected to grassroots movements that organize and not just advocate."[2]

Weaknesses and risks facing transnational feminists also should be acknowl-edged. Like many women's groups, TFNs often lack the necessary financial and other resources for real growth or more effective participation and lobbying. In the absence of a mass membership base, or due to the difficulties and expenses of col-lecting dues in a variety of currencies, they rely on "soft money" from external grants or foundation assistance, with its attendant problems of sustainability or legitimation.

Another weakness or danger is co-optation. There is always the possibility that states or international agencies can co-opt activists and especially "experts" who work with TFNs. After all, some transnational feminist activists have become UN officials or consultants, and they consult governments as well. The question of pos-sible co-optation has been raised especially in connection with the World Bank's outreach activities, although there is no evidence thus far that participation in the many gender seminars organized by the World Bank has led to dilution of the critical analysis of those feminist political economists who accept the invitations.[3]

"Political purity" or a willful disengagement from multilateral organizations can attenuate the potential effectiveness of a TFN. For example, Women Living Under Muslim Laws (WLUML) leaders have admitted that they were not as effective as they could have been with respect to an issue that has been of central importance to the network—the fate of Algerian women, and especially fellow feminists, during the terrible years of the Algerian civil conflict.[4] WLUML was quite active in supporting Algerian feminists in their encounter with Islamist groups, but the efficacy of their work was hampered by the network's reluctance to engage with UN bodies as extensively as other TFNs have done, in favor of an approach that prioritized networking, solidarity, and appeals to feminists and other progressives around the world. On the other hand, their co-authorship of a shadow report on Algeria, submitted to the Convention on the Elimination of All Forms of Discrimination against Women (CEDAW) Committee, did represent a shift in their approach.

I would conclude, nevertheless, that TFN accomplishments outweigh their weaknesses or the risks that they face. Without TFN activity the world would hardly have known about the atrocities facing Algerian and Afghan women in the 1990s. Indeed, the worldwide excoriation of the Taliban, its diplomatic isolation, and the defeat of the UNOCAL oil pipeline project is a success story of transnational feminism. Here, WLUML and its Lahore branch, ShirkatGah, played a critical role, especially in the early years. In the area of economic policy, the trenchant and sustained critiques of structural adjustment by TFNs compelled the World Bank to retreat from its earlier disregard for the social sectors and to adopt a policy of gender-sensitivity in its research and policy work. The UN, World Bank, and international development agencies recognize the role of women's organizations in the development process and in the making of civil society, and they have adopted transnational feminist concepts such as gender approach, gender equality, empowerment, and autonomy.

In fact, the study of TFNs shows that women's organizations have become major nonstate political actors on the global, regional, and national scenes. They are in a dynamic relationship with states, the media, intergovernmental organizations, and other transnational social movements (TSMOs) and transnational activist networks (TANs). They use the global, intergovernmental arena and the transnational public sphere to accomplish national priorities in the areas of women's human rights (such as violence against women and the rights of women in Muslim societies) and economic policies (such as structural adjustment and the new global trade agenda), as well as to influence international norms and conventions. As such they challenge and engage with the state and global forces alike. They also refute stereotypical notions that women's organizations are exclusively local, or that they are concerned primarily with issues of identity and sexuality, or that they do not engage with economic policy issues.

The TFNs that I have described offer a critique of neoliberal capitalism and advocate for the welfare state and for global Keynesianism. They have actively responded to adverse global processes, including economic restructuring and the expansion of fundamentalism, and are offering alternative frameworks. In order to realize their goals of equality and empowerment for women and social justice and democratization in the society and globally, TFNs engage in information exchange, mutual support, and a combination of lobbying, advocacy, and (at times) direct action. In so doing they take advantage of other global processes, including the development and spread of information and computer technologies.

TFNs confirm the importance of networks for women—whether in the form of micro-level personal relations that spawn formal groups and organizations, or macro-level organizations that operate transnationally. Transnational feminists have devised an organizational structure that consists of active and autonomous local/national women's groups but that transcends localisms or nationalisms. And as we have seen with all case-study TFNs, including those working on Muslim or Mediterranean women's human rights, their discourses are not particularistic but universalistic; they emphasize solidarity and commonality rather than difference. This finding runs counter to some arguments that have been made by feminist scholars situated in postmodernist or postcolonialist frames.

Feminism, Labor, and Human Rights

The global women's movement, and in particular transnational feminist networks, may offer lessons to other social movements and their organizations, not least the labor movement. According to two analysts, "no major American institution changed less than the labor movement. At the end of the twentieth century, American unions are as poorly adapted to the economy and society of their time as were the craft unions of iron puddlers and corwainers to the mass production industries of seventy years ago."[5] This can hardly be said of transnational feminist networks, who have become remarkably ICT-savvy. At the dawn of the new millennium, transnational feminist networks evince the organizational form and supranational solidarities that socialists had expected of the labor movement in the early twentieth century. In fact, just as the labor movement historically emerged from the involvement of workers in social production and the exploitation they experienced, so has the feminist movement emerged from women's involvement in the labor force and from the exploitation and inequality they experience at the workplace and in society more broadly.

Historically, trade unions and communist and socialist parties were the organizational expressions of the labor movement. The social movement of women has produced women's organizations; moreover, in a reflection of their incorporation in the paid labor force, women are becoming increasingly involved in unions. If the emergence of the workers' movement represented the contradictions of early capitalism, the emergence of the global women's movement and of transnational women's organizations are indicative of the contradictions of late capitalism in an era of globalization. It is worth pointing out that in the early 1990s, when the labor movement and left parties alike were in retreat, it was the emerging transnational women's movement, and specifically a number of TFNs, that were consistently critical of economic globalization. Since then, labor unions have become increasingly skeptical of the neoliberal capitalist agenda; the participation of U.S. unions in the Battle of Seattle and in various antiwar protests could represent the beginnings of "social movement unionism." But it remains to be seen whether the labor movement as a whole—within the United States and across the world-system—will follow the lead of the women's movement in its approach to globalization and collective action.

Indeed, it is my view that a formidable alliance would be one between feminism and labor—that is, between the social movement of women and social movement unionism—along with other elements of the global justice movement. Such an alliance is entirely possible, given global feminism's concern with the exploitation of female labor in the global economy, and given the growing participation of women in trade unions. Trade union women, and especially feminists within trade unions, could bridge the divide between the feminist movement and the labor movement. Such an alliance would call for a more activist and transnational labor movement than we have been accustomed to seeing in recent decades—although a number of commentators feel that social movement unionism and transnational alliances are now on the agenda. There is increasing recognition that unions, social movement organizations, and NGOs will need to work together to counter the dominance of neoliberal economic policies, as a roundtable held in Bangkok concluded.[6] Many trade union activists "are able to recognize their affinity and resemblance to other social movements, while links particularly with women's and democratic movements are now common, accepted and welcomed."[7] Dan Gallin refers to the need for unions and NGOs to coalesce around "a program of radical democracy diametrically opposed to the currently hegemonic neoliberalism," and to "reconstitute the social movement worldwide, with the means provided by globalization and its technologies."[8] A formal alliance among the women's, environmental, and labor movements could help move forward the project of global Keynesianism or transnational socialism.

This is not to say that there are no tensions between the women's movement and other social movements, or tensions within the global women's movement. As we have seen, Mahnaz Afkhami of SIGI and WLP has indicated that human rights organizations do not consistently take gender issues on board; there is sometimes distance and distrust between women's human rights organizations and the nonfeminist human rights organizations. DAWN has voiced concern that women's reproductive rights could be sidelined in a broad progressive movement that includes religious groups that are against abortion. DAWN also has raised concerns about divisions between feminist groups in the South and the North concerning trade and labor standards.[9] In 2003, as the global justice movement morphed into a global justice and peace movement and as dozens of Muslim groups in some countries joined antiwar mobilizations in the wake of the American and British invasion of Iraq, secular feminists from Muslim countries and communities began to wonder if women's issues would again be glossed over. Ideally, transnational social movement organizations and the global justice and peace movement will recognize that women's rights are human rights and that the demands, objectives, and methods of the women's movement and of global feminism are essential to the broader project of global change.

Globalization, the State, and Gender Justice

TFNs contribute several new ideas to current discussions of, and collective action around, globalization. One idea pertains to understandings and definitions of globalization. We have seen that transnational feminists are not, strictly speaking, anti-globalization. They are anti-neoliberal capitalism, but they view globalization as a multifaceted phenomenon whose most positive feature is its opportunities for transnational networking and solidarity. They would like to help reinvent globalization and reorient it from a *project of markets* to a *project of peoples*. Their literature is replete with condemnations of the ills of neoliberal capitalism. But their stated solutions and strategies are to remake (*democratize* and *engender*) global governance, not to destroy it. After all, they frequently engage with institutions and norms of global governance in order to influence policymakers or affect legal frameworks at the state level. Thus they endorse redistributive mechanisms and global social policies because these would lead to greater investments in human development, increase the likelihood of gender budgets, reduce social and gender inequalities, and redirect globalization. It is worth pointing out that in late February 2004, the ILO released a report entitled *A Fair Globalization: Creating Opportunities for All,* which noted the inequalities, exclusions, and imbalances resulting from globalization's focus on the market. In calling for a shift in emphasis on people's well-being, it echoed a prominent transnational feminist theme. Many of the ILO report's recommendations—a democratic and effective state, sustainable development, solidarity and partnerships, greater accountability to people, an effective United Nations—have been among the objectives of the transnational feminist networks examined in this chapter.[10]

A second idea pertains to the state. For transnational feminists, the state remains a key institutional actor—even though they eschew nationalist politics in favor of internationalism and transnational solidarity. The state matters because of women's stakes in the areas of reproductive rights, family law, and social policy; and because transnational feminists oppose the neoliberal and patriarchal state and favor the welfarist, developmentalist form of the state that is also democratic and woman-friendly. I have called this the critical realist approach to the state. Thus the focus of TFN activity is simultaneously the state, the region (e.g., Latin America, the European Union, the Mediterranean), and the global economy and institutions of global governance.

A third distinctive idea pertains to the transnational feminist call for women's human rights and for "gender justice." At the UN's international conference on human rights in 1993, feminists popularized the slogan "women's rights are human rights," thereby rejecting the idea that women's rights may be subject to cultural or religious conditions. Since then, they have consistently opposed fundamentalist views on women and gender. Representative of the global feminist view of women and human rights is the following statement by the Association for Women's Rights in Development (AWID):

> Women should be able to actualize their rights, to celebrate their cultures, and to live in freedom and security. No tradition, cultural practice or religious tenet can

justify the violation of a fundamental human right. . . . The human rights of women are indivisible, interdependent and universal, not subject to a religious veto. We must oppose all fundamentalisms and the erosion of women's enjoyment of their rights.[11]

This call was first made in the context of cooperation with the broader global economic justice movement and campaigns such as Jubilee 2000. To be sure, transnational feminists do not want women's rights, including reproductive rights, to be placed on the back burner or postponed until after the triumph of the anti-globalization movement, as has been the case with so many national political movements. But they also believe that global justice is rendered a meaningless, abstract concept without consideration of the gendered (and racial) makeup of working people—or of "working families."[12] Without due consideration of the sexual division of labor and the care economy, of the traffic in women's bodies, of working women's human rights (including rights to bodily integrity and reproductive rights), and of their social rights (e.g., paid maternity leaves, paternity leaves, and quality child care), there can in fact be no economic justice for women. As such, the slogan "gender justice *and* economic justice" may be understood as a variation of the slogan "women's rights *are* human rights"—both of which are key concepts of global feminism that have been developed and disseminated by transnational feminist networks.

These are still early days in the study of gender and globalization, of transnational social movements, and certainly of transnational feminist networks. This book has drawn on globalization studies, social movements research, and the scholarship on women's organizations to examine global change and the role of transnational feminist networks. I have argued that in an era of globalization, the capitalist world-system is comprised not only of a global economy and unequal nation-states, but also of transnational movements and networks—including transnational feminist networks. By analyzing several representative feminist networks, I hope to have generated a more powerful understanding of their structure and their agency, along with their links to globalization processes. And by discussing the ideas, activities, strategies, and goals of TFNs, I hope to have elucidated what I have called global feminism.

CHAPTER 8

Designing Capitalism 3.0

Dani Rodrik

Capitalism is unequaled when it comes to unleashing the collective economic energy of human societies. That great virtue is why all prosperous nations are capitalist in the broad sense of that term: they are organized around private property and allow markets to play a large role in allocating resources and determining economic rewards. Globalization is the worldwide extension of capitalism. Indeed, so intertwined has capitalism become with globalization that it is impossible to discuss the future of one without discussing the future of the other.

TOWARD CAPITALISM 3.0

The key to capitalism's durability lies in its almost infinite malleability. As our conceptions of the institutions needed to support markets and economic activity have evolved over the centuries, so has capitalism. Thanks to its capacity for reinvention, capitalism has overcome its periodic crises and outlived its critics, from Karl Marx on.

Adam Smith's idealized market society required little more than a "night-watchman state." All that governments needed to do to ensure the division of labor was to enforce property rights, keep the peace, and collect a few taxes to pay for a limited range of public goods such as national defense. Through the early part of the twentieth century and the first wave of globalization, capitalism was governed by a narrow vision of the public institutions needed to uphold it. In practice, the state's reach often went beyond this conception (as when Bismarck introduced old-age pensions in Germany in 1889). But governments continued to see their economic roles in restricted terms. Let's call this "Capitalism 1.0."

As societies became more democratic and labor unions and other groups mobilized against capitalism's perceived abuses, a new, more expansive vision of governance gradually took hold. Antitrust policies that broke up large monopolies came first, spearheaded by the Progressive movement in the United States. Activist monetary and fiscal policies were widely accepted in the aftermath of the Great Depression. The state

111

began to play an increasing role in providing welfare assistance and social insurance. In today's industrialized countries, the share of public spending in national income rose rapidly, from below 10 percent on average at the end of the nineteenth century to more than 20 percent just before World War II. In the wake of World War II, these countries erected elaborate social welfare states in which the public sector expanded to more than 40 percent of national income on average.

This "mixed-economy" model was the crowning achievement of the twentieth century. The new balance that it established between states and markets underpinned an unprecedented period of social cohesion, stability, and prosperity in the advanced economies that lasted until the mid-1970s. Let's call this "Capitalism 2.0."

Capitalism 2.0 went with a limited kind of globalization—the Bretton Woods compromise. The postwar model required keeping the international economy at bay because it was built for and operated at the level of nation-states. Thus the Bretton Woods–GATT regime established a "shallow" form of international economic integration, with controls on international capital flows, partial trade liberalization, and plenty of exceptions for socially sensitive sectors (agriculture, textiles, services) as well as developing nations. This left individual nations free to build their own domestic versions of Capitalism 2.0, as long as they obeyed a few simple international rules.

This model became frayed during the 1970s and 1980s, and now appears to have broken down irrevocably under the dual pressures of financial globalization and deep trade integration. The vision that the hyperglobalizers offered to replace Capitalism 2.0 suffered from two blind spots. One was that we could push for rapid and deep integration in the world economy and let institutional underpinnings catch up later. The second was that hyperglobalization would have no, or mostly benign, effects on domestic institutional arrangements. The crises—of both finance and legitimacy—that globalization has produced, culminating in the financial meltdown of 2008, have laid bare the immense size of these blind spots.

We must reinvent capitalism for a new century in which the forces of economic globalization are much more powerful. Just as Smith's lean capitalism (Capitalism 1.0) was transformed into Keynes's mixed economy (Capitalism 2.0), we need to contemplate a transition from the national version of the mixed economy to its global counterpart. We need to imagine a better balance between markets and their supporting institutions at the global level.

It is tempting to think that the solution—Capitalism 3.0—lies in a straightforward extension of the logic of Capitalism 2.0: a global economy requires global governance. But the global governance option is a dead end for the vast majority of nations, at least for the foreseeable future. It is neither practical nor even desirable. We need a different vision, one that safeguards the considerable benefits of a moderate globalization while explicitly recognizing the virtues of national diversity and the centrality of national governance. What we need, in effect, is an updating of the Bretton Woods compromise for the twenty-first century.

This updating must recognize the realities of the day: trade is substantially free, the genie of financial globalization has escaped the bottle, the United States is no longer the world's dominant economic superpower, and major emerging markets

(China especially) can no longer be ignored or allowed to remain free riders on the system. We cannot return to some mythical "golden era" with high trade barriers, rampant capital controls, and a weak GATT—nor should we want to. What we can do is recognize that the pursuit of hyperglobalization is a fool's errand and reorient our priorities accordingly. What this means is laid out in this chapter.

PRINCIPLES FOR A NEW GLOBALIZATION

Suppose that the world's leading policy makers were to meet again at the Mount Washington Hotel in Bretton Woods, New Hampshire, to design a new global economic order. They would naturally be preoccupied with the new problems of the day: global economic recovery, the dangers of creeping protectionism, the challenges of financial regulation, global macroeconomic imbalances, and so on. However, addressing these pressing issues requires rising above them to consider the soundness of global economic arrangements overall. What are some of the guiding principles of global economic governance they might agree on?

I present in this chapter seven commonsense principles. Taken together, they provide a foundation that would serve the world economy well in the future.

1. Markets Must Be Deeply Embedded in Systems of Governance

The idea that markets are self-regulating received a mortal blow in the recent financial crisis and should be buried once and for all. As the experience with financial globalization demonstrates, "the magic of markets" is a dangerous siren song that can distract policy makers from the fundamental insight of Capitalism 2.0: markets and governments are opposites only in the sense that they form two sides of the same coin.

Markets require other social institutions to support them. They rely on courts and legal arrangements to enforce property rights and on regulators to rein in abuse and fix market failures. They depend on the stabilizing functions that lenders-of-last-resort and countercyclical fiscal policy provide. They need the political buy-in that redistributive taxation, safety nets, and social insurance programs help generate. In other words, markets do not create, regulate, stabilize, or sustain themselves. The history of capitalism has been a process of learning and relearning this lesson.

What is true of domestic markets is true also of global ones. Thanks to the trauma of the interwar period and the perspicacity of Keynes, the Bretton Woods regime sought a fine balance that did not push globalization beyond the ability of global governance to uphold it. We need a return to that same spirit if we are going to save globalization from its cheerleaders.

2. Democratic Governance and Political Communities Are Organized Largely Within Nation States, and Are Likely to Remain So for the Immediate Future

The nation-state lives, and even if not entirely well, remains essentially the only game in town. The quest for global governance is a fool's errand, both because national governments are unlikely to cede significant control to transnational institutions and because harmonizing rules would not benefit societies with diverse needs and preferences. The European Union is possibly the sole exception to this truism, but the one that proves the rule.

Overlooking the inherent limits to global governance contributes to globalization's present frailties. We waste international cooperation on overly ambitious goals, ultimately producing weak results that go little beyond the lowest common denominator among major states. Current efforts at harmonizing global financial regulations, for example, will almost certainly end up there. When international cooperation does "succeed," it often spawns rules that reflect the preferences of the more powerful states and are ill-fitting to the circumstances of others. The WTO's rules on subsidies, intellectual property, and investment measures typify this kind of overreaching.

The pursuit of global governance leaves national policy makers with a false sense of security about the strength and durability of global arrangements. Bank regulators with a more realistic sense of the efficacy of Basel rules' impact on capital adequacy or the quality of U.S. credit rating practices would have paid more attention to the risks that their financial institutions at home were incurring.

Our reliance on global governance also muddles our understanding of the rights of nation-states to establish and uphold domestic standards and regulations, and the maneuvering room they have for exercising those rights. The worry that this maneuvering room has narrowed too much is the main reason for the widespread concern about the "race to the bottom" in labor standards, corporate taxes, and elsewhere.

Ultimately, the quest for global governance leaves us with too little real governance. Our only chance of strengthening the infrastructure of the global economy lies in reinforcing the ability of democratic governments to provide those foundations. We can enhance both the efficiency and the legitimacy of globalization if we empower rather than cripple democratic procedures at home. If in the end that also means giving up on an idealized, "perfect" globalization, so be it. A world with a moderate globalization would be a far better place to live in than one mired in the quixotic pursuit of hyperglobalization.

3. There Is No "One Way" to Prosperity

Once we acknowledge that the core institutional infrastructure of the global economy must be built at the national level, it frees up countries to develop the institutions that suit them best. Even today's supposedly homogenized industrial societies embrace a wide variety of institutional arrangements.

The United States, Europe, and Japan are all successful societies; they have each produced comparable amounts of wealth over the long term. Yet the regulations that cover their labor markets, corporate governance, antitrust, social protection, and even banking and finance have differed considerably. These differences enable journalists and pundits to anoint a succession of these "models"—a different one each decade—as the great success for all to emulate. Scandinavia was everyone's favorite in the 1970s; Japan became the country to copy in the 1980s; and the United States was the undisputed king of the 1990s. Such fads should not blind us to the reality that none of these models can be deemed a clear winner in the contest of "capitalisms." The very idea of a "winner" is suspect in a world where nations have somewhat different preferences—where Europeans, for example, would rather have greater income security and less inequality than Americans are used to living with, even if it comes at the cost of higher taxation.[1]

This surfeit of models suggests a deeper implication. Today's institutional arrangements, varied as they are, constitute only a subset of the full range of potential institutional possibilities. It is unlikely that modern societies have managed to exhaust all the useful institutional variation that could underpin healthy and vibrant economies.[2] We need to maintain a healthy skepticism toward the idea that a specific type of institution—a particular mode of corporate governance, social security system, or labor market legislation, for example—is the only type that works in a well-functioning market economy. The most successful societies of the future will leave room for experimentation and allow for further evolution of institutions over time. A global economy that recognizes the need for and value of institutional diversity would foster rather than stifle such experimentation and evolution.

4. Countries Have the Right to Protect Their Own Social Arrangements, Regulations, and Institutions

The previous principles may have appeared uncontroversial and innocuous. Yet they have powerful implications that clash with the received wisdom among boosters of globalization. One such implication is that we need to accept the right of individual countries to safeguard their domestic institutional choices. The recognition of institutional diversity would be meaningless if nations were unable to "protect" domestic institutions—if they did not have the instruments available to shape and maintain their own institutions. Stating principles clearly makes these connections transparent.

Trade is a means to an end, not an end in itself. Advocates of globalization lecture the rest of the world incessantly about how countries must change their policies and institutions in order to expand their international trade and become more attractive to foreign investors. This way of thinking confuses means for ends. Globalization should be an instrument for achieving the goals that societies seek: prosperity, stability, freedom, and quality of life. Nothing enrages WTO critics more than the suspicion that when push comes to shove, the WTO allows trade to trump the environment, human rights, or democratic decision making. Nothing infuriates the critics of the international financial system more than the idea that the interests of global bankers and financiers should come before those of ordinary workers and taxpayers.

Opponents of globalization argue that it sets off a "race to the bottom," with nations converging toward the lowest levels of corporate taxation, financial regulations, or environmental, labor, and consumer protections. Advocates counter that there is little evidence of erosion in national standards.

To break the deadlock we should accept that countries can uphold national standards in these areas, and can do so by raising barriers at the border if necessary, when trade demonstrably threatens domestic practices enjoying broad popular support. If globalization's advocates are right, then the clamor for protection will fail for lack of evidence or support. If they are wrong, there will be a safety valve in place to ensure that these contending values—the benefits of open economies and the gains from upholding domestic regulations—both receive a proper hearing in the domestic political debate.

The principle rules out extremism on both sides. It prevents globalizers from gaining the upper hand in cases where international trade and finance are a back door for eroding widely accepted standards at home. Similarly, it prevents protectionists from obtaining benefits at the expense of the rest of society when no significant public purpose is at stake. In less clear-cut cases where different values have to be traded off against each other, the principle forces internal deliberation and debate—the best way of handling difficult political questions.

One can imagine the questions a domestic political debate might raise. How much social or economic disruption does the trade in question threaten? How much domestic support is there for the practices, regulations, or standards at stake? Are the adverse effects felt by particularly disadvantaged members of society? How large are the compensating economic benefits, if any? Are there alternative ways of achieving the desired social and economic objectives without restricting international trade or finance? What does the relevant evidence—economic and scientific—say on all these questions?

If the policy process is transparent and inclusive, these kinds of questions will be generated naturally by the forces of competition among interest groups, both pro- and anti-trade. To be sure, there are no fail-safe mechanisms for determining whether the rules in question enjoy "broad popular support" and are "demonstrably threatened" by trade. Democratic politics is messy and does not always get it "right." But when we have to trade off different values and interests, there is nothing else to rely on.

Removing such questions from the province of democratic deliberation and passing them on to technocrats or international bodies is the worse solution. It ensures neither legitimacy nor economic benefits. International agreements can make an important contribution, but their role is to reinforce the integrity of the domestic democratic process rather than to replace it.

5. Countries Do Not Have the Right to Impose Their Institutions on Others

Using restrictions on cross-border trade or finance to uphold values and regulations at home must be sharply distinguished from using them to impose these values and regulations on other countries. Globalization's rules should not force Americans or Europeans to consume goods that are produced in ways that most citizens in those countries find unacceptable. Neither should they require nations to provide unhindered access to financial transactions that undercut domestic regulations. They also should not allow the United States or the European Union to use trade sanctions or other kinds of pressure to alter the way that foreign nations go about their business in labor markets, environmental policies, or finance. Nations have a right to difference, not to impose convergence.

In practice, upholding the first right may lead sometimes to the same consequence as upholding the second. Suppose that the United States decides to block imports from India made with child labor because of concern that such imports constitute "unfair competition" for domestically produced goods. Isn't that the same as imposing a trade sanction on India aimed at changing India's labor practices to make them look more like those in the United States? Yes and no. In both cases, India's exports are restricted, and the only way India can get unhindered access to the U.S. market is by converging toward U.S. standards. But intentions matter. While it is legitimate to protect our own institutions, it isn't equally legitimate to want to change others'. If my club has a dress code that requires men to wear ties, it is reasonable for me to expect that you will abide by these rules when you join me at dinner—no matter how much you hate wearing ties. But this doesn't give me the right to tell you how you should dress on other occasions.

6. The Purpose of International Economic Arrangements Must Be to Lay Down the Traffic Rules for Managing the Interface Among National Institutions

Relying on nation-states to provide the essential governance functions of the world economy does not mean we should abandon international rules. The Bretton Woods regime, after all, did have clear rules, even though they were limited in scope and depth. A completely decentralized free-for-all would not benefit anyone; one nation's decisions can affect the well-being of others. An open global economy— perhaps not as free of transaction costs as hyperglobalizers would like, but an open one nonetheless—remains a laudable objective. We should seek not to weaken globalization, but to put it on a sounder footing.

The centrality of nation-states means that the rules need to be formulated with an eye toward institutional diversity. What we need are traffic rules that help vehicles of different size and shape and traveling at varying speeds navigate around each other, rather than impose an identical car or a uniform speed limit on all. We should strive to attain the maximum globalization that is consistent with maintaining space for diversity in national institutional arrangements. Instead of asking, "What kind of multilateral regime would maximize the flow of goods and capital around the world?" we would ask, "What kind of multilateral regime would best enable nations around the world to pursue their own values and developmental objectives and prosper within their own social arrangements?" This would entail a significant shift in the mindset of negotiators in the international arena.

As part of this shift we can contemplate a much larger role for "opt-outs" or exit clauses in international economic rules. Any tightening of international disciplines should include explicit escape clauses. Such arrangements would help legitimize the rules and allow democracies to reassert their priorities when these priorities clash with obligations to global markets or international economic institutions. Escape clauses would be viewed not as "derogations" or violations of the rules, but as an inherent component of sustainable international economic arrangements.

To prevent abuse, opt-out and exit clauses can be negotiated multilaterally and incorporate specific procedural safeguards. This would differentiate the exercise of

opt-outs from naked protectionism: countries withdrawing from international disciplines would be allowed to do so only after satisfying procedural requirements
that have been negotiated beforehand and written into those same disciplines. While
such opt-outs are not riskless, they are a necessary part of making an open international economy compatible with democracy. In fact, their procedural safeguards—
calling for transparency, accountability, evidence-based decision making—would
enhance the quality of democratic deliberation.

7. Non-democratic Countries Cannot Count on the Same Rights and Privileges in the International Economic Order as Democracies

The primacy of democratic decision making lies at the foundation of the international economic architecture outlined so far. It forces us to recognize the centrality
of nation-states, given the reality that democratic polities rarely extend beyond their
boundaries. It requires us to accept national differences in standards and regulations
(and therefore departures from hyperglobalization), because it assumes that these
differences are the product of collective choices exercised in a democratic fashion.
It also legitimizes international rules that limit domestic policy actions, as long as
those rules are negotiated by representative governments and contain exit clauses
that allow for and enhance democratic deliberation at home.

When nation-states are not democratic, this scaffolding collapses. We can no
longer presume a country's institutional arrangements reflect the preferences of its
citizenry. Nor can we presume that international rules could apply with sufficient
force to transform essentially authoritarian regimes into functional democracies.
So non-democracies need to play by different, less permissive rules.

Take the case of labor and environmental standards. Poor countries argue that
they cannot afford to have the same stringent standards in these areas as the advanced
countries. Indeed, tough emission standards or regulations against the use of child
labor can backfire if they lead to fewer jobs and greater poverty. A democratic country such as India can argue, legitimately, that its practices are consistent with the
needs of its population. India's democracy is of course not perfect; no democracy is.
But its civil liberties, freely elected government, and protection of minority rights
insulate the country against claims of systematic exploitation or exclusion.[3] They
provide a cover against the charge that labor, environmental, and other standards
are inappropriately low. Non-democratic countries, such as China, do not pass the
same prima facie test. The assertion that labor rights and the environment are
trampled for the benefit of the few cannot be as easily dismissed in those countries. Consequently, exports of non-democratic countries deserve greater international scrutiny, particularly when they have costly ramifications—distributional
or otherwise—in other countries.

This does not mean that there should be higher trade or other barriers against
non-democratic countries across the board. Certainly not every regulation in such
countries has adverse domestic effects. Even though China is an authoritarian
regime, it has an exemplary economic growth record. And since countries trade to
enhance their own well-being, blanket protectionism would not be in the interest

of the importing countries in any case. Still, it would be legitimate to apply more stringent rules to authoritarian regimes in certain instances.

For example, there could be a lower hurdle for imposing restrictions on a non-democratic country's trade in cases where that trade causes problems in an importing country. If there is a requirement that compensation be paid to exporting countries when an escape clause is triggered, the requirement could be waived when the exporting country is non-democratic. And the burden of proof may need to be reversed in instances where an authoritarian regime seeks to exercise an opt-out—they should be required to demonstrate that the measure in question serves a real developmental, social, or other domestic purpose.

The principle of discrimination against non-democracies already has a place in the present trade regime. Duty-free market access to the United States under the African Growth and Opportunity Act of 2000 requires that the exporting country be democratic. When an African regime represses its political opposition or appears to rig an election, it is removed from the list of countries eligible for trade preferences.[4]

Universalizing this principle would no doubt be controversial. It is likely to be opposed both by trade fundamentalists and, more predictably, by authoritarian regimes. Nevertheless, it makes a lot of sense, especially in the context of the full set of principles considered here. Democracy, after all, is a global norm. It ought to be one of the cornerstone principles of the international trade regime, trumping non-discrimination when necessary.

WHAT ABOUT THE "GLOBAL COMMONS"?

There are a number of possible objections to the principles outlined here, and I need to take up one major objection in this chapter, as it derives from a fundamental misunderstanding. Some argue that the rules of a globalized economy cannot be left to individual nation-states. Such a system, the objection goes, would greatly reduce international cooperation, and as each nation pursues its own narrow interests, the world economy would slide into rampant protectionism. Everyone would lose as a result.

The logic relies on a false analogy of the global economy as a global commons. To see how the analogy works (or rather fails), consider global climate change, the quintessential case of global commons. Ample and mounting evidence suggests that global warming is caused by atmospheric accumulations of greenhouse gases, primarily carbon dioxide and methane. What makes this a global rather than national problem, requiring global cooperation, is that such gases do not respect borders. The globe has a single climate system and it makes no difference where the carbon is emitted. What matters for global warming is the cumulative effect of carbon and other gases in the atmosphere, regardless of origin. If you want to avoid environmental catastrophe, you need everyone else to go along. One might say that all our economies are similarly intertwined, and no doubt that would be true to an important extent. An open and healthy world economy is a "public good" which benefits all, just like an atmosphere with low levels of greenhouse gases.

But there the parallel ends. In the case of global warming, domestic restrictions on carbon emissions provide no or little benefit at home. There is a single global climate system, and my own individual actions have at best small effects on it. Absent cosmopolitan considerations, each nation's optimal strategy would be to emit freely and to free ride on the carbon controls of other countries. Addressing climate change requires that nation-states rise above their parochial interests and work in concert to develop common strategies. Without international cooperation and coordination, the global commons would be destroyed.

By contrast, the economic fortunes of individual nations are determined largely by what happens at home rather than abroad. If open economy policies are desirable, it's because openness is in a nation's own self-interest—not because it helps others. Remember Henry Martyn's case for free trade: buying cheaper cotton textiles from India is just like technological progress at home. As we have seen repeatedly in this book, there are legitimate reasons why countries may want to stop at less than free trade. Barriers on international trade or finance may fortify social cohesion, avoid crises, or enhance domestic growth. In such instances, the rest of the world generally benefits. When trade barriers serve only to transfer income from some groups to others, at the cost of shrinking the overall economic pie, domestic rather than foreign groups bear the bulk of these costs.[5] In the global economy, countries pursue "good" policies because it is in their interest to do so. Openness relies on self-interest, not on global spirit. The case for open trade has to be made and won in the domestic political arena.

A few wrinkles complicate this picture. One is that large economies may be able to manipulate the prices of their imports and exports in ways that shift more of the gains from trade to themselves—think about the impact of OPEC on oil, for example. These policies certainly harm other nations and need to be subject to international disciplines. But today such motives are the exception rather than the rule. Foreign economic policies are shaped largely by domestic considerations, as they should be. Another wrinkle involves the adverse effects on others of large external imbalances—trade deficits or surpluses. These also need international oversight.

The principles outlined in this chapter leave plenty of room for international cooperation over these and other matters. But they do presume a major difference, when compared to other areas like climate change, in the degree of international cooperation and coordination needed to make the global system work. In the case of global warming, self-interest pushes nations to ignore the risks of climate change, with an occasional spur toward environmentally responsible policies when a country is too large to overlook its own impact on the accumulation of greenhouse gases. In the global economy, self-interest pushes nations toward openness, with an occasional temptation toward beggar-thy-neighbor policies when a large country possesses market power.[6] A healthy global regime has to rely on international cooperation in the first case; it has to rely on good policies geared toward the domestic economy in the second.

APPLYING THE PRINCIPLES

A common but misleading narrative shapes our collective understanding of globalization. According to this narrative, the world's national economies have become so inextricably linked that nothing short of a new kind of governance and a new global consciousness can address adequately the challenges we face. We share a common economic destiny, we are told. We have to rise up above our parochial interests, responsible leaders implore us, and devise common solutions to common problems.

This narrative has the ring of plausibility and the virtue of moral clarity. It also gets the main story wrong. What is true of climate change, say, or human rights—genuine areas of "global commons"—is not true of the international economy. The Achilles' heel of the global economy is not lack of international cooperation. It is the failure to recognize in full the implications of a simple idea: the reach of global markets must be limited by the scope of their (mostly national) governance. Provided the traffic rules are right, the world economy can function quite well with nation-states in the driving seats.

CHAPTER 9

The Global Network Society[1]

Manuel Castells

A network society is a society whose social structure is made around networks activated by microelectronics-based, digitally processed information and communication technologies. I understand social structures to be the organizational arrangements of humans in relationships of production, consumption, reproduction, experience, and power expressed in meaningful communication coded by culture.

Digital networks are global, as they have the capacity to reconfigure themselves, as directed by their programmers, transcending territorial and institutional boundaries through telecommunicated computer networks. So, a social structure whose infrastructure is based on digital networks has the potential capacity to be global. However, network technology and networking organization are only means to enact the trends inscribed in the social structure. The contemporary process of globalization has its origin in economic, political, and cultural factors, as documented by scholarly analyses of globalization (Beck 2000; Held and McGrew 2000, 2007; Stiglitz 2002). But, as a number of studies have indicated, the forces driving globalization could only be effectuated because they have at their disposal the global networking capacity provided by digital communication technologies and information systems, including computerized, long-haul, fast, transportation networks (Kiyoshi et al. 2006; Grewal 2008). This is, in fact, what separates, in size, speed, and complexity, the current process of globalization from previous forms of globalization in earlier historical periods.

Thus, the network society is a global society. However, this does not mean that people everywhere are included in these networks. For the time being, most are not (Hammond et al. 2007). But everybody is affected by the processes that take place in the global networks that constitute the social structure. The core activities that shape and control human life in every corner of the planet are organized in global networks: financial markets; transnational production, management, and the distribution of goods and services; highly skilled labor; science and technology, including higher education; the mass media; the Internet networks of interactive, multipurpose communication; culture; art; entertainment; sports; international institutions managing the global economy and intergovernmental relations; religion; the criminal economy; and the transnational NGOs and social movements that assert the rights and values of a new, global civil society (Held et al. 1999; Volkmer 1999; Castells 2000; Jacquet et al. 2002; Stiglitz 2002; Kaldor 2003; Grewal 2008; Juris 2008). Globalization is better understood as the networking of these socially decisive global networks. Therefore, exclusion from these networks, often in a cumulative process of exclusion, is tantamount to structural marginalization in the global network society (Held and Kaya 2006).

The network society diffuses selectively throughout the planet, working on the pre-existing sites, cultures, organizations, and institutions that still make up most of the material environment of people's lives. The social structure is global, but most of human experience is local, both in territorial and cultural terms (Borja and Castells 1997; Norris 2000). Specific societies, as delineated by the current boundaries of nation-states, or by the cultural boundaries of their historical identities, are deeply fragmented by the double logic of inclusion and exclusion in the global networks that structure production, consumption, communication, and power. I propose the hypothesis that this fragmentation of societies between the included and the excluded is more than the expression of the time-lag required by the gradual incorporation of previous social forms into the new dominant logic. It is, in fact, a structural feature of the global network society. This is because the reconfiguring capacity inscribed in the process of networking allows the programs governing every network to search for valuable additions everywhere and to incorporate them, while bypassing and excluding those territories, activities, and people that have little or no value for the performance of the tasks assigned to the network. Indeed, as Geoff Mulgan observed, "networks are created not just to communicate, but also to gain position, to outcommunicate" (1991: 21). The network society works on the basis of a binary logic of inclusion/exclusion, whose boundaries change over time, both with the changes in the networks' programs and with the conditions of performance of these programs. It also depends on the ability of social actors, in various contexts, to act on these programs, modifying them in the direction of their interests. The global network society is a dynamic structure that is highly malleable to social forces, to culture, to politics, and to economic strategies. But what remains in all instances is its dominance over activities and people who are external to the networks. In this sense, the global overwhelms the local—unless the local becomes connected to the global as a node in alternative global networks constructed by social movements.

Thus, the uneven globalization of the network society is, in fact, a highly significant feature of its social structure. The coexistence of the network society, as a global structure, with industrial, rural, communal, or survival societies, characterizes the reality of all countries, albeit with different shares of population and territory on both sides of the divide, depending on the relevance of each segment for the dominant logic of each network. This is to say that various networks will have different geometries and geographies of inclusion and exclusion: the map of the global criminal economy is not the same as the map resulting from the international location patterns of high-technology industry.

In theoretical terms, the network society must be analyzed, first, as a global architecture of self-reconfiguring networks constantly programmed and reprogrammed by the powers that be in each dimension; second, as the result of the interaction between the various geometries and geographies of the networks that include the core activities—that is, the activities shaping life and work in society; and, third, as the result of a second-order interaction between these dominant networks and the geometry and geography of the disconnection of social formations left outside the global networking logic.

The understanding of power relationships in our world must be specific to this particular society. An informed discussion of this specificity requires a characterization of the network society in its main components: production and appropriation of value, work, communication, culture, and its mode of existence as a spatiotemporal formation. Only then can I meaningfully introduce a tentative hypothesis on the specificity of power relationships in the global network society—a hypothesis that will guide the analysis presented throughout this chapter.

WHAT IS VALUE IN THE NETWORK SOCIETY?

Social structures, such as the network society, originate from the processes of the production and appropriation of value. But what constitutes value in the network society? What moves the production system? What motivates the appropriators of value and controllers of society? There is no change here in relation to earlier social structures in history: value is what the dominant institutions of society decide it is. So, if global capitalism shapes the world, and capital accumulation by the valuation of financial assets in the global financial markets is the supreme value, this will be value in every instance, as, under capitalism, profit-making and its materialization in monetary terms can ultimately acquire everything else. The critical matter is that, in a social structure organized in global networks, whatever the hierarchy is between the networks will become the rule in the entire grid of networks organizing/dominating the planet. If, for instance, we say that capital accumulation is what moves the system, and the return to capital is fundamentally realized in the global financial markets, the global financial markets will assign value to every transaction in every country, as no economy is independent of financial valuation decided in the global financial markets. But if, instead, we consider that the supreme value is military power, the technological and organizational capacity of military machines will structure power in their spheres of influence, and create the conditions for other forms of value—for example, capital accumulation or political domination—to proceed under their protection. However, if the transmission of technology, information, and knowledge to a particular armed organization is blocked, this organization becomes irrelevant in the world context. Thus, we may say that global networks of information and technology are the dominant ones because they condition military capacity which, in turn, provides security for the market to function. Another illustration of this diversity of value-making processes is this: we can assert that the most important source of influence in today's world is the transformation of people's minds. If it is so, then the media are the key networks, as the media, organized in global conglomerates and their distributive networks, are the primary sources of messages and images that reach people's minds. But if we now consider the media as primarily media business, then the logic of profit-making, both in the commercialization of media by the advertising industry and in the valuation of their stock, becomes paramount.

Thus, given the variety of the potential origins of network domination, the network society is a multidimensional social structure in which networks of different kinds have different logics of value-making. The definition of what constitutes value depends on the specificity of the network, and of its program. Any attempt to reduce all value to a common standard faces insurmountable methodological and practical difficulties. For instance, if profit-making is the supreme value under capitalism, military power ultimately grounds state power, and the state has a considerable capacity to decide and enforce new rules for business operations (ask the Russian oligarchs about Putin). At the same time, state power, even in non-democratic contexts, largely depends on the beliefs of people, on their capacity to accept the rules, or, alternatively, on their willingness to resist. Then, the media system, and other means of communication, such as the Internet, could precede state power, which, in turn, would condition the rules of profit-making, and thus would supersede the value of money as the supreme value.

Thus, *value is, in fact, an expression of power:* Whoever holds power (often different from whoever is in government) decides what is valuable. In this sense, the network society does not innovate. What is new, however, is its global reach, and its networked architecture. It means, on one hand, that relations of domination between networks are critical. They are characterized by constant, flexible interaction: for instance, between global financial markets, geopolitical processes, and media strategies. On the other hand, because the logic of value-making, as an expression of domination, is global, those instances that have a structural impediment to exist globally are at a disadvantage vis-à-vis others whose logic is inherently global. This has considerable practical importance because it is at the root of the crisis of the nation-state of the industrial era (not of the state as such, because every social structure generates its own form of state). Since the nation-state can only enforce its rules in its territory, except in the case of alliances or invasion, it has to become either imperial or networked to relate to other networks in the definition of value. This is why, for instance, the U.S. state, in the early twenty-first century, made a point of defining security against terrorism as the overarching value for the entire world. It was a way of building a military-based network that would assure its hegemony by placing security over profit-making, or lesser goals (such as human rights or the environment), as the supreme value. However, the capitalist logic often becomes quickly overlaid on security projects, as the profitable business of American crony companies in Iraq strikingly illustrates (Klein 2007).

Capital has always enjoyed the notion of a world without boundaries, as David Harvey has repeatedly reminded us, so that global financial networks have a head start as the defining instances of value in the global network society (Harvey 1990). Yet, human thought is probably the most rapidly propagating and influential element of any social system, on the condition of relying on a global/local, interactive communication system in real time—which is exactly what has emerged now, for the first time in history (Dutton 1999; Benkler 2006). Thus, ideas, and specific sets of ideas, could assert themselves as the truly supreme value (such as preserving our planet, our species, or else serving God's design), as a prerequisite for everything else.

In summary, the old question of industrial society—indeed, the cornerstone of classical political economy—namely, "What is value?," has no definite answer in the global network society. Value is what is processed in every dominant network at every time in every space according to the hierarchy programmed in the network by the actors acting upon the network. Capitalism has not disappeared. Indeed, it is more pervasive than ever. But it is not, against a common ideological perception, the only game in the global town.

CHAPTER 10

The Googlization of Us
Universal Surveillance
and Infrastructural Imperialism

Siva Vaidhyanathan

In 2006, *Time* declared its Person of the Year to be you, me, and everyone who contributes content to new-media aggregators such as MySpace, Amazon, Facebook, YouTube, eBay, Flickr, blogs, and Google. The flagship publication of one of the most powerful media conglomerates in the world declared that flagship publications and powerful media conglomerates no longer choose where to hoist flags or exercise power. "It's about the many wresting power from the few and helping one another for nothing and how that will not only change the world, but also change the ways the world changes," Lev Grossman breathlessly wrote in *Time*. "And for seizing the reins of the global media, for founding and framing the new digital democracy, for working for nothing and beating the pros at their own game, TIME's Person of the Year for 2006 is you."[1]

Almost every major marketing campaign these days is likewise framed as being about "you." "You" have freedom of choice. "You" can let yourself be profiled so that "you" receive solicitations only from companies that interest "you." "You" could customize "your" mobile phone with a ringtone. "You" go to the Nike Store to design your own shoes.

This emphasis on "you," however, is only a smokescreen for what is actually happening online. The Googlization of everything entails the harvesting, copying, aggregating, and ranking of information about and contributions made by each of us. This process exploits our profound need to connect and share, and our remarkable ability to create together—each person contributing a little bit to a poem, a song, a quilt, or a conversation. It is not about "you" at all. It should be about "us"—the Googlization of us.

Google, for instance, makes money because it harvests, copies, aggregates, and ranks billions of Web contributions by millions of authors who tacitly grant Google the right to capitalize, or "free ride," on their work. So in this process of aggregation, who are you? Who are you to Google? Who are you to Amazon? Are you the sum of your consumer preferences and MySpace personas? What is your contribution worth? Do "you" really deserve an award for allowing yourself to be rendered so flatly and cravenly? Do you deserve an award because Rupert Murdoch can make money capturing your creativity with his expensive toy, MySpace?

Because Google makes its money by using our profiles to present us with advertisements keyed to the words we search, precision is its goal. Google wants advertisers to trust that the people who see their paid placements are likely customers for the advertised products or services. These advertisers have little interest in broadcasting. That's a waste of money. The more Google knows about us, the more effective its advertising services can be. Understanding the nature of this profiling and targeting is the first step to understanding the Googlization of us.

How much does Google know about us? How much data does it keep, and how much does it discard? How long does it keep that information? And why?[2] Our blind faith in Google has allowed the company to claim that it gives users substantial control over how their actions and preferences are collected and used. Google pulls this off by telling the truth: at any time, we may opt out of the system that Google uses to perfect its search engine and its revenue generation. But as long as control over our personal information and profiles is granted at the pleasure of Google and similar companies, such choices mean very little. There is simply no consistency, reciprocity, or accountability in the system. We must constantly monitor fast-changing "privacy policies." We must be willing to walk away from a valuable service if its practices cause us concern. The amount of work we must do to protect our dignity online is daunting. And in the end, policies matter less than design choices. With Google, the design of the system rigs it in favor of the interests of the company and against the interests of users.

Google complicates the ways we manage information about ourselves in three major ways. It collects information from us when we use its services; it copies and makes available trivial or harmful information about us that lies in disparate corners of the Internet; and it actively captures images of public spaces around the world, opening potentially embarrassing or private scenes to scrutiny by strangers—or, sometimes worse, by loved ones. In theory, Google always gives the victim of exposure the opportunity to remove troubling information from Google's collection. But the system is designed to favor maximum collection, maximum exposure, and the permanent availability of everything. One can only manage one's global electronic profile through Google if one understands how the system works—and that there is a system at all.[3] Google is a system of almost universal surveillance, yet it operates so quietly that at times it's hard to discern.

Google's privacy policy is not much help in this regard. In fact, it's pretty much a lack-of-privacy policy. For instance, the policy outlines what Google will collect from users—a reasonable, yet significant amount: IP (Internet Protocol) addresses (numbers assigned to a computer when it logs into an Internet service provider, which indicate the provider and the user's general location), search queries (which constitute a record of everything we care about, wonder about, or fantasize about), and information about Web browsers and preference settings (fairly trivial, but necessary to make Google work well). Google promises not to distribute this data—with two major exceptions. First, "We provide such information to our subsidiaries, affiliated companies or other trusted businesses or persons for the purpose of processing personal information on our behalf." Second, "We have a good faith belief that access, use, preservation or disclosure of such information is reasonably necessary to (a) satisfy any applicable law, regulation, legal process or enforceable governmental request, (b) enforce applicable Terms of Service, including investigation of potential violations thereof, (c) detect, prevent, or otherwise address fraud, security or technical issues, or (d) protect against imminent harm to the rights, property or safety of Google, its users or the public as required or permitted by law." [4]

Google's privacy policy is a pledge from the company to us. It is binding in that if the company violated its policy, a user could sue Google in the United States for deceptive trade practices (though proving deception is always a difficult burden). However, Google changes its policy often and without warning. So today's policy—for all its strengths and weaknesses—might not be the policy tomorrow or next year. You might have engaged with Google and donated your data trail to it under the provisions of an early version of the policy, only to discover that Google changed the policy while you were not looking. The policy does pledge that "we will not reduce your rights under this Privacy Policy without your explicit consent, and we expect most such changes will be minor." But that is cold comfort, because the policy already gives Google substantial power over the data.

If you read the privacy policy carefully, it's clear that Google retains the right to make significant decisions about our data without regard for our interests. Google will not share information with other companies without user consent, but it asserts the right to provide such information to law enforcement or government agencies as it sees fit.

If another company were to acquire Google, the policy states, the company would inform users of the transfer of the data. But there is no promise that users would have a chance to purge their data from Google's system in time to avoid a less scrupulous company's acquisition of it. Although Google's commitments to fairness and transparency are sincere and important, they are only as durable as the company. If Google's revenues slip or its management changes significantly, all the trust we place in the company today might be eroded.

To complicate matters more, each Google service has its own privacy policy. The index page for these policies contains a series of videos that outline the terms by which Google collects and retains data. One of the videos echoes the statement that Google retains personally identifiable information for only eighteen months after acquiring it. After eighteen months, information such as IP addresses is "anonymized" so that it's difficult to trace a search query to a particular user. However, that pledge is not made in the policy itself. Anonymization simply involves the removal of the last few digits of a user's IP address, and many cases of anonymization by information brokers have been exposed as ineffective at untethering people's identities from their habits.[5] The "cookies" left by many websites on users' computers contain information that could still be employed to identify a user.[6]

Although Google's public pronouncements about privacy and its general privacy statement fail to explain this point, Google actually has two classes of users, and consequently two distinct levels of data accumulation and processing. The larger, general Google user population simply uses the classic blank page with the search box in the center. Such general users leave limited data trails for Google to read and build services around. The second class might be called power users: those who have registered for Google services such as Gmail, Blogger, or iGoogle. Google has much richer and more detailed dossiers on these users. In exchange for access to this information, Google rightly claims that it serves these power users better than it serves general users. They get more subtle, personalized search results and a host of valuable services.

Google does empower users to control the information the company holds about them, but not in subtle or specific ways. Google's settings page offers a series of on-off switches that can prevent Google from placing cookies in a browser or from retaining a list of websites a user has visited. Power users can delete specific items from the list of website visits.

The default settings for all Google interfaces grant Google maximum access to information. Users must already be aware of and concerned about the amount and nature of Google's data collection to seek out the page that offers all these choices.

Google's data-retention policies have come under significant scrutiny, especially in Europe. Most of the changes in its privacy policies in recent years have resulted from pressure by European policy officials. The United States government has offered consumers and citizens no help in these matters. In fact, it has acted to erode privacy. In 2006, the U.S. Department of Justice issued subpoenas to collect general information from the major search-engine companies in an effort to support its unsurprising contention that Internet users often search for pornography. The department wanted to use such data—which would not have been linked to any particular user, but instead would have offered generalized, statistical information about what users like to do online—in its legal defense of a law called the Child Online Protection Act. Of the major search companies, only Google resisted the subpoena, and then not to protect its users' privacy but to protect its trade secrets. Google's ability to analyze search queries for patterns is its greatest strength in the market. To give up such data could reduce the company's chief competitive advantage.[7] Google prevailed, and the government abandoned its efforts to collect such information.

Understandably, Google officials have practiced responses to questions about data retention and privacy. For instance, Google vice president Marissa Mayer explained to U.S. television host Charlie Rose in early 2009: "In all cases it's a trade-off, right, where you will give up some of your privacy in order to gain some functionality, and so we really need to make those trade-offs really clear to people, what information are we using and what's the benefit to them, and then ultimately leave it to user choice."[8] Mayer, who is very disciplined in her answers to questions about privacy, always offers statements very close to this. But Mayer and Google in general both misunderstand privacy. *Privacy* is not something that can be counted, divided, or "traded." It is not a substance or collection of data points. It's just a word that we clumsily use to stand in for a wide array of values and practices that influence how we manage our reputations in various contexts. There is no formula for assessing it: I can't give Google three of my privacy points in exchange for 10 percent better service. More seriously, Mayer and Google fail to acknowledge the power of default settings in a regime ostensibly based on choice.

THE IRRELEVANCE OF CHOICE

In their 2008 book *Nudge: Improving Decisions about Health, Wealth, and Happiness,* the economist Richard Thaler and law professor Cass Sunstein describe a concept they call "choice architecture." Plainly put, the structure and order of the choices offered to us profoundly influence the decisions we make. So, for instance, the arrangement of foods in a school cafeteria can influence children to eat better. The positions of restrooms and break rooms can influence the creativity and communality of office staff. And, in the best-known example of how defaults can influence an ostensibly free choice, studies have demonstrated that when employer-based retirement plans in the United States required employees to opt in to them, more than 40 percent of employees either failed to enroll or contributed too little to get matching contributions from their employers. When the default was set to enroll employees automatically, while giving them an opportunity to opt out, enrollment reached 98 percent within six months. The default setting of automatic enrollment, Thaler and Sunstein explain, helped employees overcome the "inertia" caused by business, distraction, and forgetfulness.[9]

That choice architecture could have such an important effect on so many human behaviors without overt coercion or even elaborate incentives convinced Thaler and Sunstein that taking advantage of it can accomplish many important public-policy goals without significant cost to either the state or private firms. They call this approach "libertarian paternalism." If a system is designed to privilege a particular choice, they observe, people will tend to choose that option more than the alternatives, even though they have an entirely free choice. "There is no such thing as a 'neutral' design."[10]

It's clear that Google understands the power of choice architecture. It's in the company's interest to set all user-preference defaults to collect the greatest quantity of usable data in the most contexts. By default, Google places a cookie in your Web browser to help the service remember who you are and what you have searched. By default, Google tracks your searches and clicks; it retains that data for a specified period and uses it to target advertisements and refine search results. Google gives us the power to switch off all these features. It even provides videos explaining how to do this.[11] But unless you act to change them, the company's default settings constitute your choices.

When Mayer and others at Google speak about the practices and policies governing their private-data collection and processing (otherwise known as privacy policies), they never discuss the power of defaults. They emphasize only the freedom and power that users have over their data. Celebrating freedom and user autonomy is one of the great rhetorical ploys of the global information economy. We are conditioned to believe that having more choices—empty though they may be— is the very essence of human freedom. But meaningful freedom implies real control over the conditions of one's life. Merely setting up a menu with switches does not serve the interests of any but the most adept, engaged, and well-informed.

Setting the defaults to maximize the benefits for the firm and hiding the switches beneath a series of pages are irresponsible, but we should not expect any firm to behave differently. If we want a different choice architecture in complex ecosystems such as the Web, we are going to have to rely on firms' acceding collectively to pressure from consumer groups or ask the state to regulate such defaults.

Google officials also don't acknowledge that completely opting out of Google's data-collection practices significantly degrades the user's experience. For those few Google users who click through the three pages it takes to find and adjust their privacy options, the cost of opting out becomes plain. If you do not allow Google to track your moves, you get less precise results to queries that would lead you to local restaurants and shops or sites catering to your interests. Google has to guess whether a search for "jaguar" is intended to generate information about the car or the cat. But if Google understands your interests, it can save you time when you shop. It can seem like it's almost reading your mind. In addition, full citizenship in the Googleverse includes use of functions like Gmail and posting videos on You-Tube, which require registration and allow Google to amass a much richer collection of data about your interests. Moreover, exploring such options can give you a pretty clear idea of the nature of the transaction between Google and its users; but for the vast majority of users, the fate of their personal data remains a mystery.

Opting out of any Google service puts the Web user at a disadvantage in relation to other users. The more Google integrates its services, and the more interesting and essential the services that Google offers, the more important Google use is for effective commerce, self-promotion, and cultural citizenship. So the broader Google's reach becomes—the more it Googlizes us—the more likely it is that even informed and critical Internet users will stay in the Google universe and allow Google to use their personal information. For Google, quantity yields quality. For us, resigning ourselves to the Google defaults enhances convenience, utility, and status. But at what cost?

THE PROBLEM WITH PRIVACY

Google is far from the most egregious offender in the world of personal data acquisition. Google promises (for now) not to sell your data to third parties, and it promises not to give it to agents of the state unless the agents of the state ask for it in a legal capacity. (The criteria for such requests are lax, however, and getting more lax around the world.) But Google is the master at using information in the service of revenue generation, and many of its actions and policies are illustrative of a much larger and deeper set of social and cultural problems.

In November 2007, Facebook, the social networking site most popular among university students and faculty, snuck in a surprise for its then almost 60 million users (by 2010 it had 150 million users). With minimal warning, Facebook instituted what it called its Beacon program, which posted notes about users' Web purchases in the personal news feeds on Facebook profiles. So if a user had purchased a gift for a friend on one of the Web commerce sites that were partners in the program, the purchase would be broadcast to all of that person's Facebook associates—most likely including the intended recipient of the gift. Facebook ruined a few surprises, but it had a bigger surprise in store for itself: a user rebellion. Within days, more than fifty thousand Facebook users signed up for a special Facebook group protesting the Beacon service and Facebook's decision to deny users the chance to opt out of it. The furor spread beyond Facebook. Major news media covered the story and quoted users who until then had been quite happy with Facebook but were now deeply alarmed at the inability to control Beacon or their Facebook profiles.[12]

This reaction caught Facebook executives by surprise. In 2006, when they had released the news feed itself as a way of letting people find out what their Facebook friends were up to, there had been a small protest. But within a few weeks, users got used to it and quieted down. Over time, users did not find news feeds too intrusive or troublesome, and they could turn off the service if they wished.

Facebook executives assumed that their users were not the sort who cared very much about personal privacy. After all, they readily posted photos from wild parties, lists of their favorite bands and books, and frank comments on others' profiles. All the while, Facebook executives were led to believe that young people today were some sort of new species who were used to online exposure of themselves and others, immersed in the details of celebrity lives via sites like PerezHilton.com and Gawker .com, obsessed with the eccentricities of reality television show contestants, and more than happy to post videos of themselves dancing goofily on YouTube.[13]

Then came the great Facebook revolt of 2010. By May of that year, users had alerted each other to the various ways that Facebook had abused their trust. Where once the service had allowed easy and trustworthy management of personal information (it was simple to choose who could and could not view particular elements of one's profile), it had slyly eliminated many of those controls. It had rendered much personal information openly available by default and made privacy settings absurdly complicated to navigate and change. In addition, Facebook suffered some serious security lapses in early 2010. Soon a movement was born to urge friends to quit Facebook in protest. There is no way to tell how many people actually did quit, largely because Facebook would never release that number; moreover, completely deleting an account is very difficult. Facebook membership continued to grow worldwide throughout 2010, as did disgruntlement. Fundamentally, Facebook had become too valuable to people's lives to allow them to quit. The value, however, is in its membership, not in its platform. Facebook was only slightly chastened by the public anger.[14]

The cultural journalist Emily Nussbaum, writing in *New York* magazine in February 2007, stitched together some anecdotes about young people who have no qualms about baring their body parts and secrets on LiveJournal or YouTube. "Younger people, one could point out, are the only ones for whom it seems to have sunk in that the idea of a truly private life is already an illusion," Nussbaum wrote. "Every street in New York has a surveillance camera. Each time you swipe your debit card at Duane Reade or use your MetroCard, that transaction is tracked. Your employer owns your e-mails. The NSA owns your phone calls. Your life is being lived in public whether you choose to acknowledge it or not. So it may be time to consider the possibility that young people who behave as if privacy doesn't exist are actually the sane people, not the insane ones."[15]

Yet if young people don't care about privacy, why do they react angrily when Facebook broadcasts their purchases to hundreds of acquaintances? In fact, a study conducted by Eszter Hargittai of Northwestern University and danah boyd of Microsoft research demonstrated that young people in America have higher levels of awareness and concern about online privacy than older Americans do.[16] But still, isn't privacy a quaint notion in this era in which Google and Amazon—not to mention MI5, the U.S. National Security Agency, and the FBI—have substantial and detailed dossiers on all of us? Despite frequent warnings from nervous watchdogs and almost weekly stories about massive data leaks from Visa or AOL, we keep searching on Google, buying from Amazon, clicking through user agreements and "privacy" policies (that rarely if ever actually protect privacy), and voting for leaders who gladly empower the government to spy on us.

Broad assumptions about the apparent indifference to privacy share a basic misunderstanding of the issue. Too often we assume that a concern with privacy merely represents a desire to withhold information about personal conduct, such as sexual activity or drug use. But privacy is not just about personal choices, or some group of traits or behaviors we call "private" things. Nor are privacy concerns the same for every context in which we live and move. *Privacy* is an unfortunate term, because it carries no sense of its own customizability and contingency. When we complain about infringements of privacy, what we really demand is some measure of control over our reputations. Who should have the power to collect, cross-reference, publicize, or share information about us? If I choose to declare my romantic status or sexual orientation on Facebook, I may still consider that I am preserving my privacy because I assume I am managing the release of that information in a context I think I understand. *Privacy* refers to the terms of control over information, not the nature of the information we share.[17]

Through a combination of weak policies, poor public discussions, and some remarkable inventions, we cede more and more control over our reputations every day. And it's clear that people are being harmed by the actions that follow from widespread behavioral profiling, whether it's done by the Transportation Security Agency through its "no-fly list" or Capital One Bank through its no-escape, high-fee credit cards for those with poor credit ratings.

Jay Gatsby could not exist today. The digital ghost of Jay Gatz would follow him everywhere. There are no second acts, or second chances, in the digital age. Rehabilitation demands substantial autonomy and control over one's record. As long as our past indiscretions can be easily Googled by potential employers or U.S. security agents, our social, intellectual, and actual mobility is limited.[18]

We learn early on that there are public matters and private matters, and that we manage information differently inside our homes and outside them. Yet that distinction fails to capture the true complexity of the privacy tangle. Because it's so hard to define and describe what we mean by privacy and because it so often seems futile to resist mass surveillance, we need better terms, models, metaphors, and strategies for controlling our personal information. Here's one way to begin to think more effectively about the issue.

We each have at least five major "privacy interfaces," or domains, through which we negotiate what is known about us.[19] Each of these interfaces offers varying levels of control and surveillance.

The first privacy interface is what I call "person to peer." Early on, we develop the skills necessary to manage what our friends and families know of our predilections, preferences, and histories. A boy growing up gay in a homophobic family learns to exert control over others' knowledge of his sexual orientation. A teenager smoking marijuana in her bedroom learns to hide the evidence. If we cheat on our partners, we practice lying. These are all privacy strategies for the most personal spheres.

The second interface is one I call "person to power." There is always some information we wish to keep from our teachers, parents, employers, or prison guards because it could be used to manipulate us or expose us to harsh punishment. The common teenage call "Stay out of my room!" exemplifies the frustration of learning to manage this essential interface. Later in life, an employee may find it prudent to conceal a serious medical condition from her employer to prevent being dismissed to protect the company's insurance costs.

The third privacy interface is "person to firm." In this interface, we decide whether we wish to answer the checkout person at Babies "R" Us when she asks us (almost always at a moment when we are feeling weak and frustrated) for a home phone number. We gladly accept what we think are free services, such as discount cards at supermarkets and bookstores, that actually operate as record-keeping account tokens. The clerk at the store almost never explains this other side of the bargain.

The fourth interface is the most important because the consequences of error and abuse are so high: "person to state." Through the census, tax forms, drivers' license records, and myriad other bureaucratic functions, the state records traces of our movements and activities. The mysterious and problem-riddled "no-fly list" that bars people from boarding commercial flights in the United States for unaccountable reasons is the best example. Because the state has a monopoly on legitimate violence, imprisonment, and deportation, the cost of being falsely caught in a dragnet warrants concern, no matter how unlikely it seems.

The fifth privacy interface is poorly understood and has only recently gained notice, although Nathaniel Hawthorne explained it well in *The Scarlet Letter.* It's what I call "person to public." At this interface, which is now located largely online, people have found their lives exposed, their names and faces ridiculed, and their well-being harmed immeasurably by the rapid proliferation of images, the asocial nature of much ostensibly "social" Web behavior, and the permanence of the digital record. Whereas in our real social lives we have learned to manage our reputations, the online environments in which we work and play have broken down the barriers that separate the different social contexts in which we move. On Facebook, MySpace, or YouTube, a coworker may be an online friend, fan, or critic. A supervisor could be a stalker. A parent could be a lurker. A prospective lover could use the same online dating service as a former lover. In real life, we may be able to keep relationships separate, to switch masks and manage what people know (or think they know) about us. But most online environments are intentionally engineered to serve our professional, educational, and personal desires simultaneously. These contexts or interfaces blend, and legal distinctions between public and private no longer hold up.[20] We are just beginning to figure out how to manage our reputations online, but as long as the companies that host these environments benefit directly from the confusion, the task will not be easy.

In *The Future of Reputation,* the law professor Daniel Solove relates the sad story of the "Star Wars Kid." In November 2002, a Canadian teenager used a school camera to record himself acting like a character from *Star Wars,* wielding a golf-ball retriever as a light saber. Some months later, other students at his school discovered the recording and posted it on a file-sharing network. Within days, the image of a geeky teen playing at *Star Wars* became the hit of the Internet. Thousands—perhaps millions—downloaded the video. Soon, many downloaders used their computers to enhance the video, adding costumes, special effects, and even opponents for the young man to slay. Hundreds of versions still haunt the Web. Many Web sites hosted nasty comments about the boy's weight and appearance. Soon his name and high school became public knowledge. By the time You-Tube debuted in 2005, the "Star Wars Kid" was a miserable and unwilling star of user-generated culture. He had to quit school. The real-world harassment drove his family to move to a new town. The very nature of digital images, the Internet, and Google made it impossible for the young man to erase the record of one afternoon of harmless fantasy. But it was not the technology that was at fault, Solove reminds us. It was our willingness to ridicule others publicly and our ease at appealing to free-speech principles to justify the spreading of everything everywhere, exposing and hurting the innocent along the way.[21]

No one made any money from this or the other events that Solove describes, and the state is neutral toward such incidents, so we can't blame market forces or security overreactions. But our appetite for public humiliation of others (undeserved or otherwise) should trouble us deeply. Like Hester Prynne in *The Scarlet Letter,* any one of us may be unable to escape the traces of our mistakes. We are no longer in control of our public personas, because so many of our fellow citizens carry with them instruments of surveillance and exposure such as cameras and video recorders. An advocate of Internet creativity and its potential to contribute to democratic culture, Solove treads lightly around any idea that might stifle creative experimentation. But even those of us who celebrate this cultural "mashup" moment would be delinquent if we ignored the real harms that Solove exposes.

The sociologist James Rule, in *Privacy in Peril,* emphasizes one point that is either muted in or absent from most other discussions about privacy and surveillance: data collected by one institution is easily transferred, mined, used, and abused by others. Companies such as Choice Point buy our supermarket and bookstore shopping records and sell them to direct-mail marketers, political parties, and even the federal government. These data- mining companies also collect state records such as voter registration forms, deeds, car titles, and liens in order to sell consumer profiles to direct-marketing firms. As a result of this cross-referencing of so many data points, ChoicePoint knows me better than my parents do—which explains why the catalogs that arrive at my home better reflect my tastes than the ties my father gives me each birthday. Each data point, each consumer choice, says something about you. If you purchase several prepaid cell phones and a whole lot of hummus, you might be profiled as a potential jihadist. If you use your American Express Platinum card to buy a latte from Starbucks the same day that you purchase a new biography of Alexander Hamilton from Barnes and Noble in an affluent Atlanta ZIP code, you might be identified as a potential donor to a Republican election campaign.[22]

The privacy laws of the 1970s, for which Rule can claim some credit after his 1974 book *Private Lives and Public Surveillance,* sought to guarantee some measure of transparency in state data retention. Individuals should be entitled to know what the federal government knew about them and thus be able to correct errors. And there were to be strong limits on how government agencies shared such data.[23] As Rule explains in *Privacy in Peril,* such commonsense guidelines were eroded almost as soon as they became law. And in recent years, following pressure from the great enemy of public transparency and accountability, former vice president Dick Cheney, they have been pushed off the public agenda altogether. It's as if Watergate, the Church Committee report (which in 1975 exposed massive government surveillance of U.S. citizens and other illegal abuses of power by the CIA), and the revelations of FBI infiltration of antiwar protest groups never happened.[24]

Mass surveillance has been a fact of life since the eighteenth century. There is nothing new about the bureaucratic imperative to record and manipulate data on citizens and consumers. Digital tools just make it easier to collect, merge, and sell databases. Every incentive in a market economy pushes firms to collect more and better data on us. Every incentive in a state bureaucracy encourages massive surveillance. Small changes, such as the adoption of better privacy policies by companies like Google and Amazon, are not going to make much difference in the long run. So the only remedy is widespread political action in the public interest, much as we had in the 1970s. Passivity in the face of these threats to dignity and personal security will only invite the deployment of more unaccountable technologies of surveillance. The challenge is too large and the risks too great.

GUIDE TO FURTHER READINGS
AND RECOMMENDED WEBSITES

The following books and websites will guide your global studies research projects more deeply into the economic and technological dimensions of globalization:

- Manuel Castells, *The Information Age: Economy, Society, and Culture,* 2nd ed. 3 vols. West Sussex, UK: Wiley-Blackwell, 2010.
- Jeffry Frieden, *Global Capitalism: Its Fall and Rise in the Twentieth Century.* New York: Norton, 2007.
- James Gleick, *The Information: A History, A Theory, A Flood.* New York: Vintage, 2012.
- David Harvey, *The Enigma of Capital and the Crisis of Capitalism.* New York: Oxford University Press, 2011.

- Robert J. Holton, *Global Finance*. New York: Routledge, 2012.
- Jack Lule, *Globalization and the Media: Global Village of Babel*. Lanham, MD: Rowman & Littlefield, 2012.
- Joseph Stiglitz, *Making Globalization Work*. New York: Norton, 2007.
- Library of Congress Business and Economics Research Advisor on Globalization: http://www.loc.gov/rr/business/BERA/issue1/history.html
  Presents literature that examines the historical aspects of globalization by looking at its origins, the history of international economics and trade, and the history of international finance, exchange, and global markets. It is the intention of this website to provide a compilation of material that presents a historical and comprehensive analysis of the discussion of economic globalization.
- International Forum on Globalization: http://www.ifg.org/
  The International Forum on Globalization is a research, advocacy, and action organization, founded in 1994, focused on the impacts of dominant economic and geo-political policies. Led by an international board of scholars and citizen-movement leaders from ten countries, IFG collaborates with environmental, social justice, and anti-militarism activists, seeking secure models of democracy and sustainability, locally and globally.
- The United Nations Human Development Reports: http://hdr.undp.org/en/
  The annual UN Human Development Report, commissioned by United Nations Development Program, focuses the global debate on key development issues, providing new measurement tools, innovative analysis, and often controversial policy proposals. The global Report's analytical framework and inclusive approach carry over into regional, national, and local Human Development Reports, also supported by UNDP.
- KOF Index of Globalization: http://globalization.kof.ethz.ch/
  The KOF Index of Globalization measures the economic, social, and political dimensions of globalization. In addition to three indices measuring these dimensions, KOF calculates an overall index of globalization and subindices referring to actual economic flows, economic restrictions, data on information flows, data on personal contact, and data on cultural proximity. Data are available on a yearly basis for 207 countries over the period 1970–2010.

PART III

Cultures and Histories

Discussion Points:

- What role(s) do human migrations play in the long-term history of globalization?
- Does the intensification of global pandemics like HIV/AIDS, H1N1, or SARS retard or accelerate globalization dynamics?
- Is the increasing popularity of mega-sport events like the Olympic Games or the Soccer World Cup evidence for the rise of a global imaginary or the staying power of nationalism?
- Does the spread of American popular culture lead to cultural homogenization, diversification, or hybridization? Explain your favored scenario.
- Can you give some examples for how the marketization and commercialization of religion has affected people you know?

CHAPTER 11

Globalization: Long-Term Process or New Era in Human Affairs?

William H. McNeill

Globalization refers to the way recent changes in transport and communication have tied humankind in all parts of the earth together more closely than ever before. One effect, the widespread breakup of older forms of village life after 1950, changed the daily experience of innumerable persons so drastically that those years may plausibly claim to mark a new era in human history. New and more capacious transport and communication were primarily responsible for that change, powerfully seconded by population growth that made older ways of life unsustainable in many rural landscapes. Massive migrations from village to city were the principal manifestations of the new order, and affected all the inhabited parts of the earth.

Yet sporadic increases in the capacity of transport and communication are age-old among humankind and have always changed behavior. That process began when our proto-human ancestors learned to control fire and to dance. Fire eventually allowed humans to accelerate the recycling of organic vegetation by deliberately setting grass and brush alight in dry seasons of the year; and to survive subfreezing temperatures even in the Arctic. Control of fire was so valuable that all surviving humans acquired that skill, beginning as long ago as 400,000 B.C.E.[1]

Dancing aroused a different kind of warmth by communicating a sense of commonality to participants that dissipated inter-personal frictions. That, in turn, allowed human bands to expand in size beyond the limits our chimpanzee relatives sustain today. The advantages of larger numbers of cooperating individuals were so great that all surviving humans learned to dance. But dancing leaves no archaeological trace, so dating is completely unknowable. Yet, like control of fire, all humans learned to dance; and in all probability it was among bands enlarged and sustained by dancing on festival occasions that language, the principal vehicle of subsequent human communication, developed between 90,000 and 50,000 B.C.E.[2] Language, too, was so advantageous that it also became universal among humankind.

These three capabilities remain unique to our species; and of the three, language is the most amazing. It proved capable of sustaining agreed upon meanings among indefinite numbers of persons—by now even among hundreds of millions. More particularly, it freed humans from the limitations of acting in response to sense experience in a rather narrow present, as other animals do. By talking about things remembered and about what might happen in times to come our ancestors became able to agree on what to do tomorrow and even further into the future. Moreover, when planned actions met disappointment, they were stimulated, indeed required, to talk things over again, seeking to change what they had done in hope of achieving better results.

That process of trial and error induced systematic change in human behavior as never before, since discrepancy between hopes, plans, and actual experience was perennial and only increased as new skills and knowledge enlarged human impact on the diverse environments into which they soon penetrated.[3] We live with the result—an ever accelerating pace of social change that strains our capability for successful adjustment.

The subsequent human past can plausibly be understood as a series of thresholds when new conditions of life rather abruptly accelerated the pace of resulting change. Control of fire, which antedated language, had particularly drastic effects, allowing humans to transform local plant life by deliberately burning grass and brush wherever they went. Mastery of movement across water by use of rafts and boats much facilitated human dispersal from their ancestral cradle in Africa. The earliest clear evidence for this capability is the initial occupation of Australia in about 40,000 B.C.E., which required crossing miles of open water.

Resort to agriculture was the next major accelerant of social change. As they spread to different parts of the earth, humans discovered a wide variety of different plants to feed on. Ways to multiply the number of such plants by weeding and seeding and transplanting roots that grew naturally may well have been familiar to many hunters and gatherers long before they ever thought of settling down in a single spot and raising food crops in fields where they did not grow of their own accord.

Why our ancestors did so remains unsure. Hunters and gatherers enjoyed a more variegated and more dependable diet than early farmers; and tilling fields was far more laborious than wandering in search of game and wild-growing plant foods. But farming did produce far more food per acre and sustained far denser populations than hunting and gathering could do. That meant that wherever farmers settled down, superior numbers soon assured them against attack by hunter-gatherers and allowed them to encroach upon hunting grounds wherever cultivable land attracted their attention.

Dense populations raising different crops in diverse landscapes arose independently in several parts of the earth between 8000 B.C.E. and 4000 B.C.E. From the start, deliberate selection of seeds and roots prevailed, sometimes changing food plants radically, as when wild teosinte turned into maize in Mexico. As food supplies increased, farming populations multiplied and established new villages wherever suitable land lay within reach. More people distributed over varying landscapes soon generated divergences of local customs and skills, so that even sporadic contacts with strangers, arriving on foot or by sea, brought attractive novelties to the attention of local communities more and more often.

Consequently, the pace of social change accelerated systematically within each of the major centers of agriculture, because more people made more inventions; and some advantageous inventions and discoveries traveled well—new varieties of seeds, for example, and preciosities like mood-altering drugs, gems for decoration, and obsidian or flint to give cutting tools a sharp edge.

In Eurasia, an impressive array of domesticated animals diversified the agricultural complex of evolving plants and people still further—dogs, cats, donkeys, cattle, horses, water buffalo, camels, and still others. Cattle, horses, and camels were particularly significant, for their size and strength far surpassed that of human beings and could be used to plow the soil and to transport heavy loads. The Americas lacked a comparable array of large-bodied domesticable animals, and much of Africa was inhospitable to them. Overland transport in those parts of the earth therefore remained more slender than in Eurasia.

Accordingly, in the Americas and sub-Saharan Africa social change in general, largely dependent on contacts with strangers, fell behind the pace of Eurasian developments. Other factors, especially the prevalence of lethal infectious diseases in much of Africa, also handicapped human populations more than in Eurasia, which therefore remained the principal setting for further advances of human power and skill.

The appearance of cities and civilizations after 3500 B.C.E. accelerated social changes still further. Cities existed only by virtue of occupational differentiation and systematic exchanges of goods and services between urban populations and their rural hinterlands. Urban specialists persistently improved their skills and extended their reach further and further, as professional traders began to spend their lives traveling to and fro across long distances.

When cities started to arise in Eurasia, merchants were already sailing overseas in ships and traveling overland with caravans of pack animals. It was not accidental that where land and sea transport routes met in the land of Sumer (southernmost Iraq), was where the first cities and civilizations appeared. Other civilizations too arose at locations where strangers mingled more than usual, exchanging skills and ideas coming from extensive hinterlands. Consequently, wherever they existed, cities and civilizations circulated goods, skills, and ideas more quickly and more widely than before.

The earliest civilizations of Mesopotamia and Egypt were in slender contact from the start; and successive West Asian empires and civilizations remained constantly in touch with Mediterranean cities and civilizations thereafter. Indian and Chinese civilizations were geographically distant; and climate as well as cultural differences limited what could travel from western Asia and Europe to India and China, and vice versa, even after merchant, military, and missionary contacts did begin to connect them loosely together. That became a reality by about 100 B.C.E. and made all of Eurasia into a single interacting web, with tentacles reaching into sub-Saharan Africa, the frozen north, and among the far-flung Pacific islands off Southeast Asia.

The vastness and variety of peoples and landscapes within that circle far exceeded similar interacting webs in other parts of the earth. It is therefore not surprising that the Eurasian web evolved levels of skill and power superior to what people elsewhere had at their command when new advances in transport and communication exposed them to Old World accomplishments after 1500 C.E.

Biological resistance to a long array of infectious diseases, from the common cold to small pox, measles, plague, and others, was the single most decisive factor in compelling previously isolated populations to submit to intruders from the disease-experienced Eurasian web. The most lethal of these diseases were transfers from animal herds. Eurasia's uniquely complex array of domesticated—and some wild—animals had exposed civilized Eurasian peoples to these diseases across millennia, not without wreaking serious damages along the way. But when one epidemic after another started to rage in rapid succession among inexperienced populations in America and other newly contacted lands, resulting die-offs were crippling. The newcomers remained little affected, thanks to immunities in their bloodstreams, partly inherited, and partly acquired or reinforced by exposure in early childhood.[4]

The human destruction that followed the opening of the oceans to sustained navigation in the decades immediately after Columbus's famous voyage of 1492 were greater than ever before, since European explorers and conquistadors encountered populous, civilized lands in both Mexico and Peru where millions of persons died of new diseases within a few decades. That massive die-off in turn provoked the trade in African slaves that carried millions of Africans across the Atlantic in subsequent centuries. Accordingly, Europeans, Africans, and Amerindians mingled in the Americas earlier and more extensively than anywhere else.

In Eurasia itself after 1500 the pace of change also accelerated. New phenomena, like the flood of silver from American mines, upset prices and social-political patterns in China as well as in Europe, and the spread of new crops from America—especially maize, potatoes, and sweet potatoes—enlarged food supplies very significantly as well.

The global pace of change accelerated yet again with the introduction of steam transport on both land and sea, together with instantaneous electrical communication after 1850. One manifestation was the spread of European empires across much of Asia and Africa. Everywhere weavers and other artisans suffered severely from a flood of cheap, machine-made goods coming from newfangled European factories, powered first by flowing water, then by steam and later by electricity. But before very long Asian factories, especially in Japan, China, and India, began to produce cheaper and, more recently, also better goods than Europeans (and Americans) did; and European empires all collapsed soon after World War II.

From the long-term point of view, therefore, recent mass migrations and widespread disruption of village patterns of life by roads, trucks, buses, radio, TV, and computers look more like another wave of intensified human interaction, comparable to its predecessors and far from unique.

Argument about whether continuity or uniqueness prevails among us today is really pointless. Each moment is unique in every human life; yet continuities are strong and undeniable, both privately and publicly. It is always tempting to exaggerate the unprecedented character of the problems we face. My personal cast of mind prefers to seek commonality; and one such indisputable commonality is that in recent centuries, as social change accelerated, each generation felt uniquely challenged, yet survived in greater numbers than before. No clear end of that process is yet in view, unsustainable though it is sure to be across any lengthy future.

Really basic is the fact that human numbers recently surpassed 6 billion, after having quadrupled in the course of the twentieth century. An equally amazing fact is that more people now live in towns and cities than labor to produce food in the countryside. Both of these facts are unprecedented and, despite a margin of inexactitude in all demographic data, are also undisputed.[5] Yet the massive flow of information, goods, services, and human migrants that sustains our cities and keeps us alive remains precarious, for political, environmental, and sociological reasons.

Politically, the threat of nuclear proliferation and reckless resort to weapons of mass destruction hangs over a world of divided sovereignties. Atomic, supplemented by biological and chemical, warfare may break out suddenly and wreak enormous, perhaps paralyzing destruction around the globe in a very short period of time. Religious fanaticism and other ideological hatreds may even provoke governments to actions that might make the whole earth uninhabitable.

The risk is old hat by now. Having safely survived the Cold War, we seldom worry much about it. But with suicidal bombers at work in Iraq and neighboring lands every day, and with several beleaguered governments trying to build atomic warheads to threaten others and protect themselves, political risks of sudden disaster seem to be rising rather than diminishing.

Ecological catastrophe is a vaguer, multiplex threat. Industrial factories, mines, and transport vehicles are changing the chemical composition of soil, air, and water at unprecedented rates. Global temperatures are rising and climates are changing very quickly. The result for human and other forms of life remain uncertain, but they may reach critical levels locally or even globally sometime soon. No one knows. Human capacity to alter natural environments has increased so rapidly in recent decades that the stability of the world's ecosystems can no longer be taken for granted. That, it seems, is all one can say for sure.[6]

A less familiar instability in human affairs rests on the fact that across millennia, cities nearly always failed to reproduce themselves biologically and depended on immigrants from surrounding healthier countrysides to maintain their numbers. Intensified exposure to disease in cities was the traditional reason for urban die-off. In the nineteenth and twentieth centuries sanitation and medical advances seemed to have conquered most lethal infections. Yet new lethal infections, most notably AIDS, have now emerged; and some old ones are coming back thanks to the emergence of germs resistant to antibiotics and other once-decisive forms of treatment.

So far, however, the introduction of cheap and effective methods of birth control have proved more significant for human affairs. Most women in rich, urbanized countries like the United States and Europe quickly began to use contraceptive pills when they became available after 1960; and their birth rates soon shrank below the figure of 2.1 per woman needed to sustain existing populations. This is a new phenomenon. Women and men, in effect, became able to insulate sex from reproduction at will, and began to give birth to fewer children with no diminution of sexual gratification.

This capability was enhanced by changes of family life in urban settings that increased the cost of raising children and diminished parental satisfactions. Beginning as far back as the eighteenth century, in more and more instances, work among city dwellers began to mean leaving home and spending daytime hours in a factory, store, or office. To begin with, it was mostly men who left their homes to work, leaving women behind to keep house and look after small children.

But in the twentieth century, modern conveniences—packaged food, vacuum cleaners, dishwashers, refrigerators, and the like—made housekeeping into a part-time job. Then, during World War II, labor shortages brought more and more women into factories and offices. Looking after small children at home became increasingly irksome for those who stayed behind, for their work remained unpaid.

Simultaneously, prolonged schooling and prohibition of child labor, often dictated by law, lengthened the time before children could contribute to family income; and the rise of distinctive, and often rebellious, forms of youth culture among adolescents strained family relations yet further. Finally, government pensions for the elderly meant that children were no longer needed to support their parents in old age.

All these changes diminished the satisfactions and increased the cost of raising children among urban dwellers everywhere, especially in Europe and other highly industrialized lands. For a while, rural populations lagged behind and continued to reproduce themselves in traditional fashion. But as radio, TV, and other exposure to urban lifestyles penetrated the rural hinterland in the more highly urbanized countries, old-fashioned family patterns of behavior among rural dwellers were strained to the breaking point, and village birth rates also began to fall.

That opened wide the door for millions of migrants from lands where rapid population growth persisted. Consequently, Europe, the United States, and other countries of European settlement overseas are now increasingly divided between newcomers, with different languages, religions, and physical appearance from those of older inhabitants.

In such circumstances, mutual accommodation is inescapable, and behavioral changes run both ways. Eventual assimilation to a single norm cannot be assumed. In the past, cities regularly accommodated diverse ethnic groups, some of which were confined to ghettos; and our recent rates of migration seem sure to sustain ethnic and cultural plurality as long as they continue.

The co-existence of lands where family patterns and economic conditions sustain rapid population growth with countries and classes who are failing to reproduce themselves is not unprecedented. As I said before, throughout history cities have usually failed to reproduce themselves biologically. As long as nearby villages supplied the deficit, and as long as something approximating ethnic and cultural homogeneity prevailed regionally, European nations could be built on the premise of a common biological and cultural heritage.

But that was exceptional. Empires bulk far larger in the historic record; and they were always multi-ethnic. Imperial capitals and large provincial cities attracted populations who maintained distinct and different ways of life indefinitely, often helped by limited rights of ethnic self-government, diverse religious institutions and, not infrequently, by occupational specialization as well. In a sense, therefore, the recent expansion of urban polyethnicity in European lands is a return to normal for Europeans. Nationwide ethnic uniformity was always somewhat mythical. Today's ethnic mixing is more massive and, obviously, not new.

An unanswered question for the longer future, however, is whether the recent disruption of traditional rural life will affect birth rates among all the peoples of the earth in the same way that it did after about 1960 in Europe and in lands of European settlement overseas. It is already true that cities of China, India, Latin America and even of Africa seem to be becoming population sinkholes. Some always were, and it is in these cities that infectious diseases have made their greatest comeback from the effect of antibiotics and other medical advances of the twentieth century.

But whether the sociological changes that make childrearing more difficult and less satisfying among richer populations will spread to the rest of the world is not sure. Rural reservoirs of poor farmers remain vast, incentives to migration remain strong, and rural birth rates in Latin America, India, Africa, and the Moslem lands of Asia have diminished only slightly. Consequently, world population is still growing rapidly and may precipitate some sort of ecological and/or political disaster before changes in private family life and birth control pills make much difference in the poorer and still mainly rural countries of the world.

Yet such changes come quickly. The collapse of French Canadian birth rates immediately after World War II to a level below that of English-speaking Canada is a case in point. No one knows whether Mexico, Nigeria, and other such countries will follow the French Canadian example, but it is worth realizing that sometime late in the twenty-first century, say about 2075, declining human populations might become general throughout the world. If so, consequences are likely to be as baffling as those our recent extraordinary population growth still continues to provoke.

Future demographic stability, allowing time to adjust to ever-accelerating social change, is most unlikely. Human numbers have tended to increase over time throughout our career on earth. Local die-offs and sharp decreases happened often enough. But globally speaking, new ecological and technological discoveries that sustained population increases soon overtook even the most massive regional losses.

We may or may not be nearing an end to that age-old process of expanding the human niche in earth's ecosystem. But we will not know ahead of time. And even if global catastrophe takes over, even a small human remnant might be able to start all over again, even in a radically different environment and maintain our privileged place at the top of the food chain.

Language, endowing us with unparalleled capabilities for cooperation, innovation, and adaptability, make us unique among the forms of life that ever existed. As long as humankind retains such capabilities, we will continue to disturb the world around us and fumble towards an uncertain, changing, and always precarious future.

That realization seems to me more important than trying to isolate changes of the past fifty years from the deeper past by emphasizing their uniqueness. All ages are unique; each moment and every person is unique. So is each atom and sub-atomic particle, for that matter. But continuities and commonalities also prevail, and recognizing them is what historians and scientists focus on when trying to understand the ever changing world of which we are a part.

I conclude that the world is indeed one interacting whole and always has been. Human wealth and power have sporadically increased, spurting towards un-exampled heights lately. Limits to that spurt may now be close at hand. But ingenu-ity and invention remain alive among us as much as ever. So we and our successors may perhaps continue to stumble onward like all preceding human generations, meeting with painful disappointments and changing behavior accordingly, only to provoke new risks and meet fresh disappointments. That has always been the human condition, and seems likely to last as long as we do.

CHAPTER 12

Slaves, Germs, and Trojan Horses

Nayan Chanda

> I saw a piece of land which is much like an island, though it is
> not one, on which there were six huts. It could be made into an
> island in two days, though I see no necessity to do so since
> these people are very unskilled in arms, as your Majesties will
> discover from seven whom I caused to be taken and brought
> aboard so that they may learn our language and return.
> However, should your Highnesses command it all the
> inhabitants could be taken away to Castile or held as slaves on
> the island, for with fifty men we could subjugate them all and
> make them do whatever we wish.
>
> —CHRISTOPHER COLUMBUS
> Letter to King Ferdinand and Queen Isabella
> of Castile after his first voyage to the New World, 1492
> From *The Four Voyages,* ed. and trans. J. M. Cohen
> (London: Penguin, 1969: 58).

It was an unbearably hot summer night at the English port of Dover. As the next day's papers would report, 18 June 2000 was the hottest day of the year. Five officers of HM Revenue and Customs at the Dover Eastern Docks Ferry Terminals waited for the midnight ferry from Zeebrugge to pull into the quay. Hours earlier, when the ferry had left the Belgian port, they had received a faxed manifest of the trucks it had on board. Most of the truckers that plied this route were familiar, well-established companies hauling goods between the Continent and Britain. That night, one manifest caught the officers' attention.

The listed cargo of tomatoes was unremarkable, but the carrier—Van Der Spek Transportation—was not one that they had heard of before. Even more curious, the ferry charge was neither prepaid nor charged to a credit card. The truck driver, it seemed, had paid cash at the ferry counter at Zeebrugge. Such anomalies tend to raise suspicions about the contents of the cargo. Hidden among boxes of onions or fruit, customs officers often discovered undeclared crates of liquor or cartons of cigarettes—the usual high-value commodities smugglers try to sneak into England.

So when Van Der Spek's white Mercedes truck rolled down the gangplank to stop near the customs checkpoint, it was not waved through after a cursory look at its papers. While some officers went to talk with the driver, another went behind the refrigerated truck to open the steel doors and look inside. He noticed that the truck was oddly silent. There was no hum of a generator to keep the produce properly chilled. The only sounds were the snap and slide of the bolt on the door and the swoosh of suction as the officer loosed the door from its seal and swung it open. A rush of warm, putrid air immediately blasted his senses. In the dim light he saw over-turned crates of tomatoes and the outlines of two human figures gasping for breath. Behind them, deeper in the shadows, half-naked bodies lay in heaps on the metal floor. The officer did not realize that he had chanced on one of the most gruesome discoveries of human trafficking in modem Europe. He shouted for his colleagues.

A forklift truck was brought in to help unload the crates of tomatoes that hid a shocking scene. "There were just piles and piles of bodies, it was absolutely sick-ening," one officer later told reporters. Fifty-four men and four women of "orien-tal" appearance found that night were later identified as illegal immigrants from China. Lured by the prospect of the good life in the West, they had paid traffickers thousands of dollars to embark on a long, tortuous—and ultimately fatal—journey across Russia and Eastern Europe. One of them was nineteen-year-old Chen Lin, who had regularly called his mother back in China throughout the harrowing voyage across the continents. In his final call home, he had told her that in a few days, he would be in Britain, where a cousin had already made it.[1]

Like thousands of slaves from Africa who perished during the journey across the Atlantic two centuries ago, Chen and his compatriots were the latest victims of one of the most noxious and tragic aspects of globalization: the international trad-ing in human beings. In 1495, Christopher Columbus had organized the first-ever shipment of slaves to reach Europe. Despairing of finding any sizable quantity of gold in the New World, he organized an armed expedition to capture Indians from the island of Hispaniola. Exactly 505 years before the customs officers' shocking discovery in Dover, a vessel carrying 550 Native Americans left for Spain in February 1495. Favorable winds made the journey relatively swift by the standards of the day. But by the time the ship reached the island of Madeira, two hundred of the slaves had died of the cold.[2]

The transatlantic east-to-west slave trade received a boost in the seventeenth century with the arrival of large-hulled ships and the desire for cheap labor to ex-ploit the virgin soil of the New World. For more than two centuries, African slaves were transported across the Atlantic in these specially constructed vessels that could pack up to 450 people sardine-like, shackled to the floor, in their large hulls.[3] During this dreaded month-long Middle Passage (which began with capture and forced march to Africa's Atlantic shores and ended with auction sales of slaves to new owners), as many as four in ten died of disease, thirst, or hunger. The bodies of the unfortunate were unceremoniously dumped overboard in the waters of what was known as the Ocean Sea.

THE EUROPEAN DREAM

For the fifty-four prospective Chinese workers headed for the "new world" of Britain, the metallic belly of a refrigeration truck became a suffocating coffin.

Unlike in the previous era, however, they had not been kidnapped by slave traders to be sold in auctions for plantation owners. Slavery was abolished in most places by the late nineteenth century. Yet opportunistic middlemen found no shortage of hopeful and vulnerable would-be immigrants to prey on for profit. The emergence of inexpensive and faster mass travel in the 1970s had brought new opportunities for human traffickers to deliver cheap and often bonded laborers to employers in countries thousands of miles away. The clandestine nature of such operations meant that the comfort and speed of modern-day travel would be sacrificed for the sake of more furtive and dangerous journeys in the hidden compartments of ships and trucks.

Poverty and despair at home, combined with the dream of a better life in Europe, led the fifty-four Chinese to the door of modern-day slave traders. Instead of the land-owning masters in the New World, who bought slaves as chattel, many European and American businesses of the modern era turned to illegal immigrants to meet their need for low-cost labor. Instead of being kidnapped from their villages to be sold abroad (although that has also happened), the unfortunate Chinese immigrants had paid about thirty thousand dollars each to international human traffickers known as "snakeheads" for the covert voyage that ended in tragedy.

The Chinese formed, however, only a small part of the growing wave of illegal immigrants from all over the world flocking to Europe—from the former Yugoslavia, Afghanistan, Congo, Iran, Iraq, Romania, Sri Lanka, and the former Zaire. In 1999 alone, some seventy-one thousand persons illegally entered Britain and sought asylum. According to a CIA report, another forty-five to fifty thousand women and children were trafficked to the United States that same year out of the seven hundred thousand to two million women and children who were trafficked globally.[4] The number of immigrants trying to enter the United States illegally has continued to rise, as has the casualty rate. According to a *Wall Street Journal* report, since 2000, an average of about four hundred immigrants have died each year trying to enter the United States illegally across the Mexican border. That compares with about 240 people who died trying to cross the Berlin Wall during its 28-year existence.[5]

The same cocktail of economic disparity, power imbalance, and desire for profit that once drove the slave trade across continents is still the intoxicating elixir of the slave trade today. As Jesse Sage, a spokesman for the American Anti-Slavery Group, puts it, "Whether it is Bangladeshi toddlers trafficked into the United Arab Emirates or Chinese children smuggled into Los Angeles by snakehead criminal gangs, there is a lucrative trade in human beings. Our global economy creates demand for cheap goods and there is no cheaper labor than slave labor."[6] Maidservants and nannies are procured from poorer countries by the hundreds of thousands to work in households in rich countries—from the petrodollar-soaked Middle East to business-enriched metropolises in Asia. According to a World Bank estimate, migrant workers, including ill-treated and abused maidservants, sent home more than $150 billion in remittances in 2004 alone.[7] Those remittances have built homes, started businesses, sent children to school, and fueled a consumer economy in their home countries.

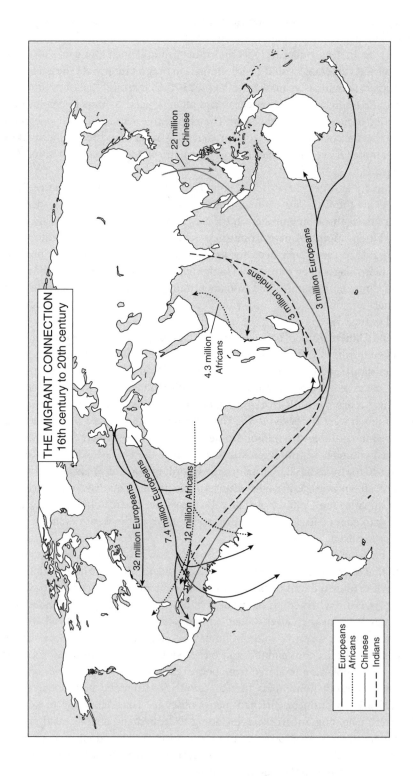

THE MIGRANT CONNECTION
16th century to 20th century

22 million Chinese

3 million Europeans

3 million Indians

4.3 million Africans

32 million Europeans

7.4 million Europeans

12 million Africans

Europeans
Africans
Chinese
Indians

The expanding economic connections among human communities, pushed by traders and propelled by consumer demand, have created an increasingly interdependent world. Imperial aggression brings far-flung communities under one ruler and produces today's interconnected world. Both of these agents of globalization—traders and warriors—have in the same process brought suffering, upheaval, and heartaches. From the beginning of human connections through warfare or trade, slavery has been an important component. Winners took back captives as slaves, and traders profited by trafficking in humans across the borders. The fact is that the process of globalization has always had a dark side. As the tragedy at Dover demonstrates, nothing has changed. In fact, with technology now speeding the process, the noxious effects of global interconnectedness may also spread and accelerate. The dark shadow falls not just on human trafficking. Both warfare and commerce have long transmitted pathogens, bringing catastrophic pandemics. That threat continues and speeds up as global trade and travel intensify. In this chapter we will see examples of how these negative consequences of globalization have evolved and how ever-faster communication and commerce have brought in their train new threats—hackers releasing destructive computer viruses, criminals stealing credit card numbers and personal information from personal computers hooked to cyberspace. The speed and ease that globalization has brought have come with a price tag.

THE OLDEST TRADE

Adam Smith saw slavery as an aberration. The Scottish economist lamented in 1776 how the beneficial new trade between Europe and the New World was spoiled by the rapacity of slave traders: "The commodities of Europe were almost all new to America, and many of those of America were new to Europe. A new set of exchanges, therefore, began to take place which had never been thought of before, and which naturally should have proved as advantageous to the new, as it certainly did to the old continent. The savage injustice of the Europeans rendered an event, which ought to have been beneficial to all, ruinous and destructive to several of those unfortunate countries."[8] The fact is, however, that although the scale and brutality of Atlantic slavery were unprecedented, slavery was, in the words of a Dutch historian, the "oldest trade" in the world. As David Christian has put it, the masters considered slaves as "living batteries, as human cattle." The importance of human beings as a source of energy helps explain why forced labor was so ubiquitous in the premodern world.[9] Many forms of slavery existed centuries before the word *slave* came into formal existence. People's insatiable search for wealth and drive for profit, combined with power imbalances between human communities, led to the growth of a system that reached its peak in the early nineteenth century and has since profoundly altered human civilization.

The word *slave* was coined in reference to the widespread enslavement of central European Slavs in the ninth century. This group constituted the main target or "resource" population for the Viking-Arab trade in the Middle Ages. Male and female "heathen" Slavs who had not yet been converted to Christianity were seen as objects, fair game for trading. From the beginning of history, war, famine, falling personal fortunes, and natural disasters have compelled people to leave their homes to find work elsewhere or accept bonded work to survive. In some cases, this has meant performing hard or dangerous tasks that could be assigned to slaves, whom Aristotle called "human instruments."[10]

Stripped of their humanity, such "working machines" were treated no better than draft animals to be bought and sold like other commodities in the marketplace. But unlike chattel, slaves brought their own races, languages, and cultures to venues far removed from their places of birth. Like migration, the slave trade brought face to face different branches of the human race that had dispersed since the ancestors left Africa more than fifty thousand years ago. The intermixing of people and their slaves (and of migrants and settlers) over the millennia has transformed the size, shape, and color of the human community and its cultures. We have seen how Egyptians' first contact with Africans in the third millennium B.C.E. led to the procurement of slaves for the pharaoh. Bartering human beings for other commodities began early in human history.

The first-century-B.C.E. historian Diodorus famously observed that Italian merchants could purchase a slave from Gaul in exchange for alcohol ("a crock of wine for a young slave boy"). Indigent parents sold their offspring to traders or handed them over to repay debts, and authorities sold convicted criminals. And of course, prisoners of war were the greatest source of able-bodied slaves. Cimon, an Athenian naval commander who fought against Persia in 468 B.C.E., sent twenty thousand prisoners to the slave market.[11] A primary occupation of these slaves was digging the earth with bare hands and stone tools for precious metals like silver. The ore played an important role in the rise of Athens. In the mid-first millennium B.C.E., silver mining in the Balkan-Aegean world employed tens of thousands of slaves and required a large-scale, well-organized slave trade. Slaves were also needed to fight as soldiers. Silver provided the means to fund wars like those Athens fought against Persia and Sparta, but the slaves themselves often were enlisted as soldiers to supplement the troops.

THE SLAVE: SOLDIER, LABORER, COMPANION

The anonymous author of the famous first-century-C.E. account of ocean trade *Periplus of the Erythraen Sea* mentions slaves as routine merchandise in Roman trade. They were imported for manual labor as well as for entertainment such as singing and companionship. The Roman author Martial mocked Caelia, who, although Roman, consorted with various foreign men, presumably slaves: "Your Egyptian lover sails to you from Alexandria, the dark-skinned Indian one from the Red Sea." But slaves were traded from both sides of Indian Ocean shores. Ancient Indian literature offers evidence of the rich owning Western slaves who may have come from the Greco-Roman world.[12] Tribute sent to the Chinese imperial court by neighbors frequently included slave girls and performers such as acrobatic "twirling girls" from Central Asia.

The Slavic population of parts of central Europe furnished the largest number of humans for sale to the Romans. While the Roman aristocracy enjoyed the high life, for the common folk life was nasty, brutish, and short, especially in south-central Europe. With their high mortality rates and low life expectancies, societies with larger populations—historians call them "population reservoirs"—became natural targets for slavers. In addition to Slavs, Greeks, and Persians, the Germanic, Celtic, and Romance peoples inhabiting lands in the north of the Roman Empire and people from sub-Saharan Africa formed the main reservoirs for those who traded in human flesh.

As the Roman Empire demanded more and more slaves to work the plantations and serve the aristocracy, the kidnapping and trading of slaves grew apace. The Greek geographer and historian Strabo wrote that ten thousand slaves could be loaded and unloaded at the Delos docks in a single day. In order to prevent solidarity (early trade unions, perhaps) or unrest among the enslaved, slaves of diverse ethnic origins from different parts of Asia Minor and the Mediterranean were intentionally combined.[13] (Interestingly, nearly two millennia later the Portuguese slave traders followed a similar course of action in supplying African slaves to Brazil. The policy was "not to allow too many from one tribe to be collected in either the whole of Brazil or in any of its captaincies, so as to avoid possible ill consequences." Despite those precautions, one tribe from Sudan organized a series of revolts.[14]) As the Roman Empire extended from the Atlantic Ocean to the Euphrates in the first two centuries of the Christian era, the large foreign slave population in Rome turned it into "a world in miniature." Rome was the center of the slave trade, and its victims from all over the world brought with them the dress, speech, customs, and cultures of their native countries.[15] Over time, intermarriage among slaves, and between Romans and slaves of different races, produced a new mixture of people.

For the succeeding millennium, slavery remained a common feature of societies around the Mediterranean, all the while growing in scale. Although slavery for domestic production in Europe was gradually supplanted by serfdom in the eleventh century, mining and farming became more reliant on slave labor due to international trade and increasing demand.[16] In the ninth and tenth centuries, Viking and Russian traders took slaves from the eastern Slavic states to Moorish Spain and North Africa as domestic servants, soldiers, and mine workers. Slave trading was not confined to Europe and the Middle East. According to seventh-century Chinese sources, slaves were brought from Zenj (sub-Saharan Africa), and by 1119 the ownership of black slaves was a mark of wealth in Canton.[17] Slavic household slaves were a common sight in the Italian city-states as late as the fourteenth century, as were African slaves in sixteenth-century Spain and Portugal. Eric Wolf notes that much of the wealth of Venice came to depend on the trade in slaves. Although slaves could not be sold at public auctions in Venice after 1386, they continued to be sold by private contract through the sixteenth century.[18]

In the Middle East, slaves were often trained to perform as entertainers, craft-workers, and soldiers.[19] For the Abbasid caliphate of Baghdad, slaves were brought in from all over Europe, as well as sub-Saharan Africa. Female slaves, who were mostly from the Middle East or India, received a lot of attention, and their relative merits were the subject of comment in contemporary accounts. One report, almost like a product review, compared slaves of different origin and concluded: "The ideal female slave was of Berber origin, left her country at age nine, spent three years at al-Medina, three in Mecca, and then went to Iraq at sixteen to acquire some of that country's culture. When resold at twenty-five, she combined the coquettishness of al-Medina, the gentle manners of Mecca, and the culture of Iraq."[20]

As Arab traders ventured deeper and deeper south along the Indian Ocean coast and into West Africa, slaves from sub-Saharan Africa emerged as a major traded item. The Prophet Muhammad himself had slaves, and he authorized the owning of slaves in certain conditions. In Arabic the word for black, *abd*, became synonymous with slave. As early as the year 652, the Christian kingdom of Nubia (today's Ethiopia) signed a treaty with the Abbasid caliphate to supply the Abbasids three hundred slaves a year. The arrangement continued for six centuries.[21]

Some of the African slaves imported into the Abbasid empire (part of today's Iraq) were enrolled in the infantry, but more were put to work in large-scale production of sugar or in farm labor.[22] Landowners in ninth-century Basra brought in several thousand East African slaves to drain the salt marshes in what is now southern Iraq, hoping to turn the marsh into breadbasket. The slaves' anger at their hard labor and minimal subsistence erupted into one of the earliest known black slave revolts, when Ali ibn Muhammad, a Persian who claimed descent from Ali, the fourth caliph, and Fatimah, Muhammad's daughter, won the support of slave work crews by promising them freedom and equality under his brand of Islam. For fourteen years, the African slave, called the Zanj, joined by Africans in the caliphate's infantry, sacked Basra and kept the power of the caliphate at bay in parts of southern Iraq and eastern Persia. They were eventually crushed by the caliph's Egyptian-backed army.[23] Despite their eventual defeat, the Zanj nevertheless shook the honor of the caliphate by exacting terrible revenge. As one contemporary historian described it: "Ali's soldiers were so outrageous as to auction off publicly women from the lineage of al-Hassan and al-Hussein and al-'Abbas [meaning descendants of 'Ali ibn abi-Talib and the ruling Abbasids] as well as others from the lineage of Hashem, Qureish [the Prophet's lineage], and the rest of the Arabs. These women were sold as slaves for a mere one or three Dirhams, and were publicly advertised according to their proper lineage, each Zanji receiving ten, twenty, and thirty of them as concubines and to serve the Zanji women as maids."[24]

Military slavery came to play an important role in the Abbasid empire as the Abbasids grew concerned about recruits from the unreliable, independent-minded Arab tribal armies and began to enlist slaves—first blacks from Africa and later mostly horse-riding Turks from Central Asia. Although it is difficult to calculate the number of military slaves in the employ of the Arab empire over the centuries, one scholar estimates it to be into the tens of millions.[25] So deep-rooted was the practice of slavery in the Middle East that it persisted in Saudi Arabia into the 1960s.

THE SLAVE-SUGAR COMPLEX

When European Crusaders arrived on the eastern shores of the Mediterranean in the twelfth century, they found a delicious product—sugar—being grown in plantations with slave labor. Sugarcane originated in the Pacific islands before reaching

India, which remained the source of that luxury for the Mediterranean world. Before then, Europe's craving for sweets was being met by sugar beets. The rise of Islam and intensified trade with the Arab world introduced sugarcane cultivation into the Levant. Italian colonies, especially Cyprus, became the principal sugar suppliers in Europe. Italian entrepreneurs in the eastern Mediterranean soon developed the so-called slave-sugar complex, an elaborate method of growing sugarcane and transforming it into sugar, made possible via the large-scale use of slaves. It became the earliest model of the system transplanted to the New World three centuries later. In this early capitalist model, land, capital, and labor were combined in a way that allowed profit to be maximized. Slaves, writes Barbara Solow, were not only "a new, improved factor of production, like a new kind of machine . . . [but] slave labor could be held as an asset in the portfolio of the slaver."[26]

Italy's experience in Crete, Cyprus, and later Sicily had shown how plantation slavery combined with exports could turn virgin lands into an enormous wealth-generating enterprise. When the Portuguese discovered the uninhabited Atlantic islands of Madeira in 1425, they followed in Italy's footsteps and introduced slave-sugar plantations. Slaves were raided or bought from the West African coast and harnessed to growing sugar to be sold in Europe. Other Europeans soon picked up the sugar-slavery model in use in Madeira, São Tomé, and the Canary Islands.

On his first voyage across the Atlantic, Columbus stopped in the Canary Islands for repair and had the opportunity to see firsthand how slave labor was being used in sugar plantations. Although he was disappointed not to find the spice or gold he had sought in Hispaniola, he did not miss the opportunity to appropriate free labor. As he wrote to the Spanish court: "I must add that this island [Hispaniola], as well as the others, belongs to your Highness as securely as the Kingdom of Castile. It only needs people to come and settle here, and to give orders to the inhabitants who will do whatever is asked of them. . . . The Indians have no weapons and are quite naked. They know nothing about the art of war and are so cowardly that a thousand of them would not stay to face three of our men . . . they need only to be given order *to be made to work, to sow, or to do anything useful.*"[27]

Columbus was the first slaver to send a group of slaves from the New World back to Europe, but the direction of this traffic across the Atlantic quickly reversed. The pressing need for labor to develop the boundless resources offered by the New World had to be met from Africa, and thus did the transatlantic slave trade take off. Europeans came to realize that not only did slavery offer a highly profitable model for producing exportable commodities but trading in slaves was itself a lucrative business. The British learned that the Portuguese method of military raids to grab slaves could be costly; they sought instead the more profitable tactic of bartering with African chiefs to trade commodities for people.

In 1562–63, John Hawkins led England's first slaving voyage to Sierra Leone, returning with three vessels loaded with three hundred slaves and other goods.[28] Despite running the gauntlet of Spain's monopoly in the slave trade, he raised a hefty profit selling the slaves in Spain's Caribbean islands. News of his expedition displeased Queen Elizabeth, who denounced it as "detestable." But after realizing the scale of profits to be reaped through the slave trade, she had a change of heart and ended up investing in Hawkins's next slaving expedition. By carrying slaves from Portuguese Africa to Spanish America, Hawkins challenged the Iberian monopoly. Other slavers soon followed, and the path was laid for slavery-based commerce in the New World.

Supported by a steady stream of imported slaves, the Portuguese colony of Brazil eclipsed Madeira to emerge as the world's leading sugar producer. In 1513 the king of Portugal sent the pope a pompous gift—a life-size image of the pontiff surrounded by twelve cardinals and three hundred candles all made of sugar.[29] From 1575 to 1650 Brazil supplied most of Europe's sugar and imported significant quantities of manufactured goods and African slaves. Slaves were later employed to grow coffee plants introduced from French Guyana, where coffee had arrived after journeying across the world from Yemen to Sri Lanka and Indonesia. A seemingly inexhaustible supply of slave labor and endless plantations turned Brazil into the world's top coffee grower. The semitropical coastal lands of Peru and Mexico offered the Spaniards land to develop sugar plantations and vineyards. Rich silver mines—worked by slaves in northern Mexico and Bolivia—became a great source of wealth for Spain, as well as currency for international commerce. African slaves working in Brazil's diamond and gold mines added to the glitter of the Portuguese empire. The British, French, and Dutch made a fortune from sugar, coffee, and cocoa plantations in the Caribbean and from cotton and tobacco plantations in North America. The prosperity of European colonial powers and the rise of international trade that forged the creation of an interdependent world were based on the ruthless exploitation of African slaves—an estimated twelve million of whom were brought to the Americas in the eighteenth and nineteenth centuries.[30]

Rumblings against slavery in the New World first circulated among the Quakers in Philadelphia as early as 1688, and nearly a hundred years later English Quakers submitted the first important antislavery petition to Parliament. The growth of an evangelical-based, powerful philanthropic movement in England accompanied the rise of laissez-faire thinking and growing opposition to protectionism in the late eighteenth century to intensify opposition to slavery. The rise of the British Empire in India—with its vast population and resources—and the declining importance of the Caribbean also lent weight to the argument to abolish sugar-slavery. In 1807, Parliament passed the first anti-slavery act, prohibiting trade in African slaves. Ten years later, Britain and Spain signed a treaty in which Spain agreed to end the slave trade north of the equator immediately and south of the equator in 1820. The treaty gave British naval vessels the right to search for suspected slavers. Thanks to loopholes in the treaty, however, slave trade continued unabated until 1830, when another Anglo-Spanish treaty officially banned slavery in most of Central and South America.

In the United States, however, the emerging antislavery movement suffered a setback with Eli Whitney's invention of the cotton gin in 1793. Soaring demand for cotton from British mills, combined with the ease of cleaning cotton with Whitney's invention, made cotton king in America's South, making slavery integral to the southern way of life. It took the South's secession from the Union and a bloody civil war finally to end slavery. The expansion of coffee plantations in Brazil also kept slavery alive for fifty years past its official abolition by an act of Parliament in 1833 that emancipated slaves in the British West Indies. In 1800 there were about 1.5 million slaves in Brazil, 857,000 in the United States, 600,000 in British West Indies, 250,000 in Spanish America, and another 150,000 in other British colonies.[31]

Laws, however, have not ended what economic inequality between different parts of the world has maintained. The world's oldest trade is alive and well even today. The testimony of an escaped Brazilian slave in 2004 provided a glimpse of the dark world beneath the country's export success.[32] Brazil's government has admitted that even now, about fifty thousand people work in "conditions analogous to slavery," clearing the Amazon forest to make tropical hardwoods accessible to loggers, open land for cattle grazing, and clear farmland for soybeans. The resultant low-cost timber, beef, and soybean boost Brazilian exports and are marketed to consumers the world over by multinational corporations. The tragedy in Dover has been followed by incidents in other parts of the world, most notably in the United States, giving us an occasional glimpse of the tip of an iceberg that continues to float darkly under the current of globalization.[33]

BRIDGING ASIA AND THE NEW WORLD

Three centuries of unfettered slave trade profoundly changed our world, meshing it ever tighter—ethnically, economically, and culturally. The slave-sugar complex that arose in the Mediterranean and conquered the New World went on, as historian Robert Harms has shown, to create a vital link in the trading system that connected the continents, forming the backbone of global commerce. The slave trade amounted to an essential bridge between Europe's New World trade and its Asia trade. In fact, in Africa a slave was known as a "piece," "uma peça d'India" in the old Portuguese expression, meaning the item of printed cotton for which he or she was exchanged.[34] French ships sailed to Africa carrying goods to be bartered for slaves. The slaves were then transported to France's New World colonies, where they were exchanged for sugar and other plantation products.

Historians are still trying to estimate the toll wrought upon Africa's population by the institution of slavery and the slave trade. Some 1.5 million slaves were brought to the British Caribbean colonies between 1650 and 1800, but by the end of that period, diseases like dysentery, yellow fever, and malnutrition had decreased the Afro-Caribbean population to just over half a million.[35] Burgeoning international commerce came at a great human price.

We have seen how the emergence of larger-hulled and speedier sailing ships in the sixteenth century and steamships in the nineteenth century helped to break the weight barrier. Instead of light, expensive items like bolts of silk, bags of spice, and boxes of pearls and diamonds, ships could carry increasingly heavier goods. Slavery helped to change the scale of production by producing more goods to fill larger ships to satisfy growing consumer demand. Hundreds of thousands of slaves contributed to the expanding production of sugar, coffee, cocoa, and tobacco, and these one-time luxuries began to reach the masses. "By 1750 the poorest English farm laborer's wife took sugar in her tea."[36] Gone were the days when a king showed off by sending the pope a gift of sugar. Newly discovered cocoa so enchanted Queen Isabella of Spain that she drank chocolate all day, gradually staining her clothes with the drink's brown color. Even on the other side of the world, in Southeast Asia, King Rama III of Siam carried on a military campaign against neighboring Cambodia to bring back bonded labor to grow sugar. Thanks to the corvée Libor, sugar had become Siam's most important export item by the first quarter of the nineteenth century.[37] As African slaves in America's South ramped up production and drove down the price of cotton, British textile manufacturing boomed, and the light cotton shirt was no longer a luxury limited to princes and peers.

Tens of thousands of African slaves toiling in the silver mines of Mexico and Peru produced the incredible amount of ingots that provided the lifeblood for world trade. Historians estimate that 130,000 to 150,000 tons of silver were extracted from the mines of Mexico and Peru between 1450 and 1800, before being shipped as bullion to Europe and to the outpost of the Spanish Empire in Asia, Manila.[38] From Manila silver bullion and minted coins circulated throughout the world to pay for the swelling volume of trade.

The slave trade, linked with other goods, tied the continents ever more closely. As Harms has noted, "The Asia trade supplied necessary trade goods for the slave ships, and the slave ships provided a steady market for the Asian products."[39] The slave trade encouraged brandy makers of Nantes and Bordeaux, but more important, the exchanges it brought about supported cloth industries in India and Hamburg, cowry diving in the Maldives, the firearms and pipe industries of Holland, and the iron industry in Sweden.[40]

The steady supply of slaves prolonged the lifespan of the colonial system, as the ready supply of labor could withstand the encroachment of new productivity-enhancing technologies, thus allowing a period of constant returns from colonial investment.[41] The wealth generated by the slavery-based plantation economy also provided a growing market for British industrial goods. As one historian has remarked, in the 1780s and 1790s "almost 60 percent of additional industrial output was exported."[42] By the nineteenth century the Atlantic slave trade had grown into a complex international trade involving East Indian textile manufacture, European metalworkers, African caravan traders, European shipping companies, and American planters.[43]

The intercontinental trading that developed primarily to trade slaves for sugar, cowries, rum, or tobacco expanded over time into other fields. And although the slave trade initially catered only to the needs of elites, soon it began providing commodities of mass consumption. As one scholar of the slave trade has noted, "In neither case did the majority of either people exhibit much knowledge of or interest in the tragic fate of those whose labors produced the goods thus consumed."[44] This is similar to today's consumers enjoying the "everyday good price" in retail outlets like Wal-Mart and Sears, which offer goods made by poor laborers in China and elsewhere working long hours in degrading conditions. Low prices have their cost! Even though consumers don't like the news they hear about working conditions abroad, buyers still flock to these stores. "Consumers are very schizo-phrenic," says Tristan Lecomte, chief executive and founder of Alter Eco, a French import company that assures decent prices to developing country producers. "On the one hand, they say that they want to be socially responsible, but then they all jump on the hard discounts."[45]

POWERING THE INDUSTRIAL REVOLUTION

The wealth generated by the slave trade contributed to the rise of some of the world's finest universities, including Harvard, Yale, and Brown. Slave traders in Providence, the home of Brown University, were involved in woolen and iron manufacturing, while Moses Brown, whose family founded the university, played a key role in developing the cotton textile industry. In 1790, Brown, then a leader of the antislavery movement, tapped English immigrant Samuel Slater (who by-passed Britain's prohibition on technology exports by memorizing machine designs) and offered him the capital to set up America's first cotton mill, in Pawtucket, just outside Providence.[46]

No power benefited more from slavery than Britain. Between 1662 and 1807 British ships carried approximately 3.4 million slaves from Africa to America, almost half of the total sent during this period.[47] At the height of the slave trade, Britain exported more slaves than any other nation. British industry prospered by selling its wares to the slave colonies, Britain's businesses racked up profits by sell-ing slave-produced goods, and the country as a whole grew rich on the profits of African slavery. Before Britain turned against slavery in 1834, the Atlantic slave system had already laid the foundation for Britain's rise to global power.

Historians estimate that about a million slaves were taken to Asian destina-tions during the nineteenth century.[48] Asia, of course, had its own intraregional slave trade, in which people from weak and politically fragmented societies were forcibly subsumed into stronger and wealthier ones. The extent of slavery in Asian societies is evident in the fact that, before 1820, a majority of the continent's urban population had been recruited in a captive state through either war or trade.[49] This was an ironic contrast to Europe, where cities emerged on a feudal landscape with a guild-based production system, and city parameters provided sanctuary to serf escapees. Legally, if a serf could manage to live in a city for a year and a day, he became a free man. Hence the German saying, "Town air makes you free" (*Stadtluft macht frei*). By contrast, Southeast Asia's colonial towns became citadels of servi-tude. Selling slaves to the towns was so lucrative that a number of states rose and flourished based primarily on slave traffic by raiding expeditions on coastal settle-ments in island Southeast Asia. The region continued supplying slave labor to the rising industrial power, Japan, late into the twentieth century. Although deeply resistant to racial intermixing, the Japanese met their acute labor shortage during World War II by employing the forced labor of seven hundred thousand Asians between 1939 and 1945.[50]

One consequence of the international slave trade was the spread of slavery in Africa itself. Of the captured total, around one-third—or 7 million—were brought into domestic slavery. Since exported slaves were overwhelmingly male, the sex ratio in west-central Africa was heavily tilted toward females. The resulting concentration of female slaves around courts led to the rise of polygyny—a form of polygamy in which one man has several wives at the same time.[51] Slavery became such an integral part of African life that "tribal leaders in Gambia, Congo, Dahomey, and other African nations that had prospered under the slave trade sent delegations to London and Paris to vigorously protest the abolition of slavery."[52] Not only did Africa lose its able-bodied population, which affected its population growth, but the warfare that ensued over the slave trade and the consequent social disruption also caused a decline in birth rates. The slave trade seriously affected and weakened African social, political, economic, and cultural institutions.

Another consequence of the slave trade was the introduction of new products in Africa, which had a lasting impact on the continent's cultural and culinary habits. On the Gold Coast (present-day Ghana) British slave traders introduced rum, cheese, beer, refined sugar, and leaf tobacco. Portuguese traders bartered slaves for sugar, brandy, tobacco, guns and gunpowder, manioc flour, and Asian and Portuguese fancy goods. As a result, African consumers became very knowledgeable about European products—a taste that far outlasted the slave trade.[53] The Portuguese also introduced the corn and manioc that became the two most important staples in the African diet, as well as sweet potato, pineapple, cashew, papaya, and dozens of other foods. Coffee plantations in Brazil sent coffee seeds back to São Tomé, from where it spread to the African mainland. Three hundred years of slave traffic left a distinctly Brazilian imprint on everyday life in West Africa, including diets, religion, popular festivals, and architecture.[54]

It was estimated that there were 1.5 million American Indians in Brazil when it was discovered by Europeans. Then 3.5 million African slaves were brought in. The impact of the African population on Brazil's demography is illustrated by the fact that, in the early 1960s, 1 percent of the population was American Indian, 11 percent of Brazilians were black, 26 percent were mixed, and the rest were of European extraction. The prominent Brazilian author Gilberto Freyre wrote that "every Brazilian, even if he is white-skinned or fair-haired, carried in his soul, and if not in his soul in his body—a shadow, or at least a spot of Negro blood."[55]

In every sphere of Brazilian life—food, clothing, religion, language, music, and folklore—centuries of slave trading have left an indelible imprint. From samba music to the *congadas* song and dance depicting the crowning of a Congolese king, from *acarajé* (a cake of baked beans in palm oil) and *carurú* (a stew of shrimp and okra) to *quibebe* (pumpkin pureé), life in Brazil is a daily reminder of the globalization that has shaped it.[56] The traditional religion brought from two major cradles of civilization, the Congo and the Gulf of Guinea, has influenced the African migrants' liturgical and visual presentation and often merged with rituals and practices of the ruling Christians. The most striking is Umbanda, considered by some to be the national religion of Brazil. As Nei Lopes explains, "Umbanda is a religion resulting from the assimilation of various elements, starting from Bantu ancestrism and the worship of the Fon-Yoruban Orishas. According to some of its scholars, Umbanda syncretizes with Hinduism, taking from it the laws of karma, evolution, and reincarnation; with Christianity, taking from it principally the rules of brotherhood and charity; and with the Native American religiosity."[57]

Similarly, Caribbean cuisine and its cultural forms—from Trinidadian calypso to Haitian vodoun—bear the hallmarks of centuries of interaction with African slaves. Creole, now spoken widely in the Caribbean, carries the imprint of years of slavery, when African languages combined with the language of French slave masters to produce a new language. The arrival of the Europeans in the New World brought more than slavery and its long-term socioeconomic consequences. It brought what some historians have called genocide—by microbial agents.

INVISIBLE DANGER FROM AFAR

On the early morning of October 12, 1492, strange-looking floating houses with masts appeared off an island in the Caribbean. Wide-eyed and naked natives gathered to watch. The pale, bearded sailors who emerged from the *Santa Maria, Niña,* and *Pinta* spoke an unknown tongue and wore strange coverings, but they seemed genuinely overjoyed to have found the rocky bay. That encounter between Europeans and American Indians reunited two human communities that had gone their separate ways on leaving Africa more than fifty thousand years earlier.

Neither the relieved Christopher Columbus and his sailors nor the curious natives could imagine what portent this encounter held for the future. Along with the unwashed and unshaven strangers in funny dress came invisible viruses and pathogens that would wreak havoc on the New World population. As Alfred W. Crosby, Jr., writes in his seminal book *The Columbian Exchange:* "When the isolation of the New World was broken, when Columbus brought the two halves of the planet together, the American Indian met for the first time his most hideous enemy: not the white man nor his black servant, but the invisible killers which these men brought in their blood and breath."[58]

Within a span of just seventy-odd years, eighty to a hundred million natives perished because of the disease brought by Europeans from across the seas: smallpox, influenza, diphtheria. "Like the rats of the medieval Black Death," Niall Ferguson comments, "the white men were the carriers of the fatal germ."[59] One of the things English pilgrims gave thanks for at Plymouth in 1621 was the fact that 90 percent of the indigenous peoples of New England had died of disease brought by previous visitors, having first—very considerately—tilled the land and buried stores of corn for the winter. As the governor of Carolina John Archdale stated in the 1690s, "The Hand of God [has been] eminently seen in thinning the *Indians,* to make room for the *English.*"[60]

The decimation of the American Indians was, however, just one episode in the long history of death and suffering that has accompanied human intercourse across the world. Along with humans, insects, cattle, and domesticated animals—all carrying viruses and pathogens—crossed borders and found new hosts. The global dissemination of disease was thus one of the earliest negative consequences of interconnectedness. It is not, however, the fact of human travel that lies behind the globalization of disease; early hunter-gatherers, who constantly moved around in search of food, appear to have been healthy. Because of their nomadic way of life, they did not live amid their waste, nor did they tend cattle or poultry. It was the rise of sedentary, agriculture-based communities that brought cattle, poultry, rodents, and insects living cheek by jowl with humans, providing vectors for the transmission of germs. As caravans and boats of traders began connecting dispersed human communities, they began inadvertently transporting, along with their goods, new pathogens: germs and germ-bearing rodents, mosquitoes, and fleas. Traded commodities like slaves carried communicable diseases that changed the recipient countries. Soldiers on expeditions carried germs to new lands and returned with new pathogens and infections ranging from the plague to influenza. With the advent of mass travel, even latter-day adventurers—tourists—have become vectors of pandemics. Thus at least three of the four agents of globalization—traders, warriors, and adventurers—were unwitting carriers of catastrophes.

Roman soldiers returning from the Parthian Wars in Mesopotamia in the second century brought with them the first documented case of an epidemic hitting the Mediterranean world of the Roman Empire. There is some debate whether it was a rat-borne plague or the first case of smallpox, but either way a terrible epidemic killed between a third and a half of those infected and triggered a decline in the Mediterranean population. The year 542 brought the first unmistakable case of bubonic plague, in which a rat-borne bacillus, *Y. pestis,* caused the swelling of lymph nodes into buboes and a fatal secondary lung infection. Called Justinius plague after the Roman emperor, the epidemic is believed to have originated in India and was brought to Egypt by rats adept in scurrying across the fastening lines that tied Arab trading ships to ports along the Red Sea. Colonies of fast-breeding rats and the fleas that fed on them spread the pestilence along the Mediterranean trade routes, all the way from Constantinople on the Bosporus to the Iberian Peninsula. The historian Procopius reported that at its peak, the plague killed ten thousand persons a day in Constantinople alone. Between 30 and 40 percent of the Roman Empire's population—estimated at sixteen to twenty-six million before the plague—perished in the pandemic.[61] A contemporary account put the loss graphically. The plague "depopulated towns, turned the country into desert and made the habitations of men to become the haunts of wild beasts."[62]

It is estimated that at least a quarter of the population in both the eastern and western halves of the Roman Empire perished. It was a record that was surpassed six centuries later by another plague pandemic, which came to be known as the Black Death (so named because of a mistranslation of Latin expression *atra mors* as "black"—rather than "terrible"—death). Commonly the appellation is attributed to the discoloration of the skin and black buboes that occur on the second day after contracting the plague.[63]

HIGHWAY OF DEATH

In 1347 Italian merchant ships from the Crimean Black Sea port of Kaffa (today's Theodosia) arrived in Constantinople and in seaports along the coasts of the Mediterranean, bringing with them the plague bacillus. The plague then spread throughout

Asia Minor, the Middle East, North Africa, and Europe. Traders crossing the rodent-infested Central Asian steppes offered themselves as unwilling carriers of the disease. As we have seen, the ancient Silk Road flourished under the Mongols' protection, but although the route was safe from bandits, it was not immune from germs passed to traders by rodents and fleas.

The Black Death, believed to have originated in China in an outbreak in 1331, reached the Crimea in 1345. By 1347 the plague had reached Constantinople, and soon Pisa and Genoa. Once the pestilence had reached the major ports in Europe it proceeded along overland routes to major cities, felling one after the other. The famous trading route that had once brought prosperity to European cities was transformed into a highway of death that traveled in the shape of furry black rats.

Historian Ole Benedictow concludes that about 60 percent of the population, or some fifty million of Europe's estimated eighty million, perished from the plague and related ailments.[64] Contemporary accounts describe mounds of rotting corpses that could not be collected, much less buried. In a city like Florence, with a population of one hundred thousand, some four hundred to a thousand people died every day. From 1347 until 1722 the plague returned to Europe periodically before dying out. For a period, trade almost came to a halt. If the word *globalization* had been known, one would have pronounced it dead as well. Europe's falling population, however, set in motion economic and social trends and medical practices that proved a turning point in world history. The devastation that followed helps to underline the interconnected nature of the world that trade had already created. The death of half or more of the population meant a sharp rise in the per capita wealth among the survivors. Newly wealthy from inheriting land, capital, and stocks of gold and silver, and exhilarated to be alive, Europeans went on a luxury buying binge that enriched Asian suppliers of silk and spices and Arab and Venetian intermediaries. Their shopping spree also caused what one historian has called the "Great Bullion Famine of the Fifteenth Century." This drastic shortage of coins led to an intensified search for precious metals, and in 1516 "one of the greatest silver strikes in history" was made in the German town of Joachimsthal. The coins produced by the town's mint were called *Joachimsthaler*. And the *thaler*, as it was later shortened was the precursor to our word *dollar*.[65] But meanwhile, the stranglehold of Venetian-Arab intermediaries on the spice trade led Europeans to intensity their search for alternate sea routes to Asia.[66] By promoting the demand growth in Europe, the Black Death in many ways foreshadowed another spurt toward formation of a consumer society that would arise from the New World's supply boom.

More immediately, the labor shortage and its high cost led to a more rational work organization, efficient production methods, and labor-saving devices. Water-powered sawmills that had been developed in the early thirteenth century came into widespread use. The death of a large number of scribes sent the price of copying manuscripts skyrocketing, pushing the need for some form of automated copying. Paper-making, learned from the Chinese, had already led to the production of cheap paper. Moveable type made of wood also was known. In 1447 Johannes Gutenberg of Mainz, Germany, combined his skill in metallurgy with printing technology to produce Europe's first moveable metal-type printing press and launched a revolution.[67] The production of cheap consumer goods in Britain and Holland shifted the center of economic gravity from the Mediterranean to the North—which would eventually pioneer modern shipbuilding and usher in the Industrial Revolution.

A catastrophe of such magnitude as the Black Death also revealed and drove long-held prejudices against "outsiders" like Jews to a new height. The theory that Jews and other "enemies of Christendom" caused these deaths by poisoning wells and other sources of drinking water led to a violent persecution of minorities in many parts of Europe. It was "a sort of medieval holocaust with extensive and indiscriminate murder of Jews, [hastening their] movement to Eastern Europe, where their descendants were, to a large extent, annihilated in a new, and even more violent holocaust 600 years later."[68]

THE BIRTH OF QUARANTINE

The Black Death had far-reaching consequences on public health policy. The first known order to quarantine passengers was issued on July 27, 1377, by the Venetian colony of Ragusa (now Dubrovnik in Croatia) on the Dalmatian coast. The order for a thirty-day period of isolation for those coming from plague-stricken areas was later extended to forty days—hence the term *quarantine,* developed from Italian *quarantenaria.* "Thus stirred by the Black Death in the middle of the fourteenth century," writes George Rosen, "public officials in Italy, southern France, and the neighboring area created a system of sanitary control to combat contagious diseases, with observation stations, isolation hospitals, and disinfection procedures. This system was adopted and developed during the Renaissance and later periods and is still a part of public health practices today, although in a more rigorously defined form."[69]

But the quarantine system did not always work. In the spring of 1720 a Levantine boat carrying cases of human plague appeared in the port of Livorno. It was turned away there and at Marseille. But after a few months of wandering in the Mediterranean, including a stop at Tripoli, the boat returned to the French port of Toulon, where many passengers managed to bribe their way out of a token quarantine. Soon plague flared in Toulon and spread to Marseille, killing nearly half of its hundred thousand residents.[70] The disaster at Marseille led to stricter enforcement of quarantine and an effort to limit or eliminate the Middle Eastern cloth trade. The effort fitted well with the rising sea-borne textile trade between India and Europe.

As noted earlier, one of the greatest ravages of globalization—in the sense of the closer integration of human communities—was the transmission of diseases to American Indians in the New World, who had no immunity against the pathogens brought from Europe. In 1519 the Spanish conquistador Hernán Cortés succeeded in defeating the more numerous Aztecs with a small army because they were enfeebled by smallpox spread from an African slave accompanying Cortés. The Aztecs interpreted the selective pestilence as a demonstration of the superior power of the god the Spanish worshipped, says historian William McNeill. As a result, Cortés and his ragtag army were able easily to subjugate the Aztec empire of some 12.5 million. From Mexico, smallpox spread to Guatemala and continued southward, reaching the Incan lands in present-day Peru around 1525. In 1563, Portuguese colonizers brought smallpox to Brazil, where it wiped out entire indigenous tribes.[71] Further north, there were probably about two million indigenous people in the territory of the modern United States in 1500. That number had fallen to 750,000 in 1700 before being further reduced to 325,000 by 1820.[72]

As the slave trade and conquest transmitted smallpox to new lands, its remedy also was passed on from one country to another. The practice of smallpox inoculation known as "buying the smallpox" or "variolation" is believed to have begun in India before 1000 B.C.E. It was spread to Tibet and then to China by monks at a Buddhist monastery in Sichuan province around the year 1000.[73] During the mid-seventeenth-century, merchant caravans brought the knowledge of variolation to Arabia, Persia, and North Africa, and it came to be practiced at the folk level throughout the Ottoman Empire. In the early eighteenth century Lady Mary Montagu, wife of the British ambassador to Constantinople and herself a survivor of smallpox, variolated her son and introduced the practice to Britain.[74]

Dr. Edward Jenner developed the technique of vaccination by inoculating people with pus from cowpox victims, which prevented the more serious small-pox infection. In his book describing the procedure in 1798, he coined the word *vaccine,* from the Latin word *vacca* for cow and named the process "vaccination." In 1881 the French microbiologist Louis Pasteur honored Jenner by expanding the use of the term *vaccination* to describe any inoculation that induced immunity against a communicable disease. More than any single medical invention, vacci-nation has since saved hundreds of millions of lives and transformed the world's demography. As J. N. Hays has noted: "One by one the perils of various infectious epidemic diseases seemed to fade away under the combined assault of enlightened public health and sanitation, the extension of the preventive principle of vaccination, and the curative powers of laboratory products, among which the antibiotics created the greatest sensation."[75]

Noted flu virologist Kennedy Shortridge believes that all flu pandemics that can be traced have always begun in China's Guangdong province, a densely popu-lated region where people, pigs, ducks, and other fowl have long lived cheek by jowl. The Spanish flu of 1918 may also have begun as bird flu in Canton in 1888. During World War I, Chinese laborers traveled to camps in France to dig trenches for the Allies and may have carried the virus strain that set off the flu pandemic. Although the suspicion that the Spanish flu is a form of avian flu has now been confirmed by DNA analysis of the victims' remains, other specialists challenge the theory of its Chinese origin.[76]

SOLDIERS, STEAMBOATS, AND SPANISH FLU

Wherever the 1918 Flu Pandemic (or Spanish flu) originated, within a year of its emergence in Europe it had infected a fifth of the world's population, including 28 percent of the U.S. population. The estimated total of victims ranges from twenty million to forty million.[77] It was called Spanish flu because, as a non-aligned country during World War I, Spain did not censor news reports, and the spread of flu there became well known in the world.

The 1918 flu was also the first truly global disease that spread as fast as the steamships and steam railways would carry people to the farthest corners of the world. Thousands of demobilized soldiers, who survived the most brutal war to date, returned home carrying the deadly infection that killed both them and their joyous family and friends. As most of the continents were by then connected by ocean liners and vast areas covered by railway networks, the flu spread out in every direction. Unlike the plague, which took three years to devastate populations from Central Asia to Europe, this flu did its damage across the world in a year and a half.

Another pandemic caused by an avian flu virus, known as an H2N2 strain, which had killed between one and four million people worldwide in 1957–58, threatened to rear its head again in early 2005. This time the threat was posed not by the emergence of a newly mutated strain but by the accidental worldwide distribution of that old strain. In late 2004 a private company, Meridian Bio-science, Inc., of Cincinnati, sent a parcel of virus samples to nearly four thousand laboratories and doctors' offices for testing as part of routine quality-control certification conducted by the College of American Pathologists. Unwittingly the samples included the H2N2 virus, against which people today have no immunity. On discovery of the mistake six months later, an alarmed World Health Organization sent out an urgent advisory to destroy the dangerous samples.[78]

When the next flu pandemic, SARS (severe acute respiratory syndrome), arose in 2003, it spread from southern China to South Africa and to Australia and Brazil in just six months. SARS originated in China's southern Guangdong province, where some diners enjoyed a meal of wild civet and along with their dinner ingested a newly mutated *Corona* virus (the cause of the common cold) against which humans had no immunity. One of the Chinese diners, bearing the highly contagious disease, went to Hong Kong and stayed in a hotel. One of the world's major tourist and business hubs was soon transformed into a giant disseminator of the world's most infectious disease. Less than a month after SARS claimed its first victim in Vietnam, the WHO issued a worldwide travel advisory. With its flight information board silently flashing CANCELLED, Hong Kong's cavernous Chek Lap Kok Airport looked desolate. Schools and businesses closed as frightened citizens in facemasks wondered if it was their turn. In a bid to prevent the spread of SARS, Beijing sealed off three hospitals and ordered nearly eight thousand people who might have been exposed to stay home. The Chinese capital's public schools, movie theaters, and discos were shut down. In Singapore wet markets were closed and hospital visits blocked. The most stringent quarantine procedures were set up at many of the world's ports and airports, and scientists in thirteen labs in ten countries raced to identify the new killer in search of an antidote.

Compared to the 2.5 percent morbidity rate of the Spanish flu, SARS was four times more virulent, killing 10 percent of its victims. Globally coordinated quarantine and preventive measures contained the virus, but only after it had caused 813 deaths in thirty countries, the vast majority in Hong Kong and mainland China.[79] Had the

WHO not issued its travel warning, and if not for the advances in science and medical surveillance and the extraordinary worldwide cooperation of scientists to identify the virus, SARS could have spread much further and faster than even the pandemic of 1918 did. Had the virus infected just 20 percent of China's population of 1.2 billion people, as many as 102 million would have died. Compared to the insignificant number of international travelers in 1918, by 2003 some 1.6 billion passengers took airplane flights, and a third of these crossed international borders, taking all manner of viruses with them on their journeys. In a race against the fast-spreading virus, scientists working in networked labs from Atlanta to Vancouver to Singapore stepped up their efforts to map the virus's genome, achieving this extraordinary feat within just one month. Thus, globalization not only gave viruses jet speed, but it accelerated the pace of countermeasures as well.

DISEASE WITHOUT BORDERS

At its annual meeting in May 2003, the WHO asserted that SARS is the first severe infectious disease to emerge in the twenty-first century and poses a serious threat to global health security, the livelihood of populations, the functioning of health systems, and the stability and growth of economies. Crossing international borders on jet airplanes and challenging the global health system, the SARS virus has been called "the first post-Westphalian pathogen."[80] The Treaty of Westphalia of 1648 marked the formal emergence of an international order based on sovereign rights within fixed borders and included public health measures. Although the great powers in Europe began international legal rules and diplomatic processes to facilitate cooperation on infectious diseases in 1851, international cooperation did not intrude much on state sovereignty. But with its advisories against visiting certain countries and its aggressive inspection regime, the WHO created a new phenomenon: the first-ever globalized response to a global disease. Even a go-it-alone President George W. Bush admitted the need for international cooperation and transparency. The lesson of the SARS experience is clear, he said: "We all have a common interest in working together to stop outbreaks of deadly new viruses—so we can save the lives of people on both sides of the Pacific."[81]

The worry that another post-Westphalian virus—that would spread like wildfire across international borders—may be brewing in the genome cauldron makes scientists worry because they now know that the deadly flu of 1918 was in its origin an avian flu.[82] In 1997, another flu crossed the species barrier in southern China, after a boy became infected by a flu common among chickens and ducks and eventually died. Since then, the so-called jumping strain of avian flu has spread beyond Hong Kong and southern China to infect chicken and bird populations in Cambodia, Indonesia, Thailand, Vietnam, Malaysia, Korea, and Japan and, by the end of 2006, had infected ninety-three humans, of whom forty-two died. The extraordinarily high morbidity rate of this avian flu—75 percent of those who caught the virus died (compared to less than 1 percent death in common human flu)—makes health officials shudder at the prospect of the avian flu's adapting itself for human-to-human transmission.[83] If SARS is any indicator, a transmuted virus of that type could spread across the world at the speed of a commercial jetliner and bring a catastrophe that would make the forty million flu deaths of 1918 look like a minor episode of early globalization.

The fact is that flu viruses mutate so quickly that an antidote for one variety may be useless for another. In collaboration with the WHO's Global Influenza Program, scientists in some 120 laboratories around the world have been constantly peering through their electron microscopes at new samples to detect any transmutation that could indicate that the flu has gained the ability to transmit among humans. Once convinced of the threat, the WHO can issue a travel advisory that could ground thousands of passenger planes crisscrossing the world's skies and quarantine entire cities or countries. This is a capability that did not exist when Black Death or Spanish flu ravaged the planet.

There is, however, no such international system of protection against another type of danger that lurks in the cyberspace.

VIRUS HUNTERS

It's late evening. The glow of the setting sun fades, and stars begin twinkling over the Pacific Ocean. But the lights are burning on the second floor of the glass-lined building of the Symantec Corporation. Banks of tall servers in glass-enclosed safe rooms glow eerily with blinking red LED lights in the software company's laboratory in Santa Monica, California. In an adjoining room, behind high partitioned cubicles, young men and women in tee-shirts and blue jeans peer intently into their screens. They come from different parts of the world and speak different languages, but they have one common goal in that quiet laboratory. They are trying to find the "signatures" of and antidotes to the newest viruses that the quietly blinking servers in the safe room have prescreened and spit out to them to fight. These young guardians of the Internet in Santa Monica and in other labs in different time zones are not fundamentally different from scientists in medical labs all over the world working with WHO. The scientists watch out for mutated flu viruses while the computer engineers scan the Web for deadly pathogens in cyberspace. The pathogens, deliberately created by humans, stalk nearly a billion computers worldwide, threatening the new highways of globalization. These malicious programs infect your computer, delete and alter your files, steal your data, and take over your machine to perform pernicious acts. To call the programs viruses is to give the natural ones a bad name. Invisible to the naked eye, biological viruses are simply doing the same basic jobs— survival and proliferation—that all life-forms struggle to do. The efforts of the Spanish flu virus and SARS to survive and proliferate by taking over hosts have been deadly to humans and other animals, but these natural viruses are not driven by malice or greed. Computer viruses function with greater intent; with each new technological innovation, some of our fellow human beings search for a way to exploit the innovation in order to steal, profit at another's expense, or simply hurt anonymous others out of sheer malice. The deliberate corruption of communications is by no means a twenty-first-century phenomenon unique to the Internet. Some of the first uses of the telegraph, for example, were to make illegal bets on horse races and to defraud unsuspecting citizens remitting money by cable. The use of computers has brought no exception to this tale of human malevolency.

There was, however, one major difference with other technologies; most technology historians agree that in the case of computers, life imitated art. In his novel *When HARLIE Was One* (1972), science fiction author David Gerrold came up with the idea of writing a rogue program and called it a virus.[84] More than a decade later, Fred Cohen, a bright graduate student at the University of Southern California, wrote as part of his class work the first program to replicate itself and self-propagate. His professor, impressed with its similarity to the biological phenomenon, suggested he call the program a "computer virus." Cohen proceeded to write his thesis on his invention and devoted his life to studying the new manmade viruses.[85] Computer lore has it that it was the Farooq Alvi brothers of Lahore, Pakistan, Amjad and Basit, who created the first worldwide virus program in 1986. Any time someone copied a software floppy disk from their computer store, a virus called Brain would place a copy of itself on the hard disk and issue a patent warning.[86]

Just as a virus in the natural world needs a host from which to extract sustenance in order to proliferate, the computer virus, too, needs a host. Before computers were connected by the Internet, the floppy disk was the vector for viruses traveling from computer to computer. Like the Pakistani virus Brain, most early computer viruses were pranks and show-offs. As the use of computers soared and the Internet created pathways, more virulent virus strains—called "malware"—proliferated. From playing a tune or displaying a funny message the viruses evolved to do nasty things like erasing your precious data and stealing your password and credit card information. New forms of malware appeared—from self-replicating viruses to worms that would install themselves in a computer and send out e-mail, to the Trojan horse, which, like the famous wooden horse of Troy that hid soldiers in its belly, pretended to do something benign but surreptitiously carried a malicious payload. A Trojan horse like Zelu, for instance, pretended to be a program that would fix the "millennium bug" but instead chewed up data from the hard drive.[87]

LOVE BITES

It was a typical summer day in 2000, when the cool interior of an office was more inviting than the color and smell of life in Hong Kong. But I was soon to find out that the cool and quiet of my office in Causeway Bay could not keep out the invasion of something unpleasant from a faraway place. I had returned from lunch and switched on the computer to check my e-mail. I had clicked on a few messages to read. Suddenly my inbox came to life with a message from someone I had no clue about. The intriguing missive with the subject line ILOVEYOU began a torrent. Within minutes, dozens of e-mails bearing the same enticing subject line were cascading down my monitor's screen. I immediately knew it was a virus attack and began block-deleting the messages that were rapidly filling up the screen. Soon the tech support manager, Vincent, poked his head through my office door, warned, "Don't open any ILOVEYOU message!" and scurried off. But the damage was done.

Some of my curious colleagues had clicked on the attachment and had given the not-so-loving e-mail access to their Outlook address books. Within minutes, hundreds of messages bearing the same profession of love had been squirted out of their computers headed for many destinations, ricocheting to computers thousands of miles apart. The virus had also begun carrying out its programmed task on the infected computers—destroying masses of data, image, and music files on the hard disk. As I learned later, it was a virus that didn't spare any user of e-mail. Singapore's powerful senior minister Lee Kuan Yew, who had only recently begun to use a computer to write his memoir, found an e-mail proclaiming love. He did not know the sender, but as he explained to me with an embarrassed laugh, "I was curious. Who would send me such a message?"[88] His computer was soon knocked out. His geek son, then Deputy Prime Minister Lee Hsien-Loong, who had coaxed him to embrace the computer, came over to disinfect the machine. Thousands of miles away, in Britain, the Parliament's computer system had to be shut down because curious members of Parliament had opened their e-mail and inadvertently sent out many more such infected missives. Throughout the day of May 4, 2000, the Love Bug tracked the path of the sun around the globe, erasing files and knocking out computer systems from Asia to Europe to the Americas. Investigators later traced the mayhem to twenty-four-year-old Onel de Guzman, a disgruntled Filipino hacker in Manila. "I hate to go to school," he wrote in a note with the malicious code, which was uploaded on one Internet server and sent out on its merry path of destruction.[89] In the course of its romp across cyberspace the Love Bug infected an estimated ten million computers worldwide, including terminals at the White House, the U.S. Congress, and the Pentagon, as well as at the British and Danish parliaments and at hundreds of European and American companies, causing, according to one estimate, economic damage worth ten billion dollars.[90]

The virus Code Red, launched in July 2001, was one of the first viruses that did not need any user interaction, no clicking on anything. It exploited a security hole in the computer's operating system and propagated itself from one computer to another through the Internet. It could infect your machine while you were sleeping. It took three weeks for a virus writer to exploit that security hole, Javier Santoyo of Symantec says, but "today that three week period has been reduced to 24 hours or less."[91] In less than fourteen hours on July 19, the Code Red worm infected 359,104 computers and servers all over the world. You can watch an animated depiction of the fast-spreading worm on the Internet.[92]

WATCHING FOR A ZERO-DAY VIRUS

In retrospect, despite the depredations of the Love Bug, it was almost an innocent prank. At the beginning, it was a matter of prestige for people who wrote virus programs. They could do something others could not. Now it is more and more motivated by profit. As the speed of the Internet has accelerated from dial-up connection to cable and DSL (digital subscriber line), so has the maliciousness of the Web-borne bugs. There are spyware programs that quietly reside in your computer and monitor what sites you visit or what you type. There are adware programs that constantly spam you with ads for cheap drugs and cheap hotels. Many computer users unknowingly have machines that have been taken over by a rogue program and turned into members of the army of slave computers that are constantly bombarding others with spam. There also are "phishing" programs that try to steal your bank and credit card information or your Social Security number. By being vigilant I had dodged the ILOVEYOU attack. But by 2004 the Internet had gotten much more troublesome and dangerous. I had been annoyed by the pop-up ads whenever I visited a Web site, but one winter morning in 2004 I could not even switch on my computer without cascading pop-up ads filling up my screen. The more I tried closing them the more popped up, covering up my monitor like college bulletin boards pasted over with notice after notice. But these were no notices for a lecture or a dance performance. These were advertisements for cheap Viagra and lottery tickets and cheap air tickets. The spyware that caused this nuisance had exploited loopholes in the Microsoft Web browser and secretly entered my hard disk to wait for the right stimuli to do their job. The result was wasted hours and frustration when I felt like picking up the damn thing and hurling it out the window. Thank you very much, globalization! How I missed my Olivetti typewriter.

In the end, I upgraded my computer's operating system and installed a whole slew of anti-spyware and anti-virus software to reclaim my computer. I was still luckier than many others whose computers had been seized by worms that deleted their files and stole their personal data without their ever suspecting anything amiss. Others have fallen for the bait used by "phishing" scammers who warn you about a security breach in your electronic banking and urge you to reactivate your closed account by providing them all your personal information.

You may have never heard of Cornell graduate student Robert Morris, Jr., Ching Ing-hau, a sergeant in the Taiwanese army, David Smith of New Jersey, Jan de Wit of the Netherlands, or for that matter a German teenager named Sven Jaschan, but their malicious creations have directly or indirectly affected computer users' lives worldwide. Morris created the so-called Morris Worm, which spread within days to about six thousand mainframes. The disgruntled Taiwanese army man's creation, the Chernobyl virus, erased an infected computer's hard drive. David Smith's Melissa virus in 1999 clogged up the mailbox, as did Jan de Wit's virus, named for Russian tennis star Anna Kournikova. From his home computer in the small town of Waffensen, German hacker Jaschan launched viruses that launched so-called denial-of-service attacks, which involved flooding target Web sites with data, causing them to crash. In the past twenty-five years some fifty-six thousand computer viruses and worms and Trojan horses have been released on the Internet, generating enough bumps and grinds on the path of globalization.[93] And they keep coming as the virus fighters sharpen their weapons.

You are unlikely to have met Yana Liu, the earnest young woman with large plastic-framed glasses and an easy smile who sits in front of two monitors in her cubicle at Symantec. A native of Chengdu, the capital of China's Sichuan province, she graduated from the University of Electronic Science and Technology of China before joining the antivirus software company's army of engineers. Hundreds like her work for such leading vendors as Symantec, Sophos, McAfee, and Trend Micro.

Each engineer can take from seven to thirty hours to find an antidote to the latest strain of malware.[94] They monitor the pattern of continuous attacks on clients' servers around the world, looking for what is known as a "zero-day virus." Once a virus is launched, it circles the world along the same path as the sun. In the morning, people wake up, open their Internet mailbox to check their messages, and innocently click on an attachment or open an e-mail, thus triggering the proliferation of the malicious virus. Often the virus is sent out to everyone in the address book on the computer, thus multiplying the virus at an accelerating rate. The task of engineers like Liu is to identify and decode the virus so that it does not have a chance to proliferate another day. The malicious software has to be killed before the sun goes down and the "zero-day virus" lives another day to infect millions more.

A CRIMINAL BAZAAR

The viruses that send out millions of spam messages or delete all the data on your hard drive are still relatively harmless compared to the hard-core criminal activity that has become the hallmark of the Internet. In 2004 *Business Week* magazine reported on a rare success scored by law enforcement against the cybercriminals who seem to operate with impunity in the Internet-connected world. The Federal Bureau of Investigation busted the aptly named cybercrime gang ShadowCrew after it had stolen nearly two million credit card numbers, accessed data from more than eighteen million e-mail accounts, and gathered identity data for thousands of people, including counterfeit British passports and U.S. driver's licenses. The FBI said that the gang, set up by a part-time student in Arizona and a New Jersey mortgage broker, ran the criminal equivalent of eBay in which they sold credit card numbers to four thousand members located throughout the world—from Bulgaria to Sweden. As one FBI official summed up the operation, "It was a criminal bazaar."[95]

ShadowCrew was only one of thousands of criminal gangs that prowl the Web. In January 2004 a new virus called MyDoom attacked the Web, installing Trojan horse software in unsuspecting computers. The malware later opened a secret door to the computer for MyDoom's author to steal credit numbers and banking information from any hard drive. By the time it was detected and stopped, MyDoom is reported to have caused $4.8 billion in damage. Another computer crime gang called HangUp, operating from Archangel, Russia, created a worm called Scob that pounced on visitors to certain sites to plant a program in their computer that spied on their keystrokes to copy and send thousands of passwords and credit card numbers to a server in Russia. As a biological virus takes over a host cell to proliferate, cybercriminals also seem to be on the lookout for countries that have weak cybercrime laws, poor enforcement, or official corruption. Thanks to the ease of operating in the high-speed Internet world, they can be located in one country and operate from servers in another country. Globalization has created a borderless world that allows me to order an iPod and have it delivered from across the ocean in a couple of days. Criminals can steal millions of credit card numbers to order much more expensive things in much shorter time. Banks and credit card companies that have been victimized do not want to admit their losses for fear of bad publicity. But according to a U.S. research firm, the total damage in 2004 from cybercrime was at least $17.5 billion, a record figure—and 30 percent higher than in 2003.

Globalization, like slavery, arouses great passion. Yet Madge Dresser, a lecturer at the University of West England, has not stopped at denouncing nineteenth-century globalization as responsible for human misery. The "slave trade," she said, "initiated globalization." In fact Dresser sees globalization as synonymous with slavery. "[Slavery] . . . epitomizes a most exploitative form of globalization, which has since resurfaced in new forms," she has written.[96] She is only partly right. As we have seen, globalization as a growing trend of connecting human societies and making them interdependent has been part of our history. The slave trade certainly played a major role in intensifying globalization, but the broad trend has meant much more than the enslavement of people. Globalization is not a morality play on a world scale. It is not the story of a ceaseless battle between the forces of good and evil. It is a never-ending saga in which the striving for a better life and greater security by millions of individuals manifests itself in the search for profit, for a livelihood, for knowledge, for inner peace, for protection for oneself, one's dear ones, and one's community. Humans' striving and searching have constantly led them to cross borders, both geographic and mental. The result of this unremitting process has been triumph for some and unbelievable misery and suffering for others. Slaves and slavers, the afflicted and the healers, the jobless and the new recruits—all have provided the warp and woof of the ever-changing texture of life and thereby created the world we know today.

The intensifying pace of human intercourse, trade, and communications has given wings to diseases and opened virtual doors to criminals and miscreants to take advantage of today's easy and fast communications. The communicable diseases that left their places of origin on trade caravans and ships and brought disasters now have new means to expand their reach and increase their speed. We have seen how the ceaseless search for knowledge and understanding of our physical world by scientists and engineers over centuries has brought us the microchip and the technology to connect with others at the speed of light. It would be ahistorical to think that the effect of this speed will always be for the good.

CHAPTER 13

Culture: The Glocal Game, Cosmopolitanism, and Americanization

Richard Giulanotti and Roland Robertson

INTRODUCTION

The cultural domain of globalization is highly debated within social science, primarily with reference to the question of agency and determination. Much debate concerns the analytical and empirical degrees of freedom that may be discerned in how local cultures engage with "the global." The arising arguments are often predicated upon conventional binary oppositions—notably between the local and the global, or the particular and the universal—and are flavored by a critical preference for one perspective over the other.[1] On one side, "cultural imperialism" arguments emphasize the determinant potency of global culture, particularly as manifested by Western (primarily American) institutions, which effectively circumscribes the critical agency of social actors at an everyday level (see, for example, Barber 1996; Latouche 1996; Ritzer 2004). Conversely, sociocultural and anthropological positions spotlight the creativity of social actors, including ways in which forms of local identity are purposively constructed "in resistance" to perceived global processes (see, for example, Hannerz 1996; Watson 1997; Tomlinson 1999; Pieterse 2007). We argue here that the most plausible perspectives on cultural globalization involve the integration of *both* of these standpoints. That is to say, social scientists need to appreciate the intensive analytical and empirical *interdependencies* of the global and the local, or the universal and the particular, when seeking to account for the complexity of cultural globalization.

Culture has been, for social scientists, the most substantially examined of all the aspects of football's globalization. Some analyses in the late 1960s and early 1970s implied that instrumental rationalization, coupled with monopoly capitalism and militaristic nationalism, had come to dominate sports culture, creating an oppressive and alienating environment for all participants (cf. Vinnai 1973; Brohm 1978; Rigauer 1981). However, from the late 1980s onward, much academic inquiry on the international aspects of football adopted a comparatively Herderian approach in exploring the distinctiveness of national football cultures, initially in Europe and Latin America, and subsequently at a more global level.[2] Particular transnational themes in football—such as the civic identities of clubs, or spectator-related violence—have provided highly fecund fields for comparative contrast and analysis. The spread of academic interest in football's international dimensions reflects a wider process of transnational exchange across the game, involving competitions, players, and finance. Most notably here, growing public and media interest in different football cultures has mushroomed, and has been reflected further in the transnational "hybridization" of young supporter fashions.

Our discussion of football's cultural globalization requires us to address analytical and substantive questions. Universalism–particularism, "relativization," and "homogenization–heterogenization" represent our initial analytical concerns, and enable us to develop our theorizations of "glocalization" and "duality of glocality" (cf. Giulianotti and Robertson 2007b). Through this analytical prism, we consider more contemporary or substantive football themes, including Americanization, cosmopolitanism, postmodernization, and nostalgia. Throughout, in broad terms, we seek to sustain the argument that, in cultural terms, the football/globalization nexus is a highly varied one in which multipolar influences are at play.

THE UNIVERSAL AND THE PARTICULAR

The interrelationships of the "universal" and the "particular" are central to football's cultural dimensions and, more generally, may be understood as "the elemental forms of global life" (Robertson 1992: 103, 1995). Any particular experience, identity, or social process is only comprehensible with reference to universal phenomena, and vice versa.

The "globewide nexus" of the particular and the universal gives rise to two interrelationships: the "universalization of particularism" and the "particularization of universalism" (Robertson 1990, 1992). First, the universalization of particularism "involves the extensive diffusion of the idea that there is virtually no limit to particularity, to uniqueness, to difference, and to otherness" (1992: 102). A "global valorization of particular identities" has intensified since the late nineteenth century, notably through principles of national identification that are underpinned by the international system. Major international football tournaments provide lively cultural arenas for the (re)production and interplay of national–societal particularities. Different national supporter groups converge and commingle, displaying their particularistic dresses, songs, and patterns of social behavior.

Second, the "particularization of universalism" involves the growing "concreteness" of the world in socio-political or "global-human" terms. This process is characterized by forms of global standardization and integration that differentiate societies along objective lines (Robertson 1990: 51–52). For example, nations are positioned within global systems of time (or time zones) or communication (such as through international telephone codes or Internet suffixes) (Robertson 1992: 102). International time-space categories were defined particularly during the take-off phase of globalization. In recent times, intensified social interconnectedness has accelerated the particularization of universalism, creating cultures of speed and immediacy wherein, for example, global communication networks enable financial markets or media transnational corporations (TNCs) to transmit information instantaneously (Tomlinson 2007).

In football, the particularization of universalism features the engagement of all institutions and actors within a pyramidal world system. The World Football Federation (FIFA) (and the International Football Association Board [IFAB]) sits at the apex, followed by the continental governing bodies, then national associations, regional and local associations, the various football clubs, and fans at the base, who literally "support" the entire edifice. Global standardization is secured through FIFA-endorsed football associations that have jurisdiction over national teams and implement the game's rules and procedures. Each nation is also located within, and helps to authorize, a world calendar of tournaments and fixtures.

These preliminary comments enable us to focus critically on commonplace assumptions regarding globalization. For example, public and academic discourses typically present "the local" and "the global" as fundamental binary opposites, as a kind of alpha and omega in the ontology of globalization (cf. Rowe 2003). Anxieties commonly arise when this binary opposition is blithely accepted, over whether the "global" is abolishing or subverting the "local" (Robertson 1992, 1995: 35). Conversely, more nuanced standpoints highlight the complex interdependencies between the local and the global.

Certainly, it might be argued that football, as a global cultural force that has been backed by potent colonial or corporate interests, has served to obliterate many local, indigenous games. In Africa, for example, Western sports were purposefully inculcated among local peoples, to the chagrin of many elders (Haruna and Abdullahi 1991; Bale and Sang 1996). Similarly, in Latin American nations such as Peru, football's social spread often coincided with the decline of traditional games such as *bochas* (Escobar 1969: 75).[3]

Nevertheless, within football, cultural exchanges between the local and the global are not unidirectional. Host societies are not passive recipients of global cultural content. Football's initial diffusion and subsequent popularization depended upon the positive reception by young males in diverse contexts. Indeed, football's "humankind" conflicts have typically featured excluded people struggling for opportunities and resources to engage in the game. Football has also enabled "local" cultures to explore fresh forms of particularity, for example through founding community clubs and developing specific styles of play.

Additionally, local cultures are not "fixed" in time and space. Rather, we need to explore the routes and roots of any culture; its mobility and its senses of "dwelling fixity" (cf. Clifford 1997), where, to borrow from John Cale, *homo sapiens* meets *hobo sapiens*. Over time, local cultures undergo processes of deterritorialization and reterritorialization. Deterritorialization relates particularly to the weakening spatial connections of cultural practices, identities, products, and communities. Strongly influenced by transnational migration and mediatization, deterritorialization processes are exemplified by Asians in Canada or Chicanos along the US–Mexico border (Canclini 1995; Appadurai 1998). Deterritorialization is accelerated in dromomanic developed nations, where national and transnational mobility is deeply entrenched. Yet, deterritorialized individuals and groups do not submerge themselves in a meaningless cultural mélange, but instead manufacture new "homes" and senses of located cultural identity: in other words, *re*territorialization occurs, abetted by the crucial resources of electronic media.

In football, deterritorialization is historically problematic. Leading clubs are historically *rooted* in communities (through stadium location, civic engagement, and regional symbolism), but the *routes* of team lore and allegiance are spread through migration and mediatization. For example, Liverpool football club is anchored in the eponymous city, with a cultural identity that claims to retain strong local "structures of feeling," in deliberate contrast to more globalist rivals, Manchester United (cf. Williams et al. 2001).[4] However, deterritorialization processes are evidenced by Liverpool's national and worldwide following since the 1970s, the dominance of mainland European players and coaches from the late 1990s, and the club's ownership by two American sports entrepreneurs.

The increasingly complex and uncertain contours of support for national teams further reveal deterritorialization processes. Nations with large migrant populations inspire internationally diffuse support for their football teams; thus, Irish President Mary Robinson claimed in 1994 that she and the national football team represented "the modern Ireland" which included Irish citizens and the children of the diaspora (Giulianotti 1996: 339). Similarly, among players, post-colonial and diasporic movements can highlight the complex ties between residency, nationality, and ethno-national identity. For example, in Paris, a "friendly match" in late 2001 between France and Algeria reportedly saw the erstwhile "visiting team" field more French-born players than the home nation.

The deterritorializing of national symbols is advanced by the international televising of some fixtures, and by football's interpenetration with other popular cultural fields. International tournaments attract wide interest across external nations and regions: for example, the Union of European Football Associations (UEFA) claimed that Euro 2004 was viewed by cumulative audiences of nearly 450 million in North America, 1 billion in Africa, and 1.1 billion in Asia.[5] Contemporary consumerism promotes diverse forms of national identification, such as through the transnational retail of replica shirts and kits. Since the late 1990s, UK fashion chains have produced many styles that imitate "classic" national football attire, with "Italia," "USSR," "Brasil" and other national signifiers emblazoned across clothing.

In these circumstances, "reterritorializing" processes acquire particular salience. Through reterritorialization, claims of cultural ownership are formulated so that even transient or migrant groups inscribe geographical marks upon their identities. On occasions when clubs "move home," reterritorialization occurs as supporters give fresh and intimate meanings to their new stadiums.[6] More potent reterritorializing occurs when supporters establish social clubs in distant settings. In southern Ontario, for example, leading English, Scottish, and Italian clubs have strong presences, with Celtic and Rangers fans boasting their own plush social clubs and memberships of over four hundred (Giulianotti 2005; Giulianotti and Robertson

2005, 2007a). More generally, the spectator cultures at leading clubs undergo continuing relativization and revitalization, typically attracting more fluid or "cosmopolitan" followers to fresh forms of sporting diversity (cf. Cowen 2002: 134). Additionally, complex de-/re-territorializing processes underpin the pride that many nations have in regard to their foreign players. For example, imported talents such as Henry, Viera, Ginola (all France), and Zola (Italy) became national celebrities in the UK, were prized for legitimizing and enhancing the domestic game within the global context, and were lauded for their general acculturation (for example, in adapting to playing styles or building particular relations with media corporations).

Clubs endeavor to reterritorialize by claiming spatial meaning for themselves in distant settings. Consider, for example, the Asian "club shops" opened by Manchester United or the summer tours of Asia and North America that are undertaken by leading European sides. Crucially, reterritorialization is not uncontested. The established, "territorialized" supporters may object to the privileges granted to outside followers. Thus, Manchester United fans based in northwest England differentiate themselves from southern-based supporters; and even among Scandinavian fans of English teams there are distinctions between long-standing and more "touristic" supporters (Brick 2001; Heinonen 2005). Thus, different social groups contest the meaning of the "local" within the global game.

RELATIVIZATION

The concept of *relativization* illuminates further the local–global interrelationship, disclosing in particular the increasingly reflexive contrasts between "local" cultures. Relativization reveals how globalization brings cultures into sharper reflexive and comparative focus, thereby compelling these cultures to respond to each other in an ever-amplifying manner across the universal domain. Indeed, in our view, it is comparison with others that makes reflexivity a possibility. Relativization also involves particular entities being shaped by the elemental reference points of individuals, national societies, international relations, and humankind (Robertson and Chirico 1985). Thus, any "national" football culture will acquire particular coherence, as a relativized entity, from interrelationships between individual citizens, the international football system, and themes of shared (or variegated) humanity.

We may unpack the interrelations of these elemental reference points with reference to Brazil's football culture and the wider society. On *individuals,* we may connect Brazil's individualistic styles of play (notably dribbling and deception) to the streetwise *malandro* (or artful rogue) who survives in Brazilian *favelas* (DaMatta 1991), or to the political power of *cartolas* ("big hats") inside football functionaries who personify the nation's dense patronage networks. In regard to *international relations,* we may tie Brazil's status in football competitions and FIFA to greater political coherence across "Third World" societies, and to transnational connectivity through the mass media and long-distance transport. With respect to *humanity,* we might explore how Brazilian football successes symbolized a sporting "pedagogy of the oppressed," showcasing the struggles of marginalized groups to participate, to express themselves, to represent "the nation" (cf. Freyre 1963; Freire 1970).

The particular Brazilian context was infused by diverse, often conflicting, social forces. On one side stood a national history of brutal colonization, charismatic authoritarianism, and rigid "racial" stratification. Beneath official discourses that have celebrated the "multi-racial democracy," there lurks an elitist and statist commitment to "whitening" the black population (Robertson 1998).[7] Yet, on the other side, a populist ideology remains, which venerates "racial hybridity," social informality, and the vibrancy of mass participation in national events. When considering the other three reference points, we gain a fuller understanding of Brazil as a *nation,* within football, as registered further by national styles of play and a fully national focus on the *seleçao* (the Brazilian national team). The nation is further revealed by football's role in constructing modem Brazilian identity, through mass media, education, language, and popular culture.

Reflection on Brazilian football also helps to challenge assumptions about uniformity and homogeneity in regard to national cultures. Brazilian football is instead a highly varied realm with complex, multidimensional relationships to the wider society. In terms of playing styles, significant variations arise between major cities, while national debates occur over the expressive *futebol-arte* or the physical *futebol-força* methods.[8] Additionally, Brazilian football does not passively reflect the national society, but represents an extraordinary domain of mass participation and global cultural success, in contrast to a painfully stratified and still-underdeveloped society.[9]

Analysis of specific football episodes helps to reveal the complex forces that are at play among the various elemental reference points within and beyond the game. Consider, for example, the visit to violence-torn Haiti by the Brazilian national team to play an exhibition match in August 2004. The event was promoted by the Brazilian Football Confederation (CBF) (national elemental reference point, football institution), Brazilian government (national, non-football), United Nations (international relations, non-football), and FIFA (international relations, football). The billed "Football for Peace" visit helped to promote the game's universalistic claims (international relations/humankind, football), carried a global humanitarian message (humanity, non-football), and advanced the standings of the Brazilian president, his government, and the UN (individual/nation/international relations, non-football). Despite pressures from the president (individual, non-football) and governing bodies (nation/international relations, football), some European clubs (international relations, football) refused to release their Brazilian players (individuals, football) to participate. These players were then dropped from Brazil's side for the next fixture (individual/nation, football). The Haiti visit fostered Brazilian pride in the team's global status (nation/international relations, football) while enhancing Brazil's standing in the UN and specific pursuit of a permanent seat on the Security Council (international relations, non-football); yet the visit also drew criticisms that the nation itself faced huge domestic problems (nation/international relations/humankind, non-football). All in all, this single match demonstrated the complex layers of relationship that arise between football and the wider social order.

The concept of relativization also facilitates a clearer understanding of particular "defense of the local" or anti-globalist discourses. These arguments are deployed, for example, to challenge global influences upon indigenous playing techniques, such as when European coaches impose their methods upon African players. But as definite cultural responses to transnational processes, these discourses emerge from relativization processes and serve to advance particular understandings of "the local" per se vis-à-vis alternative meanings.

More simplistic "defense of the local" discourses assume that global flows are largely unidirectional, from international society into particular nations or continents. Yet, even in settings where local identities are strongly sustained, complex matrices of relativization serve to mold and refashion "the local." For example, to return to Brazil, it may seem initially that "the local" (in this case, national) playing style is an uncontested concept, in being renowned globally as highly expressive, aesthetically pleasing, and indicative of a unique, "Lusotropical" national society (cf. Freyre 1963). However, Brazilian football history reveals a rather more complex story, with the national team having long been influenced by European sides and tactical systems. In the 1970s, the Brazilians explored Dutch "total football" (itself something of an invented concept), then switched to a "native" style in the 1980s. Lack of competitive success then sparked a move to a cautious, quasi-Italian style in the 1990s; victories at the 1994 and 2002 World Cup finals thereby featured tactical caution, defensive solidity, and occasional improvisational brilliance. Thus, over three decades, the "local" Brazilian style was recast and relativized in a variety of complex ways.

We should note too that relativization processes produce very different emphases on the assertion of the local, depending upon the particular societies or the social practices in question. In most nations, formidable relativization is apparent in the nationalistic rituals of football spectators, but is perhaps less apparent in regard to national styles of play. In South America, nations that understand themselves in terms of particular "schools" of play include Argentina (*criollo* style), Brazil (balletic, spectacular), and Colombia (intricate short passing); conversely, Chile, Paraguay, and Uruguay tend not to advance these local-making assertions, although they tend to compensate by advocating strongly competitive virtues (such as the brave combative methods of Paraguay's *guarani*).

HOMOGENIZATION–HETEROGENIZATION

We turn now to an axial problem in the sociology of globalization, namely the homogenization–heterogenization debate. Homogenization arguments generally posit that globalization is marked by growing cultural convergence at the transnational level. Conversely, heterogenization arguments contend that global processes maintain or facilitate cultural diversity or divergence. The rival "schools of thought" tend not to strike absolutist poses—for example, most homogenization theorists recognize significant instances of cultural diversification—yet the broad differences between the two sides remain intact. In the following discussion, we consider homogenization theories before exploring the heterogenization position.

Homogenization

Homogenization theories posit that social actors and their local cultures are orchestrated into passively absorbing or otherwise reproducing the cultural products, practices, and predilections of the world's most powerful corporations and nations. Perhaps ironically, these theories of global cultural convergence have produced a diversity of keywords and theories, such as cultural imperialism, synchronization, Americanization, Westernization, and grobalization (Schiller 1969; Hamelink 1983; Tomlinson 1991; Latouche 1996; Ritzer 2004).

Early convergence arguments emerged in the preliminary analysis of global mass communications. McLuhan (1964) is widely credited with initially exploring the possible genesis of a "global village" through heightened forms of media connectivity. However, we should recall that McLuhan did appreciate the complexity of contemporary international politics by noting the magnitude of global conflicts and East/West cultural differences (McLuhan and Fiore 1989).

However, other writers on global communications have argued that political–economic rather than cultural–technological factors lie behind global cultural convergence. Schiller (1976: 9), for example, contends that Western media corporations are rapacious, culturally imperialistic forces that dominated international markets, such that, in Wallersteinian language, "a largely one-directional flow of information from core to periphery represents the reality of power" (1976: 6). Hamelink (1983, 1994, 1995) highlights the global diffusion of Americanized consumer lifestyles and products through corporations like McDonald's and Disney (Hamelink 1995: 111). Thus, even in Mexican football, Hamelink reports the symbolic importance of Coca-Cola to pre-match rituals (noted in Tomlinson 1999: 109). Overall, he contends that Western corporations "reduce local cultural space" by controlling negative information and obstructing indigenous initiatives.

Homogenization theorists argue that, when TNCs micro-market their products, little meaningful engagement occurs with local cultures. Thus, while Western media corporations translate their programmes into local languages, the substance remains alien to peripheral cultures and must still "bear the ideological imprint of the main centers of the capitalist world economy" (Schiller 1976: 10). Hamelink (1995: 113) argues that such adaptations merely ensnare "consumers, particularly young ones, to watch programmes and in the process influence their tastes, lifestyles, and moral values."

In turn, these theorists celebrate episodes and strategies of cultural resistance toward media imperialism. France and the European Commission have sought to protect indigenous film and cultural industries from the worldwide "flood" of cheap, low-grade American media products (Hamelink 1994: 180–81, 1995: 114).[10] Schiller (1976: 106–109) advocates popular public participation in alternative forms of mass communication, which Hamelink (1994) understands as a contemporary human right.

Sports broadcasting provides some evidence for this strand of homogenization theory. Most obviously, television TNCs and powerful European football systems (such as *Serie A,* the EPL, UEFA) ensure that images of major continental tournaments are beamed remorselessly into developing societies, notably Africa, East Asia, and even South America. The core-to-periphery flow of media content is very rarely reversed, for example through live UK screening of Latin American fixtures. In turn, TNCs advertise their standardized products, and the generalized Western consumerist lifestyle, to football audiences across developing nations (cf. Sklair 2002).

However, staunch applications of homogenization theory can stretch the cultural evidence. Importantly, some reverse flows do occur across global and "mini-global" plains. For example, Argentinian and Brazilian leagues attract international interest, particularly across Iberia for obvious ethno-historical reasons. In non-core football nations, television stations add crucial contextualization and "vernacularization" to their coverage of leading European or South American fixtures (cf. Appadurai 1998). Thus, for example, in South Korea, local television stations have their own studio discussions and commentators to interpret English Premier League matches; special attention is paid, wherever possible, to the performances of Korean players.

Some homogenization arguments might borrow from Wallerstein (1974, 2000) to differentiate "core" (high-income), "peripheral" (low-income) and "semi-peripheral" (middle-income) societies, but it is problematic to translate these categories directly into world football. For example, core global nations like the United States and Japan have semi-peripheral football systems that rarely grace European television screens. Similar hazards surround the core/semi-peripheral classification of small Western European national league systems.

Where football does fit Wallerstein's categories, the vitality of "peripheral" nations is still evidenced, for example by the state subsidizing of national teams or airing of local sports events on television. In football, as in the wider context, national groups are more focused on the challenge from neighboring or historically significant "others," rather than "core" nations as a whole. For Argentinians, fixtures against Brazil germinate the strongest sentiments; for the Dutch, it is the German game; for the Chinese or South Koreans, it is the Japanese; and for the Scots, it is the English. Moreover, core nations have themselves become at least partly "peripheralized" through the mass entry and settlement of peoples from developing nations. Thus, in football, we find Zimbabwean sides in England, or North African teams in France, playing friendly fixtures before thousands of local and migrant spectators.

We may ask, too, when elite European leagues are being watched by African or Asian populations, whether the homogenization thesis provides the most plausible explanation. To those with little football engagement, it may appear so. However, if we appreciate that viewers critically engage with television content, and that many will be inured in football's cultural complexities, then an alternative judgment is fairer: that these audiences have, quite rationally, chosen to view and to appreciate the world's most aesthetic, technically sophisticated displays of football skill. Indeed, young players actively seek to imitate and emulate these global talents, thus football's diverse aesthetic and technical qualities hold a stronger currency than its simple consumerist adjuncts.

Finally, the homogenization thesis is far less controversial when explaining aspects of the "particularization of universalism" which, in short, gives rise to global similarities that structure national differences. Some insightful convergence arguments identify a transnational social isomorphism across nation states whereby national identities, practices, and structures are constructed according to universal standards and procedures (Robertson 1995: 30–1; Meyer et al. 1997). In football, such convergence is evidenced in the standardized structures of *particular* national football associations, league systems, and calendars of competition.

Heterogenization

Theories of cultural heterogenization pivot on a variety of keywords, notably "creolization," "indigenization," and "vernacularization." To begin considering these, the concept of "creolization" describes the "creative interplays" between cultural cores and peripheries, creating creole cultural forms and rhizomic identities, such as in language, cuisine, and film (Hannerz 1992: 264–6; Vergès 2001: 179). For Hannerz, creolization enables the periphery to "talk back" to the center, for example as Third World music becomes "world music," or "ghetto" phrases enter mainstream society.

In football, cross-civilizational exchanges fire intensive creolization processes. For example, Western observers are often struck by Asian football cultural values and practices that, in contrast to Europe and South America, emphasize consensus, orderliness, and politeness (see Moffett 2003). In Africa, Levi-Strauss (1966: 31) noted that the Gahuku-Gama people of New Guinea ritualized football in accordance with indigenous values, wherein the social humiliation of defeat was purposively alleviated by staging fixtures on consecutive days, thereby providing losers with further chances to win (Bromberger 1995: 299). Football's popular history has many wider instances whereby the periphery "talks back" to the center, for example when South Americans developed particular technical skills (for instance, the *chilena* or "bicycle kick," or the swerving free kick) that were then mimicked in "core" European nations.

Problematically, creolization implies that, prior to the making of creole cultural forms, there existed authentic and sharply distinctive "core" and "peripheral" phenomena. Alternatively, creolization features the interplay of already creolized cultural forms. Thus, in football, for example, it is impossible to trace the histories of playing styles back to particular, autonomously generated national techniques and philosophies.

For Friedman (1999), the alternative concept of "indigenization" portrays center–periphery relationships in more cultural political terms. Particularly for developed societies, indigenization registers "an increasing fragmentation of identities, the break-up of larger identity units, the emergence of cultural politics among indigenous, regional, immigrant, and even national populations" (Friedman 1999: 391). In football, indigenization is evidenced in the strategic resistance of Western Europe's ethnic minorities toward their racial abuse, and in their intensification of ethnonationalist or regionalist identities at clubs in southern Europe and Australia.

The idea of "vernacularization" is deployed by Appadurai (1998) to explain the discursive "domestication" that occurs within general cultural forms, including sport. Appadurai explores how Indians have "vernacularized" cricket, "hijacking" the quintessential English imperial sport, notably through television commentaries; meanwhile, "the game is inscribed in particular ways upon local male bodies" to become "an emblem of Indian nationhood" (1998: 103, 112). This conception of local–global processes has notable continuities with the Japanese concept of *dochakuka* (or "glocalization"), discussed later in this chapter.

Similar observations may be advanced regarding football, notably in explaining how television has served to narrate and to popularize distinctive playing styles across nations, especially in South America.

For Pieterse (1995), "hybridization" describes the mixing of cultures and the move toward translocal cultural forms that range from diasporic communities to cyborg beings and virtual reality. Cultural hybridity is identifiable in particular in the "global mélange," for example through "fusion food" or cross-cultural artistic ventures, and helps to foreground the shift from anti-colonial to postcolonial social orders (Pieterse 2007: 142–3). By way of criticism, we may note that the concept of hybridization harbors some potentially risky biological metaphors (Beck 2004: 26), and may promote the false assumption that phenomena which are "hybridized" had been initially in a state of distinctive cultural purity. However, the concept of hybridization has been deployed most effectively by Archetti (1998) to explain the construction of cultural identities in the New World, particularly in relation to football in Argentina, wherein the vibrancy of a hybrid society receives translucent expression in sport.

Evidently, each concept is persuasively founded upon substantial research, particularly in peripheral contexts, and encapsulates the agency of quotidian social actors in critically engaging with and transforming global cultural phenomena. However, we forward four caveats for utilization of these terms.

First, noteworthy differences in emphasis and position exist between these keywords—for example, indigenization foregrounds the centrifugal nature of cultural politics in developed societies, while vernacularization illuminates the linguistic and (by extension) corporeal aspects of cultural appropriation.

Second, we should dispute the assumption that societies which ground football are themselves homogeneous entities. Alternatively, for example, Latin American societies are highly variegated, mobile, and dynamic social formations that, in turn, formulate diverse and contested kinds of football-centered practices and beliefs (cf. Leite Lopes 1999: 89–90).

Third, emphasis upon processes of improvisation and heterogenization does not preclude consideration of socio-economic influences and themes. In football, for example, some commentators have interpreted the dribbling skills of lower-class Brazilian players to be both a sporting extension of the street-wise habitus and a crucial component of public theater within a highly stratified society, wherein the oppressed defeat their oppressors and so are acclaimed as heroes. Similarly, albeit somewhat reductively, some European coaches attribute the individualism of African players to wider problems of daily survival in the poorest locales.

Finally, there are important regional and indeed "civilizational" differences in the way in which these processes come into play. In historical terms, multiple modernities or multiple globalizations may be said to have occurred (see Arnason 1991, 2001; Wagner 2000). Therborn (1995), for example, has argued that modernity developed relatively autonomously in four major sites: in *Europe*, where revolution or reform involved "endogenous change"; in the *New World*, where transcontinental migration, genocide, and independence occurred; in large parts of the *Middle* and *Far East*, where much modernization was viewed as an external threat or fit for selective importation; and, in most of *Africa, southern and southeast Asia*, where modernity brought conquest, subjugation, and colonialism. Thus, football's spread throughout Europe was symptomatic of the continent's endogenous modern development; the game's limited entry to the New World (specifically, North America) reflected the cultural differentiation of settler populations; its uneven penetration of the Middle and Far East reflected selective cultural importation strategies; and its highly localized relevance in Africa and southern Asia reflected the subjugated position of the indigenous peoples. Thus, at least in the early twentieth century, creolization, vernacularization, and indigenization functioned in different ways within these contexts: for example, with little impact in the Middle and Far East, but with rich vitality in Europe and in South America.

GLOCALIZATION

Ritzer: The Grobal and the Glocal

The homogenization–heterogenization debate has made a significant advance through the work of Ritzer (2003, 2004) on the globalization of culture. Ritzer's thesis is largely built around his binary opposition of the keywords "grobalization" and "glocalization." "Grobalization" describes a sweeping process of homogenization, wherein the powerful subprocesses of "capitalism, Americanization and McDonaldization" overwhelm the indigenous cultures of local individuals and social groups (2004: 73). Conversely, the idea of "glocalization," for Ritzer, encaptures an increasingly heterogeneous world, wherein individuals and social groups are intensively innovative and creative in their dealings with global culture.[11] Ritzer's binary opposition has significant continuities with earlier theories, notably the Jihad/McWorld couplet advanced by Barber (1992, 1996).

Ritzer's grobal/glocal binary represents the two extreme poles on an ideal–typical continuum; in reality, most cultural commodities fall somewhere between the two ends. He concludes, pessimistically, that local cultures typically fail to resist grobalization processes. He accepts too that his standpoint is "both elitist and incurably romantic, nostalgic about the past" in its veneration of particular local cultural commodities (2004: 213).

Ritzer's analysis does benefit from its succinct case studies of cultural production and consumption, and its critical empathy for struggles against dehumanizing rationalization processes. However, we identify four particular differences between his position and our own. First, while his grobal–glocal continuum has significant continuities with our position on universalism/particularism, we adopt a longer-term view of globalization's impact upon, and construction of, "the local."

Second, Ritzer's analysis may underplay the highly varied ways in which McDonald's restaurants, or other paragons of rationalization, have originated or been introduced within different historical and cultural contexts. The modus operandi of McDonald's restaurants was in significant part inspired by the White Castle fast-food chain founded in 1921 (Steel 2008: 233–6). Moreover, different social practices and cultural impacts obtain in McDonald's restaurants in Asia compared to North America; for example, in terms of unseated customers "hovering" at tables, or promoting hygiene standards across all local restaurants (cf. Watson 1997).

Third, Ritzer's analysis is restricted to cultural *commodities*, and so omits to explore fully cultural *meanings* and *institutions*. Indeed, we might argue that his emphasis on cultural commodities may itself be understood as a distinctively American interpretation (or "glocalization") of the homogenization/heterogenization debate.[12] Football highlights some of the analytical limitations to this focus on commodities. As we have noted, any football-playing social grouping will produce varied cultural innovations—most obviously in playing styles—that reflect its particular "ethos," and which are more generally indicative of the *multidimensionality* of globalization.[13]

To substantiate this criticism, we may begin by noting that club football reveals a continuing cross-cultural diversity of institutional frameworks and practices. For example, traditional match days fall on Sundays in much of southern Europe, but on Saturdays in the north. In Spain, football matches frequently kick off far later in the evening than would be permissible in northern Europe. Since the late 1990s, many South and Central American nations feature two league championships inside one season, usually with play-offs to determine the overall champions. Conversely, in Europe, the standard one-championship season remains intact, although nations differ significantly over their format (for example, teams may play two, three, or four times each season) and calendar (for example, many European nations have winter breaks of varying length). In Europe, the team coach is responsible for training senior players, team selection, and tactics, while the general manager conducts player negotiations and other organizational business. In the United Kingdom, by contrast, both roles have traditionally fallen to the team manager, although assistant managers and coaches provide back-up. In southern Europe and Latin America, autocratic club presidents can produce extremely high turnovers of managers and players, whereas in northern Europe, managers have tended to be more secure.[14] UK and South American players (most obviously Brazilians) are more renowned for significant drinking or party cultures, unlike Scandinavian or southern European talents. In Italy and Latin America, the entire team typically spends the eve of fixtures together, in practices known as *ritiro* or *la concentratión*, but in northern Europe players only tend to congregate on match day. These and numerous other diverging institutional frameworks and practices are integral to football's culture, but would be overlooked if analysis were restricted to commercial issues.

Fourth, crucially, we differ with Ritzer on the meaning of glocalization. Whereas Ritzer associates glocalization with processes of heterogenization and critical social agency, we understand the term as featuring the possibility of *both* homogeneity and heterogeneity, as we explain next.

Glocalization and the "Duality of Glocality"

It is useful to consider the historical and social-scientific development of the concept of glocalization. The word *glocalization* itself may be traced to the Japanese term *dochakuka*, meaning "global localization" or "localized globalization," which was widely used in business circles in the late 1980s to describe the micro-marketing techniques of Sony and other companies, whereby generic products and industrial practices are adapted to suit local conditions (cf. Dicken and Miyamachi 1998: 73; Rothacher 2004: 185, 189).[15] Subsequently established as "one of the main marketing buzzwords of the beginning of the nineties," glocalization appeared in recent times to underpin the advertising discourses of TNCs like HSBC, which projected itself as "the world's local bank" (*Oxford Dictionary of New Words* 1991: 134, quoted in Robertson 1992: 174; cf. Gertler 1992: 268).

In football, this original form of glocalization is evident in club and league marketing. For example, some European clubs recruit players from the United States or East Asia in part to build consumer/fan bases in these regions. In the United States, Major League Soccer (MLS), which controls the professional club system, has sought to boost crowds by micro-marketing to Latinos in California, notably by having the popular Mexican club Guadalajara open a U.S. "franchise."

The social scientists Robertson and Swyngedouw developed the concept of glocalization at around the same time in separate and different ways in the early 1990s. For urban political economists, glocalization has come to describe the rescaling and intensified complexity of networks and systems, notably in the interrelationships between institutional actors at subnational, national, and supranational levels (Swyngedouw 1992, 2004; Brenner 1998, 2004). Despite complaints that glocalization is inconsistently defined and applied within this field, the "scalar" approach certainly chimes with related arguments on the "cascading" and "turbulence" of global politics (Rosenau 1990; Jessop and Sum 2000). In socio-cultural theory, Robertson (1992, 1994, 1995, 2007) introduced the concept of glocalization in part to update the old anthropological theory of cultural diffusion by allowing for the intensification of social connectivity and stronger forms of global consciousness. Capturing the broad interplay of the universal and the particular, glocalization registers the "real world" endeavors of individuals and social groups to ground or to recontextualize global phenomena or macroscopic processes with respect to local cultures (Robertson 1992: 173–4, 1994, 1995). Thus, "glocalization projects," as practiced by different cultures, represent "the constitutive features of contemporary globalization" (Robertson 1995: 41). Long-running processes of transnational commingling and interpenetration have resulted in a profusion of "glocal" cultures, such that the old binary distinction between "here-it-is" local and "out-there" global cultures becomes increasingly untenable.

Both socio-cultural and urban political–economic theories of glocalization have significant continuities with Rosenau's (2003) concept of "fragmegration," which notes the simultaneously fragmenting and integrating forces of globalization. Moreover, our interpretation of glocalization has strong elective affinities to the theorization of relativization set out previously in this chapter (see Robertson 1992, 1995).

In some contrast to Ritzer, our socio-cultural reading of glocalization allows for the production of both cultural divergence *and* convergence, or homogenization *and* heterogenization (Robertson 1995; cf. Ritzer 2004: 73). In other words, a *duality of glocality* is apparent, which foregrounds the societal co-presence of sameness and difference, and the "mutually implicative" relationships between homogenizing and heterogenizing tendencies (Robertson and White 2003: 4; Giulianotti and Robertson 2007a, 2007b). Notably, Ritzer (2004: 73) himself recognized that, in earlier work, Robertson "is certainly interested in both sides of the local–global, homogenization–heterogenization continua." We recognize, of course, that much social-scientific discussion on glocalization has focused hitherto on the heterogenization side, partly to rebut more reductive arguments regarding cultural homogenization. Yet, as Miller et al. (1999: 19) put it, glocalization is an important term "because global forces do not override locality, and because homogenization and heterogenization are equally crucial." Hence, we concur with Cowen's (2002: 16, 129) observation that "cultural homogenization and heterogenization are not alternatives or substitutes; rather, they tend to come together" and frequently produce cultures that are "commonly diverse."

Duality of Glocality and Football

Football provides a rich substantive field for exploring the complex "duality of glocality" in regard to convergence and divergence. If we examine the game historically in regard to the five phases, we may identify how football's global diffusion has been underpinned by different interrelationships between the universal and the particular.

During football's *germinal* and *incipient* phases, football's initial diffusion was facilitated through social contacts with the British and its cultural appeal to Anglophile local elites. In more extreme circumstances, some cultures marginalized football to develop alternative national sports.

During the *take-off* phase (the 1870s to the mid-1920s), upon its favorable cultural reception, football was glocalized through a universalization of particularism. Specific local cultures worked inside the game's universal rules to establish their own football "traditions," as illustrated by distinctive corporeal techniques, playing styles, aesthetic codes, administrative structures, and interpretative vocabularies.

During the *struggle-for-hegemony* phase (the 1920s to the late 1960s), football's glocalization also featured a particularization of universalism, as international tournaments and governing bodies were established, and as standardized national football institutions were created across the world, notably through affiliation with FIFA.

During the *uncertainty* phase (the 1970s to the early 2000s), glocalization processes were accelerated by intensified transcultural flows of labour, information, capital, and commodities, all of which may engender non-national forms of cultural identity. Glocalization registered stronger forms of global compression, thus the world appears as a kind of cultural switchboard, as different identity forms come more frequently into mutual co-presence.

Football provides many specific case studies for unraveling the "duality of glocality" in regard to homogenization and heterogenization. Here, we provide four illustrations of such interdependency in regard to laws, belief systems, media framing and interpretation of matches, and playing styles.

First, homogenization is evidenced in the global diffusion of football's *laws*, and in FIFA's endeavor to synchronize the interpretations of different national referees, for example by running intensive courses for officials before each World Cup finals. As one English official concluded, "There is no such thing as an English, Italian or French football set of rules. There is one football and one set of rules." Similar convergence strategies have been evidenced by FIFA's "Fair Play" slogan, which appeals globally to the ethical consciousness of football participants. According to Sepp Blatter, the Fair Play "catchphrase" is "a welcome intruder into all languages and cultures," and has "succeeded in building bridges across communication and cultural gaps."

However, significant pressures toward cultural divergence remain intact. On rule interpretation, UK referees, for example, continue to permit robust challenges that central and southern European officials tend to penalize. FIFA's own research revealed significant differences among European players over the parameters of "fair play": German and French players disagreed over the moral status of "revenge fouls" or "professional fouls" that prevented goals being scored, while English players were particularly intolerant of players who faked injuries.[16]

Second, *religious and supernatural belief systems* display significant forms of convergence and divergence. Players, teams, and fans in many cultures utilize religious divination to help secure their goals, but there are obviously significant cultural differences on this matter. In Europe, many players have their own distinctive pre-match superstitions, such as eating particular meals, wearing lucky amulets, or being last onto the pitch. In Latin America, notably Brazil, the remarkable growth of evangelical and Pentecostal religious movements has directly impacted upon grassroots football culture. The "Athletes for Christ" movement in Brazil has an estimated seven thousand members, most of them footballers, including *seleção* stars Kaka, Jorginho, Mazinho, Lucio, Edmilson, and Taffarel (Bellos 2002: 219). Members of this movement celebrate goals and victories with the display of proselytizing messages, such as "God Loves You."

In some contrast, in sub-Saharan Africa, witchcraft or *juju* practices are more prominent, as teams seek to deflate the energies of opponents, or to ward off malignant spirits, for example by wearing certain amulets, carrying human or animal bones to games, casting spells on the pitch before kick-off (for example, by burying sacrificed animals or urinating on markings), and spreading *muti* (magic medicine) around the ground (Igbinovia 1985: 142–3; Leseth 1997). African football authorities sought to "modernize" their international image by comparing these practices to cannibalism and banning "juju-men" from fixtures, but with little success. Thus, while the transnational existence of divination practices confirms cultural homogenization, the very varied forms and contents of these religious belief systems point to heterogenization.

Third, *media framing and interpretation* of major football events harbor both cross-cultural convergence and divergence. At the game's international mega-events, most nations share the same television images from fixtures, yet different national broadcasters employ their own journalists, commentators, summarizers, and analysts to narrate and interpret the game in distinctive national ways (Hafez 2007: 26). Television audiences may show strong convergence in terms of the global teams and players that they prefer to watch (Brazil, for example, are particular global favorites); yet, like players, significant cultural differences remain in how viewers interpret the crucial incidents, such as free-kick and penalty decisions (cf. Katz and Liebes 1993).

Fourth, the convergence/divergence debate is especially lively in regard to football's *playing styles, techniques, and tactics.* Some pessimists lament the perceived worldwide influence of technocratic, instrumental coaches who impose standardized, sterile, and disenchanting tactics upon games. Historical changes in playing formations have tended to be defensive and, through successful implementation, have spread internationally.

"Football science" too has undergone international diffusion since the 1980s. The world's best teams are increasingly prepared and organized according to identical principles, while individual performances are measured according to performative criteria, such as pass completion or tackle rates, shots on- or off-target, and distances run during matches. Unpredictable clashes of playing style rarely occur at international tournaments since the world's elite players now play in the same leagues, compete regularly against each other, and are drilled in similar tactical thinking.

On the heterogenization side, the very criticism of standardization in football points to its contestation by coaches, players, and fans. Players who receive the greatest adulation and richest rewards are renowned for transcending standardized forms of play, for redefining the technical and geometric possibilities of football, for their stunning unpredictability. Some clubs—like Ajax, Real Madrid, Celtic, or Manchester United—have constructed potent "traditions" of highly fluid, entertaining, even spectacular styles that resist regimentation. These discourses sometimes acquire a strong national inflection, for example Spanish football followers dismiss the Italian penchant for such cautious, inflexible tactical systems as "anti-football."

Additionally, playing formations still continue to display much variation in form and implementation. Some nationally distinctive line-ups do appear, such as Argentina's 3-3-1-3 formation in the early 2000s. More commonly, even where a standardized team formation like 4-4-2 is favored, major cultural differences arise over its implementation, as illustrated by the titles of coaching videos and DVDs, such as *Coaching the Dutch 4-3-3; Futbol! Coaching the Brazilian 4-4-2; The Italian 4-4-2; Coaching the English Premier League 4-4-2*; and *Coaching the European 3-5-2.* Team formations may be similar, but the national or regional flavor defines how the team actually plays.

However, we should avoid advancing an oversimplified version of the heterogenization thesis in two senses. First, it may be argued that we should beware of slipping into a simple essentializing or "Orientalizing" of cultural difference in terms of playing style. Although the theory of Orientalism needs to be considered with caution, we may consider how Orientalism is evident in the way that Europeans tend to classify African and Latin American playing styles in rather ethnocentric ways, as anti-modern, rhythmic, expressive, flamboyant, unpredictable, inconsistent, magical, and irrational, in contradistinction to the self-congratulatory Western qualities of consistency, reliability, and rationality (cf. Said 1995). Evidence of Orientalist discourses may also be identified in the media stereotyping of football regions and nations, and in the language of some leading football officials who have, for example, complained that the "natural juice" of African football is being "squeezed out" by European coaches (cf. O'Donnell 1994).

Second, we should remind ourselves that heterogenization in peripheral contexts is typically marked by creolization processes, through diverse kinds of engagement between core and periphery. For example, African football has long been influenced by other football cultures through forms of colonial, post-colonial, and media-centered social contact, thereby engendering different playing styles across the regions. East African nations such as Uganda and Kenya were weaned on British styles of play, emphasizing highly energetic, combative, long-ball methods. The recruitment of European coaches, such as Yugoslavs in west Africa, produced better passing games and stronger organization. Alternatively, some nations such as Zambia and Zaire were more directly influenced by fluid and artistic Brazilian styles, in large part through watching videos of great South American players.

The convergence–divergence debate on playing style acquires additional layers of complexity through the intensive reflexivity of different societies on this very subject. In Latin America, the playing style debates become particularly polarized over the extent to which nations should homogenize toward employing scientific, "European" methods, or retain and advance their cultural diversity. Some analysts suggest that, when confronted with strong global competition, Brazil and Argentina have tended to adopt markedly different glocalization strategies. From the 1960s onward, Brazil looked strongly to scientific rationalism and organization, emphasizing physical preparation and elaborate medical support. Conversely, Argentina emphasized cultural differentiation through a veneration of a highly technical, criollo style. Yet in Argentina itself, a fundamental ideological division between convergence and divergence strategies is understood to be embodied by two World Cup–winning coaches: the pro-improvisational, leftist, divergent César Luis Menotti (in 1978); and the ultra-pragmatic, convergent Carlos Bilardo (in 1986) (Archetti 1998). Various Latino writers, coaches and football analysts have lent support to the divergent position, by castigating football's over-theorization by "pseudo-scientists." The renowned Uruguayan writer Eduardo Galeano celebrates football as "the art of the unforeseeable," while former Real Madrid and Argentina star Jorge Valdano insists that in popular football culture, a "seduction by the sphere" occurs wherein "you can't interrupt emotion" (quoted in Arbena 2000: 88).

Overall, we might observe that, in regard to the homogenization–heterogenization debate, football games themselves serve to narrate or to dramatize the dilemmas of standardization and differentiation. In broad terms, matches continually pit the technical efficiency of homogenization against the mold-breaking divergence of improvisation and innovation. While standardization is more associated with defensive play, differentiation is more commonly identified in attack. As Guillermo

Stábile, Argentina's manager during the 1940s and 1950s, once insisted, "you can organize a defence, but you had better not try to organize your attack" (Lodziak 1966: 13). In defense, organization is paramount, with players tutored to fulfill set roles and duties that usually correspond to global coaching manuals. In attack, while set plays (such as free-kicks and corners) may be studiously rehearsed, building attacks in open play is best achieved through creativity, improvisation, and the outfoxing of opponents. In this way, in the shifting balance between calculated defense and improvisational attack, the football match itself becomes a potent and unresolved dramatization of the duality of glocality.

CHAPTER 14

The American Global Cultural Brand

Lane Crothers

While American movies, music, and television programs are important parts of the U.S. global pop culture, they are not the whole of it. The values, ideals, mores, attitudes, behaviors, norms, and rituals that embody life in the United States can be found embedded in a host of other artifacts. Consumer goods and other values combine with the products of the audiovisual pop culture industry to create a seemingly seamless, integrated American popular culture that can be found almost everywhere in the world.

This chapter examines some of the other features of globalized American pop culture. Whether the product in question is a car, a restaurant, clothing, or a sport, American brands, styles, and even identities have had a profound impact on markets, values, and attitudes across the planet. Moreover, the relatively new phenomenon of social networking adds layers of complexity and subtlety to both the marketing and the branding of pop culture artifacts. Understanding the impact of American popular culture on the process of globalization necessarily entails exploring at least some of the other ways American pop culture crosses national and cultural boundaries. This chapter offers a partial look at this multifaceted phenomenon.

FRANCHISING AMERICA

One factor crucial to the global expansion of American popular culture across the globe has been a commercial concept known as the franchise. A franchise is a contractual relationship between a company that controls a brand label for a good or service and private individuals and companies that buy the right to use the brand's name and products but otherwise operate the business on their own. Such arrangements have proved to be useful, flexible means for corporations to spread their brands at minimal risk to their bottom lines. After all, when a company owns a store—which does happen, even in some franchised businesses—the company assumes the risks associated with purchasing or leasing business space, hiring staff, marketing and building a market, and other matters. If a company-owned store fails, it costs the company a substantial amount of money. By contrast, in a franchise arrangement, the franchisee accepts most of this risk. As a consequence, franchisers can offer franchise opportunities in places and markets that might be too uncertain for the company to invest in otherwise. The franchise brand can therefore spread more quickly and into otherwise unreachable markets more easily than could an unfranchised company.

Franchises have a number of advantages that have encouraged their use. Some of these are practical and some are matters of loyalty and brand identity. From a franchisee's point of view, for example, buying a franchise can significantly reduce the cost and complexity of starting a business. One does not need to establish contracts with local vendors to provide things like hamburger to a restaurant; instead, the franchiser has preexisting networks of vendors the new franchisee can tap into to get the goods needed to run the business. In addition, franchisers usually have management-training programs so that new franchisees can learn how to recruit and manage their employees. The franchiser is also likely to have a complex set of rules and regulations defining workers' rights and responsibilities—a fact that means that franchisees do not have to develop rules and policies on their own. Even rules governing the layout of floor space simplify the task of opening and managing a new business. By buying a franchise, the new owner gives up some freedom to run things as he or she might wish but also simplifies running the business by relying on the skills and expertise of the franchiser.

Another major benefit of the franchise derives from the concept of economies of scale. Franchisers typically buy large volumes of goods and services from vendors. They are able to negotiate price reductions from these vendors that smaller purchasers (who are often local, individually owned businesses) are not able to negotiate: vendors accept lower prices for bulk sales in order to get the contract for the major sale. Franchisers pass these cost reductions on to their franchisees, meaning that the franchisee can often provide a good or a service to the customer at a lower price than an independent business can. If necessary, then, franchisees can beat independent businesses on price, enhancing their market competitiveness.

Franchises also provide regularity and predictability to both franchisees and consumers. Colas from the same franchise taste pretty much the same wherever they are concocted, just as the hamburgers taste the same, just as the coffee tastes the same. Consumers can be pretty sure that they will get a predictable and safe product from any of a chain's stores, just as franchise owners can be pretty sure that competing franchises will not be opened in the area—at least not competing franchises from the same company. This uniformity may strike some people as unfortunate, since it often entails the destruction of local businesses unable to compete with the franchise's economies of scale, but given a choice, consumers seem to flock to franchise businesses instead of local ones. Predictability and regularity are powerful market forces.

Perhaps the biggest benefit to buying a franchise is not managerial at all. Instead, it is perceptual. Franchisers invest substantial amounts of money establishing their brand identities. The most important part of the process of building brand identity is advertising. Franchisers spend a great deal of money advertising their product's label to a broad audience. This advertising both builds brand awareness and creates a public image for the franchiser's goods and services. For example, Ford, the automobile manufacturer, once offered a campaign centered on the notion that "quality is job one," suggesting that if consumers wanted safe and reliable cars they should buy Fords. Starbucks' advertising suggests it is not just a coffee shop but a destination for those who have discriminating taste and demand superior coffee. McDonald's offers decent food served quickly in a way that is supposed to mimic the feeling of home. And Coca-Cola ties itself to wholesome imagery, once promising that it would "like to buy the world a Coke, and keep it company."

This brand identity-making is not an accident. Franchisers establish brand identities to create and maintain markets for their products. One goes to Starbucks not simply because of the coffee; one goes to Starbucks to be seen as someone who goes to Starbucks. Starbucks-goers form a subculture with their own rituals and norms—in this case organized around elaborate processes for ordering cups of coffee. Nike buyers "just do it." Mountain Dew drinkers "do the Dew." "Nothing," the model-turned-actress Brooke Shields once declared, "comes between me and my Calvins" (a brand of blue jeans).

Franchisers augment this subcultural identity-making by physically labeling their customers and turning consumers into walking (and driving) advertisements for their products. Coffee cups can be emblazoned with the brand label, as can shopping bags. Automobiles and many brands of clothing come with labels that advertise the product's maker—and label the driver/wearer/user as someone who uses that company's goods and services. Some consumers respond to this labeling and identification by buying gift items emblazoned with the product's labels. Brand identity is a central feature of creating and maintaining markets for a franchiser's products.

Buying a franchise therefore means buying a brand identity and its associated market. Franchisees are largely freed of the need to convince consumers to come to their store. Instead, franchisees merely have to inform consumers about the location of their stores in order to give customers who appreciate the brand's identity the chance to shop for that store's products—and to be seen to shop for those goods and services.

Through franchising, consumers across the world have become aware of the brand identities of American clothing, restaurants, vehicles, sports, and innumerable other things. Brand identity can combine with price advantages to make American goods popular with foreign consumers, and of course American tourists appreciate the predictability of franchise brands. People across the globe seem willing to pay to associate themselves with American brands of clothing and food and other products. America has become, at least in part, a global franchise.

A BRIEF HISTORY OF THE FRANCHISE

Franchising began in Europe. It began as a way to link taverns to specific types of beer: at franchised pubs, only beer of a particular brand would be sold. However, franchising never became as important in Europe as it did in the United States. Whether for reasons of an entrepreneur-friendly culture or the vast geographic size of the United States, franchising began in America in the 1800s and quickly expanded. It took off after World War II when the automobile came to dominate American life.[1]

The earliest American franchises were in manufactured goods. As early as the 1850s, suppliers like Isaac Singer and the makers of the McCormick Harvesting Machine offered sewing machines and tractors to franchisees, who sold these products out of their stores. The franchiser, then, did not own the store in which the franchiser's goods were sold. Instead, the franchiser sold the goods to the franchisee. The franchisee then made a profit (or tried to) by marking up the price of the item, offering service, and perhaps earning incentive payments from the franchiser if the company sold a large number of units.

While Singer's first attempts at a franchise ultimately failed, the Singer model was adopted by the automobile industry as it grew. The first automobile franchise was granted in 1898, just a decade or so after the first recognizably modern car had been invented. Auto franchises allowed dealers to establish businesses at which to sell and service vehicles purchased from the manufacturer at a discount. This arrangement remains the way most cars are sold today.

The franchising concept branched out into food and services starting in the 1880s. The first truly successful franchise of a food product was Coca-Cola, the invention of an Atlanta, Georgia, druggist named John S. Pemberton. Pemberton, who sold the formula for his concoction before his death in 1888, mixed kola root, caffeine, and coca extract into a sweet, soothing formula. The person who bought the secret formula (which remains secret to this day), Asa Candler, created a franchising deal in which the Coca-Cola Company sold premixed syrup base to franchisees. (Coca was eventually removed as an ingredient of the formula.) The franchisees then added water, bottled the soda, and marketed it in their areas of operation. In time, as is discussed later in this chapter, Coca-Cola, aka Coke, would be bottled and drunk around the world—always with the same base syrup shipped from the Coca-Cola Company.

Restaurants were added to the list of goods and services that were franchised early in the twentieth century. After Roy Allen bought the formula for a new drink called root beer from an Arizona druggist in 1919, he and his partner, Frank Wright, founded the A&W restaurant franchise in 1922. A few years later Harland Sanders invented a flavor packet that he added to the fried chicken he had learned to cook quickly at the restaurant he ran at his gas station and motel complex in Corbin, Kentucky. He began selling the flavor packets and licensing his quick-cook technology to other entrepreneurs in 1930. While that business ultimately failed, his model became the foundation for the Kentucky Fried Chicken (KFC) restaurant chain. In the same period, Howard Johnson, a pharmacist from Quincy, Massachusetts, began to sell ice cream and a small selection of other items in his store; he franchised the concept in 1935. In time both the menu and the ice cream choices expanded, and distinctive, orange-roofed Howard Johnson's restaurants spread across the United States.

The emergence of the automobile as the major mode of American transportation after World War II provided the opportunity for massive expansions in franchising across the United States. Americans began traveling on wide, well-built highways in comfortable cars. They also moved to suburbs with their attendant large yards and commuter lifestyles. Travelers sought reliable, consistent places in which to eat and spend the night; car owners desired the security of knowing they could get their cars serviced at reliable, reputable chains across the United States; and consumers with money to spend pursued whatever fashion, music, or fad was hot at the moment. (One of Harland "Colonel" Sanders's innovations was to put a facsimile of one of the rooms of his motel inside his restaurant so that potential guests could see the quality of his rooms. Women wishing to use the restroom in his restaurant had to actually enter the display room in order to reach their destination.) Franchised restaurants, hotels, automobile service chains, and clothing stores rushed in to fill this market. Chains like McDonald's, Kentucky Fried Chicken, Holiday Inn, and Western Auto grew dramatically.

Table 14.1 summarizes the franchises that have at least one thousand locations outside the United States. Fast-food restaurants are disproportionately represented, although service industries like real estate sales, tax preparation, and janitorial services also make the list. The chain of 7-Eleven convenience stores is by far the largest international chain; however, McDonald's remains the sales champion among global franchises. Subway, notably, now has more restaurants than McDonald's overall, but McDonald's has more than a $60 billion advantage in global sales. In any case, it is clear that the American way of eating is spreading around the world in ever-expanding networks of franchises.

Fast food, services, and convenience stores are of course not the only global franchises for American products, goods, and services. Ford and General Motors sell millions of cars globally, for example. (Chrysler, the third major American car manufacturer, has recently been taken over by Italian manufacturer Fiat.) Even in what have been relatively hard times in the American automobile industry, Ford sold more than two million vehicles outside North America in 2010.[2] General Motors, long the world's largest car company until the recent global slowdown in auto sales, controls the Cadillac, Chevrolet, Buick, Opel, Vauxhall, and Holden brands. It sold more than five million automobiles in areas outside North America in 2010. This included 1.3 million vehicles in Europe, and some 800,000 in Africa, Latin America, and the Middle East. It sold almost 3.4 million vehicles in Asia, including 2.26 million in China alone.[3] Buick is particularly popular in China.

Other aspects of American cultural life have also expanded across the world in recent years. The megaretailer Walmart has a global presence now, and it influences both how products are created and how they are sold to people around the world. For example, Walmart has 352 stores in China, and its focus on the quality of its products is pressuring Chinese producers and vendors to increase the quality of the goods and services they provide to Chinese consumers.[4] The National Football League (NFL) now plays a regular season game in London every year. The National Basketball Association (NBA) is aggressively seeking to expand in global

Table 14.1 Top Global Franchises

RANK	FRANCHISE	U.S. LOCATIONS	INTERNATIONAL LOCATIONS	TOTAL LOCATIONS	GLOBAL SALES ($M)
1	McDonald's	14,027	18,710	32,737	77,380
2	7-Eleven	6,137	33,345	39,482	63,000
3	KFC	5,055	11,798	16,583	19,400
4	Subway	23,850	10,109	33,959	15,200
5	Burger King	7,523	4,998	12,251	14,800
7	Circle K	3,367	4,056	7,423	12,500
8	Pizza Hut	7,542	5,890	13,432	10,200
11	Hertz	4,942	3,576	8,518	7,600
15	RE/MAX	3,411	2,873	6,284	6,625*
16	Domino's Pizza	4,929	4,422	9,351	6,268*
17	Dunkin' Donuts	6,772	2,988	9,760	6,004
18	Tim Hortons	602	3,424	4,026	5,625
27	H&R Block	11,506	1,643	13,149	3,874*
31	ampm (BP)	1,225	1,592	2,817	3,415
38	Dairy Queen	4,514	1,384	5,898	2,750
49	GNC	3,651	1,606	5,257	2,050*
56	Century 21	3,000	5,000	8,000	1,800*
58	ServiceMaster	3,021	1,804	4,825	1,791*
61	Snap-on Tools	1,464	1,350	4,814	1,666
62	Baskin-Robbins	2,547	3,886	6,433	1,653
81	Curves	4,956	3,076	8,032	1,000
110	Jani-King	9,245	2,209	11,454	647*
111	ERA Real Estate	695	1,852	2,547	641*

*Revenues estimated.

Source: 2011 Franchise Times, "Top 200 Franchise Systems," http://www.franchisetimes.com/content/page.php?page=00141 (accessed January 26, 2012).

markets; players like the now-retired Chinese-born Yao Ming provided the league with entrée into that vast nation.

Not all American goods and services are marketed globally by franchises, of course. Some companies own the stores in which they sell their products globally, and other distinctively American items like blue jeans have developed a global presence separate from the original manufacturers' control. Starbucks, for example, does not offer a traditional franchise to its operators. Instead, it owns most of its stores, but it licenses some independent businesspersons to run particular stores on its behalf. Such arrangements have made it possible, as of October 2011, for Starbucks to operate 17,003 stores in fifty-eight countries worldwide.[5]

Whether franchised or not, brands like McDonald's, Coca-Cola, Starbucks, and 7-Eleven carry an American identity and an American set of cultural values and practices to the larger world. They are as embedded in American culture as movies, music, and television programming are. They offer entangling threads in which American pop culture spins into global prominence.

AMERICAN BRANDS, GLOBAL PRESENCE

This section of the chapter explores the ways in which specific American brands, franchises, and cultural forms have been integrated into global life. In particular, it offers brief histories of Coca-Cola, McDonald's, and blue jeans as case studies of the many ways American pop culture has gone worldwide. These companies and products offer insight into brands that have been long established as global forces. Their international prominence offers evidence of the power of American popular culture on a global scale.

Note that the fact that this section focuses on these companies and products should not lead anyone to the conclusion that they stand as *the* examples of American pop culture corporate globalization. The discussion offered here of how these companies and products have grown to global prominence is intended to explore the ways in which American pop culture has gone global. It is not an exhaustive list of those corporations that have spread across the planet. Indeed, both Coca-Cola and McDonald's are but branches of a complex tree of fast-food and beverage companies with a global scope. The analyses offered here are presented as a way to explore the ways American brands became global. While each is presented individually, they and the other forces of American pop culture globalization have a collective impact on the people who use American products and integrate them into their lives.

A Brief Global Cultural History of Coca-Cola

The Coca-Cola label has been called the most profitable brand in world history. Interbrand, an international consulting firm, lists the international trademarks that are understood to have generated the highest economic returns for their owners. Only those that generate more than one-third of their sales outside the United States are considered. For 2010, Interbrand estimated the Coke brand to be worth $70 billion, far outpacing the next biggest soda giant, Pepsi, at $14 billion. Coca-Cola exceeded the brand value of the second-place company, IBM, by $5.5 billion.[6] It is a global powerhouse.

This is quite a change for a company that started as a store-mixed, coca-extract-laced drink developed to supplement sales at an Atlanta, Georgia, pharmacy. John S. Pemberton, an Atlanta pharmacist, developed the drink in May 1886 and sold it from a local pharmacy. Pemberton sold the rights to his drink to several people before his death in 1888; by 1891 Asa Candler bought back all the rights Pemberton had sold. This cost Candler $2,300. Candler and his brother John joined with several other local businessmen to incorporate the Coca-Cola Company in 1892. The company's distinctive, script-based logo was registered as an official trademark in 1893.[7] It has gone on to the status of global icon.

Coca-Cola is a mix of a secret syrup, sugar, and carbonated water. The key to its success is its syrup, which has been manufactured on a large scale since 1894.

In the company's early years, the syrup was shipped to pharmacies and other stores. These stores used so-called "soda jerks"—so named because they pulled the large handles that controlled the flow of the syrup and water like draft beer is dispensed in bars today—to mix the sodas on the spot. In 1894, a Vicksburg, Mississippi, businessman named Joseph Biedenharn decided that he would bottle Coca-Cola so that his customers could store the concoction at home or work rather than needing to come to the store for a soda. Bottled Coca-Cola has been available ever since.

Nationwide franchising began in 1899. A group of Chattanooga, Tennessee, businessmen secured the rights to bottle Coca-Cola across the United States that year. However, they quickly discovered that they could not raise enough capital to build bottling plants around the United States to serve the national demand for the product. They identified bottling partners across the country and created zones of operation guaranteeing each control of a specific territory. Over a thousand bottling plants were established across the United States in the next twenty years.

Coca-Cola's growth was international in these years, although not to the degree it would later enjoy. Asa Candler's oldest son took a batch of syrup with him on a trip to England in 1900, for example, and the company received an order for five gallons of the concoction from the UK later that year. The company had more success in Latin America and American territories in the Far East. Bottling plants opened in Cuba, Panama, Puerto Rico, the Philippines, and Guam in the early years of the twentieth century. Plants also opened in Canada and France by 1920. In 1926, Coca-Cola established an international marketing unit, and in 1928, the company shipped one thousand cases of the soda to the Olympic Games in Amsterdam. This began a long association between the company and the world's premiere sporting event. The soda was bottled in forty-four countries by the late 1930s. That number would double through the 1960s.

In a striking example of the cultural relevance and significance Coca-Cola had achieved by the middle of the twentieth century, Coca-Cola became part of the U.S. war effort during World War II. While in North Africa in 1943, for example, General Dwight Eisenhower's headquarters sent a message to the company asking it to ship enough material to build ten bottling plants. It also requested that three million bottles of the soda be shipped to the front immediately, along with supplies needed to fill a quota of 6 million bottles a month.

The Coca-Cola Company also made a commitment to provide five-cent bottles of Coke to all servicemen regardless of what it cost the company to produce the drink. In all, Coca-Cola shipped materials for sixty-four bottling plants around the world, including to far-flung outposts like New Guinea. Military personnel drank some five billion bottles of soda during the war—a number that does not include soda and automatic fountain dispensaries. By the end of the war, a generation of Americans, and for that matter a generation of people touched by American military operations around the world, had been introduced or otherwise exposed to Coca-Cola.

While Coca-Cola was the dominant soda brand in the United States in the postwar period, competition from its main rival, Pepsi, induced the company to make what, in retrospect, was one of the biggest marketing and branding mistakes of all time. Concerned that Pepsi's sweeter formula was stealing market share from its products, Coca-Cola executives initiated plans to replace traditional Coca-Cola with a new formula labeled, simply enough, New Coke. The new formula had won numerous blind taste tests against both the old formula of Coca-Cola and Pepsi as well, and in 1985, company leaders decided that it was time to launch a new chapter in the product's history. "Old" Coke ceased production and New Coke was presented as "the" Coca-Cola.

To say the new product flopped would be kind. Executives received hate mail about the new flavor even as consumer lobbying groups formed to boycott the new drink and demand the return of "real" Coke—all in days before the Internet made such communications comparatively easy. Company claims that sales were good and the new formula was popular were met with howls of derision. National news broadcasts covered the marketing disaster. When news leaked that the original Coca-Cola was to return to store shelves in July 1985, barely three months after New Coke was presented to the world as "Coke," then–U.S. senator David Pryor (D-Arkansas) announced on the floor of the Senate that the news "was a meaningful moment in American history."[8] "Old" Coke, renamed "Classic," was marketed alongside New Coke until New Coke was pulled from the market entirely. (It should be noted that by the end of 1985, Coca-Cola's market share had grown dramatically, leading some to conclude that the introduction of New Coke was a cunning advertising strategy. The company has always denied this.) In January 2009, the company announced that Coca-Cola Classic would drop the "Classic" from its name. (Notably, the word "Classic" on the label had been reduced in size several times in the twenty years between New Coke's rise and the decision to remove "Classic" from the soda's package.) Coke would be just Coke again.

At the heart of this disaster was the failure to appreciate the iconic position Coca-Cola had come to hold in American society. Coca-Cola had worked hard to make itself a brand affiliated with the notion of America itself. Changes to the brand meant change to the emotional connection many consumers felt toward not just the soda but also the idea of the soda's existence as a cultural touchstone. To drink Coke was to be an American, and if Coke could change then so could America—and not in a good way. Changing to New Coke was a betrayal of the brand identity that Coca-Cola had worked hard to create.

Notably, Coca-Cola faced a similar, if less intense, controversy during Christmas season 2011. The company decided to change the color of its cans from red to white during the Christmas holidays to honor polar bears and to raise awareness of the loss of Arctic habitat for the bears and other regional wildlife. The campaign caused confusion among some drinkers who thought they were buying Diet Coke, which is sold in silver cans, and got "real" Coke instead. But others were outraged that Coke had abandoned its iconic red color. Coca-Cola, it seems, had to be offered for sale only in red to be "real" Coca-Cola.

Notably, the popular sense that Coca-Cola had an iconic, cultural identity that ought not be violated by silly issues like marketing and flavor was in many ways itself a result of Coke's efforts to turn itself into a quintessentially American product. From its early decision to use the script-lettered Coca-Cola label (drawn by John S. Pemberton's partner and bookkeeper, Frank Robinson), the company showed remarkable creativity and success in branding its product. In 1916, for example, the company created the iconic Coke contour bottle as a tool to ensure consumers were getting—and choosing—Coca-Cola instead of a competitor's products. (This shape was granted a trademark by the U.S. Patent Office in 1977.) In 1929, the company introduced a distinctive fountain glass to be used in pharmacies, restaurants, and other venues that served Coke products; this glass is still used in many restaurants and can be purchased for home use as well. In 1933, the company introduced the automatic fountain dispenser at the Chicago World's Fair. This device allowed consumers to pour their own sodas as the water and syrup were mixed in the dispenser rather than by a soda jerk. It made it possible for millions more drinks to be dispensed than ever could be before.

Coke also invented Santa Claus. Or, put another way, it was Coca-Cola's marketers who helped establish the now-classic vision of Kris Kringle as a jolly fat man with a white beard dressed in red from top to bottom. Coca-Cola co-opted Santa's image in an effort to get people to drink soda in the winter, and in the process created the modern image of Santa Claus. Prior to 1931, when a series of magazine ads for Coca-Cola featuring Santa Claus first hit American magazines, Father Christmas had been portrayed in an array of ways. In some cases he was seen as an elf; in others as a tall, thin, somewhat austere man. (This image remains popular in some parts of the world.) At times he wore a clerical robe, and at other times he was dressed in the furs of a Norse hunter. When cartoonist Thomas Nast drew Santa in the U.S. Civil War era, the character's clothes were tan, although in time Nast changed them to red.

Consumers became so obsessed with the images Coke produced that they actually scanned each year's drawings for changes. One year, when Santa appeared without a wedding ring, people wrote in wondering about Mrs. Claus. Another year readers asked why Santa's belt was on backwards. An icon was thus made, courtesy of Coca-Cola.

What was true for Santa Claus was true for a stunning array of consumer collectibles as well. It is possible to collect a vast amount of Coca-Cola labeled products, ranging from trays and bottles and bottle caps to advertising, games, smoking paraphernalia, and company gifts.[9] If it has a logo on it, it is a potential collectible; if it is older and genuine, it is likely to have substantial economic value. But of course economic value is not the only reason people collect: surrounding oneself in Coca-Cola labeled products links one to the brand and the values it expresses. Many people collect Coca-Cola for its distinctive colors and logos rather than its potential sales value. It is a subculture.

It is also a global symbol. At least two international movies have put Coca-Cola paraphernalia at the center of their films. The 1980 cult hit *The Gods Must Be Crazy* makes the brand's distinctive glass bottle the point of dramatic tension around which the movie hinges, for example. When a Coke bottle falls from a passing airplane into the hands of a tribe of hunter-gatherers in the Kalahari desert in southern Africa, the tribe's people find it useful for grinding food and other matters until, in a fit of jealousy, one tribesperson hits another over the head with the bottle. One member, Xi, decides that the gods were crazy to give them the bottle and goes on a quest to return it to its rightful owners. Along the way, viewers get a travelogue of life in the modern world as seen through the eyes of one tribesman— and his Coke bottle.

Another film, *The Cup*, a cult hit from 1999, is less focused on Coke, but uses one of its iconic symbols, its distinctively colored aluminum can, as an evocative introduction to the film. The movie is set in a Buddhist monastery in India filled with young monks obsessed by the World Cup soccer tournament. It chronicles their efforts to rent a satellite dish and television so they can watch the competition despite the supposed asceticism of life in a monastery. The film opens with a scene of young monks using a Coke can as a soccer ball in their courtyard. An older monk interrupts to take the can to his master; we see that the master has used many such cans to create oil lamps in his study. Coke is quite literally everywhere— and quite literally recognizable around the world.

Along with its iconography, Coca-Cola has become a force of economic globalization. At one level, this is the result of the substantial economic impact Coca-Cola has around the world. The opening of bottling plants brings an array of other jobs and services to the communities that house them. Coca-Cola bottling facilities rely on local water and local sweeteners to mix with the base syrup, meaning that local bottlers have to establish relationships with local providers for these services. Bottles, whether plastic or glass or aluminum, have to be produced locally, delivered to the plant and used to store the soda. Trucking firms have to hire drivers to deliver the product to the many venues in which it is sold. Then, in a process known as the multiplier effect, the employees of the trucking company and the water provider and the sweetener company and the employees of the bottling plant and the places that sell Coke all have money to spend on new goods and services. People with money in their pockets tend to go to restaurants and movies and buy cars and better televisions—or televisions in the first place. In turn, this financial boon causes other businesses to hire workers as restaurant servers and car sales staff and television repair people. Bringing a large business like a Coca-Cola bottling facility to a new area is expected to promote economic growth broadly throughout the community.

Yet Coke is not always perceived as a good force in global affairs. In part this is because the reality of local economic development is never as clearly beneficial as the process just described. Corrupt officials and their cronies do better than they ought to from the deals the company strikes in the local area, and many people do not see the economic benefit that is expected under the logic of the multiplier effect. There are also concerns that as local suppliers of water, sweeteners, and bottles and distribution networks expand to meet the company's demands, they replace rain forests and other natural areas with sugar fields and build roads across previously undisturbed countryside, displacing endangered animals and plants in the process. The diversion of large amounts of water from their natural sources to satisfy the demand for soda can likewise harm the local environment.

Many people also wonder if addicting the planet to sweetened, caffeinated beverages in a world of limited resources and growing obesity is really a very good idea from a public health perspective. Indeed, since sodas are American beverages, the criticism arises that American soda manufacturers are contributing to making the world obese, all while destroying the local culture, flavors, and styles of consumption innate to other cultures. For some, then, Coke is a symbol of cultural degradation rather than a tool of global economic development.

One other critique has been aimed at Coke: its alleged role in repressing global labor movements, particularly in Colombia. Organizers of the "Killer Coke" campaign argue that Coca-Cola officials have been complicit in or have actually caused the murders and/or kidnappings of numerous labor organizers at Coke bottling plants in Colombia.[10] Coca-Cola, then, is seen to be a central player in the efforts of global megacorporations to dominate the worldwide labor market by keeping costs low and profits high. The company, of course, denies these claims.

Regardless of one's position on the economic or moral significance of the Coca-Cola Company, it is clear nonetheless that it is an iconic representative of American pop culture across the globe. Its products, its logos, its values, and its brand identity have found a worldwide market and a worldwide audience. It is hard to imagine going pretty much anywhere on the planet that is inhabited by people who have ever had contact with groups from the outside world without expecting to be able to buy a Coke or a similar product when visiting. Indeed, it seems probable that one could visit a tribe or group that has pretty much been left alone by the outside world and find, quite by chance, someone wearing a Coca-Cola T-shirt or, a la *The Gods Must Be Crazy*, using a Coke bottle as a tool. It is a global symbol of American popular culture.

A Brief Global Cultural History of McDonald's

McDonald's is, like Coca-Cola, a global powerhouse. It is, first of all, ubiquitous. There are McDonald's restaurants all over the world. They serve as a haven for American tourists, of course—many a weary traveler has eaten at a McDonald's elsewhere, even if they rarely eat at McDonald's at home. But McDonald's attracts customers all over the world. When McDonald's opened stores in Moscow and Beijing, the lines of local people waiting for service stretched for blocks. Its 32,737 stores seem to be quite literally everywhere.

In addition, McDonald's stands as a powerful symbol of American cultural globalization. Its symbolic golden arches logo is as distinctive as the American flag. Its restaurants grew in concert with the American love of the automobile, a fact reflected in the presence of drive-through lanes at many of its stores. What could be more American than to not have to get out of one's car even to eat? McDonald's is thus both an indicator of globalization and evidence of the American cultural way of life.

The success of McDonald's was grounded on a simple idea: providing desirable food and drink at low cost, fast. This was by no means a new idea: Ray Kroc, the creator of McDonald's as a nationwide chain, discovered the technique when he visited a group of restaurants in Los Angeles, California, to which he had sold a large number of Mix-master automatic milkshake machines. Kroc was the national salesman for these machines, which could make five milkshakes at the same time. He could not understand why some of the Los Angeles restaurants needed as many as eight of these machines in a single store. On visiting this mini-chain, called McDonald's, Kroc was impressed with the production-line nature of the store's operations—and also with the line of customers who waited outside the restaurants' doors from the moment they opened until the moment they closed. The stores sold hamburgers for 15 cents; cheese was 4 cents extra. In 1954, at the age of 52, Kroc bought into the McDonald's partnership and in 1955 began franchising its stores nationwide. The first modern McDonald's opened in Des Plaines, Illinois, on April 15, 1955. It stands as a museum today.[11]

Not only was the idea not new to Ray Kroc, it wasn't new in the United States. Chains like Burger King, Carl's Jr., In-N-Out Burger, Krystal, Steak 'n Shake, White Castle, and Burger Chef all sold hamburgers before Kroc franchised his first McDonald's.[12] There were, moreover, competitive chains selling chicken, sandwiches, and ice cream across America in those years, along with an array of more formal, sit-down, full-service restaurants catering to the ever wealthier and ever more mobile American market. However, through a combination of factors like picking good sites for stores, systematizing operations across all restaurants, and effective marketing, McDonald's caught on with American consumers quite quickly. By 1958, there were 34 McDonald's restaurants in the United States; 67 more opened the next year, for a total of 101. Sales escalated accordingly: in 1963, the company sold its one-billionth hamburger, and in 1968 it opened its one-thousandth store. In 1972 the company had $1 billion in sales, and by 1976 the company passed $3 billion in sales—and twenty billion in total hamburger sales.

McDonald's updated its product offerings regularly in order to attract repeat business and entice new customers into its restaurants. It added the Filet-O-Fish sandwich to its national line in 1965 after a Cincinnati, Ohio, franchisee noted that he was losing a great deal of business on Fridays, when Catholics were supposed to avoid eating meat. Kroc initially rejected the idea of a fish sandwich for the restaurant, but he was persuaded when the local owner developed a sandwich on his own and proved that it sold well. Local pressures likewise inspired the Big Mac: a Pittsburgh, Pennsylvania, storeowner discovered that local steel mill workers weren't satisfied with the size of a single burger. The Big Mac was added to the McDonald's menu in 1968. McDonald's developed the Egg McMuffin breakfast sandwich in 1973 and expanded to offer a full breakfast menu in 1977. By 1987, 25 percent of all breakfasts eaten outside the home in the United States were eaten at McDonald's. In time, products like the Happy Meal for children, Chicken McNuggets, and salads were added to the franchise's lineup. While not all of these product innovations succeeded—the McLean burger, with less fat, was a notable failure—they continued to draw consumers to the restaurants.

McDonald's greatest product accomplishment may well have been the french fry. The original McDonald's restaurants in Los Angeles made fresh fries daily. They were a big hit. However, when Kroc tried to duplicate this item in the franchise, the results were failures: potato storage took a large amount of floor space in each facility, and potatoes had to be dried under a fan to become starchy enough to withstand washing and frying. A McDonald's potato supplier, Jack Simplot, invented a technique to cut, freeze, and prepare fries at his facilities. These could be shipped directly to the restaurants, where they could then be fried. This process saved space in the stores—and guaranteed product uniformity throughout the McDonald's chain.

Other innovations made McDonald's a destination restaurant with strong brand identity. The chain moved from its "Speedee man" mascot to a circus clown-like character, Ronald McDonald, in 1963. Ronald McDonald would become the instantly recognizable face of the franchise and would also become the character and face of Ronald McDonald House Charities, which provides places for the parents and loved ones of children with cancer to stay during their children's treatment. Eating at McDonald's could thereafter be justified as an act of charity, not just self-indulgence.

McDonald's offered other innovations to attract customers. In 1971, it opened its first McDonald's Playland, a play area for children common in many roadside McDonald's restaurants. It became heavily involved in movie cross-promotions, regularly providing figurines based on popular films as part of Happy Meals and thereby drawing in more children and their families. And while the company did not invent the idea of a drive-through lane for its restaurants, it added them in 1975. The drive-through would eventually account for more than half of all McDonald's sales across the franchise.

At least one other aspect of McDonald's success deserves attention: its linkage of architecture and advertising. McDonald's integrated its distinctive golden arches logo into the actual architecture of its early restaurants. In time, the arches were moved from the building to the restaurant's sign, with the arches linked together to form an instantly recognizable "M" at the beginning of McDonald's. Intrade now ranks the McDonald's brand as the sixth most valuable in the world, worth $33.6 billion in 2010.[13]

After first establishing restaurants across the United States and Canada, McDonald's went global in the 1970s. Starting in Costa Rica, the company opened stores in Germany, Holland, Australia, and Japan in the early years of the decade. The five-thousandth store the chain opened was in Japan, in 1978.

While expansion continued throughout the 1980s, it was the fall of the Berlin Wall and the end of the Cold War that really made McDonald's a ubiquitous global presence. It operated in fifty-eight foreign countries with more than 3,600 restaurants in the early 1990s; it only opened its ten-thousandth store in April 1988, thirty-three years after it was first franchised. Since then, its growth has been explosive. It only took the company eight more years, until 1996, to add another ten thousand stores to its portfolio, for a total of twenty thousand in 1996. By the end of 1997, the chain was opening two thousand new restaurants a year. That works out to an equivalent of one every five hours.

International growth drove much of this increase. The chain added over 7,400 new stores overseas in the years 1991–1998. It had franchises in 114 countries in that time. It entered the Middle East (Israel) in 1993; it entered India in 1996. It developed the McSki-thru in Lindvallen, Sweden, that same year. When a McDonald's opened in Kuwait City, Kuwait, in 1994, the line at the drive-through was seven miles long. This growth led to a shift in the sources of McDonald's revenues: in 1992, the company generated 60 percent of its sales in the United States, but by 1997 that percentage had fallen to 42.5.

The opening of two stores, one in the heart of the former Soviet Union in Moscow, and the other in Beijing, China, near Tiananmen Square, stand as particularly striking examples of the global growth of McDonald's. The openings of these two stores were highly symbolic acts that seemed to confirm political theorist Francis Fukuyama's claim that the fall of the Soviet Union meant the "end of history," the end of great global ideological struggles. American-style liberal capitalist democracy had won.[14] Indeed, the Moscow McDonald's, opened in 1990, quickly became the city's biggest attraction, serving 27,000 customers a day.[15] Some of them waited for hours to be served. The situation in Beijing was if anything more dramatic: opened on August 23, 1992, the Beijing McDonald's served 40,000 people its first day.[16] (In July 2011 the company was opening a restaurant in China every other day, and expected to open one per day for the next three to four years.[17])

One reason McDonald's has been so successful is its adaptability. Company stores and franchisees have been careful to shape their products in ways that meet the needs and expectations of the local communities they serve. It has had its restaurants inspected as kosher for Jewish customers and as halal, the equivalent standard for Muslims. It has changed the composition of its fry oil, which once was based on beef fat, to accommodate the religious requirements of India's Hindu population. (Problems achieving this standard are addressed later in the chapter.) The company also adapts its menus to meet the expectations of its local consumers. It is possible to buy beer in McDonald's restaurants in Germany, for example.

The adaptability of McDonald's is reflected in a series of studies compiled by James Watson in his book *Golden Arches East: McDonald's in East Asia*. The restaurant offers espresso and cold pasta in Italy; chilled yogurt drinks in Turkey; teriyaki hamburgers in Japan, Taiwan, and Hong Kong; a grilled salmon sandwich called the McLak in Norway; and McSpaghetti in the Philippines. It offers the McHuevo in Uruguay. Waiters in Rio de Janeiro serve Big Macs with champagne at candlelit restaurants. McDonald's restaurants in Caracas, Venezuela, have had hostesses seat customers, place orders, and bring customers their meals. It has thus integrated itself as a provider of local cuisines around the world.[18]

McDonald's has also shaped Asian cultures in several ways. Some of these ways are quite predictable, while others are less so. For example, the restaurants are common hangouts for young people, serving as a place where teenagers can escape the relative strictures of life at home. The restaurants have at times been turned into leisure centers and after-school meeting places. Unsurprisingly, french fries have become a staple part of younger people's diets across Asia—fries are in fact the most globally consumed item in the McDonald's line.[19]

But such fairly predictable changes do not fully describe the many ways in which the chain's restaurants have influenced Asian culture. Many Asian women apparently find McDonald's a safe place to relax and avoid aggressive, often sexual, harassment. Additionally, McDonald's has made birthday parties a central feature of life in parts of East Asia: in Hong Kong, for example, it was historically the practice to record dates of birth only for use later in life, like checking horoscopes of prospective marriage partners, but to make little of annual birthdays. McDonald's made birthday parties a central part of its marketing, thereby placing a premium on families knowing and celebrating—and being seen to celebrate—their children's birthdays. On another front, it was once very rare for people to eat with their hands in Japan. The spread of McDonald's and other fast-food restaurants has made this both more common and more acceptable.[20]

McDonald's has also shaped consumer culture. Even something as seemingly common as standing in a line to wait one's turn to order from a preset and limited menu is in fact a cultural adaptation. As McDonald's restaurants opened, their employees and advertising had to teach potential customers how to behave. For example, employees at the Moscow McDonald's moved up and down the line explaining that at McDonald's smiles were an expected part of the service and should not be confused with threats or a form of mockery, which were what smiles were previously seen to indicate in Russia. Even cleanliness standards changed under pressure from McDonald's: the restaurant has strict standards for hygiene in its kitchens and its restrooms, and competitors were forced to change their practices as consumers grew accustomed to the McDonald's way of doing business.[21]

As was true of Coca-Cola, the global scope and significance of McDonald's has led to serious criticisms of the company as a global entity. International concerns about increasing global obesity have focused on the chain's offerings; American documentarian Morgan Spurlock filmed *Supersize Me,* named after the restaurant's "supersized" drink and fries offerings, to chronicle his experiences eating only McDonald's for thirty consecutive days. His doctor forced him to quit before the thirty days were up because of the severe impact that its high-fat, high-calorie offerings were having on his health. (McDonald's subsequently eliminated its supersize menu.) Eric Schlosser offered a broader indictment of fast-food restaurants and the lifestyles that developed to accommodate them in his 2001 book, *Fast Food Nation: The Dark Side of the American Meal.*[22]

Lifestyle changes like those seen across East Asia provoke further worries on the part of many commentators and analysts. McDonald's has changed various consumer cultures, eating styles, and social relationships. Such changes inevitably engender substantial resistance, fear, uncertainty, and even anger. People worry that local cultural products will be replaced by those offered by the global corporation, even as they see local business practices and relationships changed to meet the needs of the global, transnational company. They also worry about the fact that their children spend their time in new places, making new contacts, and, perhaps most worryingly, adopting new styles and cultural behaviors—like eating lots of french fries or learning English from a McDonald's menu board. Such changes can—or can be seen to—cause a wide range of cultural changes that work as a subtle form of cultural imperialism. Local cultures might be displaced in favor of a global, consumerist, effectively American one.

McDonald's has also not always lived up to its dietary commitments. On entering the Indian market, for example, the chain promised that no beef fat would be used in the oil in which its fries were cooked. This promise was made to meet the dietary restrictions of Hindus, for whom cows are sacred and beef is forbidden. However, McDonald's continued to add a small amount of beef fat to its fry oil mixture in order to assure the desired taste for the fries. The company was forced to change its oil formula when this practice was discovered and it lost a lawsuit. The incident left many people with concerns about whether the restaurant would live up to its other dietary promises.

Like Coca-Cola, McDonald's has also faced an array of criticisms from environmentalists. McDonald's is a hamburger restaurant, after all, meaning that its growth necessitates an increase in the amount of beef available to feed its customers. This is quite separate from the chain's reliance on vast amounts of chicken, potatoes, and other crops it needs to produce its food. Beef production is particularly troubling to many environmentalists because it takes a large amount of grain to feed cows to the point that they gain enough weight to take to slaughter. Growing large amounts of grain, in turn, requires both that new land be brought into production and that large amounts of chemicals be used to fertilize crops and protect them from infestation and disease. Rain forests and other delicate ecosystems have been destroyed to serve the planet's growing demand for beef, sparking concerns that humans are both driving some species to extinction and promoting global warming to satisfy their fast-food desires. McDonald's is not the only source of this pressure, of course, but it is the largest and most globally recognizable symbol of the global love affair with beef. It therefore takes a leading role in debates about human-caused environmental degradation and species extinction worldwide. Its demand for cheap chicken causes similar questions to be raised in terms of the mass-production chicken farms needed to satisfy its requirements.

In just fifty-four years, McDonald's has gone from a small number of restaurants offering quick meals at low prices to the symbol of global fast food. (As an aside, the restaurant only sells Coca-Cola soft drinks at its stores, further linking two brands as planetary forces.) Today it has stores in 119 countries across six continents. It has annual revenues over $24 billion.[23] It is a global symbol of America and a major force in contemporary globalization.

A Brief Global Cultural History of Blue Jeans

It is not strictly correct to say that Levi Strauss, a German-born entrepreneur who moved to San Francisco during the Gold Rush that hit California after gold was discovered there in 1848, invented blue jeans. A thick, heavy cotton called denim preexisted Strauss's use of it, as did the color, a type of blue named after the Italian city of Genoa, which was later translated as "jeans." Indeed, Strauss went to California with the intent of selling tents and other supplies to the miners. When that plan failed, Strauss discovered that the miners complained that their cotton clothes wouldn't stand up to the rigors of mining. He went into business with Jacob Davis, a local tailor who hit upon the idea of adding copper rivets to the pockets and other weak points of the denim pants he made. Thus Levi's blue jeans were born.[24]

Blue jeans quickly became a standard item for American workers. Cowboys wore them as they rode. Farmers wore them as they planted and reaped. Workmen relied on their sturdiness as they laid pipes, built roads, and worked in factories. Manufacturers produced women's sizes in World War II to accommodate the many women who moved into the war production work force. Jeans were reliable. They also signaled the wearer's status as working class.

Notably, the nascent film industry helped bring jeans into global consciousness. Cowboys were seen to wear jeans in generations of early movie westerns. This established blue jeans as quintessentially American clothing. Whether good guys or bad guys, cowboys were American, and so were jeans.

Blue jeans began to move out of the world of work in the 1950s. Blue jeans were adopted by beatnik poets and cultural nonconformists as expressions of their rejection of mainstream culture, which they thought was symbolized by the grey flannel suit that characterized the "organization man" who went to work in a big, anonymous office building to sell insurance or do some other apparently boring and conformist job. Beats and "bad boys," symbolized by actors like James Dean and Marlon Brando and movies like *Rebel without a Cause* and *The Wild Bunch*, expressed their refusal to conform to dominant norms and values by wearing tight jeans rolled up at the ankles, often matched with black leather jackets and white T-shirts with cigarette packs rolled up in the sleeves. Likewise, Elvis Presley challenged the sexual mores of the times as he wore denim pants while performing hits like "Jailhouse Rock." Jeans were a way for wearers to publicly declare their unwillingness to comply with the values of McCarthyite, Cold War America.

Like most cultures facing challenge, 1950s America fought back against the threat it perceived was posed by the growing number of apparent deviants across society wearing blue jeans. Dress codes were instituted and aggressively enforced in schools; not only were jeans banned, but women were often denied the right to wear pants at all. Police treated bands of jeans-wearing youths as likely criminals and sought to break up any group as quickly as possible. Mainstream movies and television shows reinforced traditional morality by showing teenagers in conformist clothing behaving as their parents wanted them to. Wearing jeans was a political act with political consequences.

The 1960s shattered whatever efforts mainstream America had undertaken to limit the cultural spread of blue jeans. The social and political protestors of the decade wore blue jeans to signal their rejection of conventional American values. In part, this was a result of the attempts to control jeans wearing in the 1950s; wearing blue jeans after society tried to stamp them out was a clear declaration of resistance. Moreover, the fact that the pants were made out of denim cotton provided another statement of difference. Fashion in the 1950s had emphasized artificial fabrics like easy-to-clean polyester. Cotton was natural—the antithesis of the corporate-dominated, anti-nature ethos of the organization man. Jeans became as much a symbol of the counterculture and student activist movements of the period as did long hair, drug use, the sexual revolution, and what is today referred to as "classic" rock.

In addition, styles of jeans proliferated, as bell-bottoms and other loose-fitting types offered young radicals a fashion-based way to reject the uptight, constrained values of their parents' generation—values that were mirrored in tight-fitting and aggressively structured clothes, even jeans, of the previous decade. Wearers decorated their jeans with beads, peace symbols, antiwar messages, marijuana leaves, and a seemingly endless number of symbols of their political, social, moral, and cultural sensibilities.

By the end of the decade, jeans were ubiquitous in the United States—especially among students. A decade that had begun with students wearing coats and ties, or at least khakis and button-down shirts, to their college classes ended with students in blue jeans, even if they did not intend to make a political statement. As a consequence, U.S. jeans sales doubled nationally in the three years from 1962 to 1965. They quintupled again from 1965 to 1970.[25]

The 1970s saw jeans embedded across American pop culture. The upscale department store chain Neiman Marcus gave Levi Strauss & Co. its Distinguished Service in Fashion Award in 1973. The American Fashion Critics gave the company a special award for making "a fundamental American fashion that . . . now influences the world." The now-defunct American Motors Corporation, maker of the Gremlin and Hornet car lines, contracted with Levi Strauss to provide blue denim fabric for the interiors of its two automobiles. Denim was believed to signal both patriotism (an ironic reversal of the values of the 1960s counterculture activists) and optimism to consumers. These decisions were confirmed by 1977, when over 500 million pairs of jeans were sold in the United States alone. This was more than double the U.S. population.[26]

The 1970s also saw the emergence of upscale, expensive designer jeans. Fashion powerhouses like Calvin Klein, Givenchy, and Oscar de la Renta produced expensive jeans as fashion statements. Calvin Klein sold 125,000 pairs of these costly pants every week in 1979.[27] Jeans had evolved from workman's staple to fashion essential.

Along the way, blue jeans became a global standard of fashion. Several different measures of their global popularity can be offered, but a particularly striking one derives from a study of consumer awareness of American brands in the Soviet Union. A 1989 survey of college students at Kharkov State University in Ukraine found that English-speaking students knew of a wide range of American brand names, including blue-jean companies. The students also recognized American automobile, cigarette, and soft drink brands.[28] (Jeans were heavily traded on the black market in the Soviet Union in this period.)

Other measures of the global success of blue jeans can be offered as well. One study found that in 2011 the average consumer worldwide owned seven pairs of jeans.[29] The average man owned six pairs, while the average woman owned seven.[30] Seventy-five percent of consumers reported that they "loved" or "enjoyed" wearing denim; 75 percent of women and 72 percent of men reported preferring to wear denim jeans to other casual pants.[31]

One of the more striking features of this global growth is that jeans sales are less dependent on franchised networks of suppliers than is the case with restaurants or soft drinks. While major producers like Levi Strauss, Wrangler, and Guess exist, blue jeans have been adapted and produced across the globe, in some cases, this production is explicit piracy, meaning that established brand labels are simply sewed directly on to pants made in factories and workshops not affiliated with the companies in any way. In many cases, however, the making of blue jeans is simply another domestic industry. It is possible to buy locally produced blue jeans in many places around the world; as one example, I found numerous denim shops in the Grand Bazaar in the heart of Istanbul, Turkey. Jeans are a transparent product, in Olson's phrase[32]: they emerged from the American cultural milieu but offered images of comfort, freedom, and even nonconformist rebellion that resonated with customers worldwide. As a consequence, it is possible to see people wearing jeans virtually anywhere on the planet regardless of, or perhaps in addition to, whatever the native standards of clothing might be.

As with Coca-Cola and McDonald's, any product that has global impact also generates social and economic concerns. The same is true for blue jeans, although in the absence of a leading, central, corporate face on which to focus concerns, the issues raised in regards to blue-jeans and the blue-jean industry are more diffuse and indirect than were those aimed at Coke and McDonald's.

One set of complaints is aimed at the creeping casualism embedded in the very notion of wearing blue jeans. Fears that jeans cause cultural change have been common in both industrial democracies and emerging societies around the world. Numerous commentators have opined that blue jeans represent a threat to proper dress codes in the office, in schools, and even in ordinary public life. Blue jeans are seen to tempt people away from proper conduct precisely because they are comfortable and convenient: their casual use is believed to promote lack of care in relation to one's job, one's studies, and one's interaction with other human beings. Such concerns are particularly noteworthy in "new" areas of jeans' global expansion. Whether the style is infiltrating the boardroom or rural Asia, concerns are raised that the norms, values, ideals, and rituals associated with normal life in these cultural enclaves are likely to be changed under the casualism that emerges when blue jeans are common.

Another focus of concern in the globalization of blue jeans has been the politics of cotton. Cotton is a globally traded product that has the potential to be a major export in many developing countries. It is also, of course, the source of denim, the foundation material for blue jeans. Building on the notion of comparative advantage discussed in chapter 1, many countries around the world have excellent growing conditions for cotton. They also have low labor costs, meaning that cotton can be grown there relatively inexpensively. According to the theory of comparative advantage, these countries ought to dominate the global trade in cotton. These nations could then use any profits generated from growing cotton to support their national development, and consumers around the planet could enjoy high-quality cotton products at low prices. The United States, however, has a well-developed cotton industry that is not globally competitive under current trade conditions, but has substantial influence in Congress and the rest of the U.S. political system. U.S. cotton farmers have used their political clout to gain national subsidies for their products, in effect using U.S. taxpayer dollars to subsidize the real price of U.S. cotton on global markets. American taxpayers pay some of their taxes to U.S. cotton producers so that these producers can sell cotton for the same price as international producers can.

This practice violates the theory of free trade in several ways. For example, it raises the actual cost of cotton goods for American consumers, since they are actually paying taxes to buy jeans at the same cost that they could buy jeans made with cotton produced by international farmers without any tax subsidy. It also means that international producers do not have the opportunity to invest their profits into local economies, thereby stimulating local demand for goods and services— including goods and services of U.S. companies and brands.

Regardless of the policy recommendations embedded in the theory of free trade and comparative advantage, U.S. cotton farmers use their political power to maintain the tax subsidies their products receive. This in turn causes significant challenges for advocates of free trade, especially when new international trade agreements are negotiated. Recent trade negotiations have been complicated by the desires of many countries to protect their politically powerful yet uncompetitive industries; one particularly contentious set of issues has been the international trade in cotton. The popularity of blue jeans is by no means the whole cause of growth in cotton farming globally, but it is a central market for the cotton industry. Blue jeans are, as a consequence, indirectly at the center of global trade fights today.

There have been environmental complaints about blue jeans as well. Cotton fields might occupy lands that could be used for growing food. Alternatively, cotton fields might replace vital habitats for native species. Concerns have also arisen about the dyes used to make jeans blue or other colors, or the techniques like acid washing used to weather jeans into fashionable looks. Chemicals can leach into—or be dumped into—local water supplies. Workers exposed to toxic fumes have experienced serious health consequences. And of course, the simple act of transporting cotton and cotton goods to markets around the world entails burning fossil fuels in trucks, trains, and ships. Global trade may well encourage global warming.

At least one other concern about the blue-jean industry deserves attention: how they are made. Most blue jeans are made in factories in the developing world, many of which are what is typically described as "sweatshops." This complaint is by no means unique to the blue-jean industry: most apparel is made in factories in places without the same standards for worker health, safety, comfort, and decent treatment that are common, if not universal, in countries across North America, Europe, and Japan. The low wages paid in many such factories stand in stark contrast to the hundreds of dollars some customers pay for so-called designer jeans (or shoes, or jackets, or other apparel items). One of the consequences of low-priced clothing is exploitative labor standards in the parts of the world that actually make the jeans worn by people elsewhere.

As was the case with the analysis of the global/cultural position of Coca-Cola and McDonald's offered earlier, whether one thinks that blue jeans are wonderful or that blue jeans are a profound symbol of globalization gone wrong, it is clear that what started as a technical solution to the problem miners had getting clothing strong enough to stand up to the demands they placed on it has become a central force in economic and cultural globalization. Blue jeans are an American phenomenon that has become a global one—and also a local one at the same time. They express rebellion, Western individualism, and personal freedom even as they are marketed by global megacorporations to an increasingly interconnected world. This convergence of economics and culture is a central feature of globalization today.

CHAPTER 15

The Religion Market

Olivier Roy

THE MARKET: METAPHOR OR FACT?

The concept of a "religion market," more recent than that of acculturation, is now well established, at least in Anglo-Saxon academic circles.[1] In 2008, a leading international research organization, the Pew Forum on Religious and Public Life, published a survey on religious practice in the United States entitled *A Very Competitive Marketplace*. The concrete experience of a number of those involved in religion also prompts them to speak in terms of a "market":

> So what have I observed? In terms of societal environment, it is clear that the religion "market" is not flourishing for the historic Churches. It is very volatile, disparate, contrasting and indefinable, etc. Of course, there are "niches" which are doing well, like that of Taizé, but they are not big enough to be significant in terms of growth. . . . The figures are there, and very much so. The laws of the market do indeed exist for everyone, and particularly for our parishes. It is up to us to recognize that for many of our contemporaries, our "spiritual church products" seem either unappealing or inappropriate, or obsolete.[2]

In contrast to the theories of acculturation (which see religion as an offer that is imposed), this concept of a market, borrowed from the economy, postulates that first of all there is a demand for religion (invoking a human nature that, in any case, has a religious "need") which seeks out what is available on the market.[3] But globalization has led to a global religion market. We now speak of "consumers," in other words people who have spiritual needs to be fulfilled and who find themselves confronted with a choice of products that are varied and accessible, wherever they may be in the world, or almost. Globalization has opened up a market once controlled by one or several mainstream groups.

Today's "consumers" of religion have choice. The political constraint, which demands that subjects share the religion of the sovereign (*cuius regio eius religio*) has either disappeared or has become devoid of meaning as a result of the development of virtual spaces (Internet, satellite television). The social constraint, bound up with peer pressure, is seriously challenged by the loosening of social ties, the individualization of behaviours, access to information, and the crisis of the denominational Churches. The "products" are standardized, the marketing languages are either the vernacular languages or the major languages of globalization (notably English). In particular, the separation of religious and cultural markers means that people can "consume" a religious product without having to be familiar with the culture that has produced it. Products circulate via universalist technical media: radio, Internet, television networks. They are promoted through marketing campaigns: shows, star appearances, use of stadiums and advertising techniques; televangelists and imams (Amr Khalid) reach an audience that no pulpit or *minbar* could give them. Each individual can adapt the "belief kit" on the market to suit his or her needs, or almost: at the same time there is a customization and standardization of the products.

Market deregulation leads both to a homogenization of the products and increased competition. Religious freedom is not only an abstract right: it helps religion to evolve. Contemporary globalization therefore echoes the general extension of the market and places all religions in competition with each other, despite local attempts at closing in. The spread of religion goes hand in hand with democratization, as we witnessed with the collapse of the Soviet Empire. Of course, there are protectionist tendencies which attempt to reterritorialize religion (Algeria, Russia), by restricting conversions or by dubbing any new product a "cult," especially if it is imported. In France in recent years the tendency of parliamentary missions has sometimes been to combat sectarian drifts—a tendency widely encouraged or boosted by the mass media.

But the opening up of the market presupposes the constitution of an individual player, more or less freed from ethnic, cultural, social and historical constraints, freely choosing the product on the religion market that best suits him or her. The market theory is vindicated by the phenomenon of free, voluntary mass conversions, carried out at the individual level, not collectively—a phenomenon that is probably typical of the modern era. We are no longer talking about the socially or politically inspired mass conversions which characterized the expansion of the major religions, but of a circulation of individual players who sometimes change "denomination" while remaining within the framework of the same religion (people switch from Sufism to Salafism or vice versa, or from Anglicanism to evangelicalism, very often as born-agains), or again by changing religion (from Islam to Christianity, or vice versa).

The use of the word "market" is nevertheless more metaphorical than truly conceptual. An interpretation that merely attempts to transpose economic theories, like those of Rodney Stark and Laurence Iannaccone,[4] soon comes up against its limitations: the idea that first of all deregulation is necessary (total religious freedom), followed by a rich and varied offer in order for religious practice to flourish (that is the theory of supply-side stimulation—the more there is of a religion on the market, the more people will consume), does not take into account either the disparities in religious practice or the fact that new religions can develop in hostile environments, like Christianity in Muslim countries (Algeria, Morocco, and especially Central Asia).[5]

The market theory is diametrically opposed to the theory of acculturation. It is interesting to see how the debate on religion is modelled on, or apes, the debate on the economy in general, caught between a neo-Marxist theory of alienation, which sees religion purely in terms of domination strategies, and a neo-liberal theory of the rational individual acting within the transparency of a globalized market, which implies that the individual has absolute freedom. Advocates of the neo-Marxist viewpoint take a protective stance (defending sovereignty, territory, national tradition, established Churches, etc.), thus treating religion similarly to an identity issue, a line taken by conservatives and right-wingers until now, but becoming more prevalent among the left too. Suffice it to mention the role the secular left plays in France in the battle against sects, accused of being "submarines" of American influence. Typical is the attitude of Jean-Pierre Brard, the mayor of Montreuil who, in February 2005, interrupted an evangelical Protestant service where the worshippers were, incidentally, chiefly black. Today, this supposedly "republican" left is "territorialist": it is opposed to delocalization of the economy, wants to re-establish national sovereignty, and is obsessed with the battle against foreign sects and missionaries, from Salafism to evangelicalism.

By contrast, exponents of the market approach defend marketization as inevitable and positive; the American Department of State has set up an office for the purpose of protecting religious freedom. Each year it publishes a report naming and shaming the countries which do not respect it, including France when it comes to the Islamic headscarf and cults. And so it follows that the upholders of "national" authenticity see Protestant proselytism as an avatar of American cultural imperialism and evidence of the desire to reduce "national markets"; authoritarian regimes all over the world also try to pass laws against proselytism (Russia, Algeria, where converts were prosecuted in 2008). On the other hand, supporters of the theory of the religion market see in it a sign of adaptation, of a marketing capacity and the exercise of freedom. The experience of conversions and of the expansion of some religions shows that, as always, "protectionism" is a rearguard action. The global religion market actually exists.

The question is, how does such a market work? How can religious goods circulate? Precisely because they are separated from their cultural origin. Culture makes the commodity unconsumable outside its cultural sphere, unless of course the indigenous culture itself is attacked. The creation of a uniform religion market presupposes the deculturation of religion, in other words the separation of the two markers. But this separation is enforced by the market and mobility, because the consumer can choose (this is the concept of availability for export). The market supposes the weakening of the social constraint and even the loss of its embeddedness. It gives people the freedom to choose and means that religious authorities cannot impose their will, at the risk of losing their customers. The current "religious revival" is not a revival at all, but a consequence of globalization.

But what makes the product marketable, apart from its ability to circulate? Effectively, the market in itself does not transform a religion into a product: the religion must have an ability to adapt to the market. It is the disconnect between cultural and religious markers that makes the product marketable. The market does not create the phenomenon, but it multiplies its effects by sanctioning the religions that have best adapted. The process of severance between religious and cultural markers is even more pronounced with globalization: in fact it becomes the norm and "crushes" traditional religiosities.

Secularization comes in not because it marginalizes religion, but because it isolates religion from culture and makes the religious object independent. Nevertheless, the detachment processes are not only linked to secularization, but also to the development of fundamentalisms which reject culture. Fundamentalism has always existed, but in globalization it finds a new space and a means of enduring. The separation of the religious marker from the cultural is both essential and unstable; the "fallout" for culture is unavoidable when fundamentalism (and all religious charismatism) appears in a real society. But globalization offers a virtual space which seems to make it possible to ignore both social and political constraints. Fundamentalism is therefore both a contributory factor and a product of globalization. It offers it a new space and it contributes to the deculturation of existing religions.

In separating religion from culture and autonomizing it, secularization and fundamentalism turn it into an export product. Free, individual conversion then becomes the proof of a religion's capacity to become globalized. The proliferation of laws against proselytism is the proof that the number of conversions rises in situations where conversion was perceived as marginal, even unthinkable (Algeria). Furthermore, even when conversions are not significant statistically, they always are symbolically, since they break a taboo and therefore help undermine a religion's social embeddedness (which is what is happening in Malaysia and Turkey).

MARKET CONDITIONS

a) Circulation
The market assumes a common space for the circulation of products, operating outside any state controls. This free religion market exists today. It has not eradicated the national "markets," any more than in the economic sphere; national and ethnic religions are holding out. There are still protected markets, where laws attempt to restrict changes of religion or, to be more exact, the abandoning of national religions in favour of globalized religions. But on the other hand, religions closely linked to a group, a territory, or a culture can suddenly put themselves on the global market and become universal.

Clearly, the circulation of religion is accentuated by migration and demographic shifts, but it goes much further. Religions can circulate independently of people, neo-Buddhism, neo-Hinduism, and a number of Sufi brotherhoods are spreading in the West independently of any mass migrations, since it is enough for the master or a few disciples to move around from place to place. There is also the increasingly frequent case of self-conversions as a result of reading or the Internet, or through fascination for a religion often evoked in the media and in some cases given a bad press (Islam in the West, Christianity in Muslim countries, but also Judaism). An interesting case is that of the African-Americans who converted to Judaism having had no contact either with a rabbi or with the local Jewish community, but from a Protestant biblical culture, as is also the case for a Ugandan community (*Abayudaya*) and a Burmese tribal group, which self-converted to Judaism, declaring themselves to be the Bnei Menashe, one of the ten lost tribes of Israel.[6] In these last three instances, the leaders who self-converted to Judaism started out as Protestants: so it seems that the choice of Judaism stems from the promotion of Israel in an evangelicalist-type Protestant culture combined with the wish no longer to identify with Christianity; but the state of Israel does not encourage these conversions and generally refuses to grant citizenship to "self-converts," especially if they are black.[7]

While migration movements automatically result in a deterritorialization (and possible reterritorialization) of religions, this can just as easily happen *in situ*. But new technologies are obviously absolute deterritorialization factors. In his excellent study *Internet et Religion,* Jean-François Mayer shows how the Internet offers a non-territorial space to people who never leave their own homes. He cites the case of a virtual parish that was also "real," since its patron was the Anglican bishop of Oxford, which only accepts parishioners who are duly signed up and active on the website; in 2007, this i-church had 258 registered followers, some of them living in New Zealand.[8]

The emergence of the Reform Jews from the ghetto in the nineteenth century is an example of circulation without migration: it was the end of a territorial segregation associated with a social, cultural, and linguistic segregation. This emergence prompted the Jews of the Enlightenment (the *Haskala* movement) to think of Judaism as "pure religion" and not as a culture (replacement of the concept of Jewish by that of Israelite). Hinduism "for export," which developed from the late nineteenth century (with the stream of Sris—or gurus—flocking to England), was not the outcome of a migration of Hindus, even if a few individuals did move around, masters going to the West and disciples going to India to study. Hinduism is traditionally the epitome of a territorialized religion: the role of the Ganges is central, and the social stratification of the caste system has difficulty surviving population movements. But Hinduism succeeded in becoming deterritorialized precisely by leaving aside the Ganges and caste and reconstituting itself as a religion for export, either to immigrant Indian populations (Jamaica), or to Western converts.

A recent example of a rapidly globalizing territorial religion is Mormonism: associated with a specific place, Utah in the United States, after a migration wave in 1847 modelled on the exodus of the Jewish people seeking a Holy Land where the Temple would be built, and victims of a persecution which served to reinforce the sense of community, highly endogamous (a tendency strengthened by the fact that the Mormons were initially polygamous), overtly racialist until the 1970s (blacks were not admitted to the priesthood), Mormonism seemed to have become the equivalent of a neo-ethnic religion through the establishment of a quasi-ethnic group around a religious identity. And then, within a few decades, swept along by an intense missionary movement (it was mandatory for young people to devote two years of their lives to preaching), Mormonism became deterritorialized[9] and gained a foothold among the black community, who were only allowed to become priests in 1978, following the civil rights movement.[10] Paradoxically, it was the civil rights movement that pushed a very conservative Church to abandon the chief obstacle to its expansion, i.e., its racial differentialism. Nowadays, the Mormon

Church is one of the world's fastest-growing religions, especially among the black population. Jamaica and Africa both now have autochthonous Mormon Churches. The Church reportedly grew from 1.7 million members in 1960 to around 13 million by 2007, 7 million of whom are outside the USA.[11]

Today's missionary movements do not start from a centre and reach out to a "periphery." The prime movers do not necessarily come from countries associated with the religion they are spreading. The figure of the white Western Christian missionary is dying out to be replaced by a redistribution of roles. There is movement in all directions.

We have already mentioned the case of the Muslim Indians of Chiapas converted by white Spanish missionaries, themselves self-converts to Islam; the latter, the Murabitun, set up an organization in Spain made up solely of converts, the Junta Islamica, with Mansur Escudero as Chairman, Yusuf Fernandez as spokesman, and Abdennur Prado as head of the Catalan branch. Meanwhile the Spanish Muslims of Arab origin are united under the umbrella of the Islamic Council of Spain. The Murabitun have also set up an organization in Dubai to mint gold dinars in order to bypass the global banking system (the company's chairman is Umar Ibrahim Vadillo). This represents a double cultural inversion: in Spain the Murabitun seem to be an Arab fifth column, albeit more culturally than ethnically, whereas in Mexico they are the expression of a Western-style deculturation.

Another reversal is the driving energy of an African Christianity which, in different guises, has set out to conquer the white West. A Protestant Pentecostalist Church, the Embassy of the Blessed Kingdom of God for All Nations, founded by a Nigerian minister, Sunday Adelaja, in Ukraine, sends missionaries to Western Europe and to the United States.[12] WASP American Episcopalians have joined the Anglican Church of Nigeria. Similarly, the Anglican Church of Kenya ordained two (white) American priests who are opposed to the ordination of gay priests; a participant in the ceremony, the Caribbean Drexel Gomez, stated: "The Gospel . . . must take precedence over culture."[13] In Denmark, a minister from Singapore, Ravi Chandran, is drawing those who feel let down by the Lutheran Church; the Lutheran bishop of Copenhagen reckons that more than a quarter of the capital's Sunday morning Protestant services are held in "foreign" Churches.[14]

In July 2007, twenty-three Korean Protestant missionaries, the majority of whom are women, were taken prisoner by the Taliban in Afghanistan, suddenly drawing attention to the huge Korean presence in Protestant missionary networks (particularly in Central Asia and West Africa). There are reportedly 16,000 Korean missionaries overseas, a figure which puts Korea (population 44 million, including 8.7 million Protestants) just behind the USA when it comes to the absolute number of Protestant missionaries abroad, and above it when it comes to the percentage of nationals with a missionary vocation.[15] It is as if Korean Protestantism were primarily an export product, like cars: the Protestant community is barely growing within the country (and, quite logically, Protestants are over-represented in the Ministry of Foreign Affairs). This is definitely an export religion.

Conversely (but the word barely has any meaning now), Westerners go to the East to become priests in Oriental religions to which they have converted in the West. The best-known examples are the members of Hare Krishna, various Zen schools, and adherents of Sufism.

A young American Buddhist moved to Japan and wrote: "Early next morning we do *zazen* [meditation], joined by two board members. They are obviously unaccustomed to it." Suddenly young Japanese people are going to the United States to learn Buddhism: "Influenced by his long stay at Doshin-ji [Buddhist monastery in New York], the younger Suzuki plans to build an 'American-style' zendo at Unsen-ji next year. It is ironic, perhaps, that a revitalized Zen Buddhism in America is being carried back to influence the ancient, but weakened, practice in Japan. This morning's sitting is a rare event at the temple."[16] Extending the metaphor, we could speak of delocalized religions re-exporting themselves back to the countries of origin.

The Hare Krishna movement, a regular feature of Western street life since the 1960s, is also a good example of this "Hinduism for export": devoted to the worship of the god Krishna, it does indeed derive from Hinduism, but it was founded in New York in 1966 under the name of the International Society for Krishna Consciousness (ISKCON), by Bhaktivedanta Swami Prabhupada, and it recruited essentially among the Western hippie community. Missionary and egalitarian (rejection of the caste system), it breaks with the territorialist Hinduism of India. And yet, at the close of the twentieth century, it became re-Hinduized in two ways, while at the same time maintaining its missionary and anti-caste aspects. Numerous Indian immigrants to the United States joined the movement because it enabled them to reconcile their two identities, Hindu and American, in a synthesis that was virtual, since it was based on the use of floating religious markers (saffron robes, repetition of a mantra in a language they generally did not speak).[17] But the movement also became established in India, from the West and thanks to Western "priests" (the Vridavan temple founded in 1975, and New Delhi, at Raja Dhirshain Marg, built in 1998): an information panel at the Delhi temple informs us that "In the temple there are beautiful paintings by Russian artists on the different past times of Radha-Krishna, Sita-Ram, Laxman, Hanuman and Chaitanya Mahaprabhu. Special programs like kirtan, aarti, pravachan and prasadam are held every Sunday."[18] There are two noteworthy points here: the paintings in the temple are the work of Russians (the icon tradition?), and the "religious service" offered by the temple is modelled on the Sunday-morning Protestant service held at a specific time. Even the board giving details of the type of services and times of the services offered has a distinctly American flavour.

The Rastafarian movement targets "globalized blacks": it emerged in Jamaica and worships Haile Selassie, the emperor of an Ethiopia which was the only black country to hold out against colonialism. But in the 1960s, the movement crystallized around reggae with the musician Bob Marley as its figurehead, to become established in Nigeria.[19] A mythical Africa—Ethiopia—was re-invented in the West, subsequently to become rooted in the real Africa: the journey was made from West to East.

Another example is the radical Islamist movement Hizb ut-Tahrir. Founded in the early 1950s in Jordan as an Islamist movement to free Palestine, it spread throughout Europe from its London base. Recruiting among second-generation and converted Muslims, it advocated the establishment of a non-territorialized caliphate (in other words having jurisdiction over all Muslims wherever they are in the world). From London, it re-exported itself to Central Asia (Uzbekistan), Pakistan, and Australia, and from Australia to Indonesia where it is becoming increasingly influential. In 2002, three British citizens were arrested in Cairo, accused of attempting to establish Hizb ut-Tahrir there: one of them, from a Pakistani family, was born in the UK; another, Ian Nisbet, was a convert; and the third, Reza Pankhurst, had an Iranian father and an English mother. This is an example of Islamic radicalism being exported to Muslim countries from the West.

Sufism is another instance of this delocalization of religion. A certain number of brotherhoods exported themselves by playing on two complementary factors: immigration and conversion. Among the first are the Tijaniya and the Mourides of Senegal, which themselves are relatively recent brotherhoods (late nineteenth century). These brotherhoods operate in a "glocal" manner: initially the group has a specific territorial base which will remain its global headquarters, i.e., the town of Touba for the Mourides. Immigrants from the brotherhood to Europe and the United States, who set off in search of work and not to proselytize, create very supportive networks: they send money back to Touba, they welcome and assist young migrants, while dignitaries circulate from one immigrant community to another. And so these networks become transnational networks for the movement of goods and people and become part of a globalized economy. But at the same time, the group converts outside its ethnic, migrant base; newcomers also find the path to Touba.

One of the best-known brotherhoods whose expansion is due to conversions rather than to emigration is the Haqqanya: originally it was a branch of the Naqshbandi family, established in the Caucasus and then in the Middle East; in the second half of the twentieth century, their Sheikh was Mawlana Shaykh Nazim Adil al-Haqqani, an Arab of Syrian origin living in the North of Cyprus. One of his disciples, Lebanese-born Muhammad Hisham Kabbani, moved permanently to Chicago in 1991. The American branch saw a meteoric growth, far surpassing the number of disciples in the Middle East. A Bosnian branch grew out of the American branch. The language of the brotherhood's websites is therefore English (with a Bosnian version).

But Sufism in the West has an older history. In 1910, Inayat Khan, an Indian musician, visited Europe with his brother. A member of the *chestiyya* Sufi movement, he founded his own order in the West, with converts. In 1923, he set up the International Sufi Movement in Geneva, with a constitution and a transnational hierarchical structure.[20] This framework is far removed from the Sufi traditions in the Muslim countries. This brand of Sufism is purely Western and is what I term "neo-Sufism," even if the word is used in various ways. Other Sufi movements transplanted in this way include the Qadiriya Boutchichiya, which came from Morocco and spread in France via converts who tended to be from the middle and upper classes. (A description from the inside can be found in the book *Self-Islam* by Abdennour Bidar.[21]) The brotherhood of the Fethullahci, led by Fethullah Gülen, is a typical case of a globalized neo-brotherhood, even if it has difficulty spreading beyond the Turkish-speaking sphere. Familiar to experts on Turkey, it found new prominence when its leader was "elected" the most influential intellectual in the world through an Internet survey carried out by the magazines *Foreign Policy* and *Prospect* (June 2008). It was of course the followers of the brotherhood who voted collectively (probably under instructions), but, as there were 500,000 online voters, this reflects the globalized nature of the brotherhood (members are connected to the Internet and capable of following instructions in English). And then there are examples of more or less imaginary "brotherhoods," like the one founded by the prolific author Idries Shah who claimed to recruit among the leading figures of the Muslim world.[22]

The development of international religious networks from local groups is not confined to Sufism but is often linked to a charismatic figure who founds a religious school of thought. These "glocal" networks can also be strengthened as a result of splits, conflicts, the reformulation and autonomization of local branches, each one affirming its authenticity. The ultra-orthodox Jewish movement has also spawned networks similar to brotherhoods since they are essentially identified with schools of thought headed by charismatic rabbis; they are all the more deterritorialized in that they are originally non-Zionist—they do not convert but are entirely globalized.[23]

b) Export Religions

Successful religions all have an export formula. They are founded on the complete separation of the religious marker from the cultural marker, and on a formatting that enables them to appear as a universal religion adapted to the new forms of religiosity, such as self-realization. This does not mean they reject the cultural marker: on the contrary, they can exhibit some cultural markers, rather like supermarket loss leaders, but detached from any real society, in a context where a certain exoticism is seen as positive, like advertising designed to appeal to floating markets: exoticism (French names for US bakeries), the assumed permanent connection (pasta and Italy) that is found in the link between Zen and Japan (from the kimono to karate terms). The saffron robes of the Hare Krishna or the *shalwar kamiz* (long white shirt and baggy trousers) of the Salafis function as imaginary references. Deculturation does not mean abandoning cultural markers, but manipulating them outside any social reality. Proclaiming the autonomy of the faith community involves a certain exhibitionism, like the headscarf. That does not mean that any religious symbol is a sign of exhibitionism, but that it is interpreted as such. Visibility is characteristic of contemporary religion.

In the strict sense, we shall term "export religion" those that exist solely in their exported form: neo-Buddhism, neo-Hinduism, neo-Sufi brotherhoods. They are utterly cut off from their roots, and when they return to them, it is in the form of a re-exportation and not the revival of a local tradition.

Hinduism is deeply rooted in a society (castes) and a territory; it is very diversified and does not really refer to a body of precise, standardized doctrines. It can only become missionary if first of all it transforms itself into something new: it is hard to imagine Hindu missionaries explaining the need to adopt the caste system. It therefore requires an explicit reformulation of the belief system, detached from its original culture and society while preserving the exotic Oriental "touch" that is its appeal (especially the gurus' dress). Beliefs also need to be standardized, simplified, and formatted so that they can operate in Western environments. In short, to export Hinduism, it must be transformed into a religion.

This reformulation process was implemented by Hindu thinkers in India, generally those with a dual culture, writing mainly in English but ultimately only finding an audience in the West. As with Buddhism, they emerged at a time of religious and political reform, at the close of the nineteenth century, as a reaction against the English hegemony of which they were nevertheless also a product—but this pre-dated exportation (it is not immigration in itself that changes a religion).[24] For them, the West was a means of affirming the universalism of their thinking. These were not Western intellectuals seeking an imaginary Hinduism, but Indian philosophers and gurus who went and "sold" a spirituality presented as universalist, as a reaction against Western materialism; but their approach also implies a critique of colonialism, which is very pronounced in thinkers such as Sri Aurobindo. The colonial background is fundamental, but it acts in both directions: the reciprocal reformatting of religion resulting in a competition to bring comparable if not similar products face to face.

The Ramakrishna Mission developed in India in the late nineteenth century; it targeted Anglicized Indians, and its first publication was in English. One of its members, Swami Vivekananda, gave a paper which attracted a great deal of attention at the 1893 World's Parliament of Religions in Chicago, one of the first examples of attempts to transcend religions in favour of spirituality and shared values (no Muslims were present at this gathering, however). The most renowned case is that of Sri Aurobindo (1872–1950), who helped popularize yoga. He instigated the Auroville project, near Pondicherry. It is interesting that these movements adopt modern legal norms (registering their organizations under legal statutes), refuse to define themselves as a religion, and prefer to be known as philosophies. They also emphasize the importance of meditation techniques that can be acquired outside their original host cultures and are often seen as providing access to an "Oriental" culture based on silence and the rejection of discourse, i.e., of the Word, thereby escaping the need for language learning and studying literature. Again, a little holy ignorance!

Other examples include the Sri Ram Chandra Mission (established in 1945 in the United States), the guru Swami Prakashanand Saraswati (whose centre is in Austin, Texas), Maharishi Mahesh Yogi (the Beatles' guru), and the Divine Light Mission, founded in 1970 by the guru Maharaj Ji and established in Denver, Colorado.

A number of similarities have been observed in Buddhism. In exporting itself, Buddhism loses two fundamental characteristics: its monasticism and the division into "vehicles" or schools of religious thought. As Raphaël Liogier points out, we are witnessing both a simplification and standardization of ideas, and a proliferation of transnational bureaucratic organizations claiming to be Buddhist but which are far removed from tradition.[25] British Buddhists have tried to re-establish Buddhism in India, as did the "Untouchables," or Dalits starting with India's first president, Bhimrao Ramji Ambedkar, who eventually converted. So in Buddhism this "deculturating" choice derives from the rejection of the caste system.

Some forms of Buddhism have prospered better in the West than in their countries of origin. Japanese Shin Buddhism began in the late nineteenth century within Japan's sphere of influence, but it quickly became established in Hawaii, and took off with "Bishop" Yemyo Imamura, between 1900 and 1932. Imamura switched to English and built a dharma school, as did the Hindus. Then he took on as his deputy a convert, Shinkaku Hunt, a former British Anglican priest. At the same time, in San Francisco, the Dharma Sangha of Buddha was established by "whites." Self-converts can also appropriate Buddhism in this way, as in Germany.[26] But generally, as with Hinduism, there is a master, in this instance from Japan, like the famous Teitaro Suzuki (1870–1966), whose master, Shako Suen, was also at the World's Parliament of Religions in Chicago in 1893. And so it is clear that the desire for internationalization (and not only to defend an existing religion) was evident in different milieus.

But this Western poaching takes on a different dimension when a movement like the Soka Gakkai appears. Here we are not dealing with a religion formatted for export: the transformation happened *in situ* in Japan where the movement has considerable influence including at a political level (embodied in a party, The New Komeito). But, as Lorne L. Dawson writes, it very consciously Westernized its organizational structure, not in order to export itself, but because it was fashionable to do so.[27] In this instance, the change is linked not to an export strategy, but to a transformation of religion setting it on a course leading to globalization.

Movements derived from Hinduism and Buddhism frequently adopt non-religious legal forms (foundations, NGOs), like the Brahma Kumaris World Spiritual University, a spiritual organization of the eponymous sect, which, as an NGO, was given consultative status to the United Nations Economic and Social Council in 1983, and then to UNICEF in 1987. It is also associated with the United Nations Department of Public Information. In 1986, it launched its "Million Minutes of Peace" appeal. The objective of the programme was to emphasize that "peace begins with the individual and the peace process therefore must start with the individual." This trend is probably a way of escaping the religion paradigm, which demands compliance with the mainstream model of religion, the concept of "religion" as it happens. Religions for export therefore challenge not only the relationship between the religious marker and the cultural marker, but also the nature itself of the religious marker.

The circulation of religions has possibly led to the erosion of religion by new forms of synthesis between belief, law, and power, in other words, tending towards humanitarian action. NGOs are akin to modern-day foreign missions. But that is another story.

c) The Deterritorialization of the Local

Another form of deterritorialization is that of the local community: the disappearance of the territorial parish in favour of a choice of place of worship depending on affinities. The Catholic Church was a territorialization factor: in many countries, the "parish" became an administrative body (as is still the case in Louisiana) and, traditionally, worshippers were obliged to frequent their parish church; they married in it and were buried there. Jesuit missions in Quebec, Paraguay (on the colonial model of the *encomiendas*), and China established indigenous Christian villages; the

Reductions of Paraguay were a sort of forerunner of the *kolkhoz* or the *kibbutz*.[28] The monasteries, often linked to an agricultural estate, were also forms of religious territorialization. The Catholic practice of worshipping local saints or associating one saint with a number of sites (Our Lady of Lourdes, our Lady of Lorette, our Lady of Guadalupe) helped to sanctify a territorial division and endow particular places with their own religious identity. Similar phenomena are to be found in Islam: the Afghan *zyarat*, the Moroccan *zawwya* and *mulud*, and the Azerbaijani *pir* are ways of pinning down sometimes nomadic tribal groups to a territory associated with a saint's tomb, or to mark the identity of local communities.

Moreover, in Islam, the identity of a neighbourhood is traditionally marked by a mosque; in Central Asia, the sudden mushrooming of mosques after the collapse of the USSR was more to do with the desire of each *mahalla*, or neighbourhood, to have its eponymous mosque than with a sudden surge of religion. Judaism, especially in North Africa, also has a long history of local "saints." In all the major religions, pilgrimages create a network across the territory, which help shape it. There is a close link between religious practices, socialization, and territorialization which the move towards "faith communities" breaks.

Effectively, in a number of today's religions, the notion of a "parish" or a territorial community is being eroded in favour of the community of affinities. The same place of worship might see not only different generations of believers passing through (newcomers who live as a diaspora, a second generation for whom culture and religion are separate), and different categories of believers (in an American Buddhist temple immigrants from South-East Asia mix with white converts), but also different religions as upward social mobility disperses communities (synagogues or churches converted to mosques).[29] These days "ethnic neighbourhoods" resulting from immigration seem to last for a shorter time than at the beginning of the twentieth century; there is no longer a "Little Italy" in the United States, and upwardly mobile groups do not seek to reconstitute ethnic neighbourhoods (the Jews of New York who settle in Florida no longer form neighbourhood communities). On the other hand, people form groups on the basis of religious affinity rather than ethnicity (orthodox Jews like the Lubavitch and the Satmar in Montreal and New York).[30] But these groupings are precarious, as for different reasons (upward mobility of their members, housing conflicts, etc.) the re-territorialization at local level remains fragile. In 2008, there was a neighbourhood conflict surrounding a Hindu temple in Fairfax county, near Washington, DC; owing to its popularity there was insufficient parking and the neighbours demanded that the temple be moved. But the priests had just completed the slow ritual process of "territorializing" the gods, which made moving difficult from a religious point of view. The gods (and the worshippers) were sent away, through the power of real estate considerations, to wander in an endless "wilderness."[31]

People now move to be near the place of worship that suits their religious sensibility. There is no longer an automatic correspondence between the social bond and the religious bond. New religious movements favour mega churches, stadiums, assemblies in secular venues (including the gatherings of young people organized by Pope John Paul II). We are seeing congregations of affinity rather than of proximity. In France, the Catholic parish is often in decline as a result of competition from new, non-territorialized congregations, in other words not under the jurisdiction of the bishop. Many parishes prefer to call themselves simply a "community" rather than a parish. Priests are increasingly asking those who come asking for a religious service, such as marriage, to demonstrate commitment and a personal link with the community; it is not enough just to be included in the register of baptisms or to reside in the parish. To be married, for example, it is no longer sufficient to have been baptized or to reside in the parish; increasingly priests are asking that the couple be members of the local community and not simply "Catholic." What is vanishing, for the Church, is the notion of the "sociological Catholic" or "nominal Catholic": people must prove their faith; one can assume no longer that subjects are believers.

The decline in the number of priests has strengthened the role of the community to the detriment of the parish, since priests are now mobile. But the Vatican is resisting this development. Sunday Assemblies in the Absence of Priests (SAAP) were curbed if not prohibited, as increasingly the priest was being replaced by lay members. In France, 10 percent of serving priests are of foreign origin—African, Polish, Lebanese, etc. Priests are being replaced by lay people for all sorts of things. Only two sacraments are reserved for priests, the Eucharist and confession, in addition to their role of community leader. Lay communities are being established, not through the will of Rome, but quite simply because the priest is being marginalized. Alpha Groups, for example, are religious and theological formations set up by a fundamentalist Anglican, with special methods and a zealous proselytism, but these are rapidly being emulated by Catholics. Their aim is to bring back or bring in all-comers in the cities in particular, based on a very modern form of conviviality: people share an apartment and day-to-day life while working on a group project.

The ultimate stage of the process could be the i-church. There are already a number of websites for all the major religions which offer religious services: liturgical moments (the equivalent of hours of monastic prayer), prayer moments, guided "retreats," sermons, confession, and also conversion, or even matchmaking to find a spouse of the same religion, since people now have only sporadic, even virtual contact with their chosen community.

This is one of the reasons for the success of Protestantism and evangelicalism: whereas the Virgin Mary is territorialized, The Holy Spirit is anywhere and everywhere. There is no need to have a real rock on which to build the Church. You can pray in a garage or a stadium. The sacredness of the place is no longer important (whereas a church is traditionally consecrated, then purified if it is desecrated). Pentecostalists and evangelicals place the emphasis on the Holy Spirit; they do not attach any importance to the sacredness of the place of prayer, and nor do they go on pilgrimages. The Holy Spirit is everywhere, place no longer matters, except perhaps the Holy Land. The Catholic Church has the same theological conception of the Holy Spirit, but it plays no part in popular religiosity, which is chiefly devoted to Mary (hence often territorial), whereas it is essential in the evangelicals' worship. This confirms that the issue is less to do with theology than with religiosity.

This refusal to sacralize places of worship, geographical places and territories is just as evident in Salafism, which does not celebrate *mawlid* and *ziyarat* (respectively Moroccan and Central Asian local pilgrimage centres), the worship of local saints and the sacralization of tombs (even that of the Prophet). Only Mecca escapes this deterritorialization, and only just. Salafism picks up on the idea that a mosque is simply a place of prayer only for the duration of the prayer (*masjid*, the place of prostration [*sajd*], which no longer has any meaning when the rites are not being performed).

But Catholicism also has its own ways of globalizing its symbols. The "transportation" of territorialized saints is interesting. A local saint, in the context of migration, becomes either a sort of tribal "totem," or is transposed to the space of a broader section of the population. For example the Virgin of Guadalupe, greatly revered in Mexico, moved to Los Angeles with refugees from the *Cristero* rebellion of the 1930s and the clandestine Mexican immigrants of today. Although she was purely Mexican in her original context, since the other Latin American countries had their own holy places, the Virgin of Guadalupe gradually became the "saint" of all the Latinos in the United States, even of all the Catholic immigrants in Los Angeles, including the Vietnamese and the Koreans. This has gone hand in hand with the creation of neo-ethnic groups, followed by de-ethnicization.[32] On Saint Patrick's Day, all of New York is Irish. Here, the totemic function of the Catholic saints (being the emblem of a corporation, a parish, a group, an ethnic group, or a nation) is also able to become globalized: the totem remains, but it becomes nomadic and its audience changes.

This is not to say that the Internet has replaced territory. There is a definite trend in this direction, but the notion of place still makes sense. However, territory is being eroded, or rather the new territories are virtual. Deterritorialization goes along with the quest for imaginary territories (*ummah*, Holy Land, Ganges, Lhasa, etc.) and with the apocalyptic second-coming brand of millenarianism that announces the end of the world. Sub-cultures are becoming globalized, but they each bring their "map" of the world with a centre and specific places of pilgrimage. Beyond these pilgrimages which territorialize by drawing on historical roots—what I call "identity pilgrimages" (such as the Chartres pilgrimage)—what we are seeing is pilgrimages that have become deterritorialized. Paradoxically this applies to the Muslim *hajj*. There is indeed a place, Mecca, but it has been cut off from its context; the pilgrim, supervised, isolated, merged into the abstract mass of Muslims from all over the world, standardized by the clothing and the rite, does not go to Saudi Arabia, but to Mecca (which is even specified on the visa). The journey is no longer "real," as pilgrims travel by air: they no longer journey by land. Apart from the Iranians (the riots of 1987) and the Saudis themselves (the storming of the Grand Mosque in 1979), no radical movement has shown an interest in Mecca. It is not an issue for political Islam because Mecca has only a virtual reality.

What is at issue in the pilgrimage is very much the territorialization of religion. For example, a controversy is currently raging in the Hassidic world. Rabbi Nachman of Breslau (1712–1810) is buried at Uman, in Ukraine. His tomb attracts tens of thousands of pilgrims every year, particularly at Jewish New Year, to the extent that special airline charters have been set up.[33] As mentioned earlier, the Nachman group puts the emphasis on "joy" as a factor in transmitting faith, and attracts followers from far beyond its traditional religious school. Historically, the group is not Zionist, like many Hasidim, and so feels non-territorialized (although that does not make it anti-Zionist). But an appeal has been launched in Israel to repatriate the rabbi's ashes to the Hebrew state, the effect of which would be for these religious, ethnic, and political maps to coincide. So here we observe the territorialization of a religious Jewish identity in favour of an Israeli identity. But then what happens to the diaspora? Either it is perceived as having a vocation to make *aliyah* (which is the official Israeli position), or it is seen as a non-territorialized political Israel (in 2008 the Chairman of the Jewish Council of Europe demanded that all Jews have the right to vote in Israel), or as a religious community living in a space other than that of political territorialization.

Territorialization is the revenge of politics.

d) The De-Ethnicization of Religion

There is a to-ing and fro-ing in the separation of religious and cultural markers: ethnic religions become universalized, but, as a result of immigration among other things, new connections between ethnicity and religion are appearing, and new ethnic groups are even emerging, like those now called the "Muslims" of Europe, irrespective of the extent of their religious practice.

But this ethnicization is often purely transient, particularly with regard to immigration. Ethnic Churches are characteristic of the first generation, such as the "white Russians" in France after 1917. The Orthodox Churches of Paris are divided between Russian, Armenian, Ukrainian, Coptic, Syriac, Greek, Chaldean, Romanian, Georgian, etc. Paris had, and still has, Polish, Vietnamese, and Tamil Catholic churches. The African Muslim brotherhoods, Vietnamese Buddhist temples after the immigration of the boat people, the Tamil Hindu temples of Reunion Island, and the Iranian Shia mosques of Los Angeles—in all these cases a religious marker and a cultural marker (either national or linguistic) are closely interlinked. But this seeming ethnicization is often merely a transitional stage before a new separation. The moment (the transition) is taken for the essence of the phenomenon.

Let us take the case of the ethnically Chinese Protestant Church in the United States, the Chinese Christian Church (CCC) of Greater Washington, analyzed by Fenggang Yang. At first glance, it may appear to be an ethnic Church which recruits primarily among the Chinese immigrants keen to integrate, who convert to Christianity while holding onto Chinese cultural markers. But the author shows that things are more complex than that: first of all, unlike the traditional immigrant Churches (Italian, Polish, and Irish for Catholicism), but like all the modern-day evangelical Churches, the CCC does not have any social integration activities (such as support or mutual aid). It devotes itself solely to preaching and worship (the only exception being that it gives Chinese classes). Furthermore, the ministers refuse to recognize any ethnic dimension (which would certainly not have been true of an Italian or Irish Church a century earlier). The congregation is made up of people of Chinese origin who are completely assimilated, who do not need a stepping stone to integration or a refuge. So why travel miles to be with others from the same background? Because here, that background is primarily religious: "Chinese Christians have chosen evangelical or fundamentalist Christianity and subsequently have formed non-denominational ethnic churches. They see themselves as a minority, not so much in the ethnic but in the religious sense. They say that, although many Americans claim to be Christian, only a few are true Christians—those who are born-again."[34] And the author goes on, emphasizing that for today's Chinese, Christianity is no longer an "imperialist" religion, but a universalist faith. In other words, it has broken away from its historical image, because it has become de-nationalized and de-ethnicized. This is an argument that I have heard among the Taliban: in answer to the question of why, if they claim to represent "true" Islam, do they define themselves (and in particular why do they act) as Pashtuns, they reply: "Because the Pashtuns are the best Muslims in Afghanistan."

Another example is that of the reconstruction of Hinduism among migrant Indians. The first stage is the ethnicization of the religion, in other words the identification of an ethnic group with a religion. The fact that in India there is a large Muslim minority and that the state is officially secular means that, except among the nationalists of the Bharatiya Janata Party (BJP)—only just—there is no strict identification between Hinduism and being Indian. The diversity of castes, languages, and regions is too enormous.

But with emigration, the socio-cultural basis of the castes disappears, even if the memory of them remains alive. Muslim Indians then tend to identify with other Muslims from the Indian sub-continent (for example, on Reunion, the *Zarab* Muslims from Gujarat define themselves as Muslim first, as opposed to the Hindu Tamils, who in this case stress their Tamil identity; and yet both groups come from India). Many expatriate Hindus then reconstruct a Hinduism common to all the groups, irrespective of caste, standardized and formatted according to the prevailing concept of what a religion is. Steven Vertovec has studied the phenomenon in depth and shows how, in the Caribbean, Hinduism becomes the ethnic religion of Indians.[35] This ethnicization process is often only the first step towards deculturation—separation of religious and cultural markers—since "ethnic" religions are formatted along the lines of the religions of the host countries. Once the religion is autonomized, it can become de-ethnicized and operate outside its original cultural environment. In fact, the deculturation of Hinduism among Indian migrants, or in the context of "religion for export," analyzed earlier, relies on processes that have much in common: challenging the caste system, standardization, simplification, and professionalization of the protagonists.

Therefore, ethnicization can be a stage in the deculturation process, because we are dealing with a neo-ethnic group, like the "Muslims" in Europe who manufacture "pure religion" which is better equipped to emancipate itself from culture than the complex constructions rooted in the original cultures. In the case of reconstructed Hinduism in Jamaica, reformulation goes hand in hand with the influence of reformist groups. The Arya Samaj movement, which was founded in 1875 by Swami Dayanand Saraswati, who rejected the caste system, promoted monotheism and placed great importance on the Vedas, or sacred texts. Universalism, monotheism, revealed book: this is clearly a theological and "ecclesiological" formatting process based on the Christian template.

Paradoxically, the ethnicization stage can also be a route to the deculturation of a religion. Ursula King shows how Hinduism cannot function outside India unless it becomes deculturated.[36] But even in India, the process of deculturation by transformation is apparent in the way in which the nationalist BJP reconstructs a homogeneous Hinduism, also overlooking the caste system. In this instance, the invention of a Hinduism modelled on a Western religion, Christianity as it happens, is not the product of postcolonial alienation, but on the contrary, of a nationalist identity claim seeking to assert itself in the global religion market, to avoid being subjected to the influence of foreign religious paradigms that are better suited to the new market.

The fabrication of European Muslims as a neo-ethnic group also has a deculturating effect, since the lowest common denominator uniting them can only be defined in opposition to concrete cultures, which means that Salafism is often the best-placed strand to define this universalist religion.

The following stage is the transition from ethnic community to faith community. It is the faithful who no longer want to be seen as "ethnic," either because their personal identity is now religious, or because the group has ceased to have an ethnic base. Karen Chai studied the transformation of a "denominational" Korean Protestant Church in the United States into a multi-ethnic Church, using English as its working language and becoming evangelical to some degree.[37] The parents are Korean, speak Korean, and want their children to marry Koreans; in the "bourgeois" Protestantism of the established Churches they are seeking a way of reconciling integration, social advancement, and maintaining their ethnic and cultural identity. The younger generation, however, are born-again evangelicals for whom faith is more important than ethnicity when choosing a marriage partner. Here too the shift to evangelicalism works in favour of deculturation. It is often in the choice of minister (must he belong to the ethnic group?) that tensions become evident.

In Tahiti, one of the Chinese Pentecostalist Churches was initially explicitly "ethnic" (of the Hakka group), but it became a multi-ethnic Church as a result of a split: the Hakka community leaders of the Alleluja Church sacked the (French) minister because he was recruiting particularly among non-Chinese communities; so he left the Church to found a new one, and 80 percent of the Chinese congregation followed him.[38] At the same time, in 1997, in an apparently unconnected move, the dances and other cultural expressions of the Bonne Nouvelle Tahitian Pentecostalist Church were rejected by the United States-trained clergy. This reflects a complex shift in the articulation between Tahitian identity, evangelicalism (which operates on the political level), and deculturation.

When the Russian Patriarch Alexis II visited France in October 2007, he requested that French Orthodox communities that are not linked with other national non-Russian Churches (Greek, Serbian, etc.) be placed under his jurisdiction. But there was a great deal of protest from the French Orthodox community, since they did not feel, or no longer felt, "Russian" and they wanted to sever the link between ethnic group, nation, and Orthodoxy. Michel Sollogoub, the secretary of the Council of the Archdiocese of Russian Orthodox Churches in Western Europe, wrote in *Le Figaro*:

> This revival of the Church in Russia should not eclipse the modest but real pres-
> ence of Orthodoxy in France. A noteworthy effect of the history of the twentieth
> century is that the Orthodox Church stepped outside its traditional geographical
> boundaries. Russian and Greek, and later Serbian, Romanian and Lebanese mi-
> grations have resulted in a firmly established Orthodox presence on French soil,
> even if these communities maintain strong ties with their original Churches.
> After eighty years of history, Orthodoxy in France is no longer a foreigners'
> Church. The awareness of a common responsibility in the witnessing of Ortho-
> doxy and the desire to overcome the divisions between ethnic dioceses led to the
> setting up of an Inter-Episcopal Committee in 1967. Following the recommenda-
> tions of the pan-Orthodox meeting of Chambésy in 1993, this body was renamed
> the Assembly of Orthodox Bishops of France (AEOF) in 1997. The aim was to
> create, in the long term, and with the support of the different original Churches,
> a unified synodal structure, admittedly temporary, but in line with Orthodox
> ecclesiology.[39]

Christian Orthodoxy became established in France as a result of ethnic immigration, but it became de-ethnicized. Those who are interested in the subject can
visit the chapel of Saint Gregory the Athonite and Anastasia the Roma at Bernwiller
in the Sundgau (south of Alsace). The icons were painted by an American convert
and the chapel is looked after by Dr. Louis Schittly, a Mount Athos convert and one
of the founders of Médecins sans frontières.

e) Deculturation

These "marketing" processes therefore assume the deculturation of religion and, once
again, some religions are in a better position than others to become deculturated.
People sometimes wonder why Pentecostalism is the religion that is experiencing the
strongest expansion. Pentecostalism places the emphasis on emotion, healing, and
speaking in tongues. Under the influence of the Holy Spirit, emulating the apostles,
some believers start "speaking in tongues," and people with whom they have no
shared language are able to understand what they say. But the Pentecostalists who
preach in "tongues" do not preach in any real language: glossolalia is purely a succession of sounds. The "message" gets through all the same: the Word of God no longer
needs to be set down in a specific language and culture. It is precisely because the
spirit is dissociated from the Word that the message is universal. The Holy Spirit is
beyond culture, even if Christ took on a human form.

However, independently of religion, we are currently witnessing a reduction of
the "substance" of languages in favour of the transmission of a message which, in order
to be univocal, must be simple. Therefore, Pentecostalism sits alongside the improvement of automatic translation systems and the decline of languages of communication. English, which is now dominant, turns into pidgin, or rather "globish," the term
coined by Jean-Paul Nerrière in his excellent book.[40] Now it's the era of "goddish."

One could cite many more signs of this trend towards deculturation, even
when the Pentecostalist Churches identify closely with a particular people; for

nstance, the Pentecostalist Assemblies of God, dominant in Tahiti, do combat traditional beliefs and advocate the use of French. Christian ministers of Pakistani origin return to their homeland and behave like the Christian version of the Tabligh: "This was part of Arif's mission: to infuse a fundamentalist faith and literalist understanding of Scripture in Pakistani 'nominalists,' a word Martin and Shehzad spoke with disdain, a word damning those who were Christians in name only, Christians by lineage but not practice, Christians who conformed to Pakistani culture rather than biblical teaching."[41] All the literature on Pentecostalism is in a similar vein: there is both an affirmation of identity and a negation of traditional identity-markers. This dual logic is taken to extremes in one particular movement: Youth With a Mission. Taking the very classical view that Jesus will only return when the Gospel has been preached the world over, the movement's aim is to identify the "unreached people," those who have never heard the preaching of the Gospel, and to enable them to be evangelized in their own language. The movement has identified eight thousand ethnic groups and proposes that young Christians adopt these groups and possibly volunteer as missionaries (see http://www.ywam.org). The anthropological knowledge which the young people are taught is then used against the cultures to be "saved"—though not in the anthropological sense.

FROM MARKET TO HUGE BAZAAR
OF RITES AND SIGNS

Once again, the separation between religious and cultural markers does not mean that one disappears in favour of the other, but that they disintegrate and recompose themselves in a loose and random manner. That enables religions to create their market and compose *à la carte* menus connecting elements from different sources. This "customization" annoys both the cultural and the religious purists, who see it as syncretism or, worse, as a profound ignorance as to the specific nature of each religion. Ultimately, the "customers" here are simply learning the lessons of a real homogenization of the religious arena, which makes it so difficult to grasp what, in a given religion, is irreducible both with regard to other religions and to culture itself.

We end this section with two examples that mean nothing from a statistical point of view but which are typical of this dance of markers. The first is the story of an "emblematic" song entitled *"e-o" nigun* (the *nigun* is a traditional Hassidic "humming tune") which spread among American Reform Jewish students in 2003 during Shabbat retreats for young people. Now this chant had been brought over from South Africa, and there is nothing Jewish about it; but, according to the author, that is precisely why it was adopted: because it allows a universal Jewish identity that is not connected to the traditional markers (Yiddish, religious, or Israeli songs). It is the same principle as the "Torah-yoga" which appeared in the 1970s, where verses and prayers are recited accompanied by movements, which is traditional, but this time the movements are based on yoga.[42]

And one last anecdote: young Chinese girls adopted by American Jewish families are given a Jewish religious upbringing and a Chinese cultural one: "Olivia R., a girl in Massachusetts who celebrated her *bat mitzvah*[43] last fall on a day when the Jewish harvest festival of *Sukkot* coincided with the Chinese autumn moon festival, said she saw no tension between the two facets of her identity either. 'Judaism is a religion, Chinese is my heritage and somewhat my culture, and I'm looking at them in a different way,' she said. 'I don't feel like they conflict with each other at all.'"[44] But in this description of a celebratory moment, nothing makes sense, either in terms of religion or in terms of culture. What "Chinese culture" had this young girl received apart from a calendar? What dual culture beyond a set of *kosher* chopsticks? How can kinship and adoption be reconciled within Judaism, *bar* and *bat mitzvah*, Chinese New Year and *Sukkot*? But that is precisely what is happening nowadays.

GUIDE TO FURTHER READINGS
AND RECOMMENDED WEBSITES

The following books and websites will guide your global studies research projects more deeply into the cultural and historical dimensions of globalization:

- A.G. Hopkins, ed., *Globalization in World History*. New York: Norton, 2002.
- Paul James, ed., *Globalization and Culture*. 4 vols. London: Sage, 2010.
- Bruce Mazlish, *The New Global History*. New York: Routledge, 2006.
- Jan Nederveen Pieterse, *Globalization and Culture*, 2nd ed. Lanham, MD: Rowman & Littlefield, 2009.
- Manfred B. Steger, ed., *Globalization and Culture*. 2 vols. Cheltenham, UK: Edward Elgar, 2012.
- George Yúdice, *The Expediency of Culture: Uses of Culture in the Global Era*. Durham, NC: Duke University Press, 2005.
- Globalism Research Center (GRC), RMIT University, Australia: http://www.rmit.com/globalism
  Founded in 2002, the GRC is concerned to facilitate and enhance activities of cultural dialogue across the continuing and positive boundaries of cultural diversity in the world today. It undertakes engaged research into globalization, transnationalism, nationalism, and cultural diversity. It seeks to understand and critically evaluate current directions of global change, with an emphasis on the cultural implications of political and economic transformation.
- Center for Global Culture and Communication at Northwestern University: http://www.communication.northwestern.edu/global_communication/
  The Center for Global Culture and Communication was founded in 2002 as a transdisciplinary forum to address the emerging importance of globalization in communication studies.
- World History Matters: http://worldhistorymatters.org/
  Housed in the Roy Rosenzweig Center for History and New Media at George Mason University, World History Matters is an award-winning portal to other world history websites.

PART IV

Spaces and Environments

Discussion Points:

- What are the most serious social and environmental consequences of rapid urbanization in the Global South?
- What the primary factors driving the development of "urban patches" in almost every city around the world?
- In your view, what are the most formidable challenges global cities face in the twenty-first century?
- Do you agree or disagree with the suggestion that some actions of unauthorized immigrants fit the civil disobedience framework developed by Dr. Martin Luther King? If so why; if not why not?
- What is "global citizenship" and how can it be linked to global migration?
- What are the principal reasons for the failure to establish a global climate regime capable of reducing greenhouse gas emissions worldwide?
- Which measures suggested in the "One-Degree War" do you consider to be the most and the least likely to be adopted within the next decades? Why?

CHAPTER 16

The Urban Climacteric

Mike Davis

> We live in the age of the city. The city is everything to us—it
> consumes us, and for that reason we glorify it.
>
> —QNOOKOME QKOM[1]

Sometime in the next year or two, a woman will give birth in the Lagos slum of Ajegunle, a young man will flee his village in west Java for the bright lights of Jakarta, or a farmer will move his impoverished family into one of Lima's innumerable *pueblos jovenes*. The exact event is unimportant and it will pass entirely unnoticed. Nonetheless it will constitute a watershed in human history, comparable to the Neolithic or Industrial revolutions. For the first time the urban population of the earth will outnumber the rural. Indeed, given the imprecisions of Third World censuses, this epochal transition has probably already occurred.

The earth has urbanized even faster than originally predicted by the Club of Rome in its notoriously Malthusian 1972 report *Limits of Growth*. In 1950 there were 86 cities in the world with a population of more than one million; today there are 400, and by 2015 there will be at least 550.[2] Cities, indeed, have absorbed nearly two-thirds of the global population explosion since 1950, and are currently growing by a million babies and migrants each week.[3] The world's urban labor force has more than doubled since 1980, and the present urban population—3.2 billion—is larger than the total population of the world when John F. Kennedy was inaugurated.[4] The global countryside, meanwhile, has reached its maximum population and will begin to shrink after 2020. As a result, cities will account for virtually all future world population growth, which is expected to peak at about 10 billion in 2050.[5]

MEGACITIES AND *DESAKOTAS*

Ninety-five percent of this final buildout of humanity will occur in the urban areas of developing countries, whose populations will double to nearly 4 billion over the next generation.[6] Indeed, the combined urban population of China, India, and Brazil already roughly equals that of Europe and North America. The scale and velocity of Third World urbanization, moreover, utterly dwarfs that of Victorian Europe. London in 1910 was seven times larger than it had been in 1800, but

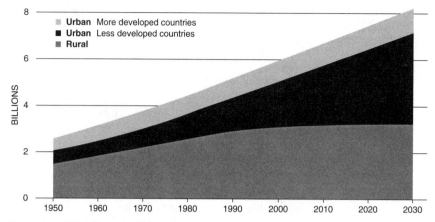

Figure 16.1 World Population Growth

Table 16.1[8] Third World Megacities (population in millions)

	1950	2004
Mexico City	2.9	22.1
Seoul-Injon	1.0	21.9
(*New York*	*12.3*	*21.9*)
São Paulo	2.4	19.9
Mumbai (Bombay)	2.9	19.1
Delhi	1.4	18.6
Jakarta	1.5	16.0
Dhaka	0.4	15.9
Kolkata (Calcutta)	4.4	15.1
Cairo	2.4	15.1
Manila	1.5	14.3
Karachi	1.0	13.5
Lagos	0.3	13.4
Shanghai	5.3	13.2
Buenos Aires	4.6	12.6
Rio de Janeiro	3.0	11.9
Tehran	1.0	11.5
Istanbul	1.1	11.1
Beijing	3.9	10.8
Krung Thep (Bangkok)	1.4	9.1
Gauteng (Witwatersrand)	1.2	9.0
Kinshasa/Brazzaville	0.2	8.9
Lima	0.6	8.2
Bogotá	0.7	8.0

Dhaka, Kinshasa, and Lagos today are each approximately *forty* times larger than they were in 1950. China—urbanizing "at a speed unprecedented in human history"—added more city-dwellers in the 1980s than did all of Europe (including Russia) in the entire nineteenth century![7]

The most celebrated phenomenon, of course, is the burgeoning of new mega-cities with populations in excess of 8 million and, even more spectacularly, hyper-cities with more than 20 million inhabitants—the estimated urban population of the world at the time of the French Revolution. In 2000, according to the UN Population Division, only metropolitan Tokyo had incontestably passed that threshold (although Mexico City, New York, and Seoul-Injon made other lists).[9] The *Far Eastern Economic Review* estimates that by 2025 Asia alone might have ten or eleven conurbations that large, including Jakarta (24.9 million), Dhaka (25 million), and Karachi (26.5 million). Shanghai, whose growth was frozen for decades by Maoist policies of deliberate underurbanization, could have as many as 27 million residents in its huge estuarial metro-region. Mumbai (Bombay), meanwhile, is projected to attain a population of 33 million, although no one knows whether such gigantic concentrations of poverty are biologically or ecologically sustainable.[10]

The exploding cities of the developing world are also weaving extraordinary new urban networks, corridors, and hierarchies. In the Americas, geographers already talk about a leviathan known as the Rio/São Paulo Extended Metropolitan Region (RSPER) which includes the medium-sized cities on the 500-kilometer-long transport axis between Brazil's two largest metropolises, as well as the important industrial area dominated by Campinas; with a current population of 37 million, this embryonic megalopolis is already larger than Tokyo–Yokohama.[11] Likewise, the giant amoeba of Mexico City, already having consumed Toluca, is extending pseudopods that will eventually incorporate much of central Mexico, including the cities of Cuernavaca, Puebla, Cuautla, Pachuca, and Queretaro, into a single mega-alopolis with a mid-twenty-first-century population of approximately 50 million—about 40 percent of the national total.[12]

Even more surprising is the vast West African conurbation rapidly coalescing along the Gulf of Guinea with Lagos (23 million people by 2015 according to one estimate) as its fulcrum. By 2020, according to an OECD study, this network of 300 cities larger than 100,000 will "have a population comparable to the U.S. east coast, with five cities of over one million . . . [and] a total of more than 60 million inhabitants along a strip of land 600 kilometers long, running east to west between Benin City and Accra."[13] Tragically, it probably will also be the biggest single footprint of urban poverty on earth.

Table 16.2[14] Urbanization of the Gulf of Guinea

CITIES	1960	1990	2020
over 100,000	17	90	300
over 5000	600	3500	6000

The largest-scale posturban structures, however, are emerging in East Asia. The Pearl River (Hong Kong–Guangzhou)[15] and the Yangze River (Shanghai) deltas, along with the Beijing–Tianjin corridor, are well on their way to becoming urban-industrial megapolises comparable to Tokyo–Osaka, the lower Rhine, or New York–Philadelphia. Indeed, China, unique among developing countries, is aggressively planning urban development at a super-regional scale using Tokyo–Yokohama and the U.S. eastern seaboard as its templates. Created in 1983, the Shanghai Economic Zone is the biggest subnational planning entity in the world, encompassing the metropolis and five adjoining provinces with an aggregate population almost as large as that of the United States.[16]

These new Chinese megalopolises, according to two leading researchers, may be only the first stage in the emergence of "a continuous urban corridor stretching from Japan/North Korea to West Java."[17] As it takes shape over the next century, this great dragon-like sprawl of cities will constitute the physical and demographic culmination of millennia of urban evolution. The ascendency of coastal East Asia, in turn, will surely promote a Tokyo–Shanghai "world city" dipole to equality with the New York–London axis in the control of global flows of capital and information.

The price of this new urban order, however, will be increasing inequality within and between cities of different sizes and economic specializations. Chinese experts, indeed, are currently debating whether the ancient income-and-development chasm between city and countryside is now being replaced by an equally fundamental gap between small, particularly inland cities and the giant coastal metropolises.[18] However, the smaller cities are precisely where most of Asia will soon live. If megacities are the brightest stars in the urban firmament, three-quarters of the burden of future world population growth will be borne by faintly visible second-tier cities and smaller urban areas: places where, as UN researchers emphasize, "there is little or no planning to accommodate these people or provide them with services."[19] In China—officially, 43 percent urban in 1993—the number of official "cities" has soared from 193 to 640 since 1978, but the great metropolises, despite extraordinary growth, have actually declined in relative share of urban population. It is, instead, the small- to medium-sized cities and recently "city-ized" towns that have absorbed the majority of the rural labor-power made redundant by post-1979 market reforms.[20] In part, this is the result of conscious planning: since the 1970s the Chinese state has embraced policies designed to promote a more balanced urban hierarchy of industrial investment and population.[21]

In India, by contrast, small cities and towns have lost economic traction and demographic share in the recent neoliberal transition—there is little evidence of Chinese-style "dual-track" urbanization. But as the urban ratio soared in the 1990s from one quarter to one third of total population, medium-sized cities, such as Saharanpur in Uttar Pradesh, Ludhiana in the Punjab, and, most famously, Visakhapatnam in Andhra Pradesh, have burgeoned. Hyderabad, growing almost 5 percent per annum over the last quarter century, is predicted to become a megacity of 10.5 million by 2015. According to the most recent census, 35 Indian cities are now above the one million threshold, accounting for a total population of nearly 110 million.[22]

In Africa, the supernova growth of a few cities like Lagos (from 300,000 in 1950 to 13.5 million today) has been matched by the transformation of several dozen small towns and oases like Ouagadougou, Nouakchott, Douala, Kampala, Tanta, Conakry, Ndjamena, Lumumbashi, Mogadishu, Antananarivo, and Bamako into sprawling cities larger than San Francisco or Manchester. (Most spectacular, perhaps, has been the transformation of the bleak Congolese diamond-trading center of Mbuji-Mayi from a small town of 25,000 in 1960 into a contemporary metropolis of 2 million, with growth occurring mostly in the last decade.[23]) In Latin America, where primary cities long monopolized growth, secondary cities such as Santa Cruz, Valencia, Tijuana, Curitiba, Temuco, Maracay, Bucaramanga, Salvador, and Belem are now booming, with the most rapid increase in cities of fewer than 500,000 people.[24]

Moreover, as anthropologist Gregory Guldin has emphasized, urbanization must be conceptualized as structural transformation along, and intensified interaction between, every point of an urban–rural continuum. In Guldin's case study of southern China, he found that the countryside is urbanizing *in situ* as well as generating epochal migrations; "Villages become more like market and *xiang* towns, and county towns and small cities become more like large cities." Indeed, in many cases, rural people no longer have to migrate to the city: it migrates to them.[25]

This is also true in Malaysia, where journalist Jeremy Seabrook describes the fate of Penang fishermen "engulfed by urbanization without migrating, their lives overturned, even while remaining on the spot where they were born." After the fishermen's homes were cut off from the sea by a new highway, their fishing grounds polluted by urban waste, and neighboring hillsides deforested to build apartment blocks, they had little choice but to send their daughters into nearby Japanese-owned sweatshop factories. "It was the destruction," Seabrook emphasizes, "not only of the livelihood of people who had always lived symbiotically with the sea, but also of the psyche and spirit of the fishing people."[26]

The result of this collision between the rural and the urban in China, much of Southeast Asia, India, Egypt, and perhaps West Africa is a hermaphroditic landscape, a partially urbanized countryside that Guldin argues may be "a significant new path of human settlement and development . . . a form neither rural nor urban but a blending of the two wherein a dense web of transactions ties large urban cores to their surrounding regions."[27] German architect and urban theorist Thomas Sieverts proposes that this diffuse urbanism, which he calls *Zwischenstadt* ("in-between city"), is rapidly becoming the defining landscape of the twenty-first century in rich as well as poor countries, regardless of earlier urban histories. Unlike Guldin, however, Sieverts conceptualizes these new conurbations as polycentric webs with neither traditional cores nor recognizable peripheries.

> Across all cultures of the entire world, they share specific common characteristics: a structure of completely different urban environments which at first sight is diffuse and disorganized with individual islands of geometrically structured patterns, a structure without a clear centre, but therefore with many more or less sharply functionally specialized areas, networks and nodes.[28]

Such "extended metropolitan regions" writes geographer David Drakakis-Smith, referring specifically to Delhi, "represent a fusion of urban and regional development in which the distinction between what is urban and rural has become blurred as cities expand along corridors of communication, by-passing or surrounding small towns and villages which subsequently experience *in situ* changes in function and occupation."[29] In Indonesia, where a similar process of rural/urban hybridization is far advanced in Jabotabek (the greater Jakarta region), researchers call these novel land-use patterns *desakotas* ("city villages") and argue whether they are transitional landscapes or a dramatic new species of urbanism.[30]

An analogous debate is taking place among Latin American urbanists as they confront the emergence of polycentric urban systems without clear rural/urban boundaries. Geographers Adrián Aguilar and Peter Ward advance the concept of "region-based urbanization" to characterize contemporary peri-urban development around Mexico City, São Paulo, Santiago, and Buenos Aires. "Lower rates of metropolitan growth have coincided with a more intense circulation of commodities, people and capital between the city center and its hinterland, with ever more diffuse frontiers between the urban and the rural, and a manufacturing deconcentration towards the metropolitan periphery, and in particular beyond into the peri-urban spaces or penumbra that surround mega-cities." Aguilár and Ward believe that "it is in this peri-urban space that the reproduction of labor is most likely to be concentrated in the world's largest cities in the 21st century."[31]

In any case, the new and old don't easily mix, and on the *desakota* outskirts of Colombo "communities are divided, with the outsiders and insiders unable to build relationships and coherent communities."[32] But the process, as anthropologist Magdalena Nock points out in regard to Mexico, is irreversible: "Globalization has increased the movement of people, goods, services, information, news, products, and money, and thereby the presence of urban characteristics in rural areas and of rural traits in urban centers."[33]

BACK TO DICKENS

The dynamics of Third World urbanization both recapitulate and confound the precedents of nineteenth- and early-twentieth-century Europe and North America. In China the greatest industrial revolution in history is the Archimedean lever shifting a population the size of Europe's from rural villages to smog-choked, sky-climbing cities: since the market reforms of the late 1970s it is estimated that more than 200 million Chinese have moved from rural areas to cities. Another 250 or 300 million people—the next "peasant flood"—are expected to follow in coming decades.[34] As a result of this staggering influx, 166 Chinese cities in 2005 (as compared to only nine U.S. cities) had populations of more than 1 million.[35] Industrial boomtowns such as Dongguan, Shenzhen, Fushan City, and Chengchow are the postmodern Sheffields and Pittsburghs. As the *Financial Times* recently pointed out, within a decade "China [will] cease to be the predominantly rural country it has been for millennia"[36] Indeed, the great oculus of the Shanghai World Financial Centre may soon look out upon a vast urban world little imagined by Mao or, for that matter, Le Corbusier.

Table 16.3[37] China's Industrial Urbanization (percent urban)

	POPULATION	GDP
1949	11	–
1978	13	–
2003	38	54
2020 (*projected*)	63	85

It is also unlikely that anyone fifty years ago could have envisioned that the squatter camps and war ruins of Seoul would metamorphose at breakneck speed (a staggering 11.4 percent per annum during the 1960s) into a megalopolis as large as greater New York—but, then again, what Victorian could have envisioned a city like Los Angeles in 1920? However, as unpredictable as its specific local histories and urban miracles, contemporary East Asian urbanization, accompanied by a tripling of per capita GDP since 1965, preserves a quasi-classical relationship between manufacturing growth and urban migration. Eighty percent of Marx's industrial proletariat now lives in China or somewhere outside of Western Europe and the United States.[38]

In most of the developing world, however, city growth lacks the powerful manufacturing export engines of China, Korea, and Taiwan, as well as China's vast inflow of foreign capital (currently equal to half of total foreign investment in the entire developing world). Since the mid-1980s, the great industrial cities of the South—Bombay, Johannesburg, Buenos Aires, Belo Horizonte, and São Paulo—have all suffered massive plant closures and tendential deindustrialization. Elsewhere, urbanization has been more radically decoupled from industrialization, even from development *per se* and, in sub-Saharan Africa, from that supposed *sine qua non* of urbanization, rising agricultural productivity. The size of a city's economy, as a result, often bears surprisingly little relationship to its population size, and vice versa. Table 16.4 illustrates this disparity between population and GDP rankings for the largest metropolitan areas.

Table 16.4[39] Population Versus GDP: Ten Largest Cities

	(1) BY 2000 POPULATION	(2) BY 1996 GDP (2000 POP. RANK)
1.	Tokyo	Tokyo (1)
2.	Mexico City	New York (3)
3.	New York	Los Angeles (7)
4.	Seoul	Osaka (8)
5.	São Paulo	Paris (25)
6.	Mumbai	London (19)
7.	Delhi	Chicago (26)
8.	Los Angeles	San Francisco (35)
9.	Osaka	Düsseldorf (46)
10.	Jakarta	Boston (48)

Some would argue that urbanization without industrialization is an expression of an inexorable trend: the inherent tendency of silicon capitalism to delink the growth of production from that of employment. But in Africa, Latin America, the Middle East, and much of South Asia, urbanization without growth, as we shall see later, is more obviously the legacy of a global political conjuncture—the world-wide debt crisis of the late 1970s and the subsequent IMF-led restructuring of Third World economies in the 1980s—than any iron law of advancing technology.

Third World urbanization, moreover, continued its breakneck pace (3.8 percent per annum from 1960 to 1993) throughout the locust years of the 1980s and early 1990s, in spite of falling real wages, soaring prices, and skyrocketing urban unemployment.[40] This perverse urban boom surprised most experts and contradicted orthodox economic models that predicted that the negative feedback of urban recession would slow or even reverse migration from the countryside.[41] "It appears," marveled developmental economist Nigel Harris in 1990, "that for low-income countries, a significant fall in urban incomes may not necessarily produce in the short term a decline in rural–urban migration."[42]

The situation in Africa was particularly paradoxical: How could cities in Cote d'Ivoire, Tanzania, Congo-Kinshasa, Gabon, Angola, and elsewhere—where economies were contracting by 2 to 5 percent per year—still support annual population growth of 4 to 8 percent?[43] How could Lagos in the 1980s grow twice as fast as the Nigerian population, while its urban economy was in deep recession?[44] Indeed, how has Africa as a whole, currently in a dark age of stagnant urban employment and stalled agricultural productivity, been able to sustain an annual urbanization rate (3.5 to 4.0 percent) considerably higher than the average of most European cities (2.1 percent) during peak Victorian growth years?[45]

Part of the secret, of course, was that policies of agricultural deregulation and financial discipline enforced by the IMF and World Bank continued to generate an exodus of surplus rural labor to urban slums even as cities ceased to be job machines.

As local safety nets disappeared, poor farmers became increasingly vulnerable to any exogenous shock: drought, inflation, rising interest rates, or falling commodity prices. (Or illness: an estimated 60 percent of Cambodian small peasants who sell their land and move to the city are forced to do so by medical debts.[46])

At the same time, rapacious warlords and chronic civil wars, often spurred by the economic dislocations of debt-imposed structural adjustment or foreign economic predators (as in the Congo and Angola), were uprooting whole countrysides. Cities—in spite of their stagnant or negative economic growth, and without necessary investment in new infrastructure, educational facilities, or public-health systems—have simply harvested this world agrarian crisis. Rather than the classical stereotype of the labor-intensive countryside and the capital-intensive industrial metropolis, the Third World now contains many examples of capital-intensive countrysides and labor-intensive deindustrialized cities. "Overurbanization," in other words, is driven by the reproduction of poverty, not by the supply of jobs. This is one of the unexpected tracks down which a neoliberal world order is shunting the future.[47]

From Karl Marx to Max Weber, classical social theory believed that the great cities of the future would follow in the industrializing footsteps of Manchester, Berlin, and Chicago—and indeed Los Angeles, São Paulo, Pusan, and today Ciudad Juárez, Bangalore, and Guangzhou have roughly approximated this canonical trajectory. Most cities of the South, however, more closely resemble Victorian Dublin, which, as historian Emmet Larkin has stressed, was unique amongst "all the slumdoms produced in the western world in the nineteenth century . . . [because] its slums were not a product of the industrial revolution. Dublin, in fact, suffered more from the problems of de-industrialization than industrialization between 1800 and 1850."[48]

Likewise, Kinshasa, Luanda, Khartoum, Dar-es-Salaam, Guayaquil, and Lima continue to grow prodigiously despite ruined import-substitution industries, shrunken public sectors, and downwardly mobile middle classes. The global forces "pushing" people from the countryside—mechanization of agriculture in Java and India, food imports in Mexico, Haiti, and Kenya, civil war and drought throughout Africa, and everywhere the consolidation of small holdings into large ones and the competition of industrial-scale agribusiness—seem to sustain urbanization even when the "pull" of the city is drastically weakened by debt and economic depression. As a result, rapid urban growth in the context of structural adjustment, currency devaluation, and state retrenchment has been an inevitable recipe for the mass production of slums. An International Labour Organization (ILO) researcher has estimated that the formal housing markets in the Third World rarely supply more than 20 percent of new housing stock, so, out of necessity, people turn to self-built shanties, informal rentals, pirate subdivisions, or the sidewalks.[49] "Illegal or informal land markets," says the UN, "have provided the land sites for most additions to the housing stock in most cities of the South over the last 30 or 40 years."[50]

Since 1970, slum growth everywhere in the South has outpaced urbanization *per se*. Thus, looking back at late-twentieth-century Mexico City, urban planner Priscilla Connolly observes that "as much as 60 percent of the city's growth is the result of people, especially women, heroically building their own dwellings on unserviced peripheral land, while informal subsistence work has always accounted for a large proportion of total employment."[51] São Paulo's *favelas*—a mere 1.2 percent of total population in 1973, but 19.8 percent in 1993—grew throughout the 1990s at the explosive rate of 16.4 percent per year.[52] In the Amazon, one of the world's fastest-growing urban frontiers, 80 percent of city growth has been in shantytowns largely unserved by established utilities and municipal transport, thus making "urbanization" and "favelization" synonymous.[53]

The same trends are visible everywhere in Asia. Beijing police authorities estimate that 200,000 "floaters" (unregistered rural migrants) arrive each year, many of them crowded into illegal slums on the southern edge of the capital.[54] In South Asia, meanwhile, a study of the late 1980s showed that up to 90 percent of urban household growth took place in slums.[55] Karachi's sprawling *katchi abadi* (squatter) population doubles every decade, and Indian slums continue to grow 250 percent faster than overall population.[56] Mumbai's estimated annual housing deficit of 45,000 formal-sector units translates into a corresponding increase in informal slum dwellings.[57] Of the 500,000 people who migrate to Delhi each year, it is estimated that fully 400,000 end up in slums; by 2015 India's capital will have a slum population of more than 10 million. "If such a trend continues unabated," warns planning expert Gautam Chatterjee, "we will have only slums and no cities."[58]

The African situation, of course, is even more extreme. Africa's slums are growing at twice the speed of the continent's exploding cities. Indeed, an incredible 85 percent of Kenya's population growth between 1989 and 1999 was absorbed in the fetid, densely packed slums of Nairobi and Mombasa.[59] Meanwhile any realistic hope for the mitigation of Africa's urban poverty has faded from the official horizon. At the annual joint meeting of the IMF and World Bank in October 2004, Gordon Brown, UK Chancellor of the Exchequer and heir apparent to Tony Blair, observed that the UN's Millennium Development Goals for Africa, originally projected to be achieved by 2015, would not be attained for generations: "Sub-Saharan Africa will not achieve universal primary education until 2130, a 50 percent reduction in poverty in 2150 and the elimination of avoidable infant deaths until 2165"[60] By 2015 Black Africa will have 332 million slum-dwellers, a number that will continue to double every fifteen years.[61]

Thus, the cities of the future, rather than being made out of glass and steel as envisioned by earlier generations of urbanists, are instead largely constructed out of crude brick, straw, recycled plastic, cement blocks, and scrap wood. Instead of cities of light soaring toward heaven, much of the twenty-first-century urban world squats in squalor, surrounded by pollution, excrement, and decay. Indeed, the one billion city-dwellers who inhabit postmodern slums might well look back with envy at the ruins of the sturdy mud homes of Çatal Hüyük in Anatolia, erected at the very dawn of city life nine thousand years ago.

CHAPTER 17

The Improbable Life
of an Urban Patch

Deciphering the Hidden Logic
of Global Urban Growth

Jeb Brugmann

We begin this chapter by exploring a typical city neighborhood to understand how it works as a microcosm of the global system of cities. To begin, imagine the classic image of Earth seen from space. You will surely see the familiar pattern of great seas and continents; deserts, polar regions, and forests; the blues, tans, whites, and greens that we have come to know through astronauts' eyes. These vast natural systems and territories are what ecologists call our planet's *biomes*. Each has its distinct currents and cycles; each has its unique, complex communities of plants and animals.

But there is something truly odd about this image. You'll note that in this view your city neighborhood does not appear. In fact, in this prevalent image of Earth—ironically photographed during Earth's most rapid period of urbanization—we see a world without a single city. This deceptive view of our planet, and its widespread embrace, epitomizes the extent to which we have left our cities, and thus our future, out of view.

To find your city neighborhood, we have to put this image aside and look at Earth from a different perspective. Imagine that same view from space, but this time at night.[1] In this view, all the natural biomes are hidden in solar shadow and a totally different reality is exposed. Dense concentrations of light dominate continents and cluster on coastlines, revealing their own patterns. The United States and Europe are completely alight. A thick band of light extends all the way from Europe and the Middle East, across Russia and Siberia, to northern Asia. The lights then spread down the brightly profiled landmasses of Japan and South Korea, spill along the eastern half of China to Indonesia, and collect into a pool that illuminates the entire Indian subcontinent. The southern and northern coasts of Africa are ringed with light, and the glow in the eastern regions of South America extends around the southern and western coastlines. Light trickles out into the Amazon basin and up the western rise of the Andes.

These vast areas of light are evidence of a new ecological order—of the urban biome we are creating.[2] We have only partial measures of urban populations, economics, health, financial flows, and resource consumption. But we know this much: we cannot see the few lights of a village from space. The dots, dense clusters, or long bands of light that extend across our continents are the growing City. The flow of energy represented by the continental constellations of light is indicative of many other Earth-changing flows that connect cities into metropolitan clusters and regional systems that, in turn, connect into the City, a phenomenon now as vast and commanding in Earth's order as the great oceans.

One point in this system of light is your city neighborhood. Zoom in from space, and the blues, tans, and greens give way to urban grays and browns. At first, the city structure looks like some kind of industrial hive or a piece of modern art, but because you have become habituated to it, you will recognize its patterns. You will discern the arrangement of streets and city blocks, of residential and industrial areas, and of canalized rivers and ports. Zoom in further and you will find the unique arrangement of streets, buildings, and green spaces that distinguish your urban patch—the urban equivalent of a tiny mountain crag or a ripple in a river. Now we can begin to understand the familiar yet ever-surprising character of the City.

To take in my own urban patch I leave my computer and go to the rooftop of my home. This is a quiet, mixed-income neighborhood in Toronto, Canada. From here I can see about five hundred feet in all directions. The two- and three-story homes of my neighbors face me to the east, across the street. Behind them lies the small neighborhood park. Beyond the park, I can see the rooftops of a small social housing project and a large high school. To the west, behind a row of trees, I see the back of another row of houses like mine. These houses face one of the bigger, mixed retail-residential avenues that border our neighborhood in each direction. There is another school across this avenue, and to the southwest I can see a high-rise housing complex. Directly to the south of my house, the single-family homes extend as far as I can see, and to the north, through the full canopy of mature maple trees and above the tops of other homes, I can glimpse the taller buildings on the district's main avenue. It seems a typical, uneventful place.

An average day unfolds. A few weeks ago, the neighborhood held its annual fireworks display and organized a cleanup in the park. Neighbors have been commiserating about the noisy, swearing teenagers on the basketball court and sharing a consoling word about the passing of an elderly neighbor who had lived here since the neighborhood was built. A century ago this man's parents saw a pasture on this place, where it met a small, wooded ravine whose stream flowed down past the old brickyard and under the train tracks, and then passed through a colony of factories and workers' houses before it reached the shore of Lake Ontario two kilometers to the south. Our urban patch sits over the filled and leveled top of that ravine.

Among the accomplished writers, actors, musicians, and artists and the established professors, journalists, advertising professionals, lawyers, and civil servants who own property here, a stunning variety of recent immigrants have also laid claim in this small area. Some came from distant villages and are building their first footholds in the City. They have brought trades, extended families, and customs with them. They have not abandoned their places of origin but use our patch to extend their opportunities across those chains of light on the darkened Earth.

Twenty years ago this area was dominated by Greek and Italian immigrants. Most came in the 1950s, leaving behind countries unsettled by war. Now the annual Greek Independence Day parade on the main avenue seems like a relic of another time. An Ethiopian family owns and runs the corner store across from the school. A Korean family owns the discount store, and a Turkish family owns the shoe repair shop. These shops are across the street from a new Starbucks. Down the sidewalk from Starbucks, a Mexican immigrant has set up a burrito shop. Across the street, a Japanese man purchased a building for his sushi restaurant, and nearby two Jamaicans run a barbershop for the local Caribbean population. Another barbershop was located near the subway station for the Greeks and other Europeans, but when the two Greek barbers retired, they leased their shop to a barber from Bangladesh. The Greek men who ambled by the shop every day to their cafés and political clubs have been replaced by the daily flow of hundreds of predominantly South Asian men on their way to prayers at the neighborhood mosque. When we take our sons into the barber's now, we are invited to sit not with a copy of *Sports Illustrated* but with a copy of the Qur'an.

In the fifteen years I have lived in this place that calls itself "the Pocket," it has developed a whole new community of Muslim immigrants from India, Pakistan, Bangladesh, Afghanistan, and East Africa. Fifty percent of the children at our neighborhood elementary school do not speak English as their primary language. Cricket has become a regular sight in the park where our sons play baseball and hockey. Single-family homes and simple retail storefronts are used in new ways. Some have been divided into rooming houses, where new arrivals first take up residence as they look for work and wait for family members to arrive. Other homes are used during the workday as informal day care centers. On the avenue immediately west, next to an old Estonian church, an extended family from a small town in Gujarat owns four homes. Here the multiple couples, parents, in-laws, aunts and uncles, siblings, and cousins have re-created a life typical of the traditional "joint homes" in their native western India. On the main avenue five hundred feet to the north, near the old Italian grocery shop and the Baptist church (that still attracts worshippers of Caribbean origin each Sunday), another successful Gujarati family has established a clothing manufacturing and retail business. When I buy my business clothes there, I am treated with a courtesy and level of service that is extremely rare in the franchised retail landscape of North America.

The public stolidity and discipline of our new Muslim village contrasts sharply with other developments in this urban patch. One of the rooming houses became the residence of a drug dealer, and then of a prostitute who openly did fast favors for her roadside recruits behind an apartment building on a nearby street. To track the drug trade, the police placed undercover agents at the local doughnut and coffee shop. One January night a dead man was dumped in the alleyway behind our neighbors' homes immediately across the street. More recently, three men threatened a couple in the park with razors when they would not surrender their wallets. Life in our patch of settled affluence and aspiring immigrants continues, although it also hosts an underworld of crime and illicit commerce that does not fit the image of a good neighborhood, even if this is a normal reality in most parts of the urban world today.

I increasingly notice similarities between life in my Toronto neighborhood and life in cities like Mumbai, Bangalore, Manila, and Johannesburg, where I have been conducting business. In those cities, low-income garbage scavengers who sell their materials to recyclers have long been an unofficial part of their city's system of solid waste management. Here in Toronto, subsistence scrap collectors do regular late-night rounds to scoop up metal appliances and furnishings that have been left for the municipal collectors. Other scavengers pick the valuable aluminum cans from our recycling bins, a practice that became so widespread that it cost the municipal recycling program an estimated million dollars each year, forcing the city to pass a law to stop it. A new deposit fee on wine bottles has spawned another specialization, whose "proprietors" have staked out territorial routes, which they "service" with repurposed shopping carts to collect the spoils from stoops and verandas of the area's wine-drinking homes.

Just a few hundred feet beyond the abstract border of our urban patch, people from other distant lands have created a microcosm of world affairs in a low-income housing complex. Women from different parts of the Caribbean run their traditional micro-banking activities, in which members make monthly contributions to savings pools and disburse the proceeds to a different woman each month. A group associated with the Dinka rebel movement of southern Sudan—refugees from their country's twenty-two-year civil war—plan their return. Afghani exiles from Taliban rule have been returning home to rebuild their businesses. Senior officials of Somalia's new national government have recently resided here, and the current prime minister of Somalia lived in a low-income housing project a few miles away.

Beyond the housing project to the southwest is a predominantly Chinese commercial district where we often shop. Here, rival extortion and drug gangs profit from the many restaurants and grocers. They occasionally have shoot-outs on the streets and have recently felled an innocent bystander. Stolen and contraband goods can be purchased from backrooms and basements. People wonder why the police cannot contain the gangs that operate so openly.

Students in our neighborhood high school, to the east, commute from an area where Sri Lanka's Tamil Tiger insurgents have long operated an extortion scheme, which generates as much as $12 million a year for their insurgency. Human Rights Watch reports that extortion fees in this neighborhood are set at $1 for each day that each Tamil family has lived in Toronto. Tamil small business owners are "asked" to pay as much as $25,000 to $100,000 per annum.[3]

These are some of the increasingly common signs of the changing life within any urban patch in the world today. I cannot begin to document or even imagine the connected worlds that are invented and taking root in this little place, which little more than a century ago was a stream, some field, and trees.

Even the natural order of things in our neighborhood defies expectations and stereotypes. People think of urban environments as depleted and spoiled, but they are not.

They are enriched by hundreds of species, native and exotic. Toronto's urban neighborhoods host substantially greater numbers of species than the temperate rural landscapes that surround the city. In addition to domestic pets, some from continents far away, our patch hosts populations of woodland raccoons and skunks that live in denser populations than those found in their natural habitats beyond the city limits.[4] These animals have fully adapted to urban living, digging nests into our rooftops and feeding surreptitiously on our leftover food. Foxes have been seen visiting the neighborhood, following the remnants of the old ravine through the train yard to the neighborhood park. The varieties of plants are even more exotic. We have avid gardeners in this patch. My twenty-foot-by-twenty-foot front yard hosts nearly one hundred perennial plant species. As a result of the exceptional ecological richness of our urban patches, greater Toronto has more plant and animal species than many whole countries.

The biology of a metropolitan area like Toronto may be unstable in comparison to natural ecosystems. Our patch depends on vast quantities of materials, commodities, and energy that are extracted from distant other ecosystems, processed in far-flung patches of the City, and shipped to us here. But managed properly, our cities are full of untapped efficiencies and potentials. For example, one of the primary efficiencies of Earth's green and blue ecosystems is the way energy is recycled along an entire food chain, passing itself in ever new nutrient forms from one species to the next. Mimicking this pattern, energy recycling is becoming an important aspect of Toronto's evolving brown and gray ecosystem. The city government established a company that uses the waste steam from four downtown energy plants to provide an efficient heating solution for 140 high-rise office buildings, running the steam through a twenty-five-mile system of pipes. Then, in 2004, the same company opened a district cooling system that draws cold water from deep in Lake Ontario to serve one hundred major office buildings. The deep lake water, which is extremely clean, then flows into the Toronto water system. From there the used water is treated and returned to the lake (albeit with many different new trace chemicals). This clever infrastructure creates an urban ecology that is more symbiotic with the natural one. It reduces the electricity used in standard air-conditioning systems by 90 percent, it reduces air pollution and massive discharges of hot water into the lake from electrical plants, and it eliminates the use of ozone-depleting CFCs.

Our five-hundred-foot patch has also hosted odd ecological conflicts. For some years, a network of Greek and Eastern European immigrants made a living by collecting large earthworms at night from, among other places, the high school playing field, to be sold along a value chain to distant recreational fishermen. One resident of Greek heritage was a veritable kingpin in the so-called dew worm trade, a supplier to a regional industry that exported more than five hundred million worms to the United States each year. Nightly worm-gathering sorties in our high school playing field so depleted the worm population that the field became barren. Even weeds struggled to survive. The municipality eventually challenged the local worm industry, which one study described as including a daily informal auction in a restaurant where freelance pickers met with refrigeration truck operators to transport the worms to the U.S. border.[5] The city's crackdown on the trade was part of a whole new regime for managing the urban environment, in which neighborhood trees, fields, wildlife, pets, waste, household chemicals, and parking spaces became, at least in theory, centrally regulated.

In spite of all this exotic detail, when guests visit our neighborhood, they remark that our area is comfortable, interesting, and charming. Our quaint neighborhood resembles many urban neighborhoods that we take for granted throughout the world. The faces and players might be different, but the dynamics of this Toronto urban patch are probably little different from the dynamics of the neighborhood that you can see from the roof of your city home or office. These are the dynamics of the fast-evolving world order that I have proposed we simply call—much as we refer to the ice caps, the steppes, the rain forests, or the seas—the City.

It is important to understand what drives the enterprising convergence of so many different undertakings in a single city block—a Starbucks located two hundred feet from a drug house in the midst of a new outpost of the Gujarati diaspora close by where distant insurgencies are financed and foreign governments planned. Further, we need to understand the imperatives that drive the merging of cities throughout the world into a single, converging system that is re-ordering the most basic dynamics of global ecology, politics, markets, and social life.

At its root, we can only comprehend and ultimately steer the City's growth and the new pressures, competitions, and struggles it creates by understanding what makes cities places of so much opportunity. People and organizations don't go to cities for their problems. If cities were primarily the problem centers of the world, as they are so often portrayed, then it would seem logical that people and money would flee them. Their populations would not be increasing. Multinational companies would not be competing for new building sites. Dubai would not be host to thirty thousand (or 24 percent) of the world's construction cranes, just as Shanghai had a quarter of the world's cranes in the 1990s. People and organizations build and flock to cities and will continue doing so because they are massive generators of opportunity. Cities offer *advantage* in the world—*unique* chances to secure greater income, to organize for political rights, to benefit from education and social services, to meet other entrepreneurs or gain competitive position in a market. Cities, relative to other forms of settlement, offer what we can simply call *urban advantage*. The further concentration of hundreds of millions in cities, whether through risk-taking squatter communities, multinational companies, ethnic groups, social movements, guerrilla movements, or transnational gangs, reflects the multitude of strategies to claim some bit of control over a city's urban advantage so they can leverage it *for their own advantage*. If we don't understand what makes up urban advantage, then we can't understand the City.

Most cities, unless they are entirely new, have accumulated a unique legacy of urban advantage, bequeathed by the strategies of earlier urban pioneers who designed and built their cities in specific ways to secure their own advantage. If your city is lucky, those pioneers had insight about the basic elements of urban advantage that could be developed from the city's location and historic circumstances. Often this took the form of a strategic location itself, like Toronto's location by a protected harbor during a time of colonial warfare, or Chicago's location at the meeting point of two great shipping basins, or Bangalore's location on a high plain between the strategic centers of Mysore and Madras. Then, if your city's fortune holds, its pioneers learned how to arrange a mix of activities—production, commerce, culture, and residential life—into a fixed spatial relationship with each other to create an efficient social and economic dynamism, which economists have explored as "agglomeration economies," but which I call a local *citysystem* to also embrace its social and ecological elements.

Take Bangalore, for instance. In the 1990s, it became a world-changing city, seemingly from nowhere. But its growth into a leading center of high-tech industry was built on a centuries-old foundation of developed urban advantage. Consider the city's historic practice of developing through distinct, specialized districts. First there was the old city where textile production, commerce, and residential activities were clustered efficiently together. Then came the nineteenth-century military cantonment, which joined barracks, housing for officers, military grounds, and later military research and production in another distinct citysystem. In the twentieth century, the city developed specialized industrial townships, where large primary manufacturers and supporting small workshops were built adjacent to workers' housing and the retail establishments and vendors that served them. Then successive national and state governments endowed the city with every imaginable kind of scientific and research institute, again using a clustered campus model of urban development. This process started with the establishment of the Indian Institute of Science in 1909 and with its numerous spin-off research institutes over the decades. The process of scientific endowment within a clustered area of the city never really stopped. It extended to the National Aeronautics Laboratories (1960), the Indian Space Research Organisation (1969), and the Indian Institute of Management (1973) and to more recent institutes on information technology (IT), telematics, electronics, physics, and every other imaginable field of scientific inquiry.

By 1980 the city had scores of colleges—and hundreds of thousands of students—producing a fresh labor supply for its technical industries. Further hands-on training was offered through an explosion of private sector training companies. By 2000, Bangalore had 760 firms offering IT training alone. As its industries and technical institutes developed, the city created and attracted young talent. And while other major Indian cities became congested and unmanageable, Bangalore had physical room to grow and intellectual room to experiment.

Repeating the industrial township approach used decades earlier, in the late 1970s Bangalore's state government created the setting for the future IT sector in the form of an industrial park called Electronics City. In the 1980s, new software start-ups like Infosys joined the city's first generation of electronics companies in Electronics City. Here their proximity, shared needs, and shared frustration with the poor infrastructure engendered both the politics and economics for the country's first scaled broadband communications system in 1992. So great was Bangalore's legacy of urban advantage that with the simple addition of a new fiber-optic infrastructure in Electronics City, the city's software companies stood ready to profitably meet the huge new challenge faced by expanding transnational companies—the integration of their separate national business operations and acquisitions into more seamless global operations through new software systems. Bangalore's rise did not appear from nowhere. It was built on a foundation of urban advantage that could support unprecedented growth.

When people are asked to describe the basic stuff of cities, they tend to mention streets, sewers, drains, housing, factories, and skyscrapers. Or they get even more basic and list concrete, steel, brick, glass—and lots of busy people. These are the *things* that visibly make what was once a marsh or village or small town a budding city. But clearly, a place like Bangalore—just one of countless specks of light on that extended global City—derives its energy from more potent forces, from some other raw stuff of a city. That stuff is the four basic elements of urban advantage, which make cities everywhere magnets for every kind of ambition: what I call their economies of *density, scale, association,* and *extension.*

The first thing that anyone notices on entering a city is the concentration of people and their activities. Simple as it is, this density has been little understood, and its benefits are too often squandered through the low-density development of cities today. The density of cities is their most basic advantage over any other kind of settlement. Without density of settlement, most of what we learn, produce, construct, organize, consume, and provide as a service in the world would simply be too expensive. Density increases the sheer *efficiency* by which we can pursue an economic opportunity.

The scale of cities is the second building block of urban advantage. It increases the sheer *volume* of any particular opportunity, producing what we call economies of scale. Scale permits the splitting of fixed costs and known risks over a large enough group of users to make an activity attractive or service profitable *in a big way.* In this way, the scale of cities increases the range of opportunities and level of ambition that can be viably pursued in them and thereby the scale of the impacts that urban pursuits can have on the world.

The scale and density of interactions among people with different interests, expertise, and objectives then combine to create the third basic economy of cities. Together they exponentially increase the variety of ways and the efficiency with which people can organize, work together, invent solutions, and launch joint strategies for urban advantage. I call this collaborative efficiency economies of association. Like-minded people have only so much time and opportunity to happen upon the people and organizations with whom they can invent, plan, and launch their strategies for advantage in the world.

Finally, economies of density, scale, and association together provide the cost efficiencies and user communities to extend their organized strategies to other cities through infrastructure investments and technology applications. Shipping ports, airports, telephone, cable television, and fiber-optic networks depend on the combined economies of density, scale, and association in cities. We accurately call these systems *urban infrastructure* because their economic viability is uncertain without the supply efficiencies created by density and scale and the demand efficiencies created by association. The net result is a new kind of advantage: economies of *extension.*

Extension is the ability to link the unique economic advantages of one city with those of other cities to create whole new strategies for advantage in the world.

These elements of urban advantage are what allowed an unknown Los Angeles neighborhood gang to develop into a transnational criminal organization in less than fifteen years, just as it allowed Bangalore software entrepreneurs to leverage their relationships with companies in Europe and North America into a new business process outsourcing industry. Cities, and specific groups within cities, design and use urban infrastructure to extend their strategies and forms of association (e.g., commerce, politics, and crime) across a network of cities. They combine the unique advantage of one city with others to create whole new strategies for advantage in the City. Globalization is this process of developing new advantage from the unique economics of an extended group of cities—from their spatial designs, infrastructures, cultures, and local markets. Local urban affairs, therefore, are more (not less) important in the global era. They define the potential and the burdens of the expanding City.

There are two aspects to density in the growth of cities. *Proximity* reduces the time and energy and therefore the cost required to move people and materials around to achieve any objective. It is easy to do the math. Take an urban water system. If we are building a water system for a suburban neighborhood where homes are 120 feet apart versus a downtown neighborhood where homes are twenty feet apart, we have to use one hundred feet of extra pipe for each home in the lower-density neighborhood. If each neighborhood has one hundred houses, then a higher-density neighborhood saves an impressive two miles of pipe—not to mention the costs for installation and maintenance and for pumping the water through it. But in my city, a person living in a low-density neighborhood pays the same rate for water as the people in my high-density neighborhood. The water department loses money on the low-density neighborhood, and our neighborhood must help make up the difference through our water rates and tax payments. The same basic math applies to every other service. If the city's average density goes down, then the underlying economics of the city deteriorate. Someone has to make up the difference. If people in low-density suburbs had to pay the full cost for their infrastructure, a great many of them would likely reconsider where they live.

When mutually supportive activities are located in proximity to each other, their *concentration* has a further synergistic effect. The economics of collaboration generally improve. Companies organize their different functions into a headquarters office or a campus to secure the other beneficial aspect of density: economies of concentration. Cities can exponentially increase these economies by clustering complementary activities together.

The economics of concentration were further driven home to me in Mumbai, where low-income vendors of bananas or tomatoes set their tables right next to each other on the street. There might be fifteen tomato vendors on one sidewalk together. On the surface this seems unwise—they are placing themselves right next to their competition. But the economic dynamics of density are such that by concentrating, they gain the benefits of a more scaled grocery operation. They create a unique go-to destination for tomatoes.

One can see this use of clustering to create the proxy advantages of scale on city streets all over the world. If you walk along the main avenue of our Toronto neighborhood you will find a group of individual stores that specialize in home décor and furnishings. They have organically concentrated together without any coordination or plan. On the surface, like the Mumbai fruit vendors, they are in competition with each other. But by concentrating together, they are using density to create what amounts to a specialized home furnishings market that attracts and serves customers from across a much larger area of the city, increasing the total pool of patrons for each individual store.

Like proximity, concentration can also provide physical economic benefits. Take high-rise apartment buildings as an example. In a world struggling to increase its energy efficiency, the high-density high-rise is an obvious solution. A free-standing home that is thirty feet long and twenty feet high has four walls of six hundred square feet each and a nine-hundred-square-foot roof—a total of thirty-three hundred square feet exposed to Toronto's winter cold or Miami's summer heat. However, a condominium of the same size that is located in the middle of an eight-story building has just one wall—six hundred square feet— exposed to the elements, through which winter cold or summer heat seeps in. Everything else being equal, the energy efficiency of a high-rise district adds in a very basic way to a city's urban advantage.

Density is the first thing that distinguishes a city from other forms of settlement because it is the city's first and most basic source of advantage. The second thing that you'll notice on entering any city is its scale. Ten years ago the restaurant and shop owners along a mile stretch of our main avenue decided to organize an annual festival in which they all sell their foods and goods on the sidewalks—to the entire city. Now the festival attracts one million visitors in a two-day period alone. Festivals in cities around the world are the most traditional and accessible form of scaled market operation. The same economic dynamic that made this work in our little urban patch also transformed a collection of competing, individual commodity traders in Chicago into the world-renowned Chicago Board of Trade or supported the investments required for dozens of clustered software start-ups in Bangalore to grow into a global high-tech hub with hundreds of thousands of employees.

The combination of density and scale economies underpins the third basic advantage of cities: association. The concentration, proximate convenience, and number of interactions between the people in a city—with their different ideas, talents, desires, and intentions—allow societies to efficiently organize into myriad groups with shared pursuits and strategies. The economics of association starts as a simple self-organizing process among small groups of like-minded people. For instance, the Muslim families in my neighborhood, from very disparate places and backgrounds, can join together into a common religious community and pool their resources to expand and upgrade their austere mosque. Like-minded neighbors can easily raise funds to upgrade and manage the activities in our neighborhood park. The businesspeople on the main avenue, from so many different countries and cultural backgrounds, can associate to create a common festival and commercial identity.

On a larger scale, city dwellers from many places and backgrounds meet, mix, plan, and engineer electorates, companies, NGOs, shadow governments, systems of criminality, and insurgencies. The economics of association in cities permits the efficient organization of talent into labor markets (like the huge new market for software technicians in Bangalore), research collaborations (like the development of e-mail and the Internet in Cambridge), and industries (like the organization of the Gounder migrants in Tiruppur). The efficiency of urban association underlies the basic process of human invention and innovation. People of all backgrounds are drawn to cities to break from the restrictions and injustices of traditional rural societies and to reorganize themselves into new communities. By facilitating new forms of association, our cities increase the pace and variety of human invention and social change.

Finally, when people and organizations associate to leverage advantages from their city, they also raise resources to build the infrastructure to tap into the opportunities of other cities. Extension from city to city is the story of my neighborhood's globally collaborating artists, activists, businesspeople, and diaspora communities, and of its criminal organizations, war extortionists, and multinational franchises alike. What starts as a local criminal gang in Hanoi or Los Angeles can extend its influence here to Toronto and thereby find new opportunities in the global City. For instance, not long ago Toronto-area police uncovered an alliance between Asian and Hungarian criminal organizations, reportedly involving one family in our urban patch, which had jointly stolen $7 million in postal checks from regional post offices. Similarly, what starts as an insurgency in Sri Lanka can develop into an international financing system that uses personal identification numbers (PINs) to track the annual payments of tens of thousands of households and small businesses in Toronto's Tamil diaspora population.

Once associates extend their reach across a group of cities—for instance, connecting New York retailers and marketers, and their unique advantages with the design industry that emerged from the unique advantages of Milan and Barcelona, with the manufacturers that emerged from the unique advantages of Tiruppur— the shared urban advantage of these places can be leveraged to support a new value chain in the global City. These alliances have developed what I call an urban strategy. Others call it something less precise: globalization.

Today, extended urban networks drive the political developments of entire countries, as in the case of my urban patch's influence on Somalia, or the earlier worldwide urban networks of South Africa's émigré anti-apartheid leadership, which sourced the finance, know-how, weaponry, and political support to overthrow the Afrikaaner apartheid regime. Likewise, local commercial communities demand and enable investments in new extension infrastructure, like the early demands of Bangalore's budding high-tech companies for a fiber-optic network. The shipping ports and airports, telephones, and Internet services that these extended networks demand provide the nervous system for the City.

Density, scale, association, and extension drive development in every urban patch, whether in a Toronto neighborhood, a Machala squatter camp, a little inner-city immigrant district like Pico-Union, or a high-tech incubator district in Bangalore.

People and organizations of every sort have joined the rough-and-tumble clamor to shape the raw economics of urban patches everywhere into spatial arrangements and building forms that offer them unique advantage. This makes the development and spatial designs of each city a constant around-the-clock competition. The most basic challenge of every city is to transform that competition into a governed negotiation to create shared urban advantages for all whose ambitions bring them to the city. The distinct ways in which cities and their different urban patches succeed or fail in creating these shared advantages determines their contributions, for better or worse, to the world City system.

CHAPTER 18

Mobile Global Citizens

Luis Cabrera

History is the long and tragic story of the fact that privileged groups seldom give up their privileges voluntarily.

—Rev. Martin Luther King, Jr.
Letter from Birmingham City Jail

Why do you want to help those wetbacks?

Young man to No More Deaths volunteers outside
the Arivaca Mercantile in Arivaca, Arizona

Sergio "Pan Duro" seemed intent on teaching a lesson. The former human smuggler, whose nickname translates literally as "hard bread," had led a group of Mexican and U.S. humanitarian-aid volunteers on a dusk patrol to the summit of a thousand-foot desert mountain. To the northeast, the lights of Agua Prieta, Sonora, and its conjoined border twin, Douglas, Arizona, shone across the valley floor. Around the group, the outlines of prickly pear and cholla cacti, thorned mesquite and ocotillo could be only dimly perceived. But they were felt, as they repeatedly snagged clothes and raked exposed skin. The U.S. walkers hung close together, pulling aside branches for one another, clutching arms when stones rolled underfoot, offering a hand after the inevitable hard backside falls. Full darkness had descended by the time they returned to the flat, and they wandered lost for a few tense minutes in dense, head-high brush, before Pan Duro appeared with a flashlight and guided them back to camp.

Pan Duro had led thousands of migrants over such terrain into the United States in a locally legendary career as a smuggler, or "pollero,"[1] that spanned twenty years. Traveling by moonlight through dry washes and along treacherously steep and rocky backcountry trails, he had slipped groups as large as thirty past the vigilant eye of the U.S. Border Patrol. After arrest and forced retirement, he worked as an officer at an Agua Prieta drug rehabilitation center. Several times a year, he and a group of patient draftees set up camp and conducted miles-long foot patrols, offering water and shelter to migrants from Mexico, Central America, and elsewhere, many of whom were already exhausted and sun-sick from walking. "When I encounter migrants, I know they're going to suffer," he later told the U.S. volunteers, noting how many border crossers become lost in the desert, just as they had. "But they also want the American dream" (author interview, July 2005).

The willingness of illicit entrants to risk grave hardships in order to enhance their own life chances, and the ways in which such actions both inform a conception of global citizenship and highlight possibilities for its institutionalization, are the subjects of this chapter. My claim is that such immigrants are practicing something akin to global civil disobedience within a nascent global civil rights movement. By offering deliberate, principled, though usually covert, resistance to restrictive entry laws, they expose tensions between the structural features of the current global system and an emerging global normative charter, or set of universal rights that its most prominent nation-states have affirmed. They are provoking the consideration of questions about membership, exclusions, and distributions that are central to accounts of global citizenship. In practice, they may be doing more than any other set of actors to compel the globally affluent to give more attention to the concerns of those in impoverished countries, as well as to highlight a need for the transformation of the current system.

GLOBAL CITIZENSHIP AND A GLOBAL CIVIL RIGHTS MOVEMENT

A civil right will be understood here as one enshrined within the body of laws governing a specific community and held by individuals who are formally recognized as members of that community (see McLean 1996: 70–72). A civil rights movement is understood as attempting to expand the set of persons who are recognized and treated by governing institutions as full members of the salient set, deserving of the full set of rights protections guaranteed under the law. For example, in the African-American civil rights movement of the 1950s and 1960s, activists pressed for the extension of equal citizen participatory and economic rights. Movement leader Martin Luther King, Jr., famously asserted that the U.S. Constitution and Declaration of Independence constituted "a promise that all men, yes, black men as well as white men, would be guaranteed the unalienable rights of life, liberty, and the pursuit of happiness" (King 1991a: 217). As numerous commentators have noted, King consistently highlighted the ways in which the U.S. founding documents promised an equality for all that still was not available to African-Americans (see Watson 2004: Vail 2006). One claim here is that, in the current global context, unauthorized immigration could represent a similar such force for constitutional recognition and expansion.

King defended his own disobedience of segregation and other narrowly discriminatory laws in his "Letter from Birmingham City Jail" (King 1991b). He noted ways in which nonviolent direct action was being used to challenge the unjust status quo. Movement actors had systematically violated laws that mandated segregation in restaurants and other commercial and public spaces (see Cook 1997; Branch 1998). King argued that such actions were necessary for creating the tensions that could open opportunities for substantive change.

King's justification for direct action in violation of the law is consonant with many offered in the more narrowly focused political theory literature on domestic civil disobedience (see Brownlee 2004). For example, the argument, and the general actions of the civil rights movement disobedient, would fit Rawls's formulation of civil disobedience as "a public, nonviolent, conscientious yet political act contrary to law, usually done with the aim of bringing about a change in the law or policies of the government" (Rawls 1999: 320). For Rawls, civil disobedience is enacted openly, its practitioners are willing to suffer arrest, and perhaps most importantly, they are acting in what is described as fidelity to the law, attempting to demonstrate how a specific law or regime of laws is out of balance with the community's prevailing sense of justice.

Rawls presumes that a conception of civil disobedience is operable in a "nearly just" society, one with relatively robust democratic institutions and mechanisms of distributive justice, but in which serious violations of justice do sometimes occur (Rawls 1999: 319). Others have questioned how far any actually existing system can or could have been considered nearly just, including the United States of the 1950s and early 1960s (Boxill 1992, chap. 10; Lyons 1998). Additionally, there has been wide debate on precisely how civil disobedience can be understood and possibly justified (see Walzer 1970; Dworkin 1977; Raz 1979; Carter 1998; Sabl 2001). That said, it will be useful here to gauge how clearly the actions of unauthorized immigrants may fit some commonly noted characteristics of permissible violations of law. The discussion will highlight some significant features shared by the practice of mass covert entry into a state and paradigm cases of civil disobedience, though it also will reveal some differences (see Simmons 2003; Brownlee 2004, 2007). The differences, I will suggest, are less significant than the similarities in demonstrating the salience of unauthorized immigration within a civil disobedience frame, and more broadly a frame of institutional global citizenship.

Publicity

Since civil disobedience is intended to call attention to potentially unjust laws, publicity is presumed to be a core defining feature. King and his co-disobedients, for example, directly challenged segregation laws by placing themselves in public spaces formally reserved for whites. How far might the actions of unauthorized immigrants similarly constitute a public challenge? We can note first some public and quite dramatic actions by groups of unauthorized immigrants. For example, the Sans-Papiers movement, launched when more than three hundred unauthorized immigrants from Africa occupied St. Ambroise church in Paris for several months in 1996, attracted global attention (McNevin 2006: 142–4; see Krause 2008). The movement has since continued and expanded to other states.

In its initial published statement, the occupying group, after declaring that its members would no longer hide in the shadows of their adopted state, said that:

> We are people like everyone else. . . . We demand papers so that we are no longer victims of arbitrary treatment by the authorities, employers and landlords. We demand papers so that we are no longer vulnerable to informants and blackmailers. We demand papers so that we no longer suffer the humiliation of controls based on our skin, detentions, deportations, the break-up of families, the constant fear. (Cited in Hayter 2004: 143)

Certainly such actions and statements would appear to satisfy a publicity requirement. Likewise, when more than 3 million unauthorized immigrants and their supporters marched and engaged in mass-absentee days and related actions in major cities across the United States in 2006–2007, it represented an extraordinarily visible public challenge to the extant membership regime (see Robinson 2006). In the most notable such event in Arizona, more than 200,000 marchers filled a central street for miles, strolling, singing, and waving tens of thousands of American flags to symbolize a desire for inclusion. The April 10, 2006, march ended on the lawn of the Arizona Capitol building, where speaker after speaker, many using only Spanish, praised the marchers' courage and their willingness to stand up against what was seen as the oppression of immigrants. They singled out for opprobrium a bill then under consideration in Congress that would have made every unauthorized immigrant in the United States liable to felony arrest. Prominent in the crowd were signs proclaiming "We are not criminals." The initial entry violations of unauthorized immigrants, while covert by nature, also have a significant publicity component. That is, if migrants' violations of entry law never became known, then the actions might pose no more challenge than some "thought crimes" would to other laws. Unauthorized immigrants, however, are often clearly present in receiving communities. In areas of high concentration in the U.S. Southwest, for example, predominantly unauthorized migrant day laborers are highly visible on street corners. Landscaping, sectors of construction, and other arduous manual fields have been dominated in the same region by recent immigrants, many of them unauthorized. Specialty groceries and other shops serving new immigrant populations are common. As noted, the United States unauthorized immigrant population is estimated at nearly 12 million persons (Passel and Cohn 2009), and their economic impacts alone are highly visible, from the billions paid into the Social Security pension system without opportunity to withdraw (Porter 2005), to acute stresses placed on some local medical and other infrastructure (Janofsky 2003). Their presence, and their impacts, would go some way toward satisfying a publicity requirement.

Accepting Consequences

Most commentators would insist that, for a violation to be characterized as civil disobedience, perpetrators must be willing to face arrest for their actions. Some would argue that courts should then be lenient in their punishment of disobedients (Dworkin 1977, chap. 8), but the willingness to face consequences in order to call attention to a potentially unjust law is seen as crucial to a defensible practice of civil disobedience. Though unauthorized immigrants may be visible in general terms, the fact remains that, unlike those who acted in concert to violate laws with King, they are not prepared to accept the consequences of their lawbreaking. Arguably that would apply also to those taking part in the U.S. street demonstrations, where their numbers so far outstrip law-enforcement numbers that arrest would seem unlikely, and possibly to the Sans-Papiers, whose members have at times publicly decried and tried to forestall threatened police action against them (BBC 2002).

Here, covert entry may diverge most significantly from civil disobedience per se. Unauthorized migrants would seem to fit better the category of "conscientious evaders," being those who deliberately but covertly violate a law on principled grounds (Rawls 1999: 324; see Feinberg 1994, chap. 6). Examples of such evaders may include those who refuse to report when drafted for a questionable war or, in the pre–Civil War United States, those who covertly violated the Fugitive Slave Acts by taking part in the Underground Railroad. The latter violations may be particularly salient here, given the characterization by some immigration restrictionists of the desert humanitarians' work as another underground railroad.[2] The actions of conscientious evaders are presumed to be morally motivated, or made within a coherent and potentially defensible moral frame, but lawbreakers do not submit to arrest. Thus conscientious evaders may be engaging in principled resistance but not formal civil disobedience. The distinction, however, does not have fundamental significance in the case of violations such as mass covert entry, where arrest is avoided but the publicity requirement is satisfied. Disobedients may not submit themselves for punishment, but the overarching aim of challenging potentially unjust laws is well met, as discussed further later in the chapter.

Conscientiousness

According to this criterion, the act of disobedience to law must be motivated by adherence to moral principles, or must be plausibly characterized as a morally defensible action. We can note first in this context that a common theme in the civil disobedience discourse has been that those engaging in deliberate yet principled violation of law, including conscientious evaders, must do so from primarily altruistic or non-self-interested motives (see Feinberg 1994: 155). The clearest examples of such evaders, Feinberg suggests, would again be those aiding fugitive slaves on the Underground Railroad. Yet slaves provided arguably a greater challenge to such laws through their own actions to free themselves, and their often eloquent later descriptions of slavery's horrors (see Equiano 2003; Still 1872 [1968]). Such individuals would have strong self-interest in being free, as well as in seeing their family members free of the harmful effects of unjust laws.

In terms of more straightforward civil disobedience, King and his co-activists in the U.S. civil rights movement, as well as those who practiced principled resistance alongside Gandhi (Brown 2008) and in a range of similar movements worldwide, also realized significant gains from their own successes. When the potentially unjust law to be targeted is one based on the exclusion of a specific group from benefits or full membership recognition, it is difficult to see how the law could be challenged by members of that group without potentially offering them benefits. That unauthorized immigrants stand to realize gains though the violation of entry laws should not significantly diminish our assessment of the potential moral significance of their actions.

In much the same way, I will suggest, the fact that most migrants are economically motivated, rather than seeking to make a moral point by breaking a specific law, does not diminish the broader moral significance of their actions. First, it can be questioned whether each individual disobedient must be acting from strictly moral motivation in order for the mass violation itself to be morally significant or ultimately defensible as principled resistance. For example, it would seem likely that some participants in any social movement are motivated to join for reasons other than a sense of indignation or outrage at possible injustice. Or they act from mixed motives that include a sense of injustice being perpetrated, but also possibly some desire to be part of a historic moment, to belong to a closely knit group which shares their values, to pursue a specific interpersonal relationship, or for other reasons. The overall significance of the movement or mass act of disobedience, presuming it can be characterized as principled resistance to an unjust law, would not seem dependent on the moral motivation of all disobedients.

By extension, while it must be true that some unauthorized immigrants enter covertly or overstay visas for reasons that are not closely connected to fundamental human rights, that should not affect the moral challenge posed by the mass movement overall. The claim is similar to some offered in the context of John Stuart Mill's intention/motive distinction (Mill 1998; Ridge 2002; see Tesón 2005). Mill emphasized the importance of the intended ultimate outcome of an act, as opposed to the underlying motive of the actor, in judging the act's moral character. For example, an action such as saving someone from drowning would ordinarily appear to be laudable, Mill observes. Yet, if it is committed with the intention of only keeping that person alive in order to be tortured, then its character is cast in a different light. It becomes one step in a larger, more morally dubious sequence of events.

By contrast, the actor's underlying motive is seen as a less important factor in judging the act when it is not part of such a sequence, that is, when it is simply a move to aid another. For example, one might save another from drowning not solely from a concern for the life of the person in peril, but in part from self-interest in avoiding whatever personal ill effects could result from witnessing such human suffering. Such motives have been explored by some social psychologists. They distinguish between empathy, understood to encompass emotions of sympathy or concern for the other, and plain sadness or distress caused by the other's suffering, where participants can be motivated by egoistic reasons to end the suffering and thus end or lessen their own distress at witnessing it (Dovidio et al. 1990; see Batson 1997; Batson et al. 2007). The revelation of such a self-interested motive, Mill would argue, may give us legitimate reason to criticize such actors or lower them in our moral estimation. If it did not change the outcome, however, the motive would not have a bearing on the moral character of the act itself. The same again could hold true in the protest context—for example, when an individual takes part in a demonstration that achieves some societal good, but does so for some motive of her own.

The motives of unauthorized entrants will generally differ from those of civil disobedients, but their intentions, and more centrally the character of their actions as morally defensible, will be quite similar. To illustrate, I will contrast the motive stated by one Mexican man intending to violate U.S. entry laws, and the motive stated by a U.S. activist in Douglas, Arizona, who had considered helping crossers violate those same laws. Miguel Sanchez, of Chiapas state in far southern Mexico, noted that he earned only the equivalent of $5.50 per day as a field laborer at home, insufficient to support his children, ages two and six. Contacted at the migrant shelter in Altar, Sonora, he was out of money for the trip after a failed attempt to reach Los Angeles, where he had hoped at least to find work as a street-corner day laborer. He told me, "In Chiapas, you don't earn anything," he said. "We work with the machete or minding horses for nothing. In the United States I think I can go and make $10 an hour." His specific motive, then, in attempting to violate laws against unauthorized entry and employment, would be to try to improve the material conditions under which his family lives.

A small number of immigration-rights activists, all themselves U.S. citizens, said they had violated, or were willing to violate, entry laws in their work. The Douglas activist noted that she and some others were going farther than No More Deaths and like groups by transporting crossers who were not in medical danger. They had considered engaging in more open violation of entry laws, she said, in a conscious civil disobedience frame that would include their own arrests and public prosecutions. In transporting a number of crossers short distances, or otherwise deliberately aiding clandestine entry, members of this group were already acting as conscientious evaders. If they had taken the next step toward open violation, they would have clearly fit the standard criteria for civil disobedience. Yet, despite their differing underlying motives, their immediate intention—to see individuals expand their access to resources and opportunities through illicit entry—would have remained the same as that of unauthorized immigrants. The moral character or defensibility of the action would have been the same, as would arguably be the kinds of effects it could have.

There is no presumption, of course, that each violation of an entry law will have precisely the same impact. Presumably, if the U.S. activist had been arrested and prosecuted, her case would have attracted significant media attention, as did the initial arrests of the No More Deaths activists noted earlier. In all likelihood, had Miguel Sanchez attempted to cross and been caught again, he would simply have been processed and deported with thousands of others like him along the border that day. The narrow claim being offered here is that the moral defensibility of an identical act is not significantly affected by the underlying motive of the actor. The broader claim is that, although most unauthorized immigrants are not primarily motivated to force a policy change in the receiving state, or normative structural change in the current global system, their actions have the same kinds of effects as would actions so motivated. Their actions thus constitute a de facto global civil disobedience movement that is potentially quite significant in a global citizenship frame.

To reinforce, motivations to challenge entry laws or membership regimes can quite clearly be ascribed to those unauthorized immigrants taking part in U.S. street demonstrations, and to Sans-Papiers members occupying churches and staging their own demonstrations in Europe. Yet the potential for those kinds of demonstrations to prompt changes within receiving states is based largely on the presence of so many unauthorized immigrants already in those states, and the

challenges their often deep participation in society poses to exclusionary understandings of membership. Even if the violation of entry laws by the less-affluent is
viewed very narrowly as permissible violation of the law, as we saw David Miller
suggest that it could be in cases of extreme deprivation (Miller 2007: 230), it is occurring on such a scale as to challenge entry laws in much the same way a more
straightforward and sustained mass protest movement would.

Consistent with the intention/motive discussion, however, it should be emphasized that not every violation of an affluent state's entry laws can be seen as
morally defensible. Implied in a conscientiousness requirement for civil disobedience, or principled resistance more broadly, is the understanding that the deliberate violation of a law will be conducted in broad fidelity to law, or to the prevailing
sense of justice. For example, the southern U.S. border is a site not only of mass
unauthorized immigration by would-be workers, but of frequent over-and-back
penetration by drug smugglers. Members of smuggling crews, each with 40- to
60-pound bales of marijuana strapped to their backs, cross in remote desert areas
and hike to drop-off points, where the drugs are left to be collected by vehicle

The act of drug smuggling, while it also involves an illicit crossing of a national boundary, is distinct from unauthorized immigration. It involves not only
the violation of laws that may be in significant tension with moral principles, as
discussed later, but the violation of laws whose effects are not so clearly seen
or presentable as unjust, including drugs and weapons laws. Drug smuggling by
its nature can lead to violence against other drug gangs, against enforcement
authorities on both sides of the border, as well as against economic immigrants
(Solís 2007). It may be possible, as some would suggest, that some level of narrowly
targeted violence is permissible in a civil disobedience context (see Brownlee 2004;
Sistare 2008). But drug smugglers, like Mill's torturer who incidentally prevents a
drowning in order to continue the torture, are engaging in more indiscriminate
violence while incidentally crossing the border as part of the process of their more
fundamentally illicit enterprise.

A harder case in this context is the human smuggler. As a result of the tighter
enforcement regime, the great majority of crossers have turned to the services of
professional guides like Pan Duro mentioned earlier (Orrenius and Coronado
2005). Hundreds each night slip their charges between strands of barbed wire at
the border and push them on foot through dry washes and over rocky desert trails.
Their role has been well chronicled in news accounts, and in the discourse of political elites and the Border Patrol, for whom they have increasingly served as vil-
lains in calls for more stringent enforcement measures. Yet, if smugglers are doing
no more than aiding a violation that may itself be justifiable, are their actions not
also justifiable, or more narrowly, taken in broad fidelity to the law? I will offer a
qualified "no" in the case of most professional smugglers, and a fairly confident
"yes" for those who assist migrants without pay—a larger group than may be generally appreciated in the U.S.–Mexico context.

Amid the stepped-up U.S. enforcement and the resultant soaring fees, the
human-smuggling industry has been transformed from one of small, often

family-based enterprises to groups more resembling crime syndicates (Orrenius and Coronado 2005: 2; see also USGAO 2000). The five former guides interviewed in Phoenix and northern Mexico all remarked that the business had been less cut-throat in their day, and the crossing much less dangerous. Numerous migrants contacted at Mexico shelters or on desert trails told of being exploited or abandoned by their paid guides. One man, Rudolfo of Guadalajara, Mexico, reported while staying at the Altar migrant shelter that his group's guide had tried to extort more money from each member just as they reached the U.S. border. When they refused, the man declined to take them across.

Others told of witnessing robbery, rape, and abandonment in remote areas (see also Singer and Massey 1998: 564–5; Alarcón 2004). A Border Patrol agent noted that "bandit" activity had increased markedly along the Arizona–Sonora border in recent years, often occurring in collusion with smuggling gangs:

> We get reports at least once a week that someone was raped, robbed, or shot at. One woman was jumped about a quarter-mile in from the border by a bunch of guys in ski masks. They spoke Spanish and told her to get on the ground. They took her money, but nothing from the smuggler. So we believe it is an organized scheme with the smugglers to get a bit more money out of these people.

Even when crossers manage to keep up with the guide, elude the Border Patrol, and reach "drop houses" in Tucson or Phoenix, they remain quite vulnerable to those in the smuggling networks. They may be effectively held for ransom, as their guides negotiate higher fees with crossers' relatives. They may even be kidnapped from their smugglers by "bajadores," or gangs that hold them hostage until relatives agree to pay large sums for their release (Gonzalez 2003; Ochoa O'Leary 2009). Given all of these factors, it is far more difficult to describe the actions of professional guides as principled resistance.

That is less true, however, of those who do not take money for their guide services. Besides the occasional transportation of individuals by those such as the Douglas, Arizona, activist noted earlier, numerous individuals contacted in Arizona reported aiding or being aided by relatives, and friends of relatives, in their crossing. The phenomenon has also been noted in the European context (see Staring 2004). Such aid is often rendered at short notice, when crossers have been abandoned by smugglers or arrangements have otherwise fallen through. One man, who had migrated without authorization from Oaxaca in the early 1980s but had later obtained his citizenship and had worked his way up to foreman on a Phoenix construction crew, said he had made five or six such trips. He recalled once receiving a phone call from a female friend-of-a-friend who had arrived in Nogales, Sonora, with her two children and was trying to find a way to cross. He arranged for a guide to take them over the line into Nogales, Arizona, where he picked them up in his car and immediately took them through a fast food drive-through so that they would appear to be nothing more than an acculturated American family, munching their burgers and fries as they drove out of town.

Casual guides such as this man, who do not charge fees for their aid, may be said to be acting in broad fidelity to the law. While migrants do violate entry laws and often related ones in order to obtain the documents that will permit them to work in the host state, the aim of most is to live and work within the legal order of the host society. In fact, contrary to common claims from nativist critics, immigrants in the aggregate have been found to violate the law at lower rates than the native-born. For example, a study using data from the 2000 U.S. Census found that in every ethnic group, rates of incarceration were lowest among immigrants, including unauthorized immigrants (Rumbaut and Ewing 2007).

Such a finding is consistent with field research conducted for this work, which identified a consistent understanding among unauthorized immigrants that they must be far more attentive to avoiding even the most minor infractions of the law than legal residents, given that a traffic stop could see them expelled. Many noted how restricted they were by their need to live as perfectly law-abiding citizens, or in fact to avoid calling any kind of attention to themselves. Said one woman, a Phoenix resident who had emigrated to the United States as a young teenager and was still without regular status more than fifteen years after filing her initial petition: "I feel caged, like I can't move. I can't go anywhere. Before I step out, even within the city, when I have to walk out of the house, I kind of think, 'Oh, am I going to get caught by the police?'" Like those immigrants holding the "We are not criminals" signs at the 2006–2007 street protests, the message most would send is that, despite the violation of a specific law involved in their entry, they intend to live in general fidelity to the law.

Necessity

Implied in the preceding discussion is some version of necessity for unauthorized immigrants. As noted earlier, there was a strong sense among many humanitarian patrollers that crossers have little choice but to violate entry laws in order to provide the subsistence minimum for themselves and their families. Here I will observe that illicit entry to pursue employment, especially on the part of those migrants from absolutely impoverished regions within Central America, sub-Saharan Africa, and elsewhere, is consistent with the "necessity defense" of domestic civil disobedience found in some legal traditions. In employing a necessity defense, defendants seek to persuade jurors that their disobedience was morally obligatory and thus effectively unavoidable. The defense has been the subject of some high-profile cases in the U.S. legal system. For example, in a case decided by the U.S. Federal Ninth Circuit Court of Appeals, the Court ruled that defendants may present a necessity defense to a jury if they can demonstrate that the law was violated to avoid an imminent harm, that there was a clear causal relationship between the violation and the imminent harm, and that there were no legal alternatives (Cavallaro 1993: 356; see Bauer and Eckerstrom 1987).

While U.S. courts have been increasingly strict in applying such evidentiary requirements and generally limiting a necessity defense, it can be noted that tens of thousands of those who flee dire economic circumstances in their home states

and enter more affluent states each year could plausibly meet the stated requirements. In fact, especially as regards the requirement that there be an absence of
legal alternatives, the illicit entrant from a desperately poor community in, for
example, Honduras,[3] might be said to have a stronger evidentiary case for claiming
necessity than even the Rev. King and his co-disobedients. As noted, King argued
that African-Americans could not afford to wait for segregation to be addressed in
the courts, and that they had to violate the laws upholding it. Yet U.S. courts in
broadly similar cases have disallowed necessity defenses, referencing potential
remedies that remained available to disobedients in the legal system (Cavallaro
1993: 359–60).

Even some prominent figures in the civil rights struggle, including U.S.
Supreme Court Justice Thurgood Marshall, the first African-American to take a
seat on the High Court, argued that the case for social equality should be pressed
primarily in the legal system, rather than in the streets (Fairclough 2004: 193–5).
The point here is not that King was not justified in his choice of methods, but to
suggest that, if King and his co-activists are seen as justified in their attempt to
bring a swifter end to unjust laws, then the same defense may apply more robustly
to those genuinely unable to meet their subsistence needs in their home states, or
more broadly, unable to reliably protect themselves and their families from a range
of general threats to well-being.

There are claims offered by Border Patrol agents that individuals from Latin
America act in morally indefensible ways when they violate entry laws, in part because they could join the queue in regular immigration channels. One agent stated
that, despite his own in-laws' unauthorized entry to the United States, he believed
that the morally correct action for even those living in extreme poverty in their
home countries would be to try to emigrate legally. Yet, amid greater restrictions
stemming from a 1996 immigration reform law, and measures put in place after
the September 11, 2001, terror attacks, non-elites within less-affluent states may
have very little chance of obtaining legal residence, especially if they are not closely
related to a current citizen. By 2007, more than 1 million workers, including highly
skilled ones such as physicians, nurses, engineers, and physical scientists, were
competing for a total of 120,000 permanent resident visas annually (Wadhwa et al.
2007). Numerous U.S. interviewees noted, like the Phoenix woman mentioned
previously, that they or family members had been living without authorization in
the United States for as long as fifteen years while their family-reunification or
other applications were pending with immigration authorities.

How applicable, then, would a necessity defense be for those in a state such as
Mexico? Again, it is the sending state for some 7 million unauthorized immigrants
in the United States (Passel and Cohn 2009), but it also is ranked relatively high on
some indicators, at least among developing states. Overall, Mexico was ranked 53rd
of 179 states in the United Nations Human Development Report (2009), which
again surveys a wide range of variables, including life expectancy, literacy, access to
medical care, clean water, and sanitation. For Durand and Massey (2004: 6),
such a ranking is evidence that should be observed in dispelling what they see as

persistent myths about Mexican migrants. Most over the past two decades, they say, sought not to escape permanently to the United States, but to work for some period in order to overcome specific economic shortfalls. As Massey states separately:

> By sending a family member to the United States to work, households diversify their income sources to reduce risks to income. With one member working abroad, a period of unemployment at home need not threaten a household's material well-being, as the family can rely on foreign earnings until the local crisis passes. (Massey 1998)

Such an understanding is consistent with the account offered here, based on individuals' needs to protect themselves and their family members against general threats. A necessity defense would plausibly be applicable for a family with no other means to insure against such threats. In addition, in a civil disobedience frame, the salient needs are not only those of immigrant sending families, but also those of the more impoverished families who cannot so easily avail themselves of the protections that migration may help provide—that is, they do not have the means to pay smugglers' fees.

In that context, it can be noted that, even within a state such as Mexico, large numbers of individuals are living lives of absolute poverty, unable to reliably meet their subsistence needs. Specifically, more than 20 million in the country were estimated to be subsisting on less than $2 per day (World Bank 2008). Five percent of children were estimated to be chronically underweight, and about the same proportion of Mexico's full population of some 108 million lacked access to clean water (UN Human Development Report 2009). Even for those relatively more fortunate, wages are often insufficient to cover basic needs. Wages in the maquiladoras, the foreign-owned factories employing hundreds of thousands of workers, mostly on Mexico's northern border, average below $90 per week (Hendricks 2005), while food and other staple items are not significantly less expensive than in the United States. Many maquila workers live in land-rush shanty towns, in homes made of found materials and with few public services (see Bean and Spener 2004: 362).

Overall, it is the case that, for tens of thousands of those in Mexico who take to the migrant trail, especially those like Miguel Sanchez who leave absolutely impoverished regions in the far south, a credible necessity defense could be mounted. Those unable to provide for themselves or their families at even the subsistence minimum could claim that they violated entry laws from need. Again, however, we need not defend a claim of sheer necessity, that individuals would not survive if they did not violate entry laws, in order to claim that unauthorized immigration can be viewed as principled resistance in a nascent movement for global civil rights. Mass unauthorized entries call attention to the widespread deprivation, or more moderate but still significant gaps in protections, that persist in even relatively high-achieving developing states such as Mexico. The violation of affluent-state entry laws is a means of addressing those gaps that is potentially defensible, according to the global community's prevailing, or perhaps emerging, sense of justice. It is that to which I now turn.

THE EMERGING GLOBAL NORMATIVE STRUCTURE

In moving across international boundaries without express permission, or in over-staying visas to take up long-term residence, unauthorized immigrants are chal-lenging the exclusions permitted to the sovereign territorial state according to the normative structure of the Westphalian states system. A core defining feature of the sovereign state is its right or ability to control its own distribution of member-ship privileges, justified in part by its role in protecting and promoting the interests of its own citizens (Walzer 2006, chap. 6). Covert entrants are implicitly claiming the right to trans-state free movement in pursuit of life opportunities that some have suggested should be viewed as a core feature of liberalism (Carens 1992) or as a fundamental human right (Ottonelli 2002; Pécoud and de Guchteneire 2006). They are acting in some ways as though there were in place the sort of fully inte-grated global institutional structure that is advocated in this work.

As noted, it is presumed in many accounts that disobedients, to achieve an expansion of rights or justice more generally, must be able to appeal to principles of justice prevalent in a society as a whole. We need not think narrowly in terms of some poll or voting mechanism to determine the sense of the prevailing majority. As in the case of the U.S. civil rights movement, it may be doubtful indeed whether the full recognition sought by disobedients would have been willingly extended under some referendum. Rather, the disobedient must be able to gain some moral purchase by referring to rights that, if not universally acknowledged or upheld, are nonetheless well established in the moral discourse. A key task again for the dis-obedient, in the case of both African-Americans and current unauthorized im-migrants, is to be able to demonstrate that the set of persons to whom such rights are applied should be expanded.

It might be argued that unauthorized migrants, as primarily conscientious evaders, are not directly appealing to a society's prevailing sense of justice in the same manner as disobedients, and that their actions will not have similar effects (see Rawls 1999: 324). Again, however, it is significant that unauthorized migrants have in recent years made very direct public appeals for regularized status or rec-ognition more broadly, as in the Sans-Papiers movement and U.S. protest actions. Not only have many migrants become eloquent spokespersons on their own behalf, but scores of nongovernmental and looser civil-society organizations have formed specifically to advocate on behalf of unauthorized migrants in relatively affluent states, especially in the United States and Western Europe.[4] Thus there are consistent direct appeals being made for more full recognition of migrants' rights or standing overall.

Further, it is the case that covert entrants generally understand their actions as morally justified within a state-transcendent frame. Virtually all of the sixty-seven unauthorized immigrants interviewed for this work in the United States, Mexico, and on Spanish territory expressed the claim, with varying levels of preci-sion or explicitness, that all individuals should be able to earn a living for them-selves and their families, regardless of their entry status. Some were highly critical of the more restrictive immigration policies being put in place virtually across the developed North. Indignantly, even angrily, an Algerian man had demanded to know why those in his country couldn't enjoy the same benefits of European integration as Spaniards, observed that he was hindered by a lack of robust opportunities in his home state, and a lack of status in Spain. He had spent some months previously in Madrid, living in the streets and eating from trash bins because he had no work papers. "I have the body to work in the fields," he said. "In the fields there is a lot of work. I want to go to Spain to earn money to help my family." Others expressed a more general desire for inclusion in their host societies, or fuller acknowledgment as individuals able to contribute and worthy of equal respect.

If such appeals are being made, however, how might they be said to have moral resonance in the existing sovereign states system? How are they appealing to a prevailing sense of justice? In fact, some recent commentators have identified an increasingly coherent conception of justice spanning borders. They note the thickening network of human rights instruments and institutions elaborating global or cosmopolitan norms (Held 2004; Benhabib 2005, 2007).

Highlighted is a transition from a body of international law whose subject is exclusively the nation-state, toward an international law which reaches within states, to provide protections to individuals, at times against their own states. Benhabib thus sees aspects of the cosmopolitan law advocated by Habermas as already being in place. Others have noted the relatively robust packages of rights elaborated in some human rights instruments widely ratified by states. Pogge (2007), in his own argument in support of a right to human development, has recently worked to reinforce the importance and possibly increasing salience of Article 25 of the Universal Declaration, affirming a right to an adequate standard of living, and Article 28, affirming a right to an international order in which core rights will be fulfilled.[5]

The Universal Declaration is not formally binding on states, and the meta-right to rights fulfilment in Article 28 is not matched to strong assurance mechanisms. However, as Pogge discusses, such "moral human rights" can figure prominently in assessments of the legitimacy of states' actions (see Sen 1982). The UNDHR has also exerted some influence on state constitutions (Clapham 2007: 42). Perhaps more significant are the formally binding human rights treaties, for which compliance is monitored by standing UN committees. Those treaties include the UN Covenant on Civil and Political Rights, which affirms numerous rights contained in the Universal Declaration, and which more than 150 states have ratified; and the International Covenant on Economic, Social and Cultural Rights, which contains provisions that reinforce the Universal Declaration's right to an adequate standard of living. States have not in general treated these treaty provisions as actionable legal rights held by individuals globally. There is, for example, no global court equivalent to the European Court of Human Rights where individuals can bring formal complaints and see them adjudicated.[6] However, such rights, and those specified and affirmed in binding UN treaties on rights possessed by women, children, workers, prisoners, members of minority groups and others, represent significant and very concrete statements of principle and obligation affirmed by states (see Nickel 2007). The claim is not that there is some cohesive global ethic already in place, but that unauthorized immigrants are posing challenges within a rights frame that most receiving states have formally acknowledged.

It seems likely that the emerging global normative structure will not for some time constitute the sort of unified "constitutional regime and publicly recognized conception of justice" that Rawls suggests is necessary for the action of lawbreakers to qualify as paradigm civil disobedience (1999: 339). Unauthorized immigration, however, is clearly a force that can highlight contradictions between the increasingly cosmopolitan character of the norms formally endorsed by migrant-receiving states and the continuing "separate but equal" character of the Westphalian system, especially where economic rights are concerned. The claim is particularly apt in the context of liberal-democratic states, which must continually navigate a path between the universal rights championed in their constitutional documents and the exclusions they put into practice as primary actors in a sovereign states system.

CHAPTER 19

An Overheated Planet

Peter Christoff and Robyn Eckersley

INTRODUCTION

In October 2009, just before the ill-fated United Nations climate conference in Copenhagen, the then President of the Maldives, Mohamed Nasheed, convened an underwater Cabinet meeting in the Indian Ocean. Dressed in scuba gear, seated around a table, and using hand signals and slates, the participants sent out an "SOS" message to the world to emphasize the perilous future of poor, low-lying nation-states if global greenhouse gas emissions continue on their upward trajectory. The Maldive Islands lie in the Indian Ocean some 430 miles from India and form the planet's lowest-lying country, with the lowest natural high point—some 2.3 meters or 7.5 feet above sea level. The population of 395,000 people live on 200 of the Maldives' 1,200 islands, most of which are no more than 3 feet above the waves. The Maldives are in the front line among the many low-lying island and coastal nations threatened with inundation by sea level rise due to global warming.[1]

Mohamed Nasheed's effort to publicize the potential obliteration of his nation highlights the central injustice of global warming: those least responsible for generating the emissions that produce global warming are likely to suffer its worst direct and indirect impacts. As we shall see, pinning down moral, political, and legal responsibility for human-induced climate change is no easy matter, because it is the cumulative effect of a wide range of activities that began well before the problem was recognized and understood—and well before the acceleration of globalization in the late twentieth century.

Since 1750, land clearing, farming, and burning fossil fuels for energy have made a discernible contribution to global warming. These activities have produced sufficient emissions to affect the planet's climate by increasing atmospheric concentrations of heat-trapping or "greenhouse" gases—in particular, carbon dioxide (CO_2) and methane. The atmospheric concentration of CO_2, the most important of the greenhouse gases, has increased from approximately 280 parts per million (ppm) pre-1750 to 400 ppm in June 2013.[2] Looked at from the point of view of Earth's CO_2 cycle, CO_2 (and other greenhouse emissions) have been entering the atmosphere at a rate beyond the planet's capacity to absorb them in its vegetation, soils, and oceans. Exceeding this "carbon budget" is, at its heart, the main cause of recent global warming.

There is no consensus about the level of global warming that constitutes "dangerous anthropogenic interference" in the Earth's climate. The critical value-laden questions we must ask are: How dangerous? Dangerous for whom? Or what? And when? Even 1.5 degrees Celsius average warming will, over time, cause seas to submerge low-lying regions and islands like the Maldives and will generate severe social and ecological impacts. Even lower levels of warming are already having considerable impacts, and there are reasons to believe that current estimates of what are "safe" levels of emissions are too high.[3] Nevertheless, we have seen an international political consensus form around keeping the planet's average temperature increase to below 2 degrees Celsius above pre-industrial levels, to avoid the worst impacts of climate change. This requires keeping atmospheric concentrations of CO_2-e to below 450 ppm (CO_2-e includes CO_2 plus other greenhouse gases converted to an equivalent CO_2 metric in terms of radiative forcing).

It is estimated that the 2 degrees Celsius threshold will be reached when a further approximately 1 trillion tonnes of CO_2 are added to the Earth's atmosphere. Since 2000, we have already used almost half that quota. The atmosphere has already accumulated some 420 ± 50 gigatonnes—a gigatonne is 1,000 million or a billion tonnes—of CO_2 since 2000, from human activities including deforestation.[4] Conservatively, only another 500 gigatonnes of CO_2 can be added if we are to have even a 75 percent chance of staying below this temperature threshold and thereby avoid causing "dangerous climate change."[5] Yet despite twenty years of international negotiations on climate change, and growing public and scientific concern, the rate and volume of greenhouse gases accumulating in the atmosphere continues to increase. At current rates of emissions, our planetary carbon budget is likely to be exhausted within the next two decades.

CURRENT CONDITIONS, FUTURE PROSPECTS

Although global warming is expressed in terms of a gradual increase in global average surface temperatures, this can translate into nonlinear changes and significant regional and local variation in temperatures, with the rate of warming much faster in polar regions than in equatorial regions. Rising temperatures are also accompanied by increases in extreme or "wild weather," such as changes in the frequency, intensity, duration, and timing of droughts and wildfires, hurricanes and wind storms, precipitation (rain, hail, and snow) and floods, and extremities of both high and low temperatures—as well as gradual changes to sea levels and in the temperature and chemical composition of oceans.[6] In combination, these slow and abrupt changes will undermine human security—particularly in terms of food production, shelter, and economic stability—and will also accelerate rates of extinction in other species. Ultimately, the impact of climate change depends on the severity of the change and the capacity of a community or a species to adapt to that change.

In 2003, Sir John Houghton, former Head of the UK Meteorological Office and co-chair of scientific assessment for the UN Intergovernmental Panel on Climate Change (IPCC), warned that "the impacts of global warming are such that I have no hesitation in describing it as a 'weapon of mass destruction.' Like terrorism, this weapon knows no boundaries. It can strike anywhere, in any form—a heat wave in one place, a drought or a flood or a storm surge in another. Nor is this just a problem for the future."[7]

Impacts of this kind are already evident. Global average temperature has risen by almost 0.8 degrees Celsius since 1850. This may not seem much, but the consequences have been increasingly dramatic. For instance, the first twelve years of the twenty-first century (2001–2012 inclusive) rank among the fourteen warmest years in the 133-year period of record keeping.[8] Moreover, since the 1970s, each decade has been hotter than the one that preceded it. Seven countries—Armenia, China, Iran, Iraq, Kuwait, Republic of the Congo, and Zambia—set all-time temperature highs in 2011. For the continental United States, 2012 was the warmest calendar year on record, with 362 record highs and no record lows, according to the National Climatic Data Center.[9] These temperatures contributed to the ferocity of the major fires that swept across Oklahoma and of Hurricane Sandy, the second most costly hurricane in the United States after Hurricane Katrina in 2005. The Northern Hemisphere summer of 2012 also produced a record melting and shrinking of Arctic sea ice.[10] Scientists warn that if this rate of melting continues, the Arctic summer could be ice-free in a decade, triggering more extreme weather, the accelerated disintegration of the Greenland ice sheet, more rapid sea level rise, and the release of carbon dioxide and methane previously locked in the once frozen but now thawing permafrost in the Arctic and sub-Arctic lowlands.

In the southern hemisphere, the Australian summer of 2012–2013 was the hottest on record in terms of both maximum and mean temperatures.[11] The previous year, 2011, was Australia's second wettest year (over land) on record, producing a flood that covered an area the size of France and Germany combined, which cost the country between $AUD 15 billion and $AUD 30 billion in damages and lost production: 2011 also brought Thailand its most expensive disaster ever recorded: flooding submerged around one-third of its provinces and caused $US 45 billion damage (equal to 14 percent of Thailand's gross domestic product).[12]

The year before that—2010—was the equal warmest year on global historical record (equal with 2005, for global surface temperatures) and also the wettest. In 2010 Russia suffered its hottest summer since records began some 130 years earlier, including a nation-wide temperature record of 44 degrees Celsius (111 degrees Fahrenheit at Yashkul). The month-long heat wave caused hundreds of wildfires that cost the economy some US$15 billion, an estimated 56,000 heat-related deaths, the declaration of a national state of emergency, and states of emergency relating to crop losses in twenty-eight provinces. Crop losses were such that the government suspended grain exports in order to limit price increases for consumers and associated political unrest.

If the volume of greenhouse emissions continues to grow at its present rate of global increase over the next two decades, our planet will experience average warming of at least 4 degrees Celsius (+7 degrees F) above preindustrial levels by the end of this century.[13] This increase is likely to have catastrophic consequences for food security, since farm output will be drastically curtailed with the increasing number and severity of droughts, floods, and storms causing crop failures. Such warming will lead to the permanent loss of summer sea ice in the North Pole (further accelerating warming); to a contraction or loss of glaciers in Asia and Latin America, causing dramatic water shortages for large, dependent populations; and to the eventual loss of land ice on Greenland and parts of the Antarctic. Warming of 4 degrees Celsius (+7 degrees Fahrenheit) is expected to lead to sea level rise of over seven meters over the next two centuries and seventy meters over the long term, causing the displacement of millions of people living in coastal settlements and low-lying islands. It is also expected to thaw frozen soils in the tundra/taiga regions, releasing methane (a highly active greenhouse gas) and causing a feedback loop that will further accelerate warming. Elevated levels of atmospheric CO_2 are also causing ocean acidification. Altered temperature, precipitation, wildfire, and storm patterns are expected to threaten or hasten the extinction of a significant percentage of the planet's terrestrial and marine species. Moreover, these various impacts and transformations are expected to continue to intensify and persist well beyond the twenty-second century. It is highly likely—given the evidence of the past—that these global changes would cause significant social crises and conflict, including conflict over diminishing food and other resources.[14]

We focus on climate change as our first major case study for two reasons. First, climate change represents the quintessential example of global environmental change. It is *the* overarching ecological problem of our epoch since most other ecological problems are invariably made worse by climate change and are therefore lost causes in the longer term if we fail to deal with this overarching threat. Climate change also offers a powerful illustration of the links between different forms of globalization and global environmental change. The core task of this chapter is to track how this environmental change has unfolded through the prism of our four domains of globalization, including their various precursors.

Second, climate change presents an almost unparalleled challenge for global governance, from the planetary to the local. The Earth's atmosphere is a global space that is owned by no one. Although it provides common benefits and, like the oceans, is often included in the list of "global commons," it has not been effectively governed for the common good.

Over the past half century, the atmospheric commons have been affected by nuclear fallout from atmospheric testing, ozone-depleting chemicals, and climate-altering emissions. Although treaties have been developed to govern and limit each of these unintended outcomes of human activities, they have so far had little success for the last and most significant global problem. Instead, we see an unfolding "tragedy of the commons" of global proportions and uneven and unjust localized impacts, as the Presidents of the Maldives and Palau have sought to highlight. Two decades of international climate negotiations and national climate policy development have produced diminishing returns, and the window for an effective response is rapidly closing. We assess the state of climate governance in the final section of this chapter.

Climate change is widely understood to be a global problem that requires global action for its resolution. But while many of the current and projected impacts on the atmospheric and marine commons—caused by changes in atmospheric concentrations of various gases and in ocean chemistry—are themselves truly planetary in their extension, they mainly arise from the incremental local actions such as driving cars, felling forests, producing goods, or using household appliances. Many climate-related impacts are also ultimately local, with very substantial variations from place to place—as the Maldives government sought to highlight. These complicated global and local linkages present a tough challenge for global climate governance, with the intertwined issues of accountability and justice at its core.

Following the structure of the previous chapter, we begin by looking at climate change in relation to the long fuse of modernization, followed by the short fuse of recent globalization. In looking at the complex interactions between the changing biophysical environment and the various domains of globalization that are producing and responding to global warming, we find that the histories in each domain fit together in surprising ways.

THE LONG HISTORY OF GLOBAL WARMING

The history of human-induced climate change involves an intertwining of two complicated stories about globalization. One is a narrative about the development and global diffusion of technological innovations and processes of industrialization, both of which are key dimensions of the broader process of modernization. The other is a tale about the long, isolated gestation of scientific ideas about the planet. The two stories only unite during the recent postwar period of hyperindustrialization and accelerated globalization.

We begin with industrialization, focusing on the activities, technologies, and fuels that have manufactured a warming planet. We then follow the parallel rise of a global scientific community that has created the highly abstract science of climate change and that now serves as the "chief informant" enabling us to understand the overarching environmental problem of our age. These two histories, and the contest between scientific awareness and the deeply embedded use of fossil fuels in economies around the world, are among the most important elements in the current struggle over climate change governance, to which this chapter will finally turn.

Manufacturing Global Warming

When, in 1848, the German political philosopher Karl Marx wrote, "All that is solid melts into air," he was reflecting on how the forces of modernization, associated with the social and economic forces of capitalism, were leading to the transformative breakup of the old certainties and restraints of traditional societies.[15] Little did he realize that the burning of coal—which was fueling the rise of industrial capitalism—was producing a gaseous residue that literally "melted into air," with unintended, unforeseen, long-term, and revolutionary transformative consequences for the global atmosphere and the Earth's species and ecosystems.

Successive energy revolutions involving the use of fossil fuels—first coal, then oil and gas—have, in combination with growth in population and energy demand, been the main contributors to human-induced climate change. However, these energy revolutions cannot be understood in isolation from the broader processes of industrialization, urbanization, and modernization that have both produced, and been propelled by, technological change. By the time science enabled us to understand the problems associated with fossil fuel use, these processes had joined forces with a globalized capitalism in ways that have made it especially hard for politics and governance to respond to the science.

The Age of Coal

Coal was first used for domestic heating and smelting in Europe, and specifically England, in the thirteenth century. Decried as a foul substance that "infected and corrupted" the air, it remained out of favor in England until the sixteenth and seventeenth centuries, when demand for it grew in response to two new pressures. First, the overharvesting of forests for ship building caused wood shortages and increased its cost as a fuel, making coal more economically competitive at a time when urbanization was accelerating. Then Europe entered the Little Ice Age—a period extending from around 1550 to 1850—and the demand for heating grew accordingly. By 1700, coal production in Britain was perhaps ten times what it was in 1550, and around five times more coal was mined there than in the rest of the world combined.[16]

Once easily accessible alluvial coal deposits were exhausted, deeper mines became a necessity. But as mines passed below the water table, drainage and dewatering—pumping out underground water—became critical practical and technological problems, especially in nations such as Britain, which were increasingly dependent on coal. At first, horse-powered, wind-powered, and occasionally water-powered pumps were used for dewatering, but none proved sufficient to the challenge and so, while demand increased, mine output began to fall. Then, in the first decade of the eighteenth century, Thomas Newcomen transformed the newly invented piston steam engine to enable it to pump water. By the 1760s, hundreds of coal-powered Newcomen engines were pumping water from coal mines all over England and Scotland. James Watt then further improved this invention: his first two coal-fired steam pumps were employed in 1776 to pump water from a coal mine and to blow the bellows in an iron foundry.

Linking coal to the steam engine underpinned the Industrial Revolution by greatly increasing machine power and productive capacity. Two further refinements then completed the industrial foundations of what we can recognize as the "Modern Age." The first was the adaptation of Watt's steam engine to transport coal, followed by people and all manner of produce. In 1825, George Stephenson's locomotive first hauled coal along a twenty-six-mile railway between Darlington and Stockton and, in 1830, commercial passengers on the Liverpool and Manchester railway. As Stephenson pushed the engine to a record thirty-five miles an hour, passengers were able to transcend the limitations of animal-power with a force and speed that compressed space and time and signaled a step forward in the seeming "conquest" of nature. This invention truly "marked a moment of acceleration in the speed of industrialization, and it fed the growing myth that technological progress was unstoppable."[17] Coal-fired trains and steamships soon linked continents, increasing the speed and volume of traffic in people and goods.

The second refinement was the invention of the turbine, which harnessed coal-fired energy to the generation of electricity. Coal gas was already widely used for lighting in industrialized cities in the latter part of the nineteenth century, but the development of the highly efficient steam turbine for electricity generation by the start of the twentieth century ensured the place of coal as a major source of energy for industrial power and urban light, and as the basis for the boom in twentieth-century production and consumption.

In all, the Age of Coal and the Industrial Revolution are inextricably linked. By the 1780s, coal was used to make coke to fuel furnaces producing cast iron, and Britain became the world's most efficient and largest manufacturer of iron. The British coal industry expanded tenfold between 1700 and 1830 (when it produced 80 percent of the world's coal), and coal production thereafter doubled between 1830 and 1854.[18] By 1848, the year of failed revolutions, Britain produced more iron than the rest of the world in total and had become the workshop of the world. While timber was plentiful in the United States, its use there as an industrial fuel was also quickly replaced by coal, which produced greater energy per unit of mass. In the United States, coal consumption doubled each decade between 1850 and 1890, and in the late 1890s, the United States became the world's largest coal producer—ahead of the United Kingdom and Germany in third place. By 1900, coal provided 71 percent of the United States' energy—while wood provided 21 percent and oil, natural gas, and hydropower less than 3 percent each.[19]

The technological, economic, and social transformations accompanying the Age of Coal were rapid and far-reaching.

Now, in the second decade of the twenty-first century, the same description can be applied with equal force to life in over a dozen Chinese cities. Globally, coal is the major source for stationary energy in most major industrialized and industrializing countries, supplying around 70 percent of total energy requirements.[21]

The Age of Oil

The other major fossil fuel contributing to global warming has been oil (and, more recently, gas), as an energy source for power, lighting, transport, and, to a lesser extent, heating. In ancient times oil, in the forms of bitumen and tar, was taken from seepages or hand-dug pits and used to caulk vessels and as medicine. Only in the mid-1800s was it sought and used in greater quantity, when a small crude oil industry developed in Eastern Europe, where it was refined into kerosene and used for lighting with special glass lamps designed for this purpose. When an American, George Bissell, innovatively employed a drilling technology developed by the Chinese several thousand years earlier to bore for subterranean salt deposits, oil could be recovered in large quantities. The combination of Eastern European lamps, Chinese drilling technology, and growing demand for an alternative fuel caused by the declining availability of sperm whale oil led to the world's first successful oil well being sunk in Pennsylvania in 1859.

By 1862 American annual production—at that time also global annual production—had risen to 3 million barrels, climbing to 3.6 million barrels by 1866. But it was not until the problems of refining oil in bulk to make kerosene, and transporting it by pipeline, rail, and sea, were solved that oil became a cheap alternative to other fuels for lighting. In 1861, the first shipment of oil was sent to Europe by sea, beginning a long upward curve in international trade to meet demand for the fuel, which was soon to become a geopolitical resource and a key dimension of U.S. energy and foreign policy.

As demand increased, alternative sources were found. In Russia, drilling began in the early 1870s. Russian oil production reached some 10.8 million barrels a year in the mid-1880s and 23 million barrels by 1888, while American production climbed to around 30 million barrels. The development of oil tankers and the opening of the Suez Canal to oil traffic in 1892 further expanded the opportunities for sea trade. Growth in demand and increased opportunities for profit encouraged exploration and speculation. Oil boomed in Texas in 1901; oil fields were discovered in Indonesia in the 1880s, in Latin America in the 1900s, and the Middle East in the 1930s. Substantial oil supplies seemed to secure a passport to national economic development—either directly through the new forms of industrialization or via wealth derived from export (although it later proved to be a curse for many developing countries).

The demand for kerosene collapsed at the end of the nineteenth century as urban centers initially adopted gas for artificial lighting and cooking, and then coal-fired electricity. However, the invention and refinement of petrol- and diesel-fueled internal combustion engines, and the automobile or "horseless carriage," created an alternative source of demand for oil that was rapidly internationalized.

Mass production made cars affordable, advertising made them desirable (not only for the leisure-oriented middle class but also the working class), and the modification and auto-dependent suburbanization of cities made car use easier and, in some cities, virtually essential. The manufacture and use of the multiplicity of commodities associated with automotive transport rapidly became a central social and economic feature of all large developed nations in the twentieth century. For instance, in 1900 there were around eight thousand cars in the United States, which would become the twentieth century's center of car culture. By 1950, that number had grown to 43 million, and to 248.5 million in 2009.[22] In 2010 alone, 78 million cars and light vehicles were produced for sale around the globe, including 18.3 million in China, 9.6 million in Japan, 7.8 million in the United States, and 5.9 million in Germany.[23] Globally, transport—including cheap mass air transport—now produces some 13 percent of all greenhouse emissions.

The Age of Oil overlaid and amplified the modernizing effects of the Age of Coal. The unearthing and harnessing of massive amounts of fossilized prehistoric solar energy have dramatically reconfigured the pace and intensity of production and consumption and transformed urban and rural life. Instead of a team of men or horses, diesel-powered engines with hundreds and thousands of "horsepower" or "manpower" now extract ores, haul earth, plow fields, lift loads, transform raw materials, and transport humans and goods. These oil-powered engines speed minerals, timber, grain, and manufactured goods in bulk to distant markets via road, rail, sea, and air. These same engines create skyscrapers illuminated day and night by thousands of fossil-fuel-fired light bulbs or fluorescent tubes. Oil has also made new, lethal, rapid forms of mechanized warfare possible. Troops are deployed by trains and trucks; machine guns are oiled; warships, trucks and tanks, fighter planes, and bombers are fueled and sent into battle. In all, oil and coal now power, lubricate, and light most aspects of everyday life in the developed world. Social, economic, and military dependency on oil evolved quickly in the twentieth century and just as quickly became deeply embedded in the transnational commodity chains that underpin contemporary patterns of production and consumption.

It is important to recognize that this new dependency has not been driven by some authorless force called globalization. Rather, it has been driven by a wide variety of different social agents including governments, the military, oil companies and oil cartels such as the Organization of Petroleum Exporting Countries (OPEC), car companies, property developers, and, above all, by the responses of eager consumers. All were initially unwitting generators, in some cases literally, of the problem of global warming. However, now that the problem has been revealed, many states, corporations, and communities are still prepared to defend their entrenched interests and resist efforts to work toward a low-carbon economy and society. Access to oil still remains a major strategic and security issue, just as access to cheap coal is seen as a source of economic strength, despite the emergence and growth of the "leave it in the ground" movement in many countries.[24]

Despite the rapid global growth in use of renewable energy (such as wind and solar power), consumption of fossil fuels continues to soar. Global production of oil was 3 million barrels in 1862. By contrast, in 2012—150 years later—the IEA forecasts global oil demand to climb to 89.9 million barrels *per day*, or 32 billion barrels per annum—a new peak, signaling a rapid rebound from the recession-driven declines of 2008–2009.[25]

Deposits of coal and oil are found on every continent, and the dispersed location of fossil fuels facilitated their global use once technologies for transporting and using them became commercially accessible. Unlike coal, however, significant oil and gas fields are far more geographically concentrated and no longer found in sufficient quantities in the United States and China to meet the needs of the planet's two biggest oil users. Both now are the world's first and second largest oil importers, respectively, and are dependent on external supplies.

By contrast China, the world's largest coal user, produces over three billion tonnes per annum and is virtually self-sufficient, although its growing demand is making it increasingly reliant on imports, while the United States, the second largest user of coal, is self-sufficient and a net exporter.[26]

Cheap and abundant oil has been central "to the vigor and growth of the American economy and to the preservation of a distinctly *American* way of life," including a car culture that equates private automobiles with personal freedom.[27] During the Cold War, oil was used by the United States as a strategic resource in pursuing its strategy of containment and in the overall management of its Western leadership.[28] Access to crude oil remains a major strategic concern, particularly for the United States. Oil provides nearly 40 percent of its total energy needs (including 94 percent in transportation and 40 percent in industry). The United States became a net importer in the late 1940s, and its dependence on oil and other liquid fuels reached a peak of 60 percent of net imports in 2005, although by 2012 this had fallen to around 41 percent mainly due to the growth in U.S. oil and gas production.[29] China became a net importer of crude oil in 1996.[30] As global oil supplies appear to have peaked in the first decade of the twenty-first century, competition for this resource will intensify and oil prices increase unless significant improvements occur in global energy efficiency and energy conservation, unconventional oil sources become viable, demand falls, or a transition to non-fossil fuel energy sources occurs.

From the outset of attempts to mitigate climate change in 1992, the struggle over emissions targets and controls has been intimately tied to the "power" struggle over energy sources and global military and economic influence, particularly between the United States, Russia, and now China. The oil fields of the Middle East in particular, and the shipping lanes and pipelines leading from them, have become objects of high and increasing strategic focus, national security, international contest, and sometimes warfare. Those countries without domestic (fossil) energy resources have had to import them in order to develop according to the energy model that now prevails globally.

Despite twenty years of climate negotiations, the price of fossil fuels remains relatively cheap compared to renewable energy sources, not only because the longer-term social and ecological impacts of their use are not factored into their price but also because they are heavily subsidized. According to the IEA's estimates, subsidies for fossil fuel consumption rose from $300 billion in 2009 to $409 billion in 2010 despite a commitment by the G20 in 2009 to phase out these environmentally perverse subsidies.[31] The relatively low price of fossil fuels has facilitated the continuing growth in their international trade and use over the past century.

The foregoing brief history should make it clear that fossil fuels have been central to the Industrial Revolution and to the rise of great powers. While Britain initiated and led this revolution, by the late nineteenth century the United States had overtaken it as the world's most significant industrial power before becoming the world's only superpower at the end of the Cold War. China, India, and other developing countries are showing no signs of forsaking fossil fuels in their development plans, despite investment in renewables, as they also seek to achieve or consolidate economic prosperity and Great Power status in the twenty-first century.

This brief history gives a sense of the extent to which fossil fuels have become structurally embedded in the material practices—and also the aspirations—of developed and developing economies and their inhabitants, of the interlocking relationships between those economies, and therefore of the structural and manifest political power of the interests associated with the use of fossil fuels. It also points to one of the greatest sources of dispute between developed and developing countries, relating to the historical responsibility for global warming and the benefits accrued over those earlier centuries. A central argument of China and the G77 has been that the nations of the "developed world" amassed their wealth through industrial development fueled by coal and oil. In doing so, they inadvertently (and more recently, knowingly) overused their share of the global atmospheric commons and have left the planet an unintended global legacy of climate change for which they are disproportionally responsible.

Tom Boden and his co-researchers report that, since 1751, approximately 356 billion tons of carbon have been released to the atmosphere from the consumption of fossil fuels and cement production (Figure 19.1). Half of these emissions have occurred since the mid-1970s.[32] Developing countries argue that countries with a historical responsibility for emissions and therefore climate change have a greater burden of responsibility for combating climate change and for assisting the development of those countries that will be denied the opportunity to enjoy the same access to the global atmospheric commons. These claims have been variously contested and reframed by certain developed countries. As we shall see, the United States, in particular, has rejected all charges of historical responsibility and focused its climate diplomacy on the future growth in emissions and on brokering a deal based on legal symmetry of commitment and shared prospective responsibility for mitigation.

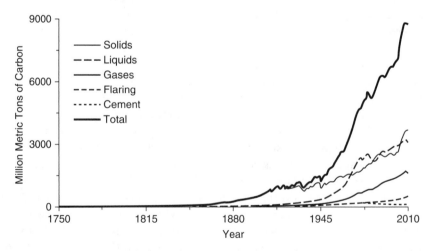

Figure 19.1 CO_2 Emissions from Industrial Sources 1750–2010

Source: Boden, T. A., G. Marland, and R. J. Andres. 2012. "Global, Regional, and National Fossil-Fuel CO_2 Emissions." Carbon Dioxide Information Analysis Center, Oak Ridge National Laboratory, U.S. Department of Energy, Oak Ridge, TN. doi 10.3334/CDIAC/00001_V2012.

Finally, mention must be made of the contribution made by agriculture and land clearing to climate change. It is estimated that between 1850 and 1990 some 124 billion tonnes of carbon were added to the atmosphere through changes in land use (predominantly the clearing of vegetation), about half that released by the burning of fossil fuels. About 108 billion tonnes came from the clearing of forests. Of this, approximately two-thirds came from tropical forests and the remainder from temperate zone and boreal forests. Another 16 billion tonnes were released from nonforested lands, mainly through cultivation of grassland soils.[33] Agriculture is also a significant source of the highly potent greenhouse gas methane.

The IPCC's Fourth Assessment Report noted that "in 2004, energy supply accounted for about 26% of greenhouse gas emissions (GHGs), industry 19%, gases released from land-use change and forestry 17%, agriculture 14%, transport 13%, residential, commercial and service sectors 8% and waste 3%."[34] Moreover, reflecting the influences of both global economic expansion and the growth in material demand accompanying population growth, "emissions of the [six major] GHGs . . . increased by about 70% (from 28.7 to 49.0 $GtCO_2$-e) from 1970–2004 . . . with CO_2 being the largest source, having grown by about 80%. The largest growth in CO_2 emissions has come from power generation and road transport. Methane (CH4) emissions rose by about 40% from 1970, with an 85% increase from the combustion and use of fossil fuels. Agriculture, however, is the largest source of CH4 emissions."[35]

Understanding Climate Change

We have argued that the material practices that have produced global warming emerged in the eighteenth century, were refined in the nineteenth century, and were widely and rapidly adopted around the world in the twentieth century. However, their climatic consequences were not recognized until an intellectual framework was created for understanding the relationship between emissions-generating activity, changing concentrations of atmospheric GHGs, global warming, and climatic impacts.

We live with weather from day to day. Asked about longer-term changes in weather, we draw on anecdotal evidence or our patchy memories of our experience of hot days, wet days, storms, droughts, or floods. In some cultures, we also call on written records of variable accuracy, which transmit traces of events that occurred in time beyond living memory.

By contrast, "climate" or "climate change" refers to long-term weather patterns and changes. Whereas changes in the weather are experienced on a day-to-day basis in particular places, "climate" and "climate change" are abstract constructs for comprehending patterns of change over different territorial scales, based on theories that organize and interpret an accumulation of longer-term observations, including primary data drawn from weather monitoring systems, and physical evidence about Earth's systems. "Climate change" in this sense is thus a thoroughly modern construction that is increasingly global in its span. Indeed, it is the abstract nature of climate science that makes it vulnerable to climate change deniers who exploit the disconnect between the immediate localized, "lived" experience of weather and the abstract historical reconstructions or future projections of climate change offered by sophisticated global climate models. They are able to draw on local experience to dispute and undermine abstract scientific claims that are, by their nature, beyond individual human experience.[36]

The capacity even to puzzle about such issues itself depended on the new spirit of questioning and empirical inquiry unleashed by the Enlightenment, and the concomitant invention of instruments to survey, record, and manipulate data about the physical environment to support the formulation and testing of more abstract theories. The development of a scientific understanding of climate change developed out of intersecting transnational scientific lines of inquiry about weather and climate, about the chemical and physical properties of air and heat, and about the Earth's geological history (including its Ice Ages) well *before* evidence of *human-induced* climate change arose.[37]

The emergence of a scientific interest in weather and climate was predicated on, and encouraged by, the broader ambitions of the Enlightenment. Considerable attention was paid to both matters in the context of emerging and competing explanations of the apparent success of certain races, cultures, and then nations, over others. At the start of the 1700s, intellectual concern about weather and climate was infused by the desire to answer the question: why was it that European (white) races seemed to be culturally and materially superior to those from elsewhere? Initially, leading Enlightenment thinkers such as Montesquieu and Hume took opposing positions—either attributing European development, deterministically, to the invigorating effects of a temperate and cold climate, or in the latter case, denying climate such influence.[38]

Concern about climate and weather was also associated with the historically new "nation-building" project. For instance, British weather and the "national climate" were regarded as more conducive to the progress of British civilization and the growth of its economic power.[39] However, this concern also extended to more practical considerations. Knowledge about weather was sought in order to better understand the influence of, to predict, and to adapt to weather's impacts on agriculture and transport (especially at sea). Starting with the Italians in 1654, and then the English, French, Germans, Russians, and Americans, "gentlemen scientists" and their emerging scientific societies began systematically to gather meteorological data and publish their interpretations of rainfall, temperature, and weather patterns more generally, in the hope of producing a rational, scientific picture of weather and climate—and to justify their hopes for national success.

By the mid-nineteenth century, meteorological records, rather than memories and "ancient authorities," provided the basis among scientists for conjecture about climate. As James Fleming notes, "The establishment of national weather services and applied climate networks [by the 1850s] was also fundamental to the emergence of effective international cooperation in meteorology and climatology. . . . International cooperation and an international bulletin of weather observations began in the 1870s."[40] The first international meteorological conference occurred in Brussels in 1853, and congresses in Vienna and Rome led to the establishment of the International Meteorological Organization (IMO) in 1873.

The creation of such an empirically oriented, transcontinental scientific endeavor and weather-observational network depended on and contributed to the development of internationally standardized scientific instruments, concepts, and empirical approaches for considering climate and weather. The development of instruments with which to measure temperature and rainfall—the thermometer and the barometer were invented in the 1600s and standardized in the 1700s—enabled the collective project of weather mapping to develop.

Already in the nineteenth century, scientific thinkers such as American geophysicist William Ferrel were beginning to consider atmospheric and marine processes on a planetary scale. These nineteenth-century scientists set in motion the evolution of a global climate-scientific epistemic community—a planet-wide body of scientists with their associated monitoring and analytical systems—that enabled the development of a more abstract understanding of changes in the Earth's climate.

A second, independent line of scientific inquiry critical to the climate change narrative also emerged in the nineteenth century through the work of two scientists whose efforts focused on temperature and atmospheric chemistry and physics. In 1824, the Frenchman Joseph Fourier provided the first rudimentary observation of the "greenhouse effect," in which the sun played a major role in determining terrestrial temperatures. This understanding was further developed by John Tyndale who, in 1859, investigated the different radiative properties of various gases—their ability to absorb or transmit heat. He determined that water vapor and CO_2 absorbed thermal radiation and therefore recognized that both were crucial in the role of atmosphere in regulating diurnal and global temperatures.

A third line of inquiry also contributed to the articulation of the puzzle of climate change. Ever since Charles Lyell had established that geological forces (rather than the hand of God) had transformed the face of the planet over "deep time," scientists had puzzled about the source of these forces. Specifically, they puzzled over the processes that drove the advance and retreat of glaciers that were recognized to have shaped many European landscapes. Clearly climates *did* change over "deep" or geological time, so what caused these changes? And was the planet stable, or warming or cooling (and therefore threatened by a new Ice Age)? In 1865 Lyell even approached Tyndale for his opinion about the possible influence of changes in the Earth's orbit on the advent of ice ages in one hemisphere or other.

In 1895, Svante Arrhenius—while puzzling over the problem of the causes of glaciation—used Tyndale's work to estimate the consequences of changes in atmospheric concentrations of CO_2 on global temperatures, and concluded that a change of about 40 percent in the atmospheric concentration of CO_2 might be responsible for initiating glacial advance and retreat.[41] He eventually calculated that "any doubling of the percentage of CO_2 in the air would raise the temperature of the earth's surface by 4 degrees [Celsius]; and if the CO_2 were increased fourfold, the temperature would rise by 8 degrees."[42] Nils Eckholm in 1899, and later Thomas Chamberlin, also nominated atmospheric CO_2—and emissions from fossil fuels—as a possible future source of climate change.

For the first four decades of the twentieth century, climate science remained speculative, unsettled, and contested internationally, with a range of competing theories proposing influences for long-term climate change and for Earth's intermittent Ice Ages. For instance, in 1920, Milutin Milanković proposed long cyclical changes corresponding to changes in the aspect of the Earth's orbit as the prime cause of these Ice Ages. Koppen and Wegener nominated continental drift. Others—with little or no evidence to support them—proposed volcanic dust, cosmic dust, and changes in solar activity (especially sunspots). Chamberlin proposed changes in ocean circulation.

The turn toward a scientific narrative emphasizing the importance of fossil fuels for climate change began with Guy Callendar's work during the 1930s. In a particular paper he read to the Royal Meteorological Society in 1938, he proposed that the burning of fossil fuels over the past half century had generated around 150 gigatonnes of CO_2, three-quarters of which had remained in the atmosphere— an increase of 6 percent in atmospheric CO_2 since 1900. Callendar suggested that the radiative properties of this additional CO_2 had caused a measurable increase in global temperature of about a quarter of a degree Celsius over the same period.[43] He later estimated a 10-percent rise in atmospheric CO_2 of 30 parts per million (from 290 ppm to 320 ppm) had occurred from the pre-1900 period to 1935, and predicted the rate of increase would accelerate due to accelerating fossil fuel use.[44] Callendar's arguments gained in authority in the immediate postwar period, during the evolving debate about the contributions of industrialization to the climatic impacts of human activity.

Warming to the Topic

Scientific attention to climate change intensified in the period immediately following World War II. This was propelled by the consolidation of scientific opinion around the importance of CO_2 as a greenhouse gas, and assisted by the formation of global institutions better able to focus and synthesize scientific discussion and the emergence of a handful of scientists prepared to project their growing concerns about their findings into the political and policy realm. Additional scientific work in the 1940s and 1950s on the radiative properties of CO_2, other gases, and water vapor, and on radiative transfer between the atmosphere and oceans, led scientists like the physicist Gilbert Plass to suggest that atmospheric accumulation of CO_2 might be a greater problem than initially believed, with a rate of increase of around 30 percent a century, and the doubling of atmospheric CO_2 leading to an average temperature increase of 3.6 degrees Celsius in the absence of other influences.[45]

Like Callendar, Plass in 1956 warned that "the accumulation of CO_2 in the atmosphere from continually expanding industrial activity may be a real problem in several generations. If at the end of this century, measurements show that the CO_2 content of the atmosphere has risen appreciably and at the same time the temperature has continued to rise throughout the world, it will be firmly established that CO_2 is an important factor in causing climatic change."[46]

Plass's warning was echoed by oceanographers Revelle and Suess, who in 1957 wrote that "human beings are now carrying out a large scale geophysical experiment of a kind that could not have happened in the past nor be reproduced in the future. Within a few centuries we are returning to the atmosphere and oceans the concentrated organic carbon stored in sedimentary rocks over hundreds of millions of years."[47]

It was on the strength of such scientific concern that David Keeling began the first rigorous monitoring of atmospheric concentrations of CO_2 in 1958 at Mauna Loa in Hawaii. By the early 1960s Keeling's work had provided conclusive empirical proof that the concentration of atmospheric CO_2 was increasing steadily and that scientific concerns about global warming were well founded.[48]

What began as individual, curiosity-driven research by scientists such as Fourier and Tyndale about the composition of the atmosphere and its influence on climate evolved, through the work of Arrhenius, Callendar, Plass, Keeling, and others, into a global scientific monitoring and research program that provided a new vantage point for the consideration of humanity's planet-transforming activities. Yet while the long fuse of modernization produced an emerging scientific consensus around the causes of global warming, the short fuse of globalization has made it harder to respond to this discovery.

TURNING UP THE HEAT, SOUNDING THE ALARM

International Scientific Institutional Responses

The global economy expanded rapidly in the second half of the twentieth century, dependent upon and reflecting consumption of fossil fuels. David Keeling's rigorous monitoring of atmospheric concentrations of CO_2 registered the resultant environmental change and injected a new note of urgency and alarm in what had hitherto been languid and detached scientific consideration of climate change as an intellectual problem. Over the ensuing decades, the growing anxieties of climate scientists became institutionalized and then disseminated into popular culture. From that point, the issue quickly became politicized and led to the construction of a new multilayered regime of climate governance, which emerged first at the national level among leading scientific nations and then was extended locally and internationally. However, this regime has been driven and riven by tensions between local, national, and international interests and has faltered in response to political movements and industry lobbies that have refused to accept the findings of climate science or the broader policy implications of those findings.

It is no small irony that the United States, as the world's largest historical emitter and a laggard in climate policy at the national level, has played a significant leadership role in fostering climate change research. The United States led in the formation of "nationally institutionalized" climate science. In 1965, the Environmental Pollution Panel of the President's Science Advisory Committee reported to President Johnson that "carbon dioxide is being added to the earth's atmosphere by the burning of coal, oil, and natural gas at the rate of 6 billion tons a year. By the year 2000 there will be about 25 percent more carbon dioxide in our atmosphere than at present."[49]

As a consequence, the U.S. National Academy of Science (NAS) took up the baton. A second warning about global warming came in 1966 from its Panel on Weather and Climate Modification, headed by geophysicist Gordon MacDonald, who later served on President Nixon's Council on Environmental Quality.[50] Less than a decade later, the NAS undertook an assessment of current knowledge about human-induced climate change and advocated for increased research funding and effort in this area.[51] In 1979, an Ad Hoc Study Group of the NAS reported that the most probable warming associated with a doubling of atmospheric CO_2 would be 3 degrees Celsius plus or minus 1.5 degrees Celsius.[52] In 1981, the Council on Environmental Quality—part of the Executive Office of the President—recommended that

> in responding to the global nature of the CO_2 problem, the United States should consider its responsibility to demonstrate a commitment to reducing the risks of inadvertent global climate modification. Because it is the largest single consumer of energy in the world, it is appropriate for the United States to exercise leadership in addressing the CO_2 problem.[53]

The development of national scientific institutions concentrating on, or significantly involved in, developing climate science and advising related policy has been paralleled in most other industrialized and now major industrializing countries. This is particularly so for those states which have been major contributors to the evolution of atmospheric science (such as Britain, through the Meteorological Office, and Germany) and increasingly now among significant recent contributors to the problem of global warming, such as China, which need to be able to participate autonomously in international climate dialogue.

Scientific debate on climate change was also fostered by the postwar growth of international scientific forums and research institutions. The World Meteorological Convention in 1947 restored confidence to an international scientific community disrupted by World War II. The professional International Meteorological Organization (IMO), founded in 1873, was superseded in 1953 by the World Meteorological Organization (WMO), an agency of the United Nations that assisted in the coordination and standardization of global weather data systems and institutional mechanisms. The International Geophysical Year in 1957 provided a transnational platform, somewhat removed from increasingly tense Cold War geopolitics, for communication about scientific climate knowledge and concerns, driven by contributions from the national behemoths for such research—the United States, Britain, and Russia.

By the 1970s, a convergence of (predominantly) scientific institutions and interests began to generate increasing political pressure for a global response to the "climate problem." Three contributions stand out: those of the WMO, the Brundtland Report, and the IPCC.

In the late 1970s and 1980s the WMO established a critically important series of climate conferences. The first World Climate Conference, held in Geneva in 1979, led to the creation of the World Climate Program, the World Climate Research Program and, ultimately, the establishment of the IPCC in 1988. Separately, through the 1980s, atmospheric scientists under the auspices of the WMO held a series of meetings in Villach, Austria. The most significant of these occurred in 1985, at which scientists considered the role of carbon dioxide and other greenhouse gases in producing climate variations and associated impacts. The conference formally concluded that, "as a result of the increasing concentrations of greenhouse gases, it is now believed that in the first half of the next century a rise of global mean temperature could occur that is greater than any in man's history."[54] The conference recommended that governments take this assessment into account in their policies and that public information campaigns on climate change and sea level rise should be increased.

The Second World Climate Conference, in November 1990, was even more important. The conference considered the IPCC's first report, and its response led directly to UN General Assembly Resolution 45/212 in the same year. This resolution established the Intergovernmental Negotiating Committee on a Framework Convention on Climate Change (INC) under the auspices of the General Assembly and with a mandate to develop a climate treaty or convention, if possible by the Earth Summit in Rio in June 1992.

A second contribution came from the United Nations' Brundtland Report, *Our Common Future*. Published in 1987, the report warned that key among environmental pressures is "the burning of fossil fuels [which] puts into the atmosphere carbon dioxide, which is causing gradual global warming. This 'greenhouse effect' may by next century have increased global temperature enough to shift agricultural production, raise sea levels, flood coastal cities, and disrupt national economies." *Our Common Future* catapulted climate change onto the global political stage, prompted debate in the UN General Assembly, and developed momentum for an international climate treaty. In Bolin's words, "The scientific community had brought the climate change issue to the political agenda with support from the two UN organizations UNEP and WMO."[55]

However, of the various international institutions established in recent times to provide scientific advice about global warming, the IPCC is the most important. Created in 1988 by the WMO and the United Nations Environment Programme (UNEP), the IPCC was established to provide periodic assessments "on a comprehensive, objective, open and transparent basis, [of] the scientific, technical and socio-economic information relevant to understanding the scientific basis of risk of human-induced climate change, its potential impacts and options for adaptation and mitigation."[56]

The IPCC's assessment reports are accepted as the most authoritative summary of the various dimensions of international climate science, based on comparisons, reviews, and summaries of climate models, data sets, and peer-reviewed published research. The lengthy process for producing each report, which requires line-by-line agreement by governments, has tended to produce especially cautious findings that are somewhat dated by their time of release. Nonetheless, the basic conclusions of the IPCC's major reports remain sound, have been widely reported, and have been highly influential in serving as a bridge between scientific climate discourse and popular climate discourse, as well as in shaping the opinions of national policy makers and negotiators. The co-authors of the IPCC's Fourth Assessment Report (2007) were joint recipients of the Nobel Peace Prize.

Contested Climate Discourses

Until the late 1980s, the problem of climate change remained predominantly a discussion between climatologists and meteorologists. However, by the end of the 1980s climate change, along with the "hole in the ozone layer," had been picked up by the media as an international environmental cause célèbre and become a matter of high public concern and political salience.[57]

In 1988, physicist James Hansen, head of the NASA Goddard Institute for Space Studies, appeared before the U.S. Congress and provided a powerful testimony on climate change that soon attracted global media attention. The *New York Times* reported Hansen as declaring that "the earth has been warmer in the first five months of this year than in any comparable period since measurements began 130 years ago, and the higher temperatures can now be attributed to a long-expected global warming trend linked to pollution." He also argued that "it was 99 percent certain that the warming trend was not a natural variation but was caused by a buildup of carbon dioxide and other artificial gases in the atmosphere."[58]

From this point onward, the rarefied and complex scientific discourse about climate change was joined by a growing cacophony of ethical, political, and economic climate discourses that have offered a variety of different characterizations of the problem and the solution. Following James Hansen's much publicized statement in 1988, global warming became a new rallying point and campaign issue for most of the major national and international environmental NGOs and networks, including Greenpeace, WWF, and Friends of the Earth, and, later, major development NGOs such as Oxfam. Growing concern over climate change also prompted the formation of a range of new NGOs and networks exclusively focused on combating climate change. The largest of these is Climate Action Network (CAN), a global network of more than seven hundred NGOs from more than ninety countries, with national and regional branches, dedicated to protecting the atmosphere while promoting sustainable and equitable development worldwide.[59]

Environmental NGOs, along with representatives of the most vulnerable nations such as low-lying island states, have been the standard-bearers of environmental justice discourses, which highlight the inverse relationship between vulnerability to climate change, on the one hand, and contribution to the problem and capacity to respond, on the other. Environmental justice discourses embrace the protection of vulnerable species, ecosystems, communities, and future human generations and argue that the division of international responsibility for emission reductions should take account of the significant differences in historical responsibility, capacity, and vulnerability between developed and developing countries. NGO campaigns have sought to draw out and amplify the ethical implications of the scientific warnings provided by the IPCC and prominent "citizen-scientists," such as Hansen and the late Stephen Schneider, to push governments for strong emissions reduction strategies and renewable energy policies, and to negotiate an ambitious international climate treaty with clear targets and timetables and significant funding for mitigation and adaptation in developing countries. NGOs in the Global South have focused on the human dimensions of the ethical discourse and given greater emphasis to poverty eradication, the historical responsibility of developed countries, and the development needs of developing countries.

The response of the corporate world to climate change has varied significantly and predictably among firms and industry groups. For example, the renewable energy industry has emerged as climate crusaders and joined discourse coalitions with environmental NGOs in support of the transition to a low-carbon society. Meanwhile, firms and industry groups, most notably the fossil fuel industry, have used their structural power to protect their threatened interests through a range of strategies, from advertising to lobbying at the national and international levels.[60] The increasing political salience of climate change has spawned some powerful "discourse coalitions" that have sought to denigrate and de-legitimize the science of climate change, exaggerate the costs of mitigation, and resist new climate policy initiatives. In some cases, this has included disinformation and outright propaganda campaigns by particular industries, scientists with strong industry ties, and/or free market think tanks (such as the Chicago-based Heartland Institute), which have willfully exploited the lay public's lack of technical expertise on complex problems such as climate change by spreading doubt and confusion.[61]

The mass media have played a critical and generative role in the development of two waves of global and national public awareness and concern over climate change, in the late 1980s and then in 2007. Media coverage of the IPCC's Fourth Assessment Report (FAR), published in 2007, galvanized public concern and political debates. So too did the documentary *An Inconvenient Truth*, which was first screened in 2006 and went on to be screened in more than fifty countries. The film won two Academy Awards in 2007 and became the seventh highest grossing documentary in history. Indeed, the combination of coverage of the IPCC's FAR and *An Inconvenient Truth* produced a renewed wave of public concern in the run up to the important 2009 Copenhagen climate negotiations.

However, the media's role has not always been one of accurate and proportionate communication of climate science. The tendency to seek out controversy and to air both sides of an argument to ensure "balanced reporting" has had the effect of overrepresenting the views of climate denialists and generating confusion and doubt among lay publics. For instance, Maxwell Boykoff and Jules Boykoff have showed that, over a fourteen-year period from 1988 to 2002, 53 percent of articles referring to the issue in four of the United States' "prestige" newspapers gave roughly equal attention to the views of climate scientists and climate denialists, while 6 percent emphasized doubts about climate science.[62] Yet a survey of the peer-reviewed scientific literature showed that 928 articles published over the decade between 1993 and 2003 supported the scientific consensus about the human contribution to global warming, with none indicating significant dissent.[63]

Similarly in 2009, the media's appetite for sensationalism and scandal led to its coverage of the so-called Climategate Affair, which concerned the publication of e-mail correspondence purportedly showing manipulation of results by climate scientists to indicate warming trends. The e-mails were obtained by unknown hackers who had gained access to the University of East Anglia's server just weeks before the Copenhagen climate conference. Although no less than eight committees of investigation into the affair subsequently found no evidence of fraud or scientific misconduct, the widespread and intense media coverage of the story greatly assisted the climate denialists' cause and appears to have contributed to diminishing support for national climate mitigation policies in English-speaking countries, particularly the United States, in the wake of the Copenhagen conference. This was aided by the widespread coverage given to errors published in the IPCC's 2007 Fourth Assessment Report, none of which affected its core findings.

Economic discourses of climate change have been particularly influential in shaping the international negotiations and national and subnational climate policy. Whereas two decades ago, the predominant economic view supported the continuing use of cheap fossil fuels to grow and strengthen national economies—deferring mitigation until there was greater certainty about climate impacts—there is now increasing recognition that deferring action merely increases the costs of mitigation and adaptation over time while also leading to irreversible and expensive economic (as well as social and ecological) losses.[64] There is also increasing support among economists for incorporating the externalized costs of climate change into the costs of production through taxes, charges, or emission trading schemes. "Putting a price on carbon" makes fossil fuels and other GHG-generating activity more expensive and renewable energy more competitive, thereby driving technological innovation toward low- or zero-carbon alternatives. Economic prescriptions for market-based instruments for climate policy to replace "old-fashioned regulation" also fitted comfortably into the neoliberal economic discourse that rose to prominence in the 1990s.

ADJUSTING THE THERMOSTAT? THE STRUGGLE FOR CLIMATE GOVERNANCE

Scientific, ethical, and economic discourses have all fed into the two-decade-long attempt by states to negotiate an international climate change regime to govern and manage global warming. However, as we shall see, different discourse coalitions have emerged among the various blocs in the negotiations, the most significant of which are the EU, the Umbrella Group (which includes the United States, Canada, Norway, Australia, and Japan), and China and the G77 (which includes around 132 developing countries).[65] The latter also contains important subdivisions that are increasingly threatening the unity of the developing country bloc. Although climate governance works at many levels,[66] here we confine our attention to the international efforts to negotiate a comprehensive international agreement under the auspices of the United Nations to guide the global effort to reduce emissions.

The Evolving Architecture of International Climate Governance

The struggle for governance of the global atmospheric commons did not begin with climate change. Public alarm over radioactive fallout from the atmospheric testing of nuclear weapons in the 1950s and early 1960s led to the Partial Test Ban Treaty in 1963. Then in the mid-1980s, the discovery of "ozone holes" over the North and South Poles—the result of ozone depletion caused by a new group of synthetic gases called chlorofluorocarbons (CFCs)—led to the formulation of what is widely hailed as one of the most successful environmental treaties of the late twentieth century.

The *Vienna Convention for the Protection of the Ozone Layer* was signed by the twenty major ozone-producing countries in 1985, less than a decade after the problems caused by CFCs were first noted and very shortly after the discovery of the "ozone hole." Two years later, the convention was strengthened and given content by the *Montreal Protocol on Substances that Deplete the Ozone Layer*, which stipulated control measures for the phaseout of CFC production, including a ban on trade in CFCs. The Montreal Protocol also enshrined the principle of differentiated responsibilities between developed and developing countries, based on different contribution to the problem and different capacities to respond. Developed countries, as the major producers of CFCs, were required to contribute to a multilateral fund that would cover the full incremental costs of compliance incurred by developing countries, and delayed compliance by developing countries was also permitted under certain special conditions.[67] The protocol, which opened for signature in 1987 and came into force in 1989, was eventually ratified by all United Nations members, and by the early 1990s had a major impact on reducing the production and emission of the main ozone-depleting substances. Scientific clarity about the causes of the problem, the limited number of contributing countries and industries, the immediate availability of commercially attractive technological solutions, and the acknowledgment of differentiated responsibilities all contributed to this rapid and effective outcome.

The climate negotiators also followed the framework convention/protocol model adopted in the ozone negotiations, which involves the negotiation of a general framework treaty (containing broad objective and principles) that authorizes the parties to negotiate more detailed legal protocols to further the objectives of the treaty. However, those who believed that the success of the ozone negotiations might be replicated in the climate negotiations would be proved wrong. In the case of the climate regime, the sources of the problem were much more varied and pervasive, the science was much more complex, the solutions much more challenging, and the burden-sharing principles more contested.

From Rio to Kyoto

Scientific concerns raised at Villach and by the IPCC's first assessment report, and public concern generated by its findings, were the major catalysts that prompted the negotiation of the *United Nations Framework Convention on Climate Change* (UNFCCC) at the United Nations Conference on Environment and Development ("the Earth Summit") at Rio de Janeiro in June 1992.[68] The ultimate objective of the UNFCCC is "the stabilization of greenhouse gas concentration in the atmosphere at a level that would prevent the dangerous anthropogenic interference with the climate system" (Article 2). The treaty came into force in 1994 and has been ratified by 194 states representing every recognized sovereign state in the world, plus the European Union (EU). However, this universal membership belies the tensions and conflicts associated with a treaty that many claim to be the most complex and testing treaty ever negotiated. Its early enthusiasts greatly underestimated the difficulties that would arise in tackling energy sources and industrial processes central to (conventional) economic development and associated national interests. The problems were not only geopolitical but also structural.

The UNFCCC was finalized at the same time as the negotiation of the Rio *Declaration on Environment and Development* (1992) and it embodies many of the Declaration's aspirations and principles.[69] It also reflects key tensions between the Global North and Global South that dominated the Earth Summit, including over the vexed questions of historical responsibility for environmental harm, burden sharing, the special situation and needs of developing countries, and the sovereign right to develop. The pivotal burden-sharing provision of the treaty provides that

> the Parties should protect the climate system for the benefit of present and future generations of humankind, on the basis of equity and in accordance with their common but differentiated responsibilities and capabilities. Accordingly, the developed country parties should take the lead in combating climate change and the adverse effects thereof.[70]

The convention divides member states into three different groupings: approximately 40 predominantly wealthy industrialized states made up of developed states and the Eastern European states undergoing a transition to a market economy (Annex I parties); 24 "developed" states, which reflects the OECD membership in 1992 (Annex II parties); and some 155 developing states (known as non-Annex I states). These groupings provide the basis for differentiated commitments under the UNFCCC, which are intended to reflect broad differences in historical and current emissions, per capita emission, capacity, development needs, and vulnerability. All the industrialized parties in Annex I are required to adopt policies and measures to reduce emissions, although the specific obligation to lead is restricted to developed countries.[71] Following the Montreal Protocol model, Annex I parties are also required to provide new and additional finance, and the transfer of technology, to help developing countries meet their commitments under the UNFCCC and to assist with adaptation to climatic impacts.[72] The obligations of developing countries under the UNFCCC are mainly confined to establishing national inventories of their emissions and reporting to the UNFCCC Secretariat.

While the UNFCCC laid down broad objectives and commitments, they were largely aspirational. Despite a pledge by industrialized countries at the Earth Summit to return their emissions to 1990 levels by 2000, little progress could be made without further clear and binding targets and timetables. Accordingly, the parties commenced a second phase of negotiations, which concluded with a legally binding protocol agreed by the third Conference of the Parties (COP 3) in Kyoto in 1997.[73]

The *Kyoto Protocol* (KP) maintained the commitment to "common but differentiated responsibilities" by requiring only the industrialized countries to commit to legally binding emissions reductions. These parties negotiated individually binding targets that would, if fully implemented, produce a net aggregate reduction in emissions of around 5 percent below a 1990 baseline by the end of its first five-year commitment period (2008–2012). The EU took the lead with an 8 percent reduction target; the United States followed with a 7 percent target.

However, in the lead-up to the negotiations, the Clinton administration had faced a hostile Senate, which had passed a unanimous resolution (the "Byrd–Hagel" resolution) in July 1997 declaring that it would not ratify the protocol if developing countries were not required to undertake emissions reduction obligations in the same commitment period, or if the treaty would harm the U.S. economy.[74] The grand bargain eventually struck at Kyoto was that the United States would accept emissions reduction targets without a corresponding commitment from developing countries in return for greater flexibility for Annex I parties in meeting their targets. This flexibility took the form of international emissions trading and offsetting (through the Clean Development Mechanism, Joint Implementation, and emissions trading), all of which would enable Annex I parties to take advantage of cheaper abatement options outside their territories (discussed in more detail later). The protocol also enshrined a related range of reporting and accounting rules and processes, including provisions that enabled Annex I parties to claim reductions from investing in "carbon sinks," such as forests.

The KP also further entrenched deep divisions within states and between blocs of states—divisions that would see its ratification jeopardized and the start of implementation delayed for years. The "firewall" between Annex I and non-Annex I countries in the KP was to generate increasing hostility toward the protocol inside the U.S. Congress. The Clinton administration never presented the protocol to the Senate for ratification, and when George W. Bush was took office in 2001, he promptly repudiated it for the same reasons as the U.S. Senate (while also questioning the climate science).[75] Australia also followed suit in declining to ratify the protocol, until the election of a new Labor government in 2007. The Bush administration's repudiation was to delay the protocol's entry into force for seven years.[76] The ongoing opposition of the United States to the KP (as distinct from the UNFCCC) continues to be a major impediment to the development of a second commitment period under the protocol. Canada, Japan, and the Russian Federation have also rejected or declined to commit to a second commitment period.

Environmental NGOs and scientists have also criticized the *Kyoto Protocol* as the product of political horse-trading rather than being based on scientific advice or an equitable formula for apportioning burdens according to responsibility, capacity, and development needs. (Australia, for instance, gained an exceptional target permitting an increase of 8 percent above its 1990 level of emissions by effectively blackmailing the assembled delegates with the possibility of its defection.[77])

Meanwhile the developing country bloc (the G77 plus China) and the European Union continued to insist that—under Article 3(1) of the UNFCCC—mitigation was rightly first and foremost a developed country obligation and a necessary first step in building developing bloc trust in a global climate regime. It was only through the provision of additional incentives (which further weakened the protocol's effectiveness) to win the support of Japan, Canada, and finally Russia for ratification that the protocol finally came into legal force in February 2005.

The Marketization of Emissions

The quest for flexibility in choosing the means for meeting national emissions reduction targets has attracted strong support from many developed countries, economists, and business groups for the establishment of an international carbon market.[78] From the standpoint of firms, carbon trading and offsetting are considered superior to prescriptive regulation or a simple tax since they enable firms to find a least-cost solution to mitigation. These mechanisms were also considered to reduce the perceived threat posed to economic growth by direct regulations and are compatible with the emphasis on market-based choice central to the neoliberal economic thinking that had become dominant in the 1990s.

The protocol's flexibility mechanisms established the foundations for a form of marketized global climate governance that also supported the underlying logic of capital accumulation. It did so through the nomination of six major GHGs, the commodification and certification of emissions of those gases, the creation of an international system for exchanging emissions certificates, and the initiation of three mechanisms as the primary vehicles for "least-cost" mitigation—the Clean Development Mechanism, Joint Implementation, and emissions trading.

The Clean Development Mechanism (CDM) is an offsetting scheme that enables Annex I countries to earn tradable "certified emissions reduction" (CER) credits by investing in additional emissions reductions projects in developing countries. The CDM has also been strongly supported by developing countries because it offers them a source of new investment, the transfer of climate-friendly technologies to promote sustainable development, the improvement of livelihoods and skills, job creation, and increased economic activity.[79] Initially believed by its proponents to be unlikely to be a significant measure, it has become the core means of climate-directed investment into the major developing countries. Of the 4,369 projects listed on the CDM registry as of mid-2012, half are located in China, and approximately one-fifth in India, with most of the investment coming from the United Kingdom, Switzerland, Japan, The Netherlands, and Sweden.[80] Annual investment in registered CDM projects rose from $US40 million in 2004 to $US47 billion in 2010 and over $US140 billion in mid-2011.[81] However, critics have questioned the robustness and environmental integrity of the CDM's accounting methodologies (which require the new investment projects to produce emissions reductions that are "additional" to what would have occurred under "business as usual") and whether the CDM has made any substantial contribution to reducing actual and prospective emissions.[82]

The second mechanism, Joint Implementation (or JI), is similar to the CDM but instead enables emissions credits to be generated by mitigation-related investment by Annex I countries in other Annex I countries (predominantly post-Soviet Central and Eastern European "economies in transition").

The KP's third mechanism is emissions trading, which allows Annex I parties that have produced more emissions than allowed under their Kyoto target to purchase "assigned amount units" from parties that have reduced their emissions more than required. The idea of a carbon emissions trading market built upon the United States' successful national sulfur dioxide cap-and-trade scheme under the U.S. Clean Air Act. The underlying logic of a cap-and-trade system is to set a tightening regulatory "cap" (the total volume of emissions to be traded in any given period) to reduce the "availability" of tradable emissions permits over time. A market in increasingly scarce and therefore increasingly expensive emissions permits is expected to increase the cost of fossil-fuel-related activities and encourage companies to invest in more financially attractive and less emissions-intensive technologies and practices.

While emissions trading had been strongly promoted by the United States prior to the Kyoto negotiations, it was initially opposed by the EU, the G77, and most environmental NGOs. The chief objection was that developed states had a moral obligation to reduce domestic emissions at source through domestic policy changes rather than pay others to reduce emissions or avoid pursuing new emissions-generating activities elsewhere. For many environmental NGOs, carbon trading and offsetting enable the evasion of national and corporate responsibility and the postponement of the necessary restructuring toward a low-carbon economy. However, during the Kyoto negotiations in 1997, the EU acceded to the United States' demands to ensure U.S. participation in the agreement and to secure the United States' expected substantial contribution—as a major emitter—to a global carbon market. The EU went on to embrace emissions trading and the international carbon market, while the United States' repudiation of the KP excluded it from this market. The EU's own regional emissions trading scheme (EU ETS), established when the KP came into force in 2005, has become the world's largest, encompassing all the twenty-seven countries of the EU plus Iceland, Liechtenstein, and Norway. The scheme, now entering its third phase, includes 72 percent of the world's volume of trade in carbon permits and 80 percent of its value. It is ironic that emissions trading has become the centerpiece of climate policy in the EU while the United States has been unable to find sufficient support in Congress to enact such a scheme and has had to resort to traditional regulation by the Environmental Protection Agency to manage greenhouse gas emissions under preexisting provisions in the Clean Air Act.

The total volume and value of global carbon trading continues to grow. The amount of carbon traded in 2011 increased by 19 percent on 2010, reaching a new high of 10.3 billion tonnes of CO_2-e and a total value of $USD 176 billion (including $148 billion in Europe)—up by 11 percent on the previous year. This is despite the ongoing influence of the global financial crisis and of the European economic downturn, which has caused a surplus in EU permits and therefore a significant depression in prices.[83] In addition to the European Union, Iceland, Liechtenstein, and Norway, national and subnational trading schemes also exist in Canada, New Zealand, Switzerland, and the United States. By 2013, there will be schemes in operation in eighteen subnational jurisdictions in Canada and the United States (including

California) and, by 2015, also in seven provinces in China,[84] the Republic of Korea, and possibly Australia. However, attempts to establish national schemes in Australia and the United States have faced stiff (and, in the United States, successful) opposition by business interests and associated political parties opposed to any carbon price.

From Bali to Copenhagen

The KP's ratification initiated a third phase of regime development, at the eleventh Conference of the Parties (COP 11) in Montreal in 2005, to determine the content—including future mitigation commitments—of the protocol's second commitment period, intended for the period 2013 to 2020. But the explicit repudiation of the protocol by the United States (supported by its close ally, Australia) in 2001 generated major problems and complications for the negotiators. Not only were the KP's targets exceedingly modest relative to the scale of the problem, but the world's biggest historical emitter and biggest aggregate emitter (at the time), and two of the world's highest per capita emitters (i.e., the United States and Australia) had refused to participate and had challenged the principle of differentiated responsibilities. The situation marked the beginning of a major standoff that has continued to stalk the negotiations. The United States would not participate in any climate treaty that did not also include all major emitters (including China and India); China, India, and other major emitters in the developing world argued that the differentiated responsibilities under the UNFCCC and KP made it clear that they were under no obligation to make international commitments for so long as developed nations had failed to discharge their leadership responsibilities.

The negotiators responded to the standoff by pursuing a two-track negotiating process, whereby the parties to the KP sought to negotiate a second commitment period, while the parties to the UNFCCC (which included the United States and Australia) would begin an informal dialogue toward a long-term treaty for the post-2012 period.

In 2007, global public concern about global warming reached new heights, fueled by widespread reportage of the findings of the IPCC's Fourth Assessment Report and the impact of *An Inconvenient Truth*, and this sentiment flowed into international negotiations. At COP 13, held in Bali at the end of 2007, Australia, under a new Labor (social democrat) government, elected in part for its promise to engage with the climate issue, ratified the KP. This left the United States isolated as the only major developed country opposing the treaty. Meanwhile, China's rapid economic growth saw it overtake the United States as the world's biggest aggregate emitter in 2006, almost more than a decade earlier than predicted, although the United States remained the largest historical emitter and its per capita emissions were around four to five times higher.[85]

At the Bali negotiations, it appeared that the United States would frustrate plans to adopt a formal negotiating process to lead to timely development of a post-2012 climate regime. Intense frustration among delegates boiled over at the COP plenary, where the United States was booed and jeered for its opposition, and then applauded when it finally decided to support the Bali Action Plan to negotiate a new treaty on long-term cooperative action. This plan, intended to come to fruition in 2009 at COP 15 in Copenhagen, aimed to determine new global and national mitigation targets, establish funding arrangements for adaptation, and finalize the design and rules for an additional area of carbon marketization and offsetting—the use of financial incentives for the reduction of emissions from deforestation and forest degradation (REDD) in developing countries. Given their leadership obligations, Annex I countries were to commit to legally binding emissions targets (while ensuring comparability of effort) while developing countries agreed to pursue "nationally appropriate mitigation actions" (NAMAs) that did not amount to legally binding international commitments.

Copenhagen was the most anxiously anticipated conference of all of the COPs to date. On the one hand, the election of President Obama raised expectations of positive U.S. engagement. On other hand, the onset and severity of the global financial crisis distracted the attention of the major economies from climate negotiations, while the "Climate-gate" affair played into the hands of those who opposed a new climate treaty. These latter elements merely added to the problem of the well-entrenched standoff between the United States and major developing countries such as India and China, which persisted despite the EU's effort to play a leadership role. The formation of a new negotiating block, the BASIC group (Brazil, South Africa, India, and China) also threatened to deepen the standoff.

The Copenhagen conference came perilously close to foundering. Negotiators at its final plenary session, which continued beyond the conference's official closure for more than forty-eight hours without break, tried desperately to salvage an acceptable outcome. In the end, no second commitment period to the KP and no new legally binding treaty were agreed. Instead, a nonbinding political agreement known as "the Copenhagen Accord" was noted in the final plenary but not accepted by the COP due to the absence of consensus.[86] This agreement, the outlines of which had been brokered by an informal meeting between the United States and the BASIC group, merely "recognized" the scientific view that warming should be kept below 2 degrees, but did not make it a specific goal. Moreover, the Accord contained no near-term (2020) or long-term (2050) collective or national targets and no timetable for when global emissions would peak and then decline. Instead, the agreement endorsed a "bottom-up" process of "pledge and review" by which all states would nominate voluntary mitigation commitments through to 2020 (and choose their own baseline). It also promised significant funding from developed states of $US10 billion per annum for three years, for adaptation assistance, and the establishment of a Green Climate Fund.[87]

The Copenhagen Accord embodied the standoff between the United States and the BASIC group. The United States refused to commit to any agreement without formal mitigation commitments from all major emitters, while the BASIC group rejected the notion of binding commitments by developing countries and reiterated the principle of differentiated responsibilities and capacities and the leadership obligations of developed countries. China also refused to accept a collective target for 2050 that might compromise its development trajectory.

From Copenhagen to Durban

Although the Copenhagen Accord was formally adopted a year later, at COP 16 at Cancun (2010), the standoff continued to thwart any progress on a second commitment period for the Kyoto Protocol or progress toward more ambitious mitigation objectives. The KP was set to expire in 2012, with no successor treaty in sight. In the lead-up to COP 17 in Durban (2011), Canada, Russia, and Japan made it clear that they saw no point in continuing the negotiations for a second commitment period in the absence of U.S. participation. Canada—unable to reach its commitments under the first commitment period—also abandoned the KP. Yet China and the G77, strongly supported by environmental NGOs, insisted on a second Kyoto commitment period given the absence of any progress on the broader post-2012 treaty.

At Durban, the EU prevented yet another derailment by agreeing to commit to a second commitment period under the KP in return for an agreement by *all* major emitters to launch negotiations for a new legally binding treaty to be signed by 2015, to come into effect in 2020. This offer was welcomed by the vulnerable developing states (especially but not only the Alliance of Small Island States), which were becoming increasingly desperate for action on mitigation, and it was eventually accepted by all major emitters. The negotiating track at Bali was wound up. A new roadmap for negotiations was agreed: the Durban Platform for Enhanced Action.

While Durban appeared to represent diplomatic progress, it produced no substantial movement toward the UNFCCC's ultimate goals.[88] The Durban Platform seeks to raise the level of mitigation ambition by recognizing the "ambition gap" between current climate science and the Copenhagen Accord's target pledges, which are unable to hold warming below 2 degrees. Yet it postponed further agreement to 2015—when the critical decade for effective action is half over—with no guarantee that a treaty containing meaningful targets will be signed then or come into legal force by 2020. As the editors of the scientific journal *Nature* summed it up: "The Durban deal may mark a success in the political process to tackle climate change, but for the climate itself, it is an unqualified disaster. It is clear that the science of climate change and the politics of climate change, which claims to represent it, now inhabit parallel worlds."[89]

CHAPTER 20

The One-Degree War

Paul Gilding

In a 2010 issue of *Nature Geosciences*, two Canadian scientists used existing models to demonstrate that if we stopped all emissions tomorrow, temperatures would stop increasing almost immediately and decrease over time.[1] In summary, the only warming that is truly "locked in" is that which we choose to create by continuing to emit. A separate study in *Science* in September 2010 found that if all existing energy and transport infrastructure was used for its natural lifetime, but no new infrastructure emitting greenhouse gasses was created, warming would peak at 1.3 degrees and then start declining.[2] Again, the conclusion is that we can physically do this—we just have to want to do it badly enough.

So if one degree is what is *necessary,* and more than this is defined as the "enemy" for our "one-degree war," what action is required to win the war, and would the required action be possible to achieve? In other words:

1. Is an agreement to achieve such a plan politically conceivable?
2. If it were, is it technically and economically possible to reduce global greenhouse gas concentrations to a level that will bring warming back below one degree?

Clearly, agreement to a one-degree war plan is hard to imagine in today's world. However, in both World War II and the recent financial crisis, there are clear examples of how quickly things can change and how apparently intractable opposition and resistance can quickly evaporate. In the case of World War II, the speed of response by the United States was extraordinary. For example, whereas in 1940 U.S. defense spending was just 1.6 percent of the economy (measured as GDP), within three years it had increased to 32 percent, and by 1945 it was 37 percent. But the GDP increased itself by 75 percent in that time, making the observed increases even more extraordinary.[3] Similarly extraordinary political decisions were made to direct the economy. For example, just four days after the bombing of Pearl Harbor, the auto industry was ordered to cease production of civilian vehicles.[4]

Gasoline and tires were rationed, campaigns were run to reduce meat consumption, and public recycling drives were held to obtain metals for the war effort. Yes, there was still plenty of resistance, but the political leadership of the day, with public and business support, simply overrode it for the greater public good—because the consequence of failure was unacceptable.

So it *can* be done. But *how* would it be done? It is unlikely that the one-degree war would result from a universal global agreement. The process around the Kyoto Protocol and the Copenhagen meeting shows how difficult global agreements are. This difficulty in reaching consensus is often put to me as evidence that we will fail to act on climate change. My response is to ask, "Can you think of other examples where a major military action or economic transformation was driven by a consensus global agreement?" On what basis did we ever believe such an approach would be possible with climate change, especially when many participants have actively sought to undermine it?

We didn't seek a single global agreement to free trade before any action was taken, for example. If we had done so, we would probably still be negotiating on the preamble fifty years later! Instead we started with consultative bodies like the General Agreement on Tariffs and Trade (GATT); we negotiated agreements between individual countries and then expanded them to regions. Meanwhile, very, very slowly, we built the global infrastructure for governance of trade, taking from 1947 with the formation of GATT until 1995 to form a body with enforcement power, the World Trade Organization (WTO). More than sixty years after GATT, even the WTO is still not global in impact, with even China joining only in 2001— that alone took fifteen years of negotiations.

So on climate change, an even more complex economic issue and with significant business opposition to change, it is hard to imagine we would jump straight to a single, legally enforceable, global agreement even in a crisis.

When we do decide to launch a rapid response, it is far more likely that a small number of powerful countries, a kind of "Coalition of the Cooling," will decide to act and then others will follow. Some will follow in order to align with the major powers, and some will be under military, economic, and diplomatic pressure to join.

In a technical sense, this process is easy. A full 50 percent of global greenhouse gas emissions will be covered if three "countries" (China, the United States, and the EU-27) agree to act. If we add another four countries (Russia, India, Japan, and Brazil), the coalition will control 67 percent of global emissions.[5] Add a few friends and we soon move to more than sufficient impact to tackle the problem. We saw this start to emerge in Copenhagen, and while it will be messy and will ebb and flow over coming years, there is no doubt in my mind that this is the primary way progress will emerge.

The answer to the first question is therefore clearly yes. When we accept the crisis, we are capable of taking the political decisions required to get to work on the action plan. So is there an action plan that would work?

Based on current knowledge and technology, a one-degree target is completely achievable and at an acceptable cost compared with the price of failure. It would be very disruptive to parts of the economy and to many people, and it would require considerable short-term sacrifice, but it certainly "solves the problem."

So from both questions, our political decision-making capacity and our technical/ economic capacity, the issue is not humanity's *capacity* to act, but the conditions being such that humanity *decides* to act. Identifying this point is simple: When the dominant view becomes that climate change threatens the viability of civilization and the collapse of the global economy, a crisis response will rapidly follow. Then society's framework will change from "what is politically possible" to Churchill's "what is necessary." Until then, little of real substance will happen except getting ready for that moment.

What would such a "war plan" look like? Can we forecast the likely response that will be implemented when the moment comes? Jorgen and I thought so. In designing our draft plan, we estimated a start date of around 2018, not as a precise prediction, but we needed a start date to model our response and its impact, and 2018 was our best judgment on when this would emerge. Post-Copenhagen, it still seems like a reasonable forecast.

We concluded that at that late stage, four types of actions would be required to take control of the crisis:

1. A massive industrial and economic shift that would see the elimination of net CO_2e emissions from the economy within twenty years, with a 50 percent reduction in the first five years.
2. Low-risk and reversible geoengineering actions to directly slow temperature increase, to safely overcome the lag between emissions reduction and temperature impact.
3. The ongoing removal of around 6 gigatons of CO_2 from the atmosphere per year for around one hundred years and the long-term storage of this CO_2 in underground basins, in soils and in biomass.
4. Adaptation measures to reduce hardship and geopolitical instability caused by then unavoidable physical changes to the climate, including food shortages, forced migration, and military conflict over resources.

It is a symptom of the magnitude of the task that even with the dramatic action proposed in our one-degree war plan, warming would continue above one degree until the middle of this century, before falling back to plus one degree centigrade by 2100.

We suggest fighting the one-degree war in three phases:

1. **Climate War. Years 1–5.** Modeled on the action following the entry of the United States into World War II, this would be the launch of a world war level of mobilization to achieve a global reduction of 50 percent in greenhouse gas emissions within five years. This crisis response would shock the system into change and get half the job done.
2. **Climate Neutrality. Years 5–20.** This would be a fifteen-year-long push to lock in the 50 percent emergency reductions and move the world to net zero climate emissions by year 20 (that is, in 2038 if we start in

2018). This will be a major global undertaking, requiring full utilization of all technological opportunities, supported by behavior and culture change.

3. **Climate Recovery. Years 20–100.** This would be the long-haul effort toward global climate control—the effort to create a stable global climate and a sustainable global economy. Achieving this will require a long period of negative emissions (i.e., removing CO_2 from the atmosphere) to move the climate back toward the preindustrial "normal." For instance, some refreezing of the arctic ice cap will require removing CO_2 from the atmosphere through geoengineering actions, like burning plantation wood in power stations and storing the emissions underground using carbon capture and storage (CCS). We believe humanity can complete the stabilization job in the first decades after 2100.

We tested our suggested emission cuts in the C-ROADS global climate model developed by Climate Interactive, an initiative of Ventana Systems, Sustainability Institute, and MIT's Sloan School of Management.[6] This confirmed that implementation would deliver broadly the following results:

The CO_2e concentration falls below 350 ppm by the end of the century, after peaking at around 440 ppm.

Global temperature does temporarily rise above plus one degree centigrade in midcentury, then falls below plus one degree centigrade around the end of this century.

Average sea level rises by 0.5 meters around 2100 and continues rising to a peak of 1.25 meters around 2300. This is still very disruptive and might trigger a tighter target, but 1.25 meters over three hundred years is at least more manageable than current forecasts with good preparation given the longer time frames.

In broad terms, what this all means is that the climate would be stabilized and manageable for global society. There would still be substantial changes to the climate, disruption to the economy and food supplies, and great loss of biodiversity. However, it would be manageable and it would reduce the risk of the collapse to a tolerable level. It would also allow stronger action if the science indicates the situation is worse than expected.

So it seems it is possible to design a plan that would achieve the required reductions. Of course this is just indicative. What is needed is a multiyear detailed modeling and planning exercise on a scale only governments could afford to devise. Our point was simply to show what is possible. So what types of real-world actions does our plan indicate would be required?

We proposed a dramatic and forceful start of the one-degree war, for two reasons:

1. There is disproportionate value in early actions.[7] As the impact of emissions is cumulative, cuts taken earlier in a program save much larger and more disruptive reductions later.

2. History indicates that successful responses to crises tend to involve urgent, dramatic actions rather than slower, steady ones. This engages the public and breaks the tyranny of tradition.

The one-degree war plan therefore proposes a series of global measures to achieve a rapid halving of CO_2 emissions during the initial five-year C-war, through linear reductions of 10 percent per year. The C-ROADS model indicated that it takes cuts of 50 percent by 2023 to reach our goal. Even then, this cut must be followed by reductions to zero net emissions by 2038 and net absorption, each year for the rest of the century, of 6 $GtCO_2e$/year (gigatons of CO_2 equivalents per year). While the initial 50 percent in five years is very challenging, it is certainly doable. Critically, a slower start would make it challenging to achieve the one-degree goal.

The good news is that cutting by 50 percent by 2023 can be achieved with the types of initiatives that studies like those by international management consultancy McKinsey & Co. indicate will cost society less than €60/tCO_2e.[8] (ton of CO_2e). The bad news is that making these cuts at a faster speed will, by conventional wisdom, increase the cost. This is based on infrastructure having to be scrapped before the end of its useful life and because technologies will have to be implemented before they are commercially mature. If this is accurate, it is the unfortunate consequence of acting late, as we will be. Delaying action would, however, just make that worse.

There is a counterargument that was not possible for us to model, but we were inclined to support, that a warlike mobilization of the global economy to transform our energy and transport infrastructure will not only be affordable, but may in fact trigger so much innovation and economic activity that it ends up being positive economically. This is argued by many analysts in this area, who see renewable energies as so immature that they will inevitably become not just cheaper than today, but cheaper than fossil fuels even without a carbon price. Certainly the types of approaches proposed in the one-degree war plan would unleash massive innovation and scale, so this would rapidly be proven either way. It is the case in previous wars that innovation drove new industries and great efficiencies because the determination to achieve an outcome forced major breakthroughs in technology and overcame normal commercial development impediments.

This debate is largely of academic interest only, as the crisis then present will dictate that the approach has to occur, largely regardless of the cost. I don't imagine there was much of a cost-benefit analysis done on the Manhattan Project when the U.S. government decided it needed to produce an atomic bomb. So we can safely leave to history the judgment of relative costs of CO_2 reduction.

To provide a flavor of what we can expect to see when the type of response we are forecasting occurs, I will list some edited excerpts from our plan. They indicate the types of actions that would be required in the first five-year period to get the global economy on the path required to ultimately bring global temperature increase below plus one degree centigrade.

CUT DEFORESTATION AND OTHER
LOGGING BY 50 PERCENT

Reduce by one half the ongoing net forest removal and land clearing across the world, including tropical deforestation. At the same time, concentrate commercial forestry operations into plantations managed to maximize carbon uptake. This will require significant payments to developing countries, for the climate services provided by their intact forests, but is surprisingly cost-effective and doable.[9]

CLOSE ONE THOUSAND DIRTY COAL
POWER PLANTS WITHIN FIVE YEARS

Close down a sufficient number of the world's dirtiest coal-fired power plants to cut the greenhouse gas emissions from power production by one third. We estimate this implies closing down one thousand plants,[10] resulting in a parallel reduction in power production of one sixth. (Power production would fall proportionally less than emissions, because the dirtiest plants emit more CO_2 per unit of energy.)

RATION ELECTRICITY, GET DRESSED FOR
THE WAR, AND RAPIDLY DRIVE EFFICIENCY

In response to lower power supply, launch an urgent efficiency campaign matched with power rationing. Include a global campaign to change the temperature by one to two degrees centigrade in all temperature-controlled buildings (increase/decrease according to season). Make this part of the "war effort" as a public engagement technique, with large immediate power savings. On the back of this, launch an urgent mass retrofit program, including insulating walls and ceilings, installing efficient lighting and appliances, solar hot water, and so on across both residential and commercial buildings. This would have significant short-term job creation impacts.

RETROFIT ONE THOUSAND COAL POWER PLANTS
WITH CARBON CAPTURE AND STORAGE

Install CCS[11] capacity on one thousand of the remaining power plants. This huge investment would be much simpler through international standardization. The CCS technology will also be needed for removal of CO_2 from the atmosphere later in the one-degree war (generating power using biomass and sequestrating the CO_2). CCS is not yet commercially viable and will require heavy government intervention. However, one of my colleagues strongly believes CCS will be mandated because it is a simple, albeit expensive, way of reducing greenhouse gas emissions, whereas I'm more skeptical. It's not important at this stage, as all technologies will develop and actions taken will adapt accordingly.

ERECT A WIND TURBINE OR SOLAR PLANT
IN EVERY TOWN

Build in every town of one thousand inhabitants or more at least one wind turbine. If there is no meaningful wind, build a solar thermal or solar photovoltaic (PV) plant instead. Beyond the CO_2 and renewable technology acceleration benefits, this would have the powerful impact of giving most people in the world a tangible physical connection to the "war effort."

CREATE HUGE WIND AND SOLAR FARMS
IN SUITABLE LOCATIONS

Launch a massive renewable energy program focused primarily on concentrated solar thermal, solar PV, and wind power—on land and offshore. Given the urgency, the initial focus will need to be on those areas with most short-term potential for mass rollout, with finance supported by global agreement. The DESERTEC initiative for large scale renewable energy generation in north Africa connected to the European grid provides an interesting concept of what would be possible with a multilateral focus.[12] On a global scale, various studies have shown how we could move to a 100 percent renewable energy system relatively rapidly. A recent global study showed how this could be achieved by 2030 with full baseload coverage. Of particular interest is that it concluded it would actually be cheaper than fossil fuels and nuclear power, due to the considerable efficiencies inherent in an energy system based on renewable generation and electricity use.[13] All such modeling exercises are problematic and subject to controversy, but there is certainly massive potential in renewables with a war effort–type approach.

LET NO WASTE GO TO WASTE

Ensure that all used materials are recycled and reused, at the very least to recover the embedded energy. To force this, limit production of virgin aluminum, cement, iron, plastics, and forest products—possibly through international agreements to restrict their use through higher prices or a special global emissions tax on virgin materials. Drive public recycling as part of the war effort (there are good examples here also from World War II, where mass public recycling drives focused on key materials).

RATION USE OF DIRTY CARS TO CUT TRANSPORT
EMISSIONS BY 50 PERCENT

Launch large-scale replacement of fossil-fuel cars with chargeable electric vehicles—running on climate-neutral power—along with a massive boost in fuel-efficiency standards, bans on gas guzzlers, and greater use of hybrid cars. Public repurchase and destruction of the most inefficient vehicles ("cash for clunkers" schemes) may help speed the transition and help address equity issues. Given the time it will take to scale up production, there will need to be rationing of the purchase of gasoline and diesel and other restrictions on their use such as special speed limits on fossil-fuel cars. Such restrictive measures would help drive acceptance of electric and efficient vehicles that would be free of such controls—the fast electric car can wave as it passes the old gas guzzler on the freeway!

In World War II, fuel in the United States was rationed at four gallons (per vehicle per week), then reduced to three gallons, and finally reduced in 1944 to two gallons. Alongside this, a national 35 mph speed limit was imposed, and anyone breaking the limit risked losing his fuel and tire rations. The government ran marketing campaigns to support these measures, such as advertisements asking, "Is this trip necessary?" and education campaigns on "how to spend a weekend without a car."[14] It seems there were early-day environmentalists at the U.S. Defense Department!

PREPARE FOR BIOPOWER WITH CCS

Interestingly, the C-war may not see a large increase in the use of biofuels for land transport (not even second-generation fuels made from cellulose). It seems better for the climate to grow the cellulose and burn it in power stations with CCS, thereby removing CO_2 from the atmosphere while making power and heat. For this reason, boosting cellulose production (in plantations and elsewhere) will be key.

STRAND HALF OF THE WORLD'S AIRCRAFT

Reduce airplane capacity by a linear 10 percent per year through regulatory intervention and pricing to achieve a 50 percent reduction in airline emissions by the end of year 5. This will force the rapid development of biofuels for aircraft because of the commercial imperative to do so and force a cultural shift to electronic communication and away from frivolous air travel.

CAPTURE OR BURN METHANE

Put in place a global program to ensure that a significant proportion of the methane from agricultural production and landfills are either captured for energy purposes or at least burned to reduce the warming effect of that methane by a factor of 23.

MOVE AWAY FROM CLIMATE-UNFRIENDLY PROTEIN

Move society toward a diet with much less climate-unfriendly meat—through public education backed by legislation and pricing. This should be not against particular meat, but against the associated emissions, so that preference is given to protein produced with lower emissions. There are large differences among protein types—emissions differ from soy, chicken, pork, and beef (and within beef, from grass vs. grain fed, particularly noting the emerging science that cattle grazed in certain ways can dramatically increase soil carbon). Therefore science-based policy should be established to encourage the most impactful behavior change and for meat to be rated CO_2e/kg and priced accordingly. We note that the U.S. government ran an effective "meat-free Tuesday" campaign during World War II. There is now already a community-based Meatless Monday campaign.

BIND 1 GIGATON OF CO_2 IN THE SOIL

Develop and introduce agricultural methods that reduce greenhouse gas emissions from agriculture and maximize soil carbon. This will require significant changes in farm technology and farmer psychology, and we are unlikely to get far during C-war. But the effort should be started immediately in preparation for the large-scale binding of carbon in forestry and agriculture that will be necessary from year 5 onward in order to remove CO_2 from the atmosphere over the rest of the century. In both cases, the object will be to grow as much plant material as possible and ensure that the bound carbon ends in the soil or in subsurface storage, not back in the atmosphere. Currently, global forests bind some 3 $GtCO_2e$/yr. Hopefully—through the use of fast-growing tropical plantations, supplemented with industrial growth of algae—we could achieve the binding (and safe storage) of some 6 $GtCO_2e$/yr from forestry and agriculture combined in future decades.

LAUNCH A GOVERNMENT- AND COMMUNITY-LED "SHOP LESS, LIVE MORE" CAMPAIGN

In order to free up finance, manufacturing capacity, and resources for critical war-effort activities, a large-scale campaign to reduce carbon-intensive consumption, or at least stabilize it, would be of great help. This will align well with the general need to shift the economy away from carbon-intensive activities toward climate-friendly experiences. We would propose a bottom-up and top-down campaign to highlight the quality-of-life benefits of low-carbon lives with less stuff.

While all these actions may seem draconian or unrealistic by the standards of today's debate, they will seem far less so when society moves to a war footing and a focus on "what is necessary." Once more, World War II demonstrated that seemingly unachievable actions quickly became normal when delivered in the context of a war effort. They ranged across dramatic increases in the level of taxation, the direction by government of manufacturing, and engagement campaigns to drive public behavior shifts. So once more, the plan asserts that the challenge is not to find appropriate actions, but to make the decision to move on the problem.

The full plan, available from the *Journal for Global Responsibility* website,[15] provides further details on these and other actions that would be required. These include how we could raise $2.5 trillion per year by year 5 via a global carbon tax and how this could be used to finance the measures required to compensate the poor, reduce disruption, and create the new industries and employment required.

We also cover the types of multinational decision-making bodies that would be required, including a Climate War Command, and more detail on the actions required after the first five-year war, including major reversible global geoengineering projects to reflect sunlight and remove CO_2 from the atmosphere and stabilize the global climate.

The point is not to say that Professor Randers and I have the right plan or have defined all the right actions. What we sought to establish, and the point I'm making here, is that a study of history indicates that we will, in the end, embark upon a crisis response to climate change, and when we do, we can see through our plan that quite extraordinary reductions and management measures are practical and achievable. The plan also indicates that the economic cost will be considerably less than unchecked climate change.

Of course, there will be significant disruption as old industries are closed and dislocation as people are moved on to new economic activity. But in a real war, such losses are caused by the decision to go to war. In our case, losses would occur anyway, because climate change would inevitably drive the collapse of the economy if strong action wasn't taken.

The exciting thing about such a plan is that, unlike in a real war, deciding to launch the one-degree war doesn't cost any lives. Instead it saves millions of them. It doesn't shift economic resources onto wasteful though necessary activities, it redirects them to build exciting new industries that will enhance the quality of life for the people of all countries involved. It doesn't waste a generation of youth and leave the survivors traumatized, it educates a generation in the technologies of the future and drives productive innovation that builds new companies and industries.

It is a war we have no choice but to fight and great benefit to gain from declaring.

GUIDE TO FURTHER READINGS
AND RECOMMENDED WEBSITES

The following books and websites will guide your global studies research projects more deeply into the spatial and environmental dimensions of globalization:

- John Agnew, *Globalization and Sovereignty*. Lanham, MD: Rowman & Littlefield, 2009.
- Tim Flannery, *Here on Earth: An Argument for Hope*. Melbourne, AUS: Text Publishing Co, 2010.
- Bill McKibben, *Eaarth: Making Life on a Tough New Planet*. New York: St. Martin's, 2011.
- Warwick E. Murray, *Geographies of Globalization*. New York: Routledge, 2006.
- Orrin H. Pilkey and Keith C. Pilkey, *Global Climate Change: A Primer*. Durham, NC: Duke University Press, 2011.
- Saskia Sassen, *The Global City*. 2nd ed. Princeton, NJ: Princeton University Press, 2001.

- The Globalization and World Cities Network (GaWC): http://www.lboro.ac.uk/gawc/ Created in the Geography Department at Loughborough University (UK), this network focuses upon research into the external relations of world cities. Today the network operates as one of the leading think tanks on cities in globalization and has diversified into related subjects where concern for inter-city relations intersects with research on issues concerning, for instance, international business, sustainability, urban policy, and logistics.

- The Global Cities Research Institute (GCRI): http://global-cities.info/ The GCRInstitute was inaugurated in 2006 to bring together key researchers at RMIT University, Melbourne (Australia), working on understanding the complexity of globalizing urban settings from provincial centers to megacities. The Institute's research is highly collaborative, linking with institutions and people around the world in long-term partnerships that are directly addressing the challenge through engaged research programs intended to have significant on-the-ground impact. The emphasis of the research is on questions of resilience, security, sustainability, and adaptation in the face of the processes of globalization and global climate change.

- Mapping Globalization: http://www.princeton.edu/~mapglobe/HTML/home.html Housed at Princeton University, the Mapping Globalization website is intended for everyone interested in globalization. The main goal of the website is to make empirical work on globalization as widely accessible as possible. The website offers an expanding set of resources for students, instructors, and researchers, and provides a forum for empirical research on globalization. In particular, it provides raw data and the visualization of such data, which includes maps and animations.

- 350.org: http://350.org/ 350.org is an NGO committed to building a global grassroots movement to solve the climate crisis. Its online campaigns, grassroots organizing, and mass public actions are led from the bottom up by thousands of volunteer organizers in over 188 countries. To preserve planet Earth, scientists tell us we must reduce the amount of CO_2 in the atmosphere from its current levels of nearly 400 parts per million to below 350 ppm. But 350 is more than a number—it's a symbol of where the planet needs to go.

References

Chapter 3

Albrow, M. 1997. *The Global Age: State and Society Beyond Modernity.* Stanford, CA: Stanford University Press.

Anderson, B. 1991. *Imagined Communities: Reflections on the Origin and Spread of Nationalism.* Rev. ed. London: Verso.

Appadurai, A. 2006. *Fear of Small Numbers: An Essay on the Geography of Anger.* Durham: Duke University Press.

Ball, T., and R. Dagger. 2004. *Political Ideologies and the Democratic Ideal.* 5th ed. New York: Pearson Longman.

Barat, L. P. 2003. *Political Ideologies: Their Origins and Impact.* 8th ed. Upper Saddle River, NJ: Prentice Hall.

Bin Laden, O. 2005. "A Muslim Bomb." In *Messages to the World,* edited by B. Lawrence, translated by J. Howarth. London: Verso.

Bourdieu, P. 1990. *The Logic of Practice.* Stanford, CA: Stanford University Press.

Calhoun, C. 1997. *Nationalism.* Minneapolis: University of Minnesota Press.

Connolly, W. E. 1988. *Political Theory and Modernity.* Cambridge: Basil Blackwell.

Devji, F. 2005a. "Osama Bin Laden's Message to the World." *Open Democracy,* December 21, 2.

Devji, F. 2005b. *Landscapes of the Jihad: Militancy, Morality, Modernity.* Ithaca, NY: Cornell University Press.

Dumont, L. 1994. *German Ideology: From France to Germany and Back.* Chicago: University of Chicago Press.

Elliott, A., and C. Lemert. 2006. *The New Individualism: The Emotional Costs of Globalization.* London: Routledge.

Festenstein, M., and M. Kenny, eds. 2005. *Political Ideologies: A Reader and Guide.* Oxford: Oxford University Press.

Freeden, M. 2003. *Ideology: A Very Short Introduction.* Oxford: Oxford University Press.

Geertz, C. 1973. "Ideology as Cultural System." In *The Interpretation of Cultures,* edited by C. Geertz, 193–233. New York: Basic Books.

George, S. 2004. *Another World Is Possible, If. . . .* London: Verso.

Gerges, F. A. 2009. *The Far Enemy: Why Jihad Went Global.* 2nd ed. Cambridge: Cambridge University Press.

Greenfeld, L. 2004. "Is Modernity Possible Without Nationalism?" In *The Fate of the Nation-State*, edited by Michel Seymour, 38–50. Montreal: McGill-Queen's University Press.

Habermas, J. 1987. *The Philosophical Discourse of Modernity*. Cambridge, MA: MIT Press.

Hazareesingh, S. 1994. *Political Traditions in Modern France*. New York: Oxford University Press.

Heywood, A. 2003. *Political Ideologies: An Introduction*. 3rd ed. Houndmills, UK: Palgrave Macmillan.

Hobsbawm, E. 1992. *Nations and Nationalism Since 1780*. Cambridge: Cambridge University Press.

James, P. 2006. *Globalism Nationalism Tribalism: Bringing the State Back In*. London: SAGE.

Karam, A., ed. 2004. *Transnational Political Islam: Religion, Ideology and Power*. London: Pluto Press.

Kautsky, K. 1922. "Das Erfurter Program: In *seinem grundsaetzlichen Teil erlaeutert*." Berlin: Verlag J. H. W. Dietz Nachfolger.

Kepel, K. 2004. *The War for Muslim Minds*. Cambridge, MA: Belknap Press.

Kepel, G., and J.-P. Milelli, eds. 2008. *Al Qaeda in Its Own Words*. Cambridge, MA: Belknap Press of Harvard University Press.

Lawrence, B. 2005. "Introduction." In Osama Bin Laden, *Messages to the World: The Statements of Osama Bin Laden*, edited by B. Lawrence, translated by J. Howarth. London: Verso.

Lenin, V. I. (1902) 1975. "What Is to Be Done?" In *The Lenin Anthology*, edited by Robert Tucker. New York: W. W. Norton.

Lewis, B. 1998. "License to Kill." *Foreign Affairs* 77 (6): n.p.

McAuley, D. 2005. "The Ideology of Osama Bin Laden: Nation, Tribe and World Economy." *Journal of Political Ideologies* 10 (3): 269–87.

Mozaffari, M. 2007. "What Is Islamism? History and Definition of a Concept." *Totalitarian Movements and Political Religions* 8 (1): 17–33.

Nairn, T. 2005. "Make for the Boondocks." *London Review of Books* 27 (9): 12–14.

Ricoeur, P. 1986. *Lectures on Ideology and Utopia*. New York: Columbia University Press.

Robertson, R. 1992. *Globalization: Social Theory and Global Culture*. Thousand Oaks, CA: SAGE.

Robertson, R. 2009. "How Useful Is the Concept of Global Society?" *International Political Sociology* 3 (1): 119–22.

Rosenau, J. N. 2003. *Distant Proximities: Dynamics Beyond Globalization*. Princeton, NJ: Princeton University Press.

Roy, O. 2004. *Globalized Islam: The Search for a New Ummah*. New York: Columbia University Press.

Ruthven, M. 2002. *A Fury for God: The Islamist Attack on America*. London: Granta Books.

Sargent, L. T. 2008. *Contemporary Political Ideologies: A Comparative Analysis*. 14th ed. Belmont, CA: Wadsworth.

Sassen, S. 2008. *Territory, Authority, Rights: From Medieval to Global Assemblages*. Princeton, NJ: Princeton University Press.

Smith, A. 1998. *Nationalism and Modernism: A Critical Survey of Recent Theories of Nations and Nationalism*. London: Routledge.

Steger, M. B. 2005. "Ideologies of Globalization." *Journal of Political Ideologies* 10: 11–30.

Steger, M. B. 2008. *The Rise of the Global Imaginary: Political Ideologies from the French Revolution to the Global War on Terror*. Oxford: Oxford University Press.

Steger, M. B. 2009a. *Globalization: A Very Short Introduction*. 2nd ed. Oxford: Oxford University Press.

Steger, M. B. 2009b. *Globalisms: The Great Ideological Struggle of the Twenty-First Century.* Lanham, MD: Rowman & Littlefield.

Steger, M. B., J. Goodman, and E. K. Wilson. 2013. *Justice Globalism: Ideology, Crises, Policy.* London: SAGE.

Steger, M. B., and E. K. Wilson. 2012. "Anti-Globalization or Alter-Globalization? Mapping the Political Ideology of the Global Justice Movement." *International Studies Quarterly* 56 (4): 1–16.

Taylor, C. 2004. *Modern Social Imaginaries.* Durham: Duke University Press.

Chapter 4

Alvarez, S., N. Faria, and M. Nobre. 2004. "Another (also Feminist) World Is Possible: Constructing Transnational Spaces and Global Alternatives from the Movements." In *World Social Forum: Challenging Empires*, edited by J. Sen, A. Anand, A. Escobar, and P. Waterman, 199–206. New Delhi: Viveka.

Ayres, J. M. 1998. *Defying Conventional Wisdom.* Toronto, ON: University of Toronto Press.

Babb, S. 2003. "The IMF in Sociological Perspective: A Tale of Organizational Slippage." *Studies in Comparative International Development* 38: 3–27.

Boli, J., and G. M. Thomas, eds. 1999. *Constructing World Culture: International Nongovernmental Organizations Since 1875.* Stanford, CA: Stanford University Press.

Brunelle, D. 2006. "Le Forum social mondial: Origine et participants." *Observatoire des Ameriques.* http://www.ameriques.uqam.ca.

Carlsson, I., and S. Ramphal. 1995. "Co-chairmen's Foreword." In *Our Global Neighborhood: Report of the Commission on Global Governance*, by the Commission on Global Governance, xii–xv. New York: Oxford University Press.

Commission on Global Governance. 1995. *Our Global Neighborhood: Report of the Commission on Global Governance.* New York: Oxford University Press.

Crozier, M., S. P. Huntington, and J. Watanuki. 1975. *The Crisis of Democracy: Report on the Governability of Democracies to the Trilateral Commission.* New York: New York University Press.

Escobar, A. 2004. "Beyond the Third World: Imperial Globality, Global Coloniality and Anti-Globalisation Movement." *Third World Quarterly* 25 (1): 207–30.

Fraser, N. 1992. "Rethinking the Public Sphere." In *Habermas and the Public Sphere*, edited by C. Calhoun, 109–42. Cambridge: MIT Press.

Gerhards, J., and D. Rucht. 1992. "Mesomobolization." *American Journal of Sociology* 8: 555–95.

Gibson-Graham, J. K. 2006. *A Postcapitalist Politics.* Minneapolis: University of Minnesota Press.

Juris, J. S. 2008. *Networking Futures: The Movements Against Corporate Globalization.* Durham, NC: Duke University Press.

Khasnabish, A. 2005. "'You Will No Longer Be You, Now You Are US': Zapitismo, Transnational Activism, and the Political Imagination." PhD diss., Department of Anthropology, McMaster University, Hamilton, ON.

Macdonald, L. 2005. "Gendering Transnational Social Movement Analysis: Women's Groups Contest Free Trade in the Americas." In *Coalitions Across Borders: Negotiating Difference and Unity in Transnational Coalitions Against Neoliberalism*, edited by J. Bandy and J. Smith, 21–42. Lanham, MD: Rowman and Littlefield.

Markoff, J. 1999. "Globalization and the Future of Democracy." *Journal of World-Systems Research* 5: 242–62.

McMichael, P. 2003. *Development and Social Change: A Global Perspective.* 3rd ed. Thousand Oaks, CA: Pine Forge.

Notes from Nowhere. 2003. *We Are Everywhere.* London: Verso.

Olesen, T. 2005. *International Zapatismo.* London: Zed Books.

Peet, R. 2003. *Unholy Trinity: The IMF, World Bank, and WTO.* New York: Zed Books.

Polletta, F. 2002. *Freedom Is an Endless Meeting.* Chicago: University of Chicago Press.

Portes, A. 1997. "Neo-liberalism and the Sociology of Development: Emerging Trends and Unanticipated Facts." *Population and Development Review* 23: 2–25.

Rice, A. E., and C. Ritchie. 1995. "Relationships Between International Non-Governmental Organizations and the United Nations: A Research and Policy Paper." *Transnational Associations* 47 (5): 254–65. http://www.uia.org/uiadocs/unngos.htm.

Robinson, W. 2004. *A Theory of Global Capitalism.* Baltimore, MD: Johns Hopkins University Press.

Rucht, D. 2000. "Distant Issue Movements in Germany: Empirical Description and Theoretical Reflections." In *Globalizations and Social Movements: Culture, Power, and the Transnational Public Sphere,* edited by J. A. Guidry, M. D. Kennedy, and M. N. Zald, 76–107. Ann Arbor: University of Michigan Press.

Rupp, L. J. 1997. *Worlds of Women: The Making of an International Women's Movement.* Princeton, NJ: Princeton University Press.

Sikkink, K. 1986. "Codes of Conduct for Transnational Corporations: The Case of the WHO/UNICEF Code." *International Organization* 40: 815–40.

Sklar, H., ed. 1980. *Trilateralism: The Trilateral Commission and Elite Planning for World Management.* Montreal, QC: Black Rose Books.

Smith, J. 2004. "Exploring Connections Between Global Integration and Political Mobilization." *Journal of World Systems Research* 10: 255–85.

Smith, J. 2008. *Global Visions, Rival Networks: Social Movements for Global Democracy.* Baltimore, MD: Johns Hopkins University Press.

Smith, P. J., and E. Smythe. 2001. "Globalization, Citizenship, and Technology." In *Culture and Politics in the Information Age,* edited by F. Webster, 183–206. London: Routledge.

Starr, A. 2005. *Global Revolt.* London: Zed Books.

Sternbach, N. S., M. Navarro-Aranguren, P. Chuchryk, and S. E. Alvarez. 1992. "Feminisms in Latin America: From Bogotá to San Bernardo." In *The Making of Social Movements in Latin America: Identity, Strategy, and Democracy,* edited by A. Escobar and S. E. Alvarez, 207–39. Boulder, CO: Westview.

UNDP. 2005. *Human Development Report 2005: International Cooperation at a Crossroads.* New York: Oxford.

Walton, J., and D. Seddon. 1994. *Free Markets and Food Riots: The Politics of Global Adjustment.* Cambridge, MA: Blackwell.

Williamson, J. 1997. "The Washington Consensus Revisited." In *Economic and Social Development into the XXI Century,* edited by L. Emmerij, 48–61. Baltimore, MD: Johns Hopkins University Press.

Chapter 9

Beck, U. 2000. *What Is Globalization?* Malden, MA: Blackwell.

Benkler, Y. 2006. *The Wealth of Networks: How Social Production Transforms Markets and Freedom.* New Haven, CT: Yale University Press.

Borja, J., and M. Castells, eds. 1997. *Local and Global: Management of Cities in the Information Age.* London: Earthscan.

Castells, M. 2000. *End of the Millennium.* 2nd ed. Oxford: Blackwell.

Dutton, W. 1999. *Society on the Line: Information Politics in the Digital Age.* Oxford: Oxford University Press.

Grewal, D. S. 2008. *Network Power: The Social Dynamics of Globalization.* New Haven, CT: Yale University Press.

Hammond, A., W. J. Kramer, J. Tran, R. Katz, and C. Walker. 2007. *The Next 4 Billion: Market Size and Business Strategy at the Base of the Pyramid.* Washington, DC: World Resources Institute.

Harvey, D. 1990. *The Condition of Postmodernity.* Oxford: Blackwell.

Held, D., and A. Kaya. 2006. *Global Inequality: Patterns and Explanations.* Cambridge: Polity Press.

Held, D., and A. McGrew, eds. 2000. *The Global Transformations Reader: An Introduction to the Globalization Debate.* Cambridge: Polity Press.

Held, D., and A. McGrew, eds. 2007. *Globalization Theory: Approaches and Controversies.* London: Polity Press.

Held, D., A. McGrew, D. Goldblatt, and J. Perraton, eds. 1999. *Global Transformations: Politics, Economics, and Culture.* Cambridge: Polity Press.

Jacquet, P., J. Pisani-Ferry, and L. Tubiana, eds. 2002. *Governance Mondiale.* Paris: Documentation Francaise.

Juris, J. S. 2008. *Networking Futures: The Movements Against Corporate Globalization.* Durham, NC: Duke University Press.

Kaldor, M. 2003. *The Global Civil Society: An Answer to War.* Cambridge: Polity Press.

Kiyoshi, K., T. R. Lakhsmanan, and W. P. Anderson. 2006. *Structural Changes in Transportation and Communication in the Knowledge Society.* Northampton, MA: Edward Elgar.

Klein, N. 2007. *Shock Therapy: The Rise of Disaster Capitalism.* New York: Double Day.

Mulgan, G. 1991. *Communication and Control: Networks and the New Economies of Communication.* Cambridge: Polity Press.

Norris, P. 2000. *A Virtuous Circle: Political Communications in Postindustrial Societies.* Cambridge: Cambridge University Press.

Stiglitz, J. 2002. *Globalization and Its Discontents.* New York: W. W. Norton.

Volkmer, I. 1999. *News in the Global Sphere: A Study of CNN and Its Impact on Global Communications.* Luton: University of Luton Press.

Chapter 13

Appadurai, A. 1998. *Modernity at Large.* Minneapolis: University of Minnesota Press.

Arbena, J. 2000. "Meaning and Joy in Latin American Sports." *International Review for the Sociology of Sport* 35: 83–91.

Archetti, E. 1998. *Masculinities.* Oxford: Berg.

Arnason, J. 1991. "Modernity as a Project and as a Field of Tension." In *Communicative Action,* edited by A. Honneth and H. Joas, 181–213. Cambridge: Polity.

Arnason, J. P. 2001. "The Multiplication of Modernity." In *Identity, Culture, and Globalization,* edited by E. B. Rafael and Y. Sternberg, 131–56. Leiden: Brill.

Bale, J., and J. Sang. 1996. *Kenyan Running.* London: Frank Cass.

Barber, B. 1992. "Jihad versus McWorld." *Atlantic Monthly* 269 (3): 53–65.

Barber, B. 1996. *Jihad vs McWorld.* New York: Ballantine.

Beck, U. 2004. "Rooted Cosmopolitan: Emerging from a Rivalry of Distinctions." In *Global America? The Cultural Consequences of Globalization?* edited by U. Beck, N. Sznaider, and R. Winter, 15–29. Liverpool: Liverpool University Press.

Bellos, A. 2002. *Futebol: The Brazilian Way of Life.* London: Bloomsbury.

Brenner, N. 1998. "Global Cities, Glocal States: Global City Formation and State Territorial Restructuring in Contemporary Europe." *Review of International Political Economy* 5 (1): 1–37.

Brenner, N. 2004. "Urban Governance and the Production of New State Spaces in Western Europe, 1960–2000." *Review of International Political Economy* 11 (3): 447–88.

Brick, C. 2001. "Can't Live With Them, Can't Live Without Them: Reflections on Manchester United." In *Fear and Loathing in World Football*, edited by G. Armstrong and R. Giulianotti, 9–21. Oxford: Berg.

Brohm, J.-M. 1978. *Sport: A Prison of Measured Time*. London: Pluto.

Bromberger, C. 1995. "Football as World-View and as Ritual." *French Cultural Studies* 6: 293–311.

Canclini, N. G. 1995. *Hybrid Cultures*. Minneapolis: Minnesota University Press.

Clifford, J. 1997. *Routes: Travel and Translation in the Late Twentieth Century*. Cambridge: Harvard University Press.

Cowen, T. 2002. *Creative Destruction*. Princeton, NJ: Princeton University Press.

DaMatta, R. 1991. *Carnivals, Rogues, and Heroes: An Interpretation of the Brazilian Dilemma*. Notre Dame: Notre Dame University Press.

Dicken, P., and Y. Miyamachi. 1998. " 'From Noodles to Satellites': The Changing Geography of the Japanese Sogo Shosha." *Transactions of the Institute of British Geographers* 23 (1): 55–78.

Escobar, G. 1969. "The Role of Sports in the Penetration of Urban Culture to the Rural Areas of Peru." *Kroeber Anthropological Society Papers* 40: 72–81.

Freire, P. 1970. *Pedagogy of the Oppressed*. New York: Continuum.

Freyre, G. 1963. *The Mansions and the Shanties*. London: Weidenfield & Nicolson.

Friedman, J. 1999. "Indigenous Struggles and the Discreet Charm of the Bourgeoisie." *Journal of World-Systems Research* 5 (2): 391–411.

Gertler, M. 1992. "Flexibility Revisited: Districts, Nation-States and the Forces of Production." *Transactions of the Institute of British Geographers* 17: 259–78.

Giulianotti, R. 1996. "Back to the Future: An Ethnography of Ireland's Football Fans at the 1994 World Cup Finals in the USA." *International Review for the Sociology of Sport* 31 (3): 323–48.

Giulianotti, R. 2005. "Towards a Critical Anthropology of Voice: The Politics and Poets of Popular Culture, Scotland, and Football." *Critique of Anthropology* 25 (4): 339–60.

Giulianotti, R., and R. Robertson. 2005. "Glocalization, Globalization and Migration: The Case of Scottish Football Supporters in North America." *International Sociology* 121 (2): 171–98.

Giulianotti, R., and R. Robertson. 2007a. "Forms of Glocalization: Globalization and the Migration Strategies of Scottish Football Fans in North America." *Sociology* 41 (1): 133–52.

Giulianotti, R., and R. Robertson. 2007b. "Recovering the Social: Globalization, Football and Transnationalism." *Global Networks* 7 (2): 144–86.

Hafez, K. 2007. *The Myth of Media Globalization*. Cambridge: Polity.

Hamelink, C. J. 1983. *Cultural Anatomy in Global Communication*. London: Longman.

Hamelink, C. J. 1994. *The Politics of World Communication: A Human Rights Perspective*. London: SAGE.

Hamelink, C. J. 1995. *World Communication: Disempowerment and Self-Empowerment*. London: Zed Books.

Hannerz, U. 1992. *Cultural Complexity: Studies in the Social Organization of Meaning*. New York: Columbia University Press.

Hannerz, U. 1996. *Transnational Connections*. London: Routledge.

Haruna, M., and S. A. Abdullahi. 1991. "The 'Soccer Craze' and Club Formation Among Hausa Youth in Kano, Nigeria." *Kano Studies*, special issue, 113–24.

Heinonen, H. 2005. *Jalkapallon Lumo.* Jyvaskyla: Atena.

Igbinovia, P. 1985. "Soccer Hooliganism in Black Africa." *International Journal of Offender Therapy and Comparative Criminology* 29: 135–46.

Jessop, B., and N. L. Sum. 2000. "An Entrepreneurial City in Action: Hong Kong's Emerging Strategies in and for (Inter) Urban Competition." *Urban Studies* 37: 2287–313.

Katz, E., and T. Liebes. 1993. *The Export of Meaning: Cross-Cultural Readings of 'Dallas.'* 2nd ed. Cambridge: Cambridge University Press.

Latouche, S. 1996. *The Westernization of the World.* Cambridge: Polity.

Leite Lopes, J. S. 1999. "The Brazilian Style of Football and its Dilemmas." In *Football, Cultures, and Identities*, edited by G. Armstrong and R. Giulianotti, 86–95. Basingstoke: Macmillan.

Leseth, A. 1997. "The Use of *Juju* in Football: Sport and Witchcraft in Tanzania." In *Entering the Field: New Perspectives on World Football*, edited by G. Armstrong and R. Giulianotti, 159–74. Oxford: Berg.

Levi-Strauss, C. 1966. *The Savage Mind.* Chicago: University of Chicago Press.

Lodziak, C. 1966. *Understanding Soccer Tactics.* London: Faber and Faber.

McLuhan, M. 1964. *Understanding Media: The Extensions of Man.* London: Routledge and Kegan Paul.

McLuhan, M., and Q. Fiore. 1989. *The Medium Is the Massage.* New York: Touchstone.

Meyer, J. W., J. Boli, G. M. Thomas, and F. O. Ramirez. 1997. "World Society and the Nation-State." *American Journal of Sociology* 103 (1): 144–81.

Miller, T., G. Lawrence, J. McKay, and D. Rowe. 1999. "Modifying the Sign: Sport and Globalization." *Social Text* 17 (3): 15–33.

Moffett, S. 2003. *Japanese Rules.* London: Yellow Jersey.

O'Donnell, H. 1994. "Mapping the Mythical: A Geopolitics of National Sporting Stereotypes." *Discourse and Society* 5 (3): 345–80.

Oxford Dictionary of New Words. 1991. Compiled by S. Tulloch. Oxford: Oxford University Press.

Pieterse, J. N. 1995. "Globalization as Hybridization." In *Global Modernities*, edited by M. Featherstone, S. Lash, and R. Robertson, 45–68. London: SAGE.

Pieterse, J. N. 2007. *Ethnicities and Global Multiculture.* Lanham, MD: Rowman and Littlefield.

Rigauer, B. 1981. *Sport and Work.* New York: Columbia University Press.

Ritzer, G. 2003. "Rethinking Globalization: Glocalization/Grobalization and Something/Nothing." *Sociological Theory* 21 (3): 193–209.

Ritzer, G. 2004. *The Leisure Industries.* Basingstoke: Palgrave.

Robertson, R. 1990. "After Nostalgia? Wilful Nostalgia and the Phases of Globalization." In *Theories of Modernity and Postmodernity*, edited by B. S. Turner, 45–61. London: SAGE.

Robertson, R. 1992. *Globalization: Social Theory and Global Culture.* London: SAGE.

Robertson, R. 1994. "Globalization or Glocalisation?" *Journal of International Communication* 1 (1): 33–52.

Robertson, R. 1995. "Glocalization: Time-Space and Homogeneity-Heterogeneity." In *Global Modernities*, edited by M. Featherstone, S. Lash, and R. Robertson, 25–44. London: SAGE.

Robertson, R. 1998. "Identidad Nacional y Globalizacion: Falacias Contemporaneas." *Revista Mexicana de Sociologia,* 1 (enero-marzo): 3–19.

Robertson, R. 2007. "Glocalization." In *Encyclopedia of Globalization*, vol. 2, edited by R. Robertson and J. A. Scholte, 524–52. London: Routledge.

Robertson, R., and J. A. Chirico. 1985. "Humanity, Globalization, and Worldwide Religious Resurgence." *Sociological Analysis* 46: 219–42.

Robertson, R., and K. E. White. 2003. "Globalization: An Overview." In *Globalization: Critical Concepts in Sociology*, 6 vols., edited by R. Robertson and K. E. White, 1–44. London: Routledge.

Rosenau, J. 1990. *Turbulence in World Politics: A Theory of Change and Continuity.* Princeton, NJ: Princeton University Press.

Rosenau, J. 2003. *Distant Proximities: Dynamics Beyond Globalization.* Princeton, NJ: Princeton University Press.

Rothacher, A., ed. 2004. *Corporate Cultures and Global Brands.* Hackensack, NJ: World Scientific.

Rowe, D. 2003. "Sport and Repudiation of the Global." *International Review for the Sociology of Sport* 38 (3): 281–94.

Said, E. 1995. *Orientalism.* Harmondsworth: Penguin.

Schiller, H. I. 1969. *Mass Communications and American Empire.* Boston, MA: Beacon.

Schiller, H. I. 1976. *Communication and Cultural Domination.* Armonk, NY: Sharpe.

Sklair, L. 2002. *Globalization.* 3rd ed. Oxford: Oxford University Press.

Steel, C. 2008. *Hungry City: How Food Shapes Our Lives.* London: Chatto & Windus.

Swyngedouw, E. 1992. "The Mammon Quest: 'Glocalization,' Interspatial Competition and the Monetary Order: The Construction of New Scales." In *Cities and Regions in the New Europe: The Global-Local Interplay and Spatial Development Strategies*, edited by M. Dunford and G. Kafkalis, 39–68. London: Belhaven Press.

Swyngedouw, E. 2004. "Globalization or Glocalization? Networks, Territories, and Rescaling." *Cambridge Review of International Affairs* 17 (1): 25–48.

Therborn, G. 1995. "Routes to/through Modernity." In *Global Modernities*, edited by M. Featherstone, S. Lash, and R. Robertson, 124–39. London: SAGE.

Tomlinson, J. 1991. *Cultural Imperialism: A Critical Introduction.* London: Pinter.

Tomlinson, J. 1999. *Globalization and Culture.* Cambridge: Polity

Tomlinson, J. 2007. *The Culture of Speed.* London: SAGE.

Vergès, F. 2001. "Vertigo and Emancipation, Creole Cosmopolitanism and Cultural Politics." *Theory, Culture, & Society* 18: 169–83.

Vinnai, G. 1973. *Football Mania.* London: Ocean.

Wagner, P. 2000. "Modernity—One or Many?" In *The Blackwell Companion to Sociology*, edited by J. Blau, 30–42. Oxford: Blackwell.

Wallerstein, I. 1976. *The Modern World System: Capitalist Agriculture and the Origins of the European World Economy in the Sixteenth Century.* New York: Academic Press.

Wallerstein, I. 2000. *The Essential Wallerstein.* New York: New Press.

Watson, J., ed. 1997. *Golden Arches East: McDonald's in East Asia.* Palo Alto, CA: Stanford University Press.

Williams, J., S. Hopkins, and C. Long. 2001. *Passing Rhythms: Liverpool FC and the Transformation of Football.* Oxford: Berg.

Chapter 18

Alarcón, A. 2004. *The Border Patrol Ate My Dust.* Translated by E. C. Brammer de Gonzales. Houston: Arte Publico Press.

Batson, D. 1997. "Self-Other Merging and the Empathy-Altruism Hypothesis: Reply to Neuberg, et al." *Journal of Personality and Social Psychology* 73 (3): 517–22.

Batson, D., J. H. Eklund, V. L. Chermok, J. L. Hoyt, and B. G. Ortiz. 2007. "An Additional Antecedent of Empathic Concern: Valuing the Welfare of the Person in Need." *Journal of Personality and Social Psychology* 93 (1): 65–74.

Bauer, S., and P. J. Eckerstrom. 1987. "The State Made Me Do It: The Applicability of the Necessity Defense to Civil Disobedience." *Stanford Law Review* 39: 1173–200.

BBC (British Broadcasting Corporation). 2002. "Immigrants Stage Sit-In in Paris Church." August 20. http://news.bbc.co.uk/1/hi/world/europe/2205064.stm.

Bean, F., and D. A. Spener. 2004. "Controlling International Migration Through Enforcement: The Case of the United States." In *International Migration: Prospects and Policies in a Global Market*, edited by D. Massey and J. E. Taylor, 352–70. Oxford: Oxford University Press.

Benhabib, S. 2005. "Borders, Boundaries, and Citizenship." *PS: Political Science and Politics* 38 (4): 673–77.

Benhabib, S. 2007. "Twilight of Sovereignty or the Emergence of Cosmopolitan Norms? Rethinking Citizenship in Volatile Times." *Citizenship Studies* 11 (1): 19–36.

Boxill, B. 1992. *Blacks and Social Justice*. Lanham, MD: Rowman & Littlefield.

Branch, T. 1998. *Pillar of Fire: America in the King Years, 1963–65*. New York: Simon and Schuster.

Brown, J. M. 2008. *Gandhi and Civil Disobedience: The Mahatma in Indian Politics 1928–1934*. Cambridge: Cambridge University Press.

Brownlee, K. 2004. "Features of a Paradigm Case of Civil Disobedience." *Res Publica* 10 (4): 337–51.

Brownlee, K. 2007. "Civil Disobedience." *Stanford Encyclopedia of Philosophy*. http://plato.stanford.edu/entries/civil-disobedience/.

Carens, J. 1992. "Migration and Morality: A Liberal Egalitarian Perspective." In *Free Movement: Ethical Issues in the Transnational Migration of People and Money*, edited by B. Barry and R. Goodin, 25–47. University Parks: Pennsylvania State University Press.

Carter, A. 1998. "In Defence of Radical Disobedience." *Journal of Applied Philosophy* 15 (1): 29–47.

Cavallaro, J. L. 1993. "The Demise of the Political Necessity Defense: Indirect Civil Disobedience and United States vs. Schoon." *California Law Review* 81 (1): 351–85.

Clapham, A. 2007. *Human Rights*. Oxford: Oxford University Press.

Cook, R. 1997. *Sweet Land of Liberty? The African-American Struggle for Civil Rights in the 20th Century*. New York: Longman.

Dovidio, J., J. L. Allen, and D. A. Schroeder. 1990. "Specificity of Empathy-Induced Helping: Evidence for Altruistic Motivation." *Journal of Personality and Social Psychology* 59: 249–60.

Durand, J., and D. S. Massey. 2004. "What We Learned from the Mexican Migration Project." In *Crossing the Border: Research from the Mexican Migration Project*, edited by J. Durand and D. S. Massey, 1–16. New York: Russell Sage Foundation.

Dworkin, R. 1977. *Taking Rights Seriously*. London: Duckworth.

Equiano, O. 2003. *The Interesting Narrative and Other Writings*. Rev. ed., edited by V. Carretta. New York: Penguin.

Fairclough, A. 2004. "Thurgood Marshall's Pursuit of Equality Through Law." *Critical Review of International Social and Political Philosophy* 7 (4): 177–99.

Feinberg, J. 1994. *Freedom and Fulfillment: Philosophical Essays*. Princeton, NJ: Princeton University Press.

Gonzalez, D. 2003. "Gangs Are Menacing 'Coyotes,' Immigrants; Assaults, Kidnapping Are Rampant." *The Arizona Republic*, August 17, A-1.

Hayter, T. 2004. *Open Borders: The Case Against Immigration Controls*. 2nd ed. London: Pluto Press.

Held, D. 2004. *Global Covenant: The Social Democratic Alternative to the Washington Consensus*. Cambridge: Polity Press.

Hendricks, T. 2005. "On the Border: Maquiladoras." *The San Francisco Chronicle*, November 27, A-1.

Janofsky, M. 2003. "Burden Grows for Southwest Hospitals." *New York Times*, April 14.

King, M. L., Jr. 1991a. "I Have a Dream." In *A Testament of Hope: The Essential Writings and Speeches of Martin Luther King, Jr.*, edited by J. M. Washington, 217–20. New York: Harper Collins.

King, M. L., Jr. 1991b. "Letter from Birmingham City Jail." In *A Testament of Hope: The Essential Writings and Speeches of Martin Luther King, Jr.*, edited by J. M. Washington, 289–302. New York: Harper Collins.

Krause, M. 2008. "Undocumented Migrants: An Arendtian Perspective." *European Journal of Political Theory* 7 (3): 331–48.

Lyons, D. 1998. "Moral Judgment, Historical Reality, and Civil Disobedience." *Philosophy and Public Affairs* 27 (1): 31–49.

Massey, D. 1998. "March of Folly: US Immigration Policy After NAFTA." *The American Prospect*, March 1.

McLean, I., ed. 1996. *Oxford Concise Dictionary of Politics*. Oxford: Oxford University Press.

McNevin, A. 2006. "Political Belonging in a Neoliberal Era: The Struggle of the Sans-Papiers." *Citizenship Studies* 10 (2): 135–51.

Mill, J. S. 1998. *Utilitarianism*, edited by R. Crisp. Oxford: Oxford University Press.

Miller, D. 2007. *National Responsibilities and Global Justice*. Oxford: Oxford University Press.

Nickel, J. W. 2007. *Making Sense of Human Rights*. 2nd ed. Oxford: Blackwell.

Ochoa O'Leary, A. 2009. "The ABCs of Migration Costs: Assembling, Bajadores, and Coyotes." *Migration Letters* 6 (1): 27–36.

Orrenius, R. M., and R. Coronado. 2005. "The Effect of Illegal Immigration and Border Enforcement on Crime Rates Along the US-Mexico Border." *Center for Comparative Immigration Studies,* Working Paper No. 131, December. www.ccis-ucsd.org/PUBLICATIONS/wrkg131.pdf.

Ottonelli, V. 2002. "Immigration: What Does Global Justice Require?" In *Global Citizenship: A Critical Introduction*, edited by N. Dower and J. Williams, 231–43. New York: Routledge.

Passel, J., and D. Cohn. 2009. *A Portrait of Unauthorized Immigrants in the United States*. Washington, DC: Pew Hispanic Center.

Pécoud, A., and P. de Guchteneire. 2006. "International Migration, Border Controls and Human Rights: Assessing the Relevance of a Right to Mobility." *Journal of Borderlands Studies* 21 (1): 69–86.

Pogge, T. 2007. "Severe Poverty as a Human Rights Violation." In *Freedom from Poverty as a Human Right*, edited by T. Pogge, 11–53. Oxford: Oxford University Press.

Porter, E. 2005. "Illegal Immigrants Are Bolstering Social Security with Billions." *New York Times*, April 5.

Rawls, J. (1971) 1999. *A Theory of Justice*. Rev. ed. Cambridge, MA: Belknap Harvard.

Raz, J. 1979. *The Authority of Law: Essays on Law and Morality*. Oxford: Clarendon Press.

Ridge, M. 2002. "Mill's Intentions and Motives." *Utilitas* 14 (1): 54–70.

Robinson, W. 2006. "Aqui Estamos, Y No Nos Vamos: Global Capital and Immigrant Rights." *Race and Class* 48 (2): 77–91.

Rumbaut, R., and W. Ewing. 2007. "The Myth of Immigrant Criminality and the Paradox of Assimilation: Incarceration Rates Among Native and Foreign-Born Men." *Immigration Policy Center/American Immigration Law Foundation*. www.immigrationpolicy.org/images/File/specialreport/Imm%20Criminality%20(IPC).pdf.

Sabl, A. 2001. "Looking Forward to Justice: Rawlsian Civil Disobedience and Its Non-Rawlsian Lessons." *The Journal of Political Philosophy* 9 (3): 307–30.

Sen, A. 1982. *Poverty and Famines: An Essay on Entitlement and Deprivation*. Oxford: Oxford University Press.

Simmons, A. J. 2003. "Civil Disobedience and the Duty to Obey the Law." In *A Companion to Applied Ethics*, edited by R. G. Frey and C. H. Wellman, 50–61. Oxford: Blackwell.

Singer, A., and D. S. Massey. 1998. "The Social Process of Undocumented Border Crossing Among Mexican Migrants." *International Migration Review* 32 (3): 561–92.

Sistare, C. 2008. "John Brown's Duties: Obligations, Violence, and 'Natural Duty.'" In *Coercion and the State*, edited by D. Reidy and W. Riker, 95–112. Dordrecht: Springer.

Solís, D. 2007. "Drug Cartels Want Migrants' Routes: Fight to Control Corridors on Arizona Border Turns Violent." *Dallas Morning News*, February 19.

Staring, R. 2004. "Facilitating the Arrival of Illegal Immigrants in the Netherlands: Irregular Chain Migration versus Smuggling Chains." *Journal of International Migration and Integration* 5 (3): 273–94.

Still, W. (1872) 1968. *The Underground Railroad*. New York: Arno Press and the New York Times.

Tesón, F. 2005. "Ending Tyranny in Iraq." *Ethics and International Affairs* 19 (2): 1–20.

United Nations Human Development Report. 2009. www.hdr.undp.org.

USGAO (United States Government Accountability Office). 2000. "Alien Smuggling Management and Operational Improvements Needed to Addressing Growing Problems." GAO/GCD-00-103. www.gao.gov/products/GGD-00-103.

Vail, M. 2006. "The 'Integrative' Rhetoric and the Rational Public." *Political Behavior* 25 (4): 341–60.

Wadhwa, V., G. Jasso, B. Rissing, G. Gereffi, and R. Freeman. 2007. "Intellectual Property, the Immigration Backlog, and a Reverse Brain-Drain." Kauffman Foundation. www.kauffman.org/Details.aspx?id=1020.

Walzer, M. 1970. *Obligations: Essays on Disobedience, War and Citizenship*. Cambridge, MA: Harvard University Press.

Walzer, M. 2006. *Just and Unjust Wars: A Moral Argument with Historical Illustrations*. 4th ed. New York: Basic Books.

Watson, M. S. 2004. "The Issue is Justice: Martin Luther King Jr.'s Response to the Birmingham Clergy." *Rhetoric and Public Affairs* 7 (1): 1–22.

World Bank. 2008. "World Development Indicators: Mexico Country Brief." www.worldbank.org.

Notes

Chapter 1

1. John Keane, *Civil Society: Old Images, New Visions* (Cambridge: Polity, 1998).
2. John L. Comaroff and Jean Comaroff (eds.), *Civil Society and the Political Imagination in Africa: Critical Perspectives* (Chicago: University of Chicago Press, 1999), 4.
3. Anthony Giddens, *Runaway World: How Globalisation Is Reshaping Our Lives* (Profile, London, 1999); and Ulrich Beck, *World Risk Society* (Cambridge: Polity, 1999).
4. Václav Havel, "The Power of the Powerless," in John Keane (ed.), *The Power of the Powerless: Citizens against the State in Central-Eastern Europe* (London: Hutchinson, 1985).
5. Jean Cohen and Andrew Arato, *Civil Society and Political Theory* (London: Verso, 1992).
6. Margaret Keck and Kathryn Sikkink, *Activists beyond Borders: Advocacy Networks in International Politics* (Ithaca, NY: Cornell University Press, 1998).
7. See Ian Clark, *Globalisation and International Relations Theory* (Oxford: Oxford University Press, 1999).
8. Chris Brown, "Cosmopolitanism, World Citizenship and Global Civil Society," *Critical Review of International Social and Political Philosophy*, 3 (2000).
9. Saskia Sassen, *Globalisation and Its Discontents* (New York: New Press, 1998).
10. Brown, "Cosmopolitanism"; David Rieff, "The False Dawn of Civil Society," *Nation*, 22 Feb. 1999.
11. See Mary Kaldor, *Global Civil Society: An Answer to War* (Cambridge: Polity, 2003), chap. 2.
12. This version of global civil society is exemplified in John Keane's essay "Global Civil Society?" in Helmut Anheier, Marlies Glasius, and Mary Kaldor (eds.), *Global Civil Society 2001* (Oxford: Oxford University Press, 2001). The term "globalization from below" is sometimes used in a narrower sense to refer to global social movements, NGOs, and networks. See Mario Piantia, *Globalizzazione dal Basso: Economia Mondiale e Movimenti Sociali* (Rome: Manifestolibri, 2001).
13. Rieff, "The False Dawn."
14. Keane, "Global Civil Society?"

Chapter 2

1. Robert Gilpin, *Global Political Economy* (Princeton, NJ: Princeton University Press, 2001), 388–9.
2. Randall D. Germain, "Global Financial Governance and the Problem of Inclusion," *Global Governance* 7, no. 4 (2001): 421.

3. "Collective" is an adjective that means "group-based." This modifier may imply universal or global participation (for example, the UN as a collective security organization), but it may imply much less participation (for example, NATO is a collective defense organization for sixteen member states). See Arnold Wolfers, *Discord and Collaboration in a New Europe* (Lanham, MD: University Press of America, 1994).

4. See James N. Rosenau and Ernst-Otto Czempiel (eds.), *Governance without Government: Order and Change in World Politics* (Cambridge: Cambridge University Press, 1992). Also see Leon Gordenker and Thomas G. Weiss, "Pluralizing Global Governance: Analytical Approaches and Dimensions," in Leon Gordenker and Thomas G. Weiss (eds.), *NCOs, the UN, and Global Governance* (London: Lynne Rienner, 1996), 17–47.

5. See Anne-Marie Slaughter, *A New World Order* (Princeton, NJ: Princeton University Press, 2004).

6. Amit Bhaduri and Deepak Nayyar, *The Intelligent Person's Guide to Liberalization* (New Delhi: Penguin, 1996), 67.

7. See, for example, Paul Hirst and Grahame Thompson, *Globalization in Question: The International Economy and the Possibilities of Governance* (Cambridge: Polity Press, 1996).

8. World Commission on the Social Dimension of Globalization, *A Fair Globalization: Creating Opportunities for All* (Geneva: International Labour Organization, 2004), xi.

9. See Deepak Nayyar (ed.), *Governing Globalization: Issues and Orientations* (Oxford: Oxford University Press, 2002).

10. See Jane Boulden, Ramesh Thakur, and Thomas G. Weiss (eds.), *The United Nations and Nuclear Orders* (Tokyo: UN University Press, 2009).

11. See Michael G. Schechter, *United Nations Global Conferences* (London: Routledge, 2005); and Ramesh Thakur, Andrew Cooper, and John English (eds.), *International Commissions and the Power of Ideas* (Tokyo: UN University Press, 2005).

12. Hedley Bull, *The Anarchical Society: A Study* (New York: Columbia University Press, 1977). A more recent treatment is Robert H. Jackson, *The Global Covenant: Human Conduct in a World of States* (Oxford: Oxford University Press, 2000).

13. For an argument on how shaming is an effective instrument in underpinning the efficacy of the European human rights regime, see Andrew Moravcsik, "Explaining International Human Rights Regimes: Liberal Theory and Western Europe," *European Journal of International Relations* 1, no. 2 (1995): 157–89. For a slightly different interpretation of the domestic impact of norms embedded in the European human rights regime, see Jeffrey T. Checkel, "International Norms and Domestic Politics: Bridging the Rationalist-Constructivist Divide," *European Journal of International Relations* 3, no. 4 (1997): 473–95. See also his "Norms, Institutions, and National Identity in Contemporary Europe," *International Studies Quarterly* 43, no. 1 (1999): 83–114.

14. See Simon Chesterman (ed.), *Secretary or General? The UN Secretary-General in World Politics* (Cambridge: Cambridge University Press, 2007).

15. See Ramesh Thakur and William Maley, "The Ottawa Convention on Landmines: A Landmark Humanitarian Treaty in Arms Control?" *Global Governance* 5, no. 3 (1999): 273–302. See also Don Hubert, *The Landmine Ban: A Case Study in Humanitarian Advocacy* (Providence, RI: Watson Institute, 2000), occasional paper no. 42; and Richard Price "Reversing the Gun Sights: Transnational Civil Society Targets Land Mines," *International Organization* 52, no. 3 (1998): 613–44.

16. This is addressed in greater detail in Ramesh Thakur and Thomas G. Weiss, "United Nations 'Policy': An Argument with Three Illustrations," *International Studies Perspectives* 10, no. 2 (2009): 18–35.

17. Paul Cammack, "The Mother of all Governments: The World Bank's Matrix for Global Governance," in Rorden Wilkinson and Steve Hughes (eds.), *Global Governance: Critical Perspectives* (London: Routledge, 2002), 36–54.

18. James E. Dougherty and Robert L. Pfaltzgraff, Jr., *Contending Theories of International Relations: A Comprehensive Survey*, 4th ed. (New York: Longman, 1997), 422.

19. John Gerard Ruggie, "International Regimes, Transactions, and Change: Embedded Liberalism in the Postwar Economic Order," *International Organization* 36, no. 2 (1982): 196.

20. Robert O. Keohane, "A Functional Theory of Regimes," in Robert J. Art and Robert Jervis (eds.), *International Politics: Enduring Concepts and Contemporary Issues*, 5th ed. (New York: Longman, 2000), 135.

21. *Report of the Panel on United Nations Peace Operations* (UN document A/55/305-S/2000/809), 21 August 2000. For an early assessment, see David M. Malone and Ramesh Thakur, "UN Peacekeeping: Lessons Learned?" *Global Governance* 7, no. 1 (2001): 11–17.

22. See Edel Hughes, William A. Schabas, and Ramesh Thakur (eds.), *Atrocities and International Accountability: Beyond Transitional Justice* (Tokyo: UN University Press, 2007).

23. See Chiyuki Aoi, Cedric de Coning, and Ramesh Thakur (eds.), *Unintended Consequences of Peacekeeping Operations* (Tokyo: UN University Press, 2007).

24. Kofi A. Annan, *"We the Peoples": The Role of the United Nations in the 21st Century* (New York: United Nations, 2000), 57–8.

Chapter 3

1. For my definitions of basic concepts related to globalization, see Steger (2009a, 2009b).

2. This essay draws on parts of my book-length study on the subject. See Steger (2008).

3. See, for example, Festenstein and Kenny (2005); Ball and Dagger (2004); Barat (2003); and Heywood (2003). The laudable exception to this rule is Sargent (2008).

4. The ideological function of "fixing" the process of signification around certain meanings was discussed as early as the 1970s by the French linguist Michel Pecheux and intellectuals associated with the French semiotic journal *Tel Quel*.

5. For a useful summary of the main functions of ideology, see Ricoeur (1986).

6. Craig Calhoun (1997: 18–20) argues that such nationalist "essentialism" represents one of the guiding assumptions in modern thinking on matters of personal and collective identity.

7. See Kautsky (1922) and Lenin (1902).

8. For a substantial discussion of these claims, see Steger (2009a).

9. See, for example, Mozaffari (2007); Roy (2004); Karam (2004); Kepel (2004); and Ruthven (2002).

10. Lawrence (2005). See also Lewis (1998). For the most recent collection of writings by al-Qaeda leaders, see Kepel and Milelli (2008).

11. For an insightful analysis of the tribal, national, and global dimensions in Bin Laden's discourse, see McAuley (2005). For a brilliant discussion of globalizing dynamics involving tribal identities, see James (2006).

12. For a more detailed exposition of the reasons behind al-Qaeda's shift from the near to the far enemy, see Gerges (2009); and Kepel (2004).

13. Bin Laden (2005: 91).

14. Devji (2005a: 2). See also Devji (2005b: 144).

15. Osama Bin Laden, untitled transcript of a video-taped message to the American people (6 September 2007).

16. For a discussion of such "fragmegration," see Rosenau (2003).

Chapter 5

1. Vaclav Havel, quoted by Jim Clancy, "Vaclav Havel: Arab Protesters Have It Harder than My Generation in '89," *CNN*, March 8. 2011. Available at http://edition.cnn.com/2011/WORLD/europe/03/07/czech.havel.arab.unrest/index.html (accessed March 23, 2011).

2. "Poll Results Prompt Iran Protests," *Al Jazeera* English, June 14, 2009, at http://english.aljazeera.net/news/middleeast/2009/06/2009613172130303995.html (accessed January 11, 2011).

3. Hamid Dabashi, quoted by Jon Leyne, "How Iran's Political Battle Is Fought in Cyberspace," *BBC News*, February 11, 2010, at http://news.bbc.co.uk/2/hi/middle_east/8505645.stm (accessed January 11, 2011).

4. Austin Heap, quoted by Leyne, "How Iran's Political Battle Is Fought in Cyberspace."

5. Leyne, "How Iran's Political Battle Is Fought in Cyberspace."

6. Habib Bourguiba served as Tunisia's first president from 1957, after Tunisia gained independence from France, until 1987, when Ben Ali took power.

7. Robert Godec, quoted by Ian Black, "WikiLeaks Cables: Tunisia Blocks Site Reporting 'Hatred' of First Lady," *Guardian*, December 7, 2010, at http://www.guardian.co.uk/world/2010/dec/07/wikileaks-tunisia-first-lady (accessed March 25, 2011).

8. Yasmine Ryan, "The Tragic Life of a Street Vendor," *Al Jazeera English*, January 20, 2011, at http://english.aljazeera.net/indepth/features/2011/01/201111684242518839.html (accessed March 25, 2011).

9. Rochdi Horchani, quoted by Yasmine Ryan, "How Tunisia's Revolution Began," *Al Jazeera* English, January 26, 2011, at http://english.aljazeera.net/indepth/features/2011/01/2011126121815985483.html (accessed March 25, 2011).

10. Mona Eltahawy, "Tunisia's Jasmine Revolution," *Washington Post*. January 15, 2011, at http://www.washingtonpost.com/wp-dyn/content/article/2011/01/14/AR2011011405084.html (accessed March 25, 2011).

11. News organizations in France reported that Ben Ali and his wife took 1.5 tons of gold bars with them as they left the country, but Tunisia's central bank insisted that the country's 6.8 tons of gold stocks remained unchanged. "Tunisian Central Bank Denies Ben Ali Fled with Gold," *Radio France Internationale,* January 22, 2011, at http://www.english.rfi.fr/africa/20110122-tunisian-central-bank-denies-ben-ali-fled-gold (accessed March 25, 2011).

12. Moncef Marzouk, quoted by Alexandra Zavis, "Former Dissident Sworn in as Tunisia's President," *Los Angeles Times*, December 13, 2011, at http://latimesblogs.latimes.com/world_now/2011/12/tunisia-president-moncef-marzouki.html (accessed December 30, 2011).

13. Najib Chebbi, quoted in "Tunisia Installs Moncef Marzouki as President," *Reuters,* December 13, 2011, at http://www.guardian.co.uk/world/2011/dec/13/tunisia-moncef-marzouki-president (accessed December 30, 2011).

14. Joe Sullivan, quoted by Alexis Madrigal, "The Inside Story of How Facebook Responded to Tunisian Hacks," *Atlantic,* January 24, 2011, at http://www.theatlantic.com/technology/archive/2011/01/the-inside-story-of-how-facebook-responded-to-tunisian-hacks/70044 (accessed February 2, 2011).

15. Rim Abida, quoted by Madrigal, "The Inside Story of How Facebook Responded to Tunisian Hacks."

16. "Mid-East Bloggers Hail Change in Tunisia," BBC *News Africa,* January 15, 2011, at http://www.bbc.co.uk/news/world-africa-12200029 (accessed February' 2, 2011).

17. Bint Masreya, at http://www.bentmasreya.net (accessed February 2, 2011).

18. Gigi Ibrahim, quoted by Mona Eltahawy, "Tunisia's Jasmine Revolution."

19. Marwa Awad, "Autopsy Says Egypt Activist Choked, Protest Planned," Reuters, June 23, 2010, at http://www.reuters.com/article/2010/06/23/egypt-activist-torture-idAFLDE65M22620100623 (accessed February 2, 2011).

20. As of February 2011, a copy of the video on YouTube had been viewed 15,559 times. See "ABO ESLAM & Mido Magdy," at http://www.youtube.com/watch?v=elTj8mErGDI&r feature=player_embedded#! (accessed February 2, 2011).

21. As of June 2011, a video of the 10-minute interview had been viewed more than 331,000 times on YouTube. See http://www.youtube.com/watch?v=JOFsuLBfnfo&feature=related (accessed June 26, 2011).

22. An English language version of the organization's website can be found at http://www.arabist.net/blog/2010/6/14/the-murder-of-khaled-said.html (accessed February 2, 2011).

23. "Activists Blame Police for Egyptian's Death," *Egyptian Gazette Online,* June 12, 2010, at http://213.158.162.45/~egyptian/index.php?action=news&id=8943&tille=Activists%20blame%20police%20for%20Egyptian's%20death (accessed February 2, 2010).

24. The website can be found at http://www.elshaheeed.co.uk. See "Mid- East Bloggers Hail Change in Tunisia," *BBC* News, January 15, 2011, at http:// www.bbc.co.uk/news/world-africa-12200029 (accessed January 31, 2011).

25. Lobna Darwish, quoted by Maha Ben Abdeladhim and Sebastian Seibt, "Thousands Call for Mubarak to Resign in Coordinated Protests across Egypt," *France 24,* January 26, 2011, at http://www.france24.com/en/20110125-tunisia-facebook-twitter-coordinate-protests-egypt-mubarak-resign-cairo (accessed January 28, 2011).

26. Maha Ben Abdeladhim and Sebastian Seibt, "Thousands Call for Mubarak to Resign."

27. Mohamed ElBaradei, at http://twitter.com/elbaradei, January 13, 2011 (accessed February 2, 2011).

28. Ayman Noor, at http://twitter.com/ayman_nour (accessed February 2, 2011).

29. Alaa Al Aswany, "Police Alone Can't Keep Rulers in Power," *Guardian,* January 27, 2011, at http://www.guardian.co.uk/commentisfree/2011/jan/27/police-power-egypt-battle-protesters (accessed January 28, 2011).

30. Abdel Halim Hafez, quoted by Anthony Shadid, "Obama Urges Faster Shift of Power in Egypt," *New York Times,* February 2, 2011, at http://www.nytimes.com/2011/02/02/world/middleeast/02egypt.html (accessed February 2, 2011).

31. Matt Bradley, "Mubarak's Trial to Start in August," *Wall Street Journal,* June 1, 2011, at http://online.wsj.com/article/SB10001424052702303657404576359283425162982.html (accessed June 22, 2011).

32. Michael R. Blood, "Cheney Calls Mubarak a Good Friend, US Ally." Associated Press, February 6, 2011, at http://news.yahoo.com/s/ap/20110206/ap_on_re_us/us_reagan_cheney (accessed February 6, 2011).

33. Craig Labovitz, quoted by Hazma Hendawi and Sarah El Deeb, "Egypt: Internet Down, Police Counterterror Unit Up," Associated Press, January 28, 2011, at http://news.yahoo.com/s/ap/20110128/ap_on_bige/ml_egypt_protest (accessed January 29, 2011).

34. Jordan Robertson, "The Day Part of the Internet Died: Egypt Goes Dark," Associated Press, January 28, 2011, at http://news.yahoo.com/s/ap/20110128/ap_on_hi_te/us_egypt_protest_internet_outage (accessed January 29, 2011).

35. Ghonim's "Farmville" comment referred to the popular Internet simulation game and not the rural town in North Carolina. See Wael Ghonim, at http://twitter.com/Ghonim (accessed February 1, 2011).

36. Wael Ghonim, quoted by Ian Black, "Wael Ghonim Anointed Voice of the Revolution by Tahrir Square Faithful," *Guardian,* February 8, 2011, at http://www.guardian.co.uk/world/2011/feb/08/wael-ghonini-tahrir square?lNT CMP=SRCH (accessed March 25, 2011).

37. Wael Ghonim, quoted in "Google Executive Is Released in Egypt," CNN, February 7, 2011, at http://articles.cnn.com/2011-02-07/world/egypt.google.executive_1_tweet-google-executive-cairo?_s=PM:WORLD (accessed March 26, 2011).

38. Reem El-Komi quoted by Ian Black, "Wael Ghonim Anointed Voice of the Revolution."

39. See http://twitter.com/minnagamal, as well as http://twitter.com/angelsavant and http://twitter.com/Desert_Dals.

40. Wael Ghonim, quoted by Sam Gustin, "Wael Ghonim Leaving Google to Launch Tech NGO in Egypt," Wired, April 25, 2011, at http://www.wired.com/epicenter/2011/04/ghonim-leaves-google (accessed June 22, 2011).

41. Leila Marzouk, quoted by Reem Abdellatif, "Thousands Rally for Alleged Torture Victim Essam Atta," Global Post, October 29, 2011, at http://www.globalpost.com/dispatch/news/regions/middle-east/egypt/111029/thousands-rally-alleged-torture-victim-essam-atta (accessed October 30, 2011).

42. Ahmed Faouzi Khenissi, quoted by Scott Sayare, "Now Feeling Free, but Still without Work, Tunisians Look toward Europe," New York Times, March 23, 2011, http://www.nytimes.com/2011/03/24/world/africa/24tunisia.html (accessed March 28, 2011).

43. Blocking the word "jasmine" proved to be a tricky business, however. As the New York Times reported, a popular Chinese folk song is named "Jasmine," and Chinese activists posted video clips of the country's president, Hu jintao, singing the song, "forcing censors to have to decide if they should take down videos of senior leaders that could be explained as an expression of patriotism." See Ian Johnson, "Calls for a 'Jasmine Revolution' in China Persist," New York Times, February 23, 2011, at http://www.nytimes.com/2011/02/24/world/asia/24china.html (accessed March 28, 2011).

44. Eunice Yoon, "Getting Harassed by the Chinese Police," CNN, February 28, 2011, at http://business.blogs.cnn.com/2011/02/28/getting-harassed-by-the-chinese-police (accessed March 28, 2011).

45. Jonathan Watts, "Inner Mongolia Protests Prompt Crackdown," Guardian, May 30, 2011, at http://www.guardian.co.uk/world/2011/may/30/mongolia-protests-communist-party-crackdown (accessed June 22, 2011).

Chapter 6

1. See Reed, Economic Change, 47.

2. Coulson, Tanzania: A Political Economy, contains an assessment of Tanzania's post-independence economic policies. See also Temu and Due, "The Business Environment in Tanzania after Socialism."

3. Data for income, life expectancy, and literacy are from the World Bank, World Development Report 2008.

4. USITC dataweb, accessed 7/22/08.

5. Hansen, Salaula. Hansen refers to salaula (the term for used clothing from the Zambian Bemba language) rather than mitumba (from Swahili).

6. Hansen, 90.

Chapter 7

1. Meyer 1999: 108. Meyer notes that while the radical feminist peace groups of the 1980s lost their focus and energy or largely disappeared, WILPF's formal organizational structure allowed it to adapt to new times (p. 119).

2. Personal interview with Rosalind Petchesky, WEDO board member, New York, 3 March 2002.

3. This statement pertains also to the present author.

4. Marieme Hélie-Lucas, in a conversation with the author, Vienna, January 2000.

5. Brecher and Costello 1998: 25.
6. The Bangkok International Roundtable of Unions, Social Movements, and NGOs was organized by Focus on the Global South and the Friedrich Ebert Foundation in Bangkok on March 11–13, 2001.
7. Cohen and Rai 2000: 11, citing the works of Sarah Ashwin, Ronaldo Munck, Peter Waterman, and others.
8. Gallin 2000: 30–31.
9. See, for example, various articles in *DAWN Informs,* 1999, 2000, 2001, 2002.
10. ILO 2004.
11. www.awid.org/campaign/globalizethis.html, accessed 28 March 2004.
12. "Justice for working families" is the motto of the AFL-CIO of the United States.

Chapter 8

1. For a detailed statistical analysis of differences between European and American attitudes toward inequality, see Alberto Alesina, Rafael Di Tella, and Robert MacCulloch, "Inequality and Happiness: Are Europeans and Americans Different?" *Journal of Public Economics* 88, nos. 9–10 (August 2004): 2009–42.
2. This argument is developed in Roberto Mangabeira Unger, *Democracy Realized: The Progressive Alternative* (London and New York: Verso, 1998).
3. There is a very large literature on the comparative economic performance of democracies versus non-democracies. This literature suggests that democratically governed economies tend to outperform authoritarian regimes on a number of dimensions: they are better at adjusting to external shocks, they provide greater stability and predictability, and they produce better social indicators and distributional outcomes. The results on long-term growth performance are more mixed, but the more recent evidence suggests that democracies have the edge there as well. See José Tavares and Romain Wacziarg, "How Democracy Affects Growth," *European Economic Review* 45, no. 8 (August 2001): 1341–79; Dani Rodrik, "Participatory Politics, Social Cooperation, and Economic Stability," *American Economic Review, Papers and Proceedings* (May 2000); Dani Rodrik, "Democracies Pay Higher Wages," *Quarterly Journal of Economics* (August 1999); Dani Rodrik and Romain Wacziarg, "Do Democratic Transitions Produce Bad Economic Outcomes? "*American Economic Review, Papers and Proceedings* 95, no. 2 (May 2005): 50–55; and Elias Papaioannou and Gregorios Siourounis, "Democratization and Growth," *Economic Journal* 118, no. 10 (2008): 1520–51.
4. In December 2009, three countries—Guinea, Niger, and Madagascar— were removed from the list for lack of progress toward democratic practices. Mauritania was reinstated following democratic elections.
5. A good example is agricultural protection in the developed countries. The costs are paid primarily by consumers and taxpayers in those same developed countries.
6. In the language of economics, the global climate is a "pure" public good whereas an open economy is a private good, from the standpoint of individual nations, with some external effects on others.

Chapter 9

1. This chapter elaborates and updates the analysis presented in my book *The Rise of the Network Society* (2000). I take the liberty of referring the reader to that book for further elaboration and empirical support of the theorization presented here. Additional supporting material can be found in some of my writings in recent years (Castells, 2000b, 2001, 2004b, 2005a, 2005b, 2008a, 2008b; Castells and Himanen, 2002; Castells et al. 2006b, 2007).

Chapter 10

1. Lev Grossman, "Time's Person of the Year: You," *Time*, December 13, 2006.

2. See Robert L. Mitchell, "What Google Knows about You," *Computer World*, May 11, 2009.

3. Michael Zimmer, "Privacy on Planet Google: Using the Theory of Contextual Integrity to Clarify the Privacy Threats of Google's Quest for the Perfect Search Engine," *Journal of Business and Technology Law* 3 (2008): 109.

4. "Privacy Policy: Google Privacy Center," Google.com, www.google.com/privacypolicy .html, accessed March 11, 2009.

5. Paul Ohm, "Broken Promises of Privacy: Responding to the Surprising Failure of Anonymization," *SSRN eLibrary*, August 13, 2009, http://papers.ssrn.com/sol3/papers.cfm? abstract_id=1450006.

6. "Privacy Policy," Google.com. March 11, 2009.

7. Arshad Mohammed, "Google Refuses Demand for Search Information," *Washington Post*, January 20, 2006.

8. *Charlie Rose Show*, 2009, available at http://video.google.com.

9. Richard Thaler and Cass Sunstein, *Nudge: Improving Decisions about Health, Wealth, and Happiness* (New Haven, CT: Yale University Press, 2008), 109.

10. Ibid., 3.

11. *Google Search Privacy: Plain and Simple*, 2007, www.youtube.com/watch?v= kLgJYBRzUXY.

12. Louise Story and Brad Stone, "Facebook Retreats on On-Line Tracking," *New York Times*, November 30, 2007.

13. Warren St. John, "When Information Becomes T.M.I.," *New York Times*, September 10, 2006.

14. Jenna Wortham, "Facebook Glitch Brings New Privacy Worries," *New York Times*, May 5, 2010; Laura M. Holson, "Tell-All Generation Learns to Keep Things Offline," *New York Times*, May 8, 2010.

15. Emily Nussbaum, "Say Everything: Kids, the Internet, and the End of Privacy: The Greatest Generation Gap since Rock and Roll," *New York*, February 12, 2007.

16. danah boyd and Eszter Hargittai, "Facebook Privacy Settings: Who Cares?" *First Monday* 15, no. 8 (2010), www.uic.edu/htbin/cgiwrap/bin/ojs/index.php/fm/article/ view/3086/2589.

17. Helen Nissenbaum, *Privacy in Context: Technology, Policy, and the Integrity of Social Life* (Stanford, CA: Stanford Law Books, 2010).

18. Michael Zimmer, "The Quest for the Perfect Search Engine: Values, Technical Design, and the Flow of Personal Information in Spheres of Mobility," PhD diss., New York University, 2007.

19. I am basing the notion of privacy interfaces on the work of the foremost philosopher of privacy and ethics in online environments, Helen Nissenbaum. See her most influential work on the subject, "Privacy as Contextual Integrity," *Washington Law Review* 79, no. 1 (2004): 101–39. Also see Nissenbaum, *Privacy in Context: Technology, Policy, and the Integrity of Social Life* (Stanford, CA: Stanford Law Books, 2010).

20. Helen Nissenbaum, "Protecting Privacy in an Information Age: The Problem of Privacy in Public," *Law and Philosophy* 17, no. 5 (1998): 559–96.

21. Daniel Solove, *The Future of Reputation: Gossip, Rumor, and Privacy on the Internet* (New Haven, CT: Yale University Press, 2007). Solove's earlier book, *The Digital Person: Technology and Privacy in the Information Age* (New York: NYU Press, 2006), set the standard for explaining what is at stake in online data collection and analysis. In it, Solove walks us through the construction of "digital dossiers" in the "person to firm"

and "person to state" interfaces and outlines the potentials for abuse. *The Digital Person* is significant because it came out long enough after September 11, 2001, to take into account the U.S. government's notorious Total Information Awareness program and other efforts at behavioral profiling. It supplemented the best previous book of social and media theory applied to massive digital data collection and private-sector surveillance, Oscar Gandy's *The Panoptic Sort* (Boulder, CO: Westview Press, 1993). But 2004 was a long time ago in matters of government surveillance. Solove could not have predicted the revelation in 2005 that the NSA was monitoring American phone calls through an illegal secret program that relied on the cooperation of the major telecommunication companies.

22. James Rule, *Privacy in Peril* (Oxford: Oxford University Press, 2007).
23. James Rule, *Private Lives and Public Surveillance: Social Control in the Computer Age* (New York: Schocken Books, 1974).
24. Ibid.

Chapter 11

1. Johan Goudsblom, *Fire and Civilization* (Middlesex, England: Alan Lane, 1992), 17.
2. William H. McNeill, *Keeping Together in Time* (Cambridge, MA: ACLS Humanities, 1995), 31.
3. J. R. McNeill and William H. McNeill, *The Human Web* (New York: W. W. Norton, 2003), 11–14, and passim.
4. William H. McNeill, *Plagues and Peoples* (New York: Anchor, 1976), passim.
5. Paul Demeny and Geoffrey McNicoll (eds.), "The Political Economy of Global Population Change, 1950–2050," *Population and Development Review,* Supplement to vol. 32 (2006) offers a convenient and authoritative discussion of these phenomena.
6. J. R. McNeill, *Something New Under the Sun: An Environmental History of the Twentieth-Century World.* (New York: W. W. Norton, 2000), passim.

Chapter 12

1. Maureen Johnson, "Another Arrest in Truck Deaths as Details of Journey Emerge," Associated Press, June 20, 2000. The account of the Dover tragedy is based on contemporary press reports.
2. Hugh Thomas, *Rivers of Gold: The Rise of the Spanish Empire from Columbus to Magellan* (New York: Random House, 2003), 155.
3. Milton Meltzer, *Slavery: A World History,* 2 vols. (New York: Da Capo, 1993), 2–39.
4. Amy O'Neill Richard, *International Trafficking in Women to the United States: A Contemporary Manifestation of Slavery and Organized Crime* (Central Intelligence Agency Center for the Study of Intelligence, April 2000), 3.
5. *Wall Street Journal,* March 11, 2006.
6. Mark Riley, "27 Million Slaves and We Look Away," *Sydney Morning Herald,* June 4, 2001.
7. Amy Waldman, "Sri Lankan Maids Pay Dearly for Perilous Jobs Overseas," *New York Times,* May 8, 2005. See *Migration in an Interconnected World: New Directions for Action* (Geneva: Global Commission on International Migration, October 2005) available at http://www.gcim.org/attachements/gcim-complete-report-2005.pdf 26.
8. Adam Smith, *An Inquiry into the Nature and Causes of the Wealth of Nations,* vol. 1, ed. R. H. Campbell and A. S. Skinner (Oxford: Clarendon Press, 1976), 448.
9. David Christian, *Maps of Time: An Introduction to Big History* (Berkeley: University of California Press, 2004), 263.

10. Meltzer, *Slavery*, 1, 71.

11. Ibid., 1, 63.

12. Grant Parker, "*Ex oriente luxuria:* Indian Commodities and Roman Experience," *Journal of the Economic and Social History of the Orient* 45, no. 1 (2002): 50.

13. Timothy Taylor, "Believing the Ancients: Quantitative and Qualitative Dimensions of Slavery and the Slave Trade in Later Prehistoric Eurasia," *World Archaeology* 33, no. 1 (2001): 34.

14. Jose Honorio Rodrigues, "The Influence of Africa on Brazil and of Brazil on Africa," *Journal of African History* 3, no. 1 (1962): 54–56.

15. Meltzer, *Slavery*, 2, 132.

16. Chris Harman, *A People's History of the World,* part 3, chap. 6: "European Feudalism," 143, available at http://www.istendency.net/pdf/3_06_european_feudalism.pdf.

17. Eric R. Wolf, *Europe and the People without History* (Berkeley: University of California Press, 1982), 42.

18. Ibid., 74.

19. Ronald Findlay, "Globalization and the European Economy: Medieval Origins to the Industrial Revolution," in Henryk Kierzkowski (ed.), *Europe and Globalization* (New York: Palgrave Macmillan, 2002), 37.

20. Mustafa al Jiddawi, "Al Riqqfi al Tarikh wafi al Islam" [Slavery throughout History and during Muslim Times] (Alexandria 1963), 92–93.

21. Robin Blackburn, *The Making of New World Slavery* (London: Verso, 1997), 79.

22. Jere L. Bacharach, "African Military Slaves in the Medieval Middle East: The Cases of Iraq (869–955) and Egypt (868–1171)," *International Journal of Middle East Studies* 13 (1981): 471–95.

23. "Zanj Rebellion," Encyclopaedia Britannica Online http://search.eb.com/eb/article?eu=80343. Another important case of slave rebellion occurred nearly a thousand years later aboard a slave ship on the Atlantic. See Mitra Sharafi, "The Slave Ship Manuscripts of Captain Joseph B. Cook: A Narrative Reconstruction of the Brig *Nancys* Voyage of 1793," *Slavery and Abolition* 24 (April 2003): 71–100.

24. Ghada Hashem Talhami, "The Zanj Rebellion Reconsidered," *International Journal of African Historical Studies* 10, no. 3 (1977): 456.

25. Patricia Risso, *Merchants and Faith: Muslim Commerce and Culture in the Indian Ocean* (Boulder, CO: Westview, 1995), 16.

26. Barbara L. Solow, "Capitalism and Slavery in the Exceedingly Long Run," *Journal of Interdisciplinary History* 17 (Spring 1987): 711–37, quotation at 715.

27. Columbus, quoted in Ibid. 722, italics added.

28. April Lee Hatfield, "A 'Very Wary People in Their Bargaining' or 'Very Good Marchandise': English Traders' Views of Free and Enslaved Africans 1550–1650," *Slavery and Abolition* 25 (December 2004): 9.

29. Fernand Braudel, *Civilization and Capitalism Fifteenth–Eighteenth Century,* vol. 2: *The Wheels of Commerce* (New York: William Collins and Sons, 1982), 191.

30. The number of slaves brought from Africa to the New World remains contested. Historian Philip D. Curtin's estimate that between 8 and 10.5 million slaves were brought during the period of Atlantic slave trade has been challenged by others and revised upward considerably. See J. E. Inikon, "Measuring the Atlantic Slave Trade: An Assessment of Curtin and Anstey," *Journal of African History* 17, no. 2 (1976): 197–223, and Curtin's reply, Philip D. Curtin, "Measuring the Atlantic Slave Trade Once Again: A Comment," Ibid. 17, no. 4 (1976): 595–605. One later estimate puts the number of slaves leaving Africa at 11,863,000, of which 10–20 percent perished during the voyage

across the Atlantic called the Middle Passage. Paul E. Lovejoy, "The Impact of the Atlantic Slave Trade on Africa: A Review of the Literature," Ibid. 30, no. 3 (1989): 365–94.

31. Blackburn, *Making of New World Slavery*, 581.

32. Kevin G. Hall, "Brazilian Slaves Help Make Products That End Up in the United States through World Trade," *San Jose Mercury News*, September 14, 2004.

33. Eighteen illegal immigrants were found dead inside a refrigerated tractor trailer in Texas (*Houston Chronicle*, 8 May 18, 2003). As a newspaper report put it, "Nearly 150 years since slavery was officially abolished about 27 million people around the world remain physically or economically shackled—the highest number ever and it is growing" (Riley, "27 Million Slaves").

34. Fernand Braudel, *A History of Civilizations*, trans. Richard Mayne (London: Penguin, 1993), 381.

35. Patrick K. O'Brien, gen. ed., *Atlas of World History* (Oxford: Oxford University Press, 2002), 126.

36. Solow, "Capitalism and Slavery," 730.

37. Puangthong Rungswasdisab, *War and Trade Siamese Interventions in Cambodia 1767–1851* (PhD diss., University of Woolongong, 1995), 148.

38. Ward Barrett, "World Bullion Flows 1450–1800," in James D. Tracy (ed.), *The Rise of Merchant Empires: Long Distance Trade in the Early Modern World, 1350–1750* (New York: Cambridge University Press, 1990), 236.

39. Robert Harms, 'Early Globalization and the Slave Trade', *YaleGlobal Online* 9 May 2003.

40. Robert Harms, *The Diligent: A Voyage through the Worlds of the Slave Trade* (New York: Basic Books, 2002), 82.

41. Solow, "Capitalism and Slavery," 732. British capital investment in the colonies amounting to 37 million pounds in 1773 was large enough to make this a significant force. As British income grew in the eighteenth century—from higher agricultural productivity at home, which released farm labor to work in newly rising industries—demand for sugar was boosted and the system was kept functioning with the elastic supply of slave labor from Africa to the New World (Ibid., 733).

42. Nicholas F. R. Crafts, "British Economic Growth," *Economic History Review* 36 (1983): 177–99.

43. Herbert S. Klein, "Eighteenth Century Atlantic Slave Trade," in Tracy (ed.), *Rise of Merchant Empires*, 289.

44. George Metcalf, "A Microcosm of Why Africans Sold Slaves: Akan Consumption Patterns in the 1770s," *Journal of African History* 28, no. 3 (1987): 393.

45. Tristan Lecomte, quoted in Doreen Carvajal, "Third World Gets Help to Help Itself," *International Herald Tribune*, May 6, 2005.

46. Rachel Chernos Lin, "The Rhode Island Slave Traders: Butchers, Bakers and Candlestick-Makers," *Slavery and Abolition* 23 (December 2002): 21–38.

47. John Richard Oldfield, "Slavery Abolition and Empire," *GSC Quarterly* 14 (Winter-Spring 2005), available at http://www.ssrc.org/programs/gsc/publications/quarterlyi4/oldfield.pdf.

48. W. G. Clarence Smith, ed., *The Economics of the Indian Ocean Slave Trade in the Nineteenth Century* (London: Frank Cass, 1989).

49. Anthony Reid, *Charting the Shape of Early Modern Southeast Asia* (Singapore: ISEAS, 2000), 208.

50. Norimitsu Onishi, "In Japan's New Texts, Lessons in Rising Nationalism," *New York Times*, April 17, 2005.

51. Paul E. Lovejoy, "The Impact of the Atlantic Slave Trade on Africa: A Review of the Literature," *Journal of African History* 30, no. 3 (1989): 388.

52. Dinesh D'Souza, "The End of Racism," cited in *Slavery and Globalization* by Marian L. Tupy, September 5, 2003, Cato Institute; available at http://www.cato.org/dailys/09-05-03.html.

53. Klein, "Eighteenth Century Atlantic Slave Trade," 291.

54. S. Elisée Soumonni, "Some Reflections on the Brazilian Legacy," in Dahomey, *Slavery and Abolition* 22 (April 2001), 42–60.

55. Quoted in Rodrigues, "Influence of Africa on Brazil," 52.

56. Ibid., 56–61.

57. Nei Lopes, "African Religions in Brazil Negotiation and Resistance: A Look from Within," *Journal of Black Studies* 34 (July 2004): 853.

58. Alfred W. Crosby, Jr., *The Columbian Exchange Biological and Cultural Consequences of 1492* (Westport, CT: Greenwood, 1972), 31.

59. Niall Ferguson, *Empire: The Rise and Demise of the British World Order and the Lessons for Global Power* (New York: Basic Books, 2002), 71.

60. John Archdale, quoted in Ibid.

61. Ronald Findlay and Mats Lundahl, *Demographic Shocks and the Factor Proportions Model: From the Plague of Justinian to the Black Death,* typescript, Columbia University, University Seminar in Economic History 28, available at http://www.econ.barnard.Columbia.edu/econhist/papers/Findlay%20Justinian.pdf.

62. Kenneth F. Kiple, "The Plague of Justinian: An Early Lesson in the Black Death," in Kiple (ed.), *Plague, Pox, and Pestilence* (London: Weidenfeld and Nicolson, 1997), 29.

63. Ole J. Benedictow, *The Black Death 1346–1353: The Complete History* (Woodbridge: Boydell, 2004), 3.

64. Ibid., 382.

65. James Burke, *Connections* (Boston: Little Brown, 1978), 70.

66. Ronald Findlay and Kevin H. O. Rourke, "Commodity Market Integration 1500–2000," in Michael D. Bordo, Alan M. Taylor, and Jeffrey G. Williamson (eds.), *Globalization in Historical Perspective* (Chicago: University of Chicago Press, 2003), 15.

67. Burke, *Connections,* 103–4. The technique of papermaking was picked up by Arabs when they overran Samarkand in 751 CE just after the Chinese had sent a team of paper makers there to set up a factory. By 1050 paper was being made in Moorish, Spain. In 1280 a paper mill running on waterpower was set up at Fabriano, Italy (Ibid., 100).

68. Benedictow, *Black Death,* 393.

69. George Rosen, *A History of Public Health,* reprint ed. (Baltimore: Johns Hopkins University Press, 1993), 43–45.

70. Ibid., 64.

71. Jonathan Tucker, *Scourge: The Once and Future Threat of Smallpox* (New York: Atlantic Monthly Press, 2001), 10–11.

72. Ferguson, *Empire,* 71.

73. Tucker, *Scourge,* 15.

74. Ibid., 16.

75. J. N. Hays, *The Burdens of Disease: Epidemics and Human Response in Western History* (New Brunswick, NJ: Rutgers University Press 1998), 240.

76. Gina Kolata, *Flu: The Story of the Great Influenza Pandemic of 1918 and the Search for the Virus That Caused It* (New York: Farrar Straus and Giroux 1999), 297–98.

77. Virologist John Oxford estimated that the worldwide death from the flu was one hundred million rather than twenty to forty million (Ibid., 285).

78. Rob Stein and Shankar Vedantam, "Deadly Flu Strain Shipped Worldwide: Officials Race to Destroy Samples," *Washington Post,* April 13, 2005, available at http://www.washingtonpost.com/wp-dyn/articles/A47841-2005Apr12.html.

79. Jong Wha Lee and Warwick J. McKibbin, *Globalization and Disease: The Case of SARS,* August 2003, Working Paper no 2003/16, Division of Economics Research School of Pacific and Asian Studies, 13.

80. David Fidler, "SARS: Political Pathology of the First Post-Westphalian Pathogen," *Journal of Law Medicine and Ethics* 31 (December 2003): 485.

81. http://www.whitehouse.gov/news/releases/2005/11/200511166.html.

82. David Heymann, "Preparing for a New Global Threat—Part I," *YaleGlobal Online,* January 26, 2005, available at http://yaleglobal yale edu/displayarticle?id=5174.

83. Thomas Abraham, "Preparing for a New Global Threat—Part II," *YaleGlobal Online* January 28, 2005, available at http://yaleglobal yale edu/display article?id=5191.

84. Cited in Eugene H. Spafford, "Computer Viruses as Artificial Life," *Journal of Artificial Life* (1994), available at http://www.scs.carleton.ca/~soma/biosec/readings/spafford-viruses.pdf.

85. Fred Cohen, *Computer Viruses* (Ph.D. diss., University of Southern California, 1985).

86. Xin Li, *Computer Viruses: The Threat Today and the Expected Future* (undergraduate thesis, Linkoping University, 2003) available at http://www.ep.liu.se/exjobb/isy/2003/3452/.

87. Dugan Haltey Virus Alert 2001 typescript available at http://eserverorg/courses/soi/tc510/foobar/virus/printable.pdf.

88. Lee Kuan Yew, interview with author, January 17, 2004.

89. Mynardo Macaraig, "Philippine Internet Providers Admit Being Love Bug Source," *Agence France Presse,* May 5, 2000; Mark Landler, "A Filipino Linked to Love Bug Talks about His License to Hack," *New York Times,* October 21, 2000.

90. John Eisinger, "Script Kiddies Beware," *Washington and Lee Law Review* 59 (2002): 1507–44.

91. Javier Santoyo, interview with author April 18, 2005.

92. "The Spread of the Code-Red Worm (CRv2)," available at http://www.caida.org/analysis/security/code-red/coderedv2_analysis.xml#animations.

93. Li, *Computer Viruses*, 42.

94. Mark Hall, "Sticky Security," *Computerworld* 19 (January 2004): 48.

95. This section on cybercrime relies on Brian Grow with Jason Bush, "Hacker Hunters," *BusinessWeek* May 30, 2005.

96. Cited by Marian L. Tupy, *Slavery and Globalization*, Cato Institute, September 5, 2003; available at http://www.cato.org/pub_displayphp?pub_id=3227.

Chapter 13

1. We appreciate that the concepts of the local and the global, and the particular and the universal, are not identical binary oppositions.

2. See, for example, Lanfranchi (1992); Giulianotti and Williams (1994); Sugden and Tomlinson (1994); Armstrong and Giulianotti (1997, 1998a, 2001, 2004); Brown (1998).

3. Also, in Turkey, football's urban appeal has weakened traditional wrestling (Stokes 1996: 26–7).

4. While Manchester United have developed a potent mythology surrounding the club's history and its local connections (notably in regard to the 1958 Munich disaster, which killed eight players), supporters of local rivals, Manchester City, tend to claim a closer attachment to the city per se.

5. See www.uefa.com/Competitions/Euro/Organisation/Kind=32768/newsId=332293.html.

6. For example, in Buenos Aires, the fans of San Lorenzo refer to their stadium as Nuevo Gasómetro, in collective memory of their old ground, the Gasómetro, which was torn down in 1979.

7. Thus, leading football stars, notably Pele, were visibly integrated into elite/white society, while white players were notably more prominent in Brazil's national team during the 1980s. On the subsequent attempts to "whiten" leading black athletes in the United States, notably Michael Jordan, see Andrews (2001).

8. Indeed, even the 1970 Brazil team blended the two logics, through brilliant expressive play and rigorous training at high altitude.

9. Similarly, outsiders typically discuss "African football" as a uniform entity, thus ignoring enormous local, national, and regional diversity (cf. Armstrong and Giulianotti 2004).

10. Elsewhere, Canada has endeavored to counteract perceived Americanization at economic, political, and cultural levels (Smith 1994).

11. Cohen and Kennedy (2000: 377) adopt a similar stance, defining glocalization in terms of the selective and adaptive capacities of local actors in relation to global culture. They contrast this definition directly with the machinations of powerful companies in "customizing" products to suit local markets.

12. Ritzer could clarify more precisely his conception concerning the "nothingness" of grobalization. In our context, it would seem to imply that "grobal" football is simply "nothing," a point that is difficult to sustain given the political and economic impact of the professional, commercial game.

13. For Cowen (2002; 48), an ethos refers to the "special feel or flavour of a culture," providing "the background network of worldviews, styles, and inspirations found in a society, or a framework for cultural interpretation. Ethos therefore is part of an implicit language for creating or viewing art."

14. For example, during his seventeen-year presidential reign at Atlético Madrid, the mercurial Jesus Gil disposed of 39 coaches and recruited 141 players (World Soccer, July 2004).

15. The co-founder of Sony, Akio Morita, understood this as involving the meeting of "local needs with local operations while developing common global concepts and technologies." See www.sony.net/Fun/SH/1-29/h1.html.

16. Nor do these observations require us to accept uncritically the lofty self-proclamations of particular nations regarding their football ethos. Brazilian football may be typologized as the "beautiful game," but domestic fixtures are typically blighted by brutal and persistent fouling. For example, in one weekend, at the 2003 Paulista (São Paulo) championship final, there were three red cards, ten yellows, over fifty fouls, and assorted brawls; a day later, at the 2003 Carioca (Rio) championship final, there were 78 fouls, three red cards, and a ten-minute fight between players and coaches.

Chapter 14

1. The following discussion of the development of the franchise in the United States is derived from Carrie Shook and Robert L. Shook, *Franchising: The Business Strategy that Changed the World* (Englewood Cliffs, NJ: Prentice Hall, 1993), 139–66; John A. Jakle and Keith A. Sculle, *Fast Food: Roadside Restaurants in the Automobile Age* (Baltimore: Johns Hopkins University Press, 1999), 139–62; and Thomas S. Dicke, *Franchising in America: The Development of a Business Method, 1840–1980* (Chapel Hill: University of North Carolina Press, 1992).

2. "World Motor Vehicle Production," http://oica.net/wp-content/uploads/ford-2010.pdf (accessed January 27, 2012).

3. Ibid.

4. Orville Schell, "How Walmart Is Changing China (and Vice Versa)," *The Atlantic* (December 2011): 80–98.

5. Starbucks Company Profile, http://news.starbucks.com/images/10041/AboutUs-CompanyProfile-Q4-2011-12_14_11-FINAL.pdf (accessed January 27, 2012).

6. "2010 Ranking of the Top 100 Brands." http://www.interbrand.com/en/best-global-brands/best-global-brands-2008/best-global-brands-2010.aspx (accessed 31 January 2012).

7. This history is adapted from http://www.thecoca-colacompany.com/heritage/pdf/Coca-Cola_l25_years_booklet.pdf (accessed January 31, 2012); "The Chronicle of Coca-Cola," http://www.thecoca-colacompany.com/heritage/chronicle_birth_refreshing_idea.html (accessed January 31, 2012); and Mark Pendergast, *For God, Country, and Coca-Cola: The Unauthorized History of the Great American Soft Drink and the Company that Makes It* (New York: Scribner, 1993).

8. Pendergast, *For God, Country, and Coca-Cola*, 354–71; quote on 365.

9. See Cecil Munsey, *The Illustrated Guide to the Collectibles of Coca-Cola* (New York: Hawthorn Books, 1972) for a guide on such matters.

10. See http://www.killercoke.org (accessed January 31, 2012).

11. Except where otherwise noted, the history of McDonald's presented here is derived from numerous sources, including Shook and Shook, *Franchising*, 139–66; Jakle and Sculle, *Fast Food*, 139–62; http://www.mcdonalds.com/us/en/our_story/our_history.html (accessed 31 January 2012); http://www.mcdonalds.com/corp/about.html (accessed February 4, 2009); and Funding Universe, "McDonald's Corporation," http://www.fundinguniverse.com/company-histories/McDonalds-Corporation-Company-History.html (accessed March 2, 2011).

12. Jakle and Sculle, *Fast Food*, 135–36.

13. "2010 Ranking of the Top 100 Brands."

14. Francis Fukuyama, *The End of History and the Last Man* (New York: Free Press, 1992).

15. Jonathan Steele, "Muscovites Find Perestroika in a Restructured Cow," *The Guardian*, February 1, 1990.

16. James L. Watson (ed.), *Golden Arches East: McDonald's in East Asia* (Stanford, CA: Stanford University Press, 1997).

17. "McDonald's to Open a Restaurant a Day in China in Four Years." http://www.bloomberg.com/news/2011-07-29/mcdonald-s-franchises-to-account-for-up-to-20-of-china-business.html (accessed January 31, 2012).

18. Watson, *Golden Arches East*, 1–38.

19. Ibid.

20. Ibid.

21. Ibid.

22. Eric Schlosser, *Fast Food Nation: The Dark Side of the American Meal* (New York: Houghton Mifflin Harcourt, 2001).

23. "Financial Highlights," "http://www.aboutmcdonalds.com/mcd/investors/financial_highlights.html" (accessed January 31, 2012).

24. This history is derived from Jeans and Accessories, "The History of Blue Jeans," http://www.jeans-and-accessories.com/history-of-blue-jeans.html (accessed January 31, 2012); and The Great Idea Finder, "Blue Jeans History," http://www.ideafinder.com/history/inventions/bluejeans.htm (accessed January 31, 2012).

25. Beverly Gordon, "American Denim: Blue Jeans and Their Multiple Layers of Meaning," in Patricia A. Cunningham and Susan Voso Lab (eds.), *Dress and Popular Culture* (Bowling Green, OH: Bowling Green State University Popular Press, 1991), 34.

26. Ibid., 36.

27. Ibid., 37.

28. Virginia Wallace-Whitaker, *Awareness of American Brand Names in the Soviet Union*, paper presented at the annual meeting of the Association for Education in Journalism and Mass Communication, August 10–13, 1989.

29. "How Many Pairs of Denim Jeans Do Consumers Own?," http://lifestylemonitor .cottoninc.com/LSM-Fast-Facts/001-How-many-pairs-denim-jeans-do-consumers-own/?category=denim&sort=viewall&mainSection=fastFacts&currentRow=3 (accessed January 31, 2012).

30. "How Many Pairs of Denim Jeans Do Men Own?," http://lifestylemonitor.cottoninc .com/LSM-Fast-Facts/002-How-many-pairs-denim-jeans-do-men-own/?category=de nim&sort=viewall&mainSection=fastFacts&currentRow=11 (accessed January 31, 2012); and "How Many Pairs of Denim Jeans Do Women Own?," http://lifestylemonitor .cottoninc.com/LSM-Fast-Facts/003-How-many-pairs-denim-jeans-do-women-own/?category=denim&sort=viewall&mainSection=fastFacts&currentRow=12 (accessed January 31, 2012).

31. "Percent of Consumers Who Love or Enjoy Wearing Denim," http://lifestylemonitor .cottoninc.com/LSM-Fast-Facts/004-Percent-consumers-wearing-denim/?category= denim&sort=viewall&mainSection=fastFacts&currentRow=13 (accessed January 31, 2012); and "Do Men and Women Prefer to Wear Denim Jeans or Causal Slacks?," http:// lifestylemonitor.cottoninc.com/LSM-Fast-Facts/009-Men-Women-Prefer-Denim-Jeans-Casual-Slacks/?category=denim&sort=viewall&mainSection=FastFacts&cur rentRow=17 (accessed January 31, 2012).

32. Scott Robert Olson, "Hollywood Planet: Global Media and the Competitive Advantage of Narrative Transparency," in Robert C. Allen and Annette Hill (eds.), *The Television Studies Reader* (New York: Routledge, 2004), 114.

Chapter 15

1. In French, see the various works by Danièle Hervieu-Léger, and Patrick Haenni's book *L'islam de marché* (City: Publisher, year). For American sources on this subject, see R. Finke and R. Stark, "Religious Economies and Sacred Canopies," *American Sociological Review* 53 (1988); P. Berger, *The Sacred Canopy* (City: Publisher, year), p. 138; and the Introduction to D. Martin, *Tongues of Fire* (City: Publisher, year).

2. Bernard Grosclaude, "Sortir des incantations" (on the Luthero-Protestant ministers of Montbéliard), *Reformation*, February 14, 2008.

3. This is a nagging question: why are humans religious? If religion is based on a quest for the sacred instead of it being part of a cultural or ideological system, then a link with "human nature" needs to be found. Scott Atran puts forward an original atheist viewpoint in *In Gods We Trust: The Evolutionary Landscape of Religion* (Oxford: Oxford University Press, 2002).

4. Laurence R. Iannaccone, Roger Finke, and Rodney Stark, "Deregulating Religion: The Economics of Church and State," *Economic Inquiry* 35, no. 2 (1997): 350–64.

5. For a critique see Steve Bruce, "The Supply-Side Model of Religion: The Nordic and Baltic States," *Journal for the Scientific Study of Religion* 39, no. 1 (March 2000): 32–46.

6. Shalva Weil, "Dual Conversion Among the Shinlung of North-East India," *Studies of Tribes and Tribals* 1, no. 1 (2003): 43–57.

7. "There are 2500 in Israel, spread across the entire country, essentially in Arad, Mitzpe Ramon and Tiberias; but Kfar Hashalom is located close to Dimona, the heart of the community of Black Hebrews. In 1969, these blacks from Chicago who claim to be from the tribe of Judah immigrated to Israel, after two years of wandering in Liberia.

Their spiritual guide, Ben Ammi Ben Israel (born Ben Carter) tells how he saw a vision of the Angel Gabriel while he was lying on his bed, in Chicago, in 1966; he entreated him to set out for Israel with his nearest and dearest"; see Nathalie Szerman, in collaboration with André Darmon, "Israël: Une visite chez les Hébreux noirs," October 9, 2006; available at http://religion.info/french/articles/article_269.shtml.

8. Jean-François Mayer, *Internet and Religion* (Gollion, Switzerland: Infolio, 2008).

9. Jan Shipps, *Sojourner in the Promised Land: Forty Years Among The Mormons* (Carbondale: University of Illinois Press, 2006).

10. There was indeed a Mormon mission in Tahiti and in the Pacific from 1844, but it was because they were looking for a lost tribe of Israel. This is indeed a case of racial exclusivity. Nowadays, 10 percent of the population of Tahiti belongs to the Morman Church; see Yannick Fer, Religioscope (website), http://religion.info/french/entretiens/article_314.shtml.

11. Mary Jordan, "The New Face of Global Mormonism: Tech-Savvy Missionary Church Thrives as Far Afield as Africa," *Washington Post,* November 19, 2007.

12. Mara D. Bellaby, "Nigerian preacher runs Ukraine's first megachurch," The Associated Press, August 4, 2006. According to the article, the mayor of Kiev, Leonid Chernovetsk, is apparently a member of the Church.

13. "Two U.S. Priests Defect to Anglicans in Kenya," *Washington Post,* August 31, 2007. They are Bill Atwood from Texas and William Murdoch from Massachusetts.

14. Kevin Sullivan, "Foreign Missionaries Find Fertile Ground in Europe: Singaporean Pastor Fires Up Staid Danes," *Washington Post,* June 11, 2007.

15. Shim Jae Hoon, "Doing God's Work for the Taliban, Korean Christian Missionaries End Up Bolstering the Terrorists in Afghanistan," *Yale Global,* September 4, 2007.

16. Henry C. Finney, "American Zen's 'Japan Connection': A Critical Case Study of Zen Buddhism's Diffusion to the West," *Sociological Analysis* 52, no. 4: Religious Movements and Social Movements (Winter 1991): 379–96. The author, a sociologist, accompanied a group of American monks to Japan to carry out a participatory observation study.

17. Michelle Boorstein, "Hare Krishna Coming of Age," *Washington Post,* August 6, 2006.

18. http://etirth.wordpress.com/2008/03/02/iskcon-temple-delhi-india.

19. Neil J. Savishinsky, "Rastafari in the Promised Land: The Spread of a Jamaican Socioreligious Movement among the Youth of West Africa," *African Studies Review* 37, no. 3 (1994).

20. See Celia Genn, "From Chishtiyya Diaspora to Transnational Sufi Movement,"Griffith University, Brisbane, site http://coombs.anu.edu.au/Special-Proj/ASAA/biennial-conference/2006/Genn-Celia-ASAA2006.pdf. See also Judith Howell's research.

21. Abdennour Bidar, *Self Islam* (Paris: Le Seuil, 2006).

22. This pseudo-brotherhood is linked to the curious case of a book telling of a journey through the Afghan resistance organized by Idries Shah's networks; but the entire book seems to be fictitious, and the only photo that could testify to the authenticity of the journey is taken in a region that does not feature on the author's itinerary, according to the map inside the book: see Louis Palmer, *Adventures in Afghanistan* (London: Octogon Press, 1991). The epitome of deterritorialization is to plunge into an imaginary world.

23. Shlomo Shamir, "Scandals and disputes plague ultra-orthodox circles in the US," *Haaretz,* January 14, 2007.

24. Ursula King, "Some Reflections on Sociological Approaches to the Study of Modern Hinduism," *Numen* 36, part 1 (June 1989): 72–97. See also "India: Does Hinduism exist? Interview with Martin Fárek," Religioscope (website), June 1, 2008.

25. Raphaël Liogier, in *Le Bouddhisme mondialisé* (Paris: Ellipses, 2004), 10, 21–24.

26. Martin Baumann, "Culture Contact and Valuation: Early German Buddhists and the Creation of a 'Buddhism in Protestant Shape,'" *Numen* 44, no. 3 (September 1997): 270–95.

27. "The Cultural Significance of New Religious Movements: The Case of Soka Gakkai," *Sociology of Religion* 62, no. 3 (Autumn 2001) 337–64.

28. Jozef Van Hecken, "Les réductions Catholiques au pays des Ordos, une méthode d'apostolat des missionaires de Schuet," *Les Cahiers de la Nouvelle Revue de Science Missionnaire*, XV, 1957.

29. There is a review of some of the major works on this subject in Rhys H. Williams, "Religion, Community, and Place: Locating the Transcendent,"*Religion and American Culture: A Journal of Interpretation* 12, no. 2 (Summer 2002): 262.

30. Jan Feldman, *Lubavitchers as Citizens: A Paradox of Liberal Democracy* (Ithaca, NY: Cornell University Press, 2003).

31. Brigid Schulte, "Temple Traffic a Mixed Blessing, Congregation's Growth Causes Parking Crisis and Threatens Closure," *Washington Post*, September 15, 2008.

32. David Rieff, "Nuevos Católicos," *New York Times*, December 24, 2006.

33. Yair Ettinger, "Rosh Hashanah Kibbutz: On New Year, Thousands Flock to Rabbi Nachman's Grave in Ukraine," *Haaretz*, September 27, 2006.

34. Fenggang Yang, "Chinese Conversion to Evangelical Christianity: The Importance of Social and Cultural Contexts," *Sociology of Religion* 59, no. 3 (1998): 243.

35. Peter van der Veer and Steven Vertovec, "Brahmanism Abroad: On Caribbean Hinduism as an Ethnic Religion," *Ethnology* 30, no. 2 (April 1991): 149–66.

36. Ursula King, "Some Reflections" (see note 24).

37. See Karen Chai, "Competing for the Second Generation: English-Language Ministry at a Korean Protestant Church," in R. Stephen Warner and Judith G. Wittner (eds.), *Gatherings in Diaspora: Religious Communities and the New Immigration* (Philadelphia, PA: Temple University Press, 1998).

38. Yannick Fer, *Pentecostalisme en Polynésie Française*, (Geneva: Labor & Fides, 2005), 85, 106, 110.

39. *Le Figaro*, October 3, 2007.

40. Jean-Paul Nerrière, *Don't speak English, Parlez Globish!* (Paris: Eyrolles, 2006).

41. Daniel Bergner, "The Believers," *New York Times*, December 30, 2007. Arif and Kathleen Khan were assassinated in Pakistan in August 2007.

42. Vanessa L. Ochs, *Reinventing Jewish Ritual* (Philadelphia: Jewish Publication Society, 2007), 16, 70.

43. Equivalent of the *bar mitzvah* for girls, which in itself is a departure from Jewish tradition.

44. Andy Newman, "Journey from a Chinese orphanage to a Jewish rite of passage," *New York Times*, March 8, 2007.

Chapter 16

1. Onookome Okome, "Writing the Anxious City: Images of Lagos in Nigerian Home Video Films," in Okwui Enwezor et al. (eds), *Under Siege: Four African Cities—Freetown, Johannesburg, Kinshasa, Lagos* (Ostfildern-Ruit: Hatje Cantz, 2002), 316.

2. UN Department of Economic and Social Affairs, Population Division, *World Urbanization Prospects*, 2001 Revision, (New York: United Nations, 2002).

3. Population Information Program, Center for Communication Programs, the Johns Hopkins Bloomberg School of Public Health, "Meeting the Urban Challenge," *Population Reports* 30, no. 4 (Fall 2002): 1.

4. Dennis Rondinelli and John Kasarda, "Job Creation Needs in Third World Cities," in John D. Kasarda and Allan M. Parnell (eds.), *Third World Cities: Problems, Policies and Prospects* (Newbury Park, CA: Sage Publications, 1993), 101.

5. Wolfgang Lutz, Warren Sanderson, and Setgei Scherbov, "Doubling of World Population Unlikely," *Nature* 387 (June 19, 1997): 803–4. However, the populations of sub-Saharan Africa will triple, and of India, double.

6. Although the velocity of global urbanization is not in doubt, the growth rates of specific cities may brake abruptly as they encounter the frictions of size and congestion. A famous instance of such a "polarization reversal" is Mexico City, widely predicted to achieve a population of 25 million during the 1990s (the current population is between 19 million and 22 million). See Yue-man Yeung, "Geography in an Age of Mega-Cities," *International Social Sciences Journal* 151 (1997): 93.

7. *Financial Times,* July 27, 2004; David Drakakis-Smith, *Third World Cities,* 2nd ed. (London: Routledge, 2000).

8. Composite of UN-HABITAT, Global Urban Indicators Database (2002); Thomas Brinkhoff "The Principal Agglomerations of the World," www.citypopulation.de/World.html (May 2004).

9. UN-HABITAT, Global Urban Indicators Database (2002).

10. *Far Eastern Economic Review: Asia 1998 Yearbook*, p. 63.

11. Hamilton Tolosa, "The Rio/São Paulo Extended Metropolitan Region: A Quest for Global Integration," *The Annals of Regional Science* 37: 2 (September 2003): 480, 485.

12. Gustavo Garza, "Global Economy, Metropolitan Dynamics and Urban Policies in Mexico," *Cities* 16: 3 (1999): 154.

13. Jean-Marie Cour and Serge Snrech (eds.), *Preparing for the Future: A Vision of West Africa in the Year 2020,* (Paris: OECD/Club du Sahel, 1998), 94.

14. Ibid., p. 48.

15. See Yue-man Yeung, "Viewpoint: Integration of the Pearl River Delta," *International Development Planning Review* 25: 3 (2003).

16. Aprodicio Laquian, "The Effects of National Urban Strategy and Regional Development Policy on Patterns of Urban Growth in China," in Gavin Jones and Pravin Visaria (eds), *Urbanization in Large Developing Countries: China, Inonesia, Brazil, and India* (Oxford: Oxford University Press, 1997), 62–63.

17. Yue-man Yeung and Fu-chen Lo, "Global Restructuring and Emerging Urban Corridors in Pacific Asia," in Lo and Yeung (eds), *Emerging World Cities in Pacific Asia* (Tokyo: United Nations University Press, 1996), 41.

18. Gregory Guldin, What's a Peasant to Do? Village Becoming Town in Southern China, (Boulder, CO: Westview Press, 2001), 13.

19. United Nations Human Settlements Programme, *The Challenge of Slums: UN-HABITAT's Global Report on Human Settlements 2003* (London: Routledge, 2003), 3.

20. Guldin, *What's a Peasant to Do?*

21. Sidney Goldstein, "Levels of Urbanization in China," in Mattei Dogon and John Kasarda (eds), *The Metropolis Era: Volume One—A World of Giant Cities* (Newbury Park, CA: Sage, 1988), 210–21.

22. Census 2001, Office of the Registrar General and Census Commissioner, India; and Alain Durand-Lasserve and Lauren Royston, "International Trends and Country Contexts," in Alain Durand-Lasserve and Lauren Royston (eds), *Holding Their Ground: Secure Land Tenure for the Urban Poor in Developing Countries* (London: Routledge, 2002), 20.

23. Mbuji-Mayi is the center of the "ultimate company state" in the Kaasai region run by the Société Minière de Bakwanga. See Michela Wrong, *In the Footsteps of Mr. Kurtz: Living on the Brink of Disaster in the Congo* (London: Harper Perennial, 2000), 121–23.

24. Miguel Villa and Jorge Rodríguez, "Demographic Trends in Latin America's Metropolises, 1950–1990," in Alan Gilbert (ed.), *The Mega-City in Latin America* (Tokyo and New York: United Nations University Press, 1996), 33–34.

25. Guldin, *What's a Peasant to Do?*, pp. 14–17.

26. Jeremy Seabrook, *In the Cities of the South: Scenes from a Developing World* (London: Verso, 1996), 16–17.

27. Guldin, *What's a Peasant to Do?*, pp. 14–17. See also Jing Neng Li, "Structural and Spatial Economic Changes and Their Effects on Recent Urbanization in China," in Jones and Visaria, *Urbanization in Large Developing Countries*, p. 44. Ian Yeboah finds a *desakota* ("city village") pattern developing around Accra, whose sprawling form (188 percent increase in surface area in 1990s) and recent automobilization he attributes to the impact of structural adjustment policies; see Ian Yeboah, "Demographic and Housing Aspects of Structural Adjustment and Emerging Urban Form in Accra, Ghana," *Africa Today* 50: 1 (2003): 108, 116–17.

28. Thomas Sieverts, *Cities without Cities: An Interpretation of the Zwischenstadt* (London: Routledge, 2003), 3.

29. Drakakis-Smith, *Third World Cities*, p. 21.

30. See overview in T. G. McGee, "The Emergence of *Desakota* Regions in Asia: Expanding a Hypothesis," in Norton Ginsburg, Bruce Koppel, and T. G. McGee (eds.), *The Extended Metropolis: Settlement Transition in Asia* (Honolulu: University of Hawaii Press, 1991). Philip Kelly, in his book on Manila, agrees with McGee about the specificity of the Southeast Asian path of urbanization but argues that *desakota* landscapes are unstable, with agriculture slowly being squeezed out; see Philip Kelly, *Everyday Urbanization: The Social Dynamics of Development in Manila's Extended Metropolitan Region* (London: Routledge, 1999), 284–86.

31. Adrián Aguilar and Peter Ward, "Globalization, Regional Development, and Mega-City Expansion in Latin America: Analyzing Mexico City's Peri-Urban Hinterland," *Cities* 20: 1 (2003): 4, 18. The authors claim that *desakota*-like development does not occur in Africa: "Instead city growth tends to be firmly urban and large-city based, and is contained within clearly defined boundaries. There is not meta-urban or peri-urban development that is tied to, and driven by, processes, in the urban core" (p. 5). But certainly Gauteng (Witwatersrand) must be counted as an example of "regional urbanization" fully analogous to Latin American examples.

32. Ranjith Dayaratne and Raja Samarawickrama, "Empowering Communities: The Peri-Urban Areas of Colombo," *Environment and Urbanization* 15: 1 (April 2003): 102. (See also, in the same issue, L. van den Berg, M. van Wijk, and Pham Van Hoi, "The Transformation of Agricultural and Rural Life Downsteam of Hanoi.").

33. Magdalena Nock, "The Mexican Peasantry and the *Ejido* in the Neo-liberal Period," in Deborah Bryceson, Cristóbal Kay, and Jos Mooij (eds.), *Disappearing Peasantries? Rural Labour in Africa, Asia and Latin America* (London: Intermediate Technology Publications 2000), 173.

34. *Financial Times*, December 16, 2003, July 27, 2004.

35. *New York Times*, July 28, 2004.

36. Wang Mengkui, Director of the Development Research Center of the State Council, quoted in the *Financial Times*, November 26, 2003.

37. Goldstein, "Levels of Urbanizaton in China," Table 7.1, p. 201; the 1978 figure is from Guilhem Fabre, "La Chine," in Thierry Paquot, *Les Monde lies Villes: Panorama Urbain de la Planéte* [*The World of Cities: Urban Panorama of the Planet*] (Brussels: Editions Complexe, 1996), 187. It is important to note that the World Bank's time series differs from Fabre's, with a 1978 urbanization rate of 18 percent, not 13 percent. (See World Bank, *World Development Indicators*, 2001, CD-ROM version.).

38. World Bank, *World Development Report 1995: Workers in an Integrating World* (New York: Oxford University Press, 1995), 170.

39. Population rank from Thomas Brinkhoff (www.citypopulation.de); GDP rank from Denise Pumain, "Scaling Laws and Urban Systems," Santa Fe Institute Working Paper 04-02-002, (Santa Fe, NM: Santa Fe Institute, 2002), p. 4.

40. Josef Gugler, "Introduction—II: Rural–Urban Migration," in Gugler (ed.), *Cities in the Developing World: Issues, Theory and Policy* (Oxford: Oxford University Press, 1997), 43.

41. Sally Findley emphasizes that everyone in the 1980s underestimated levels of continuing rural–urban migration and resulting rates of urbanization; see Sally Findley, "The Third World City," in Kasarda and Parnell, *Third World Cities: Problems*, p. 14.

42. Nigel Harris, "Urbanization, Economic Development and Policy in Developing Countries," *Habitat International* 14: 4 (1990): 21–22.

43. David Simon, "Urbanization, Globalization and Economic Crisis in Africa," in Carole Rakodi (ed.), *The Urban Challenge in Africa: Growth and Management in Its Large Cities* (Tokyo: United Nations University Press, 1997), 95. For growth rates of English industrial cities 1800–1850, see Adna Weber, *The Growth of Cities in the Nineteenth Century: A Study in Statistics* (New York: Macmillan, 1899), 44, 52–53.

44. A. S. Oberai, *Population Growth, Employment and Poverty in Third-World Mega-Cities: Analytical Policy Issues,* (London: St. Martin's Press, 1993), 165.

45. *United Nations Environment Programme (UNEP), Africa Environment Outlook: Past, Present and Future Perspectives,* quoted in *Al Abram Weekly (Cairo)* (October 2–8, 2003); Alain Jacquemin, *Urban Development and New Towns in the Third World: Lessons from the New Bombay Experience* (Aldershot: Ashgate, 1999), 28.

46. Sébastien de Dianous, "Les Damnés de la Terre du Cambodge," *Le Monde diplomatiaue* (September 2004): 20.

47. See Josef Gugler, "Overurbanization Reconsidered," in Gugler, *Cities in the Developing World,* pp. 114–23.

48. Foreword to Jacinta Prunty, *Dublin Slums, 1800–1925: A Study in Urban Geography,* (Dublin: Irish Academic Press, 1998), ix. Larkin, of course, forgets Dublin's Mediterranean counterpart: Naples.

49. Oberai, *Population Growth,* p. 13.

50. UN-HABITAT, *An Urbanising World: Global Report on Human Settlements* (Oxford: Oxford University Press, 1996), 239.

51. Priscilla Connolly, "Mexico City: Our Common Future?," *Environment and Urbanization* 11: 1 (April 1999): 56.

52. Ivo Imparato and Jeff Ruster, *Slum Upgrading and Participation: Lessons from Latin America* (Washington, DC: World Bank Publications, 2003), 333.

53. John Browder and Brian Godfrey, *Rainforest Cities: Urbanization, Development, and Globalization of the Brazilian Amazon* (New York: Columbia University Press, 1997), 130.

54. Yang Wenzhong and Wang Gongfan, "Peasant Movement: A Police Perspective," in Michael Dutton (ed.), *Streetlife China* (Cambridge: Cambridge University Press, 1998), 89.

55. Dileni Gunewardena, "Urban Poverty in South Asia: What Do We Know? What Do We Need To Know?," working paper, Conference on Poverty Reduction and Social Progress, Rajendrapur, Bangladesh, April 1999, p. 1.

56. Arif Hasan, "Introduction," in Akhtar Hameed Khan, *Orangi Pilot Project: Reminiscences and Reflections* (Karachi: Oxford University Press, 1996), xxxiv.

57. Suketu Mehta, *Maximum City: Bombay Lost and Found* (New York, 2004), 117.

58. Gautam Chatterjee, "Consensus versus Confrontation," *Habitat Debate* 8: 2 (June 2002): 11. Statistic for Delhi from Rakesh K. Sinha, "New Delhi: The World's Shanty Capital in the Making," *OneWorld South Asia*, August 26, 2003.

59. Harvey Herr and Guenter Karl, "Estimating Global Slum Dwellers: Monitoring the Millennium Development Goal 7, Target 11," working paper (Nairobi: UN-HABITAT, 2003), p. 19.

60. Gordon Brown, quoted in *Los Angeles Times,* October 4, 2004.

61. UN statistics, quoted in John Vidal, "Cities Are Now the Frontline of Poverty," *Guardian,* February 2, 2005.

Chapter 17

1. An excellent NASA image of Earth at night can be found at http://apod.nasa.gov/apod/apoo1127.html.

2. The use of satellite imagery and remote sensing has opened a new dimension of scholarship in the study of cities. No single remote-sensing methodology has yet been established as a standard for measuring the cityscape, but a general consensus exists that the described light patterns are one of the primary indictors of urbanized terrain. Measurement of the density of light, in particular, is an established proxy used to measure the geography of urbanized territories. See Mark R. Montgomery, "The Urban Transformation of the Developing World," *Science* 319 (February 8, 2008): 761–64. Among a number of research endeavors recently established to document and model the land areas and growth patterns of cities worldwide, the tri-university research project managed by the University of Connecticut's Center for Land Use Education and Research (CLEAR) offers the fullest data set. This study, as well as the research of Karen Seto of the Center for Environmental Studies and Policy at Stanford University, uses land cover data and not visible surface light to determine urbanized area. Seto's work uses infrared photography to distinguish different land covers. The CLEAR Project clusters micro (pixel-level) data from daytime imagery into fifty different land-type clusters and then sorts these into urban and nonurban land uses. In an interview for this report, Seto noted that visible light intensity is also used as an accepted technical measure of urbanized area, particularly for industrialized countries, although it is a more accurate measure of energy intensity. In higher income, industrialized countries, she explains, the intensity of light creates a "bloom effect," or glow, that extends beyond the actual land area from which the light is emanating. This has to be corrected for in measuring urbanized area in these countries. Conversely, in lower-income developing countries there may be urbanized areas with low energy intensity and little light marker.

3. "Funding the 'Final War': LTTE Intimidation and Extortion in the Tamil Diaspora," *Human Rights Watch* 18, no. 1 (March 14, 2006). http://www.hrw.org/reports/2006/ltte0306/ltte0306webwcover.pdf (accessed December 27, 2013).

4. See C. A. Schubert, I. K. Barker, R. C. Rosatte, and C. D. MacInnes, "Density, Dispersion, Movements and Habitat Preference of Skunks (*Mephitis mephitis*)and Raccoons

(*Procyon lotor*) in Metropolitan Toronto," in D. R. McCollough and R. Barrett (eds.), *Wildlife 2001: Populations* (London: Elsevier Science, 1992), 932–44.

5. A. D. Tomlin, "The Earthworm Bait Market in North America," in J. E. Satchell (ed.), *Earthworm Ecology* (London: Chapman and Hall, 1983), 331–38. http://sci.agr.ca/london/faq/tomlinoi_e.htm (accessed September 2007).

Chapter 18

1. Literally, herder of chickens, "pollo" being the colloquial term among guides for migrant clients. Smugglers also are referred to as "coyotes" in media accounts and by U.S. public officials.

2. Said Minuteman co-founder Simcox after the 2005 arrests of No More Deaths patrollers Daniel Strauss and Shanti Sellz, "I think once and for all, hopefully, this will be a deterrent to break up this underground railroad" (Mendoza 2006).

3. Honduras reported a GDP per capita of US $3,796 in 2007, while nearly 30 percent of its more than 6 million people were subsisting on less than $2 per day in U.S. purchasing power parity (United Nations Human Development Report 2009).

4. For example, in Western Europe, the Platform for International Cooperation on Undocumented Migrants (PICUM) has organized a range of NGO conferences and related events to promote migrant rights (www.picum.org).

5. Article 25(1): Everyone has the right to a standard of living adequate for the health and well-being of himself and of his family, including food, clothing, housing and medical care and necessary social services, and the right to security in the event of unemployment, sickness, disability, widowhood, old age or other lack of livelihood in circumstances beyond his control. Article 28: Everyone is entitled to a social and international order in which the rights and freedoms set forth in this Declaration can be fully realized.

6. The First Optional Protocol of the UN Civil and Political Rights covenant does offer individuals the right to file a complaint directly to the Human Rights Committee of the covenant after they have exhausted all domestic remedies. The Committee does not have formal compliance powers, however (Camp Keith 1999; see Neumayer 2005).

Chapter 19

1. *Global warming* refers to the overall increase in average global temperature, but also involves complex changes to the planet's climatic systems. We use the terms *global warming* and *climate change* interchangeably in this chapter to mean anthropogenic (i.e., human-induced) changes in climatic conditions.

2. See http://keelingcurve.ucsd.edu.

3. See Michael C. MacCracken, Frances Moore, and John C. Topping (eds.), *Sudden and Disruptive Climate Change* (London: Earthscan Books, 2008), especially the chapter by Barry A. Pittock, "Ten Reasons Why Climate Change May Be More Severe than Projected," 11–28.

4. Jos G. J. Oliver, Greet Janssens-Maenhout, and Jeroan A. H. W. Peters, *Trends in Global CO_2 Emissions; 2012 Report* (The Hague: PBL Netherlands Environmental Assessment Agency; Ispra: Joint Research Centre, 2012), 18.

5. Hans J. Schellnhuber, Wolfgang Cramer, Nebojsa Nakicenovic, Tom Wigley, and Gary Yohe, *Avoiding Dangerous Climate Change* (Cambridge: Cambridge University Press, 2006); WGBU (German Advisory Council on Global Change), *Solving the Climate Dilemma: The Budget Approach* (Berlin: German Advisory Council on Global Change, 2009); and Malte Meinshausen, N. Mein-shausen, William Hare, S. C. B. Raper,

K. Frieler, R. Knutti, Dave J. Frame, and M. R. Allen, "Greenhouse-Gas Emission Targets for Limiting Global Warming to 2°C," *Nature* 458 (2009): 1158–62, doi: 10.1038/nature08017.

6. IPCC, *Managing the Risks of Extreme Events and Disasters to Advance Climate Change Adaptation—A Special Report of Working Groups I and II of the Intergovernmental Panel on Climate Change. Summary for Policymakers* (Cambridge: Cambridge University Press, 2012), 1–19; Jean-Pierre Gattuso and Lina Hansson (eds.), *Ocean Acidification* (Oxford and New York: Oxford University Press, 2011); and NAS (National Academy of Sciences, U.S.), *Ocean Acidification: A National Strategy to Meet the Challenges of a Changing Ocean* (Washington, DC: National Academy of Sciences Press, 2010).

7. John Houghton, "Global warming is now a weapon of mass destruction: It kills more people than terrorism, yet Blair and Bush do nothing," *The Guardian*, July 28, 2003.

8. National Climatic Data Center, "Global Analysis—Annual 2012." At www.ncdc.noaa.gov/sotc/global/2012/13 (accessed 17 April 2013).

9. Christopher C. Burt, "Weather Extremes," January 2, 2013. At www.wunderground.com/blog/weatherhistorian/comment.html?entrynum=112.

10. National Oceanic and Atmospheric Administration, "Arctic Report Card: Update for 2012." At www.arctic.noaa.gov/reportcard/ (accessed 14 January 2013).

11. Australian Government, Bureau of Meteorology, "Australia in Summer 2012–2013." At www.bom.gov.au/climate/current/season/aus/summary.shtml (accessed 17 April 2013).

12. Janet Larsen and Sara Rasmussen, "2011—A Year of Weather Extremes, with More to Come," February 1, 2012 (IPS). This article was originally published by the Earth Policy Institute. Data and additional resources at www.earth-policy.org.

13. World Bank, *Turn Down the Heat: Why a 4C Warmer World Must Be Avoided, A Report for the World Bank by the Potsdam Institute for Climate Impact Research and Climate Analytics* (Washington, DC: World Bank, 2012), xiii. At climatechange.worldbank.org/sites/default/files/Turn_Down_the_heat_Why_a_4_degree_centrigrade_warmer_world_must_be_avoided.pdf.

14. David D. Zhang, Harry F. Lee, Cong Wang, Baosheng Li, Qing Pei, Jane Zhang, and Yulun An, "The Causality Analysis of Climate Change and Long-Term Human Crisis," *PNAS Early Edition* (2012). www.pnas.org/cgi/ doi/10.1073/pnas.1104268108 (accessed February 12, 2012).

15. Karl Marx and Friedrich Engels, *The Manifesto of the Communist Party* (London: Penguin Books, 1967 [1848]).

16. John Hatcher, *Before 1700: Towards the Age of Coal,* The History of the British Coal Industry, Volume 1 (Oxford: Oxford University Press, 1993), 55; E. A. Wrigley, *Continuity, Chance and Change: The Character of the Industrial Revolution in England* (Cambridge: Cambridge University Press, 1988), 54.

17. Barbara Freese, *Coal: A Human History* (London and New York: Penguin Books, 2003), 95.

18. Michael W. Flinn, *History of the British Coal Industry: Volume 2. 1700–1830: The Industrial Revolution,* (Oxford: Oxford University Press, 1984), 442.

19. Carl N. Degler, *The Age of the Economic Revolution 1876–1900* (Glenview: Scott Foresman, 1977), 29; S. H. Schurr, B. C. Netschert, V. F. Eliasberg, J. Lerner, and H. H. Landsberg, *Energy in the American Economy* (Baltimore: Johns Hopkins Press, 1960), 69, quoted in Barbara Freese, *Coal,* 137.

20. Industrial and domestic coal use became so intensive in certain cities that it contributed to heavy, sometimes life-threatening, smogs in major Victorian cities like London and

Manchester, and in the United States in Pittsburgh and Chicago. By the late nineteenth century, new "smoke abatement" laws and regulations to govern industrial air pollution were being implemented in these places as part of a general response to public pressure to make cities healthy and livable spaces. These innovations provided early models of pollution control that were communicated and copied internationally as similar problems emerged in industrializing countries worldwide in the nineteenth and twentieth centuries. See Freese, *Coal*, 73.

21. See: www.eia.gov/countries/cab.cfm?fips=CH.

22. U.S. Department of Energy (US DoE), *Transportation Energy Data Book*. At cta.ornl .gov/data/chapter8.shtml.

23. OICA (International Organization of Motor Vehicle Manufacturers), *OICA Production Statistics 2012*. At oica.net/category/production-statistics/ (accessed April 12, 2013).

24. See Thomas Princen, "Leave It in the Ground: The Politics and Ethics of Fossil Fuels and Global Disruption." Paper presented at the International Studies Association annual conference, Montreal, March 16–19, 2011.

25. IEA (International Energy Agency), *Oil Market Report*, June 13, 2012. At homrpublic .iea.org/archiveresults.asp?formsection=full+issue&formdate= 2012&Submit=Submit.

26. William Watson, Nicholas Paduano, Tejasvi Raghuveer, and Sundar Thapa, *U.S. Coal Supply and Demand: 2010 Year in Review* (Washington, DC: U.S. Energy Information Administration, 2011). At 205.254.135.7/coal/review/pdf/feature10.pdf (accessed June 20, 2012).

27. Michael Klare, *Blood and Oil* (New York: Metropolitan Books, 2004), xiii–xiv. See also Matthew Paterson, *Automobile Politics: Ecology and Cultural Political Economy* (Cambridge: Cambridge University Press, 2007).

28. Simon Bromley, *American Hegemony and World Oil* (Cambridge: Cambridge University Press, 1991); Simon Bromley, "The United States and the Control of World Oil," *Government and Opposition* 40, no. 2 (2005): 225–55.

29. U.S. Energy Information Administration, *Annual Energy Outlook 2013*. At www.eia .gov/forecasts/aeo/lF_all.cfm#petroleum_import (accessed April 18, 2013).

30. Zhe Daojiong, "China's Energy Security and Its International Relations." Paper presented at the Third IISS Global Strategic Review, Geneva, September 16–18, 2005. At www.silkroadstudies.org/new/docs/CEF/Zha_Daojiong.pdf.

31. IEA, World Energy Outlook, "Energy Subsidies" (2012). At www.worldenergyoutlook .org/subsidies.asp.

32. T. A. Boden, G. Marland, and R. J. Andres, *Global, Regional, and National Fossil-Fuel CO_2 Emissions* (Oak Ridge, TN: Carbon Dioxide Information Analysis Center, Oak Ridge National Laboratory, U.S. Department of Energy, 2011). doi: 10.3334/ CDIAC/00001_V2011.

33. R. A. Houghton, "The Annual Flux of Carbon to the Atmosphere from Changes in Land Use 1850–1990," *Tellus* 51b (1999): 298–313.

34. T. Barker et al., "Contribution of Working Group III to the Fourth Assessment Report of the Intergovernmental Panel on Climate Change: Technical Summary," in B. Metz, O. R. Davidson, P. R. Bosch, R. Dave, and L. A. Meyer (eds.), *Climate Change 2007: Mitigation of Climate Change* (Cambridge: Cambridge University Press, 2007), 27. The authors also noted that "these figures should be seen as indicative, as some uncertainty remains, particularly with regards to CH4 [methane] and N20 [nitrous oxide] emissions (error margin estimated to be in the order of 30–50%) and CO_2 emissions from agriculture and forestry with an even higher error margin."

35. Barker et al., "Technical Summary," 27.

36. See Paul N. Edwards, *A Vast Machine: Computer Models, Climate Data, and the Politics of Global Warming* (Cambridge, MA: MIT Press, 2010).

37. See, for instance, Tim Flannery, *The Weather Makers: How Man Is Changing the Climate and What It Means for Life on Earth* (Melbourne: Text Publishing, 2005); James Roger Fleming, *Historical Perspectives on Climate Change* (Oxford: Oxford University Press, 1998); and Spencer R. Weart, *The Discovery of Global Warming* (Cambridge, MA: Harvard University Press, 2003).

38. For instance, in 1784 Montesquieu wrote, "We have already observed that great heat enervates the strength and courage of men, and that in cold climates they have a certain vigor of body and mind which renders them capable of long, painful, great and intrepid actions" (quoted in Fleming, *Historical Perspectives,* 16).

39. See Jan Golinski, *British Weather and the Climate of the Enlightenment* (Chicago: University of Chicago Press, 2007).

40. Fleming, *Historical Perspectives,* 41 and 44.

41. Svante Arrhenius, "On the Influence of Carbonic Acid in the Air upon the Temperature of the Ground," *Philosophical Magazine* 5, no. 41 (1896): 237–76.

42. Arrhenius's predicted 4 degrees Celsius increase is remarkably close to more recent predictions by the Intergovernmental Panel on Climate Change. However, many would argue that this was merely a coincidental outcome, given the crudeness of Arrhenius's underlying model. See Svante Arrhenius, *Worlds in the Making: The Evolution of the Universe* (New York: Harper and Brothers, 1908), 52.

43. G. S. Callendar, "The Artificial Production of Carbon Dioxide and Its Influence on the Atmosphere," *Quarterly Journal of the Royal Meteorological Society* 64 (1938): 223–40.

44. Like Arrhenius before him, Callendar welcomed this change as a potential benefit to humanity, increasing plant growth and the northern extension of agriculture, and possibly delaying a new Ice Age. See G. S. Callendar, "The Composition of the Atmosphere through the Ages," *The Meteorological Magazine* 74, no. 878 (March 1939).

45. Gilbert N. Plass, "Effects of Carbon Dioxide Variation on Climate," *American Journal of Physics* 24, no. 5 (1956): 377–80.

46. Plass, "Effects of Carbon Dioxide Variation," 387.

47. Roger Revelle and Hans E. Suess, "Carbon Dioxide Exchange between Atmosphere and Ocean and the Question of an Increase of Atmospheric CO_2 during the Past Decades," *Tellus* 9, no. 1 (1957): 19.

48. An additional comment can be made about how evolving technological capacities contributed to the development of this global scientific narrative about climate. From the 1950s onward, technological developments in the capacity to survey the planet and to manipulate data—through the advent and use of satellites and the development of computers with the capacity to run elaborate climatic models—enabled the articulation of complex climate scenarios based around an increasing number of interactive factors. These developments were also influenced by the tensions of the Cold War. Concerns were raised in the 1960s about the use of weather as a weapon and about climatic implications for national security. Artificial satellites were quickly used to generate new knowledge of planetary atmospheric, terrestrial, and marine conditions. They were simultaneously contributors to a fierce ideological and technological struggle for supremacy between the leading states of the capitalist and socialist worlds—signaled, for instance, by the launch of the world's first satellite, the Russian Sputnik 1, as part of the International Geophysical Year in 1957. The United States launched its first

meteorological satellite, TIROS 1, on April 1, 1960, and its first successful photo-reconnaissance satellite, Discovery 14, in August that year. The first results of a general circulation model (GCM) were presented in 1975, and the first GISS global temperature analysis was published in 1981, analyzing surface temperatures at meteorological stations from 1880 to 1985. As Edwards notes, full global consolidation of technical work on climate change did not really begin until 1992, with the establishment of the Global Climate Observing System, created to support the UN Framework Convention on Climate Change (see Edwards, *A Vast Machine*, 15).

49. EPP (Environmental Pollution Panel), *Restoring the Quality of Our Environment*, report of President's Science Advisory Committee (Washington, DC: U.S. Government Printing Office, 1965).

50. NAS (National Academy of Sciences, U.S.), *Weather and Climate Modification Problems and Prospects*, vol. 1, final report of the Panel on Weather and Climate Modification, NAS-NRC Publication 1350 (Washington, DC: NAS Press, 1966).

51. NAS (National Academy of Sciences, U.S.), *Energy and Climate*, Geophysical Study Committee (Washington, DC: NAS Press, 1977).

52. NAS (National Academy of Sciences, U.S.), *Carbon Dioxide and Climate: A Scientific Assessment*, Report of an Ad Hoc Study Group on Carbon Dioxide and Climate, Woods Hole, Massachusetts, July 23–27, 1979 (Washington DC: National Academy of Sciences, 1979).

53. Council on Environmental Quality, cited in Bert Bolin, *A History of the Science and Politics of Climate Change: The Role of the Intergovernmental Panel on Climate Change* (Cambridge: Cambridge University Press, 2007), 34.

54. World Meteorological Organization, *Report of the International Conference on the Assessment of the Role of Carbon Dioxide and of Other Greenhouse Gases in Climate Variations and Associated Impacts*, Villach, Austria, October 9–15, 1985, WMO no. 661. At www.scopenvironment.org/downloadpubs/scope29/statement.html.

55. Cited in Bolin, *A History of the Science and Politics of Climate Change*, 40.

56. IPCC (Intergovernmental Panel on Climate Change), *Principles Governing IPCC Work* (1988). At www.ipcc.ch/pdf/ipcc-principles/ipcc-principles. pdf (accessed February 17, 2012).

57. While Fleming (*Historical Perspectives*, 118 and 131) suggests that "global warming was on the public agenda in the late 1940s and early 1950s," its occasional mentions in the popular press in the 1950s do not compare with the high salience of climate debate in the late 1980s.

58. Philip Shabecoff, "Global Warming Has Begun, Expert Tells Senate," *New York Times*, June 24, 1988.

59. www.climatenetwork.org/about/about-can.

60. See, for example, Peter Newell and Matthew Paterson, "A Climate for Business: Global Warming, the State and Capital," *Review of International Political Economy* 5, no. 4 (1998): 679–704; and David Levy and Peter Newell (eds.), *The Business of Global Environmental Governance* (Cambridge, MA: MIT Press, 2005).

61. See, for example, Aaron M. McCright and Riley E. Dunlap, "Anti-reflexivity: The American Conservative Movement's Success in Undermining Climate Science and Policy," *Theory, Culture & Society* 27, no. 2–3 (2010): 100–133; Naomi Oreskes and Erik Conway, *Merchants of Doubt* (New York: Bloomsbury Press, 2010); and Riley E. Dunlap and Aaron M. McCright, "Organized Climate Change Denial," in J. S. Dryzek, R. B. Norgaard, and D. Schlosberg (eds.), *The Oxford Handbook of Climate Change and Society* (Oxford: Oxford University Press, 2011), 144–60.

62. Jules Boykoff and Maxwell Boykoff, "Balance as Bias: Global Warming and the U.S. Prestige Press," *Global Environmental Change* 15, no. 2 (2004): 125–36.

63. Naomi Oreskes, "Beyond the Ivory Tower: The Scientific Consensus on Climate Change," *Science* 306, no. 5702 (2004): 1686. doi: 10.1126/science.1103618. PMID 15576594.

64. Nicholas Stern, *The Economics of Climate Change: The Stem Review* (Cambridge: Cambridge University Press, 2007); Ross Garnaut, *The Garnaut Climate Change Review* (Cambridge: Cambridge University Press, 2008). However, significant trans-Atlantic differences have emerged over the construction of economic cost-benefit analyses and appropriate discount rates.

65. The complete list of Umbrella Group members are the United States, Canada, Australia, Norway, Iceland, Japan, the Russian Federation, and Ukraine. This group evolved out of an alliance known as JUSCANZ, made up of Japan, the United States, Canada, Australia, and New Zealand.

66. See, for instance, Harriet Bulkeley and Peter Newell, *Governing Climate Change* (London: Routledge, 2010).

67. Mathew J. Hoffman, *Ozone Depletion and Climate Change: Constructing a Global Response* (Albany: State University of New York Press, 2005), 120.

68. *United Nations Framework Convention on Climate Change,* United Nations, 1992. FCCC/1NFORMAL/84 GE.05-62220 (E) 200705. At unfccc.int/resource/docs/convkp/conveng.pdf.

69. *The Rio Declaration on Environment and Development* (1992). At www.unesco.org/education/information/nfsunesco/pdf/RIO_E.PDF.

70. UNFCCC, Article 3(1). The convention also acknowledges the development needs, and the special vulnerability to climate change, of developing countries (Preamble, Article 3(2), 3(3), and 4(5)). In terms of specific commitments, Article 4(2) (a) requires developed countries to undertake policies and measures that demonstrate that they are taking the lead in reducing emissions. Article 4(3) also requires them to provide the financial resources (including technology transfer) to enable developing countries to meet their commitments. The principle of CBDR was also articulated in Principle 7 of the Rio Declaration.

71. UNFCCC, Article 4(2)(a).

72. UNFCCC, Article 4(2) and Article 12(1).

73. The Kyoto Protocol to the United Nations Convention on Climate Change, United Nations, 1998. At unfccc.int/resource/docs/convkp/kpeng.pdf.

74. The Byrd–Hagel Resolution was passed unanimously (95–0) by the U.S. Senate on July 25, 1997, during the 105th Congress. When the U.S. Senate rejected the protocol, it argued that the KP was contrary to the United States' national economic interest and was environmentally flawed—its exemption for developing country parties being seen as inconsistent with the need for global action on climate change.

75. The United States—then clearly the world's biggest GHG emitter—objected that developing countries such as China and India had made no commitment to reduce their emissions despite the prospect of them becoming significant aggregate GHG contributors over coming decades.

76. Joanna Depledge, "Against the Grain: The United States and the Global Climate Change Regime," *Global Change, Peace and Security* 17, no. 1 (2005): 11–28.

77. Peter Christoff, "From Global Citizen to Renegade State: Australia at Kyoto," *Arena Journal* 10 (1998): 113–28.

78. At the 2005 World Economic Forum, twenty-three multinational corporations, including British Airways, BP, Ford, Toyota, and Unilever, formed the G8 Climate Change

Roundtable Group. In June 2005, the group published a statement affirming the need for action on climate change and stressing the importance of market-based solutions. It called on governments to establish "clear, transparent, and consistent price signals" through a long-term policy framework that would include all major producers of GHGs. At www.weforum.org/pdf/g8_climatechange.pdf.

79. UNFCCC, *The Benefits of the Clean Development Mechanism* (2011), 5. At cdm.unfccc.int/about/dev_ben/pg1.pdf.

80. At cdm.unfccc.int/Statistics/index.html.

81. UNFCCC, *The Benefits of the Clean Development Mechanism*, 6.

82. See Matthew Paterson, "Selling Carbon: From International Climate Regime to Global Carbon Market," in J. S. Dryzek, R. B. Norgaard, and D. Schlosberg (eds.), *The Oxford Handbook of Climate Change and Society* (Oxford: Oxford University Press, 2011), 616; and UNFCCC, *The Benefits of the Clean Development Mechanism*.

83. Andre Kossoy and Pierre Guinon, *The State and Trends of the Carbon Market 2012* (Washington, DC: World Bank, 2012).

84. Ibid.

85. Netherlands Environmental Assessment Agency, "China Now No. 1 in CO_2 Emission; USA in Second Position." At www.pbl.nl/en/dossiers/Climat-echange/moreinfo/China nownolinCO2emissionsUSAinsecondposition.

86. The Copenhagen Accord, *Report of the Conference of the Parties on Its Fifteenth Session, Held in Copenhagen from 7 to 19 December 2009 Addendum Part Two: Action Taken by the Conference of the Parties at Its Fifteenth Session*, Decision 2/CP.15 (2009). At unfccc.int/resource/docs/2009/cop15/eng/lla01.pdf.

87. See also Peter Christoff, "Cold Climate in Copenhagen: China and the United States at COP15," *Environmental Politics* 19, no. 4 (2010): 637–56.

88. Draft decision -/CP.17, Establishment of an Ad Hoc Working Group on the Durban Platform for Enhanced Action (advanced unedited version). At unfccc.int/files/meetings/durban_nov_2011/decisions/application/pdf/cop17_durbanplatform.pdf.

89. Editorial, "The Mask Slips," *Nature* 480, no. 292 (December 14, 2011).

Chapter 20

1. H. Damon Matthews and Andrew J. Weaver, "Committed Climate Warming," *Nature Geoscience* 3 (2010): 142–43.

2. Steven J. Davis, Ken Caldeira, and H. Damon Matthews, "Future CO_2 Emissions and Climate Change from Existing Energy Infrastructure," *Science* 328, no. 5997 (September 2010): 1330–33.

3. Economic History Association, website, http://eh.net/encyclopedia/article/tassava.WWII.

4. Robert G. Ferguson, "One Thousand Planes a Day: Ford, Grumman, General Motors and the Arsenal of Democracy," *History and Technology* 21 (2005): 149.

5. World Resources Institute, Climate Analysis Indicators Tool, available at http://cait.wri.org/cait.php?page=yearly (accessed May 11, 2009). These percentages are based on 2005 emissions, excluding Land Use, Land Use Change, and Forestry.

6. We ran our assumed emission scenario (along with an IPCC "business as usual" scenario) through the C-ROADS model with the kind help of Lori Siegel. See T. Fiddaman, L. Siegel, E. Sawin, A. Jones, and J. Sterman, *2009: C-ROADS Simulator Reference Guide*, Ventana Systems, Sustainability Institute, and MIT Sloan School of Management, www.climateinteractive.org.

7. McKinsey & Co., *Pathways to a Low-Carbon Economy* (2009), shows how for every year of delay, the peak atmospheric concentration of CO_2e could be expected to be

5 ppm higher for the same level of action. Available at http://www.mckinsey.com/clientservice/ccsi/. Stern also argues the economic value case for "strong and early action" in Nicholas Stern, *Executive Summary, Stern Review on the Economics of Climate Change,* 2006. Available at http://www.sternreview.org.uk/.

8. Dollars or euros per ton of CO_2e is a measure of the estimated cost to take actions to achieve a ton of CO_2e reduction. The McKinsey study referred to categorized various actions (for instance, energy efficiency, nuclear power, solar panels, auto efficiency) into various cost categories.

9. See The Prince's Rainforests Project, *An Emergency Package for Tropical Forests,* March 2009, http://princes.3cdn.net/7052d2e7f785f953cc_uvm6vtxpe.pdf (accessed December 30, 2013).

10. In this chapter we assume there will be some six thousand major power plants in operation in 2018 (against some five thousand today). We assume that one thousand of these are closed down during the C-war in 2018–2023 (reducing emissions by 5 $GtCO_2e$/yr) and that a further one thousand plants will be retrofitted with CCS equipment (reducing emissions by a further 2 $GtCO_2e$ by 2023). A big CCS plant sequesters on average 2 $MtCO_2$/yr—roughly 1 in a gas-fired utility and roughly 3 in a coal-fired utility.

11. CCS refers to various technologies designed to capture the carbon emitted from burning coal in power plants, then concentrating it and transporting it to underground basins, where it can be locked up indefinitely.

12. See http://www.desertec.org.

13. See Mark Z. Jacobson and Mark A. Delucchi, (November 2009) "A Plan to Power 100 Percent of the Planet with Renewables," *Scientific American* 301, no. 5 (November 2009): 58–65, which summarizes their full study.

14. See V. R. Cardozier, *The Mobilization of the United States in World War II: How the Government, Military and Industry Prepared for War,* especially chapter 10 (Jefferson, NC: McFarland, 1995).

15. Jorgen Randers and Paul Gilding, "The One Degree War Plan," *Journal of Global Responsibility* 1, no. 1 (2010): 170–88.

Credits

Chapter 1
Reprinted in the UK and rest of world excluding North America, from *Global Civil Society* by Mary Kaldor (ISBN 9780745627571), with permission from Polity Press, Cambridge, UK.

Chapter 2
From: "Framing Global Governance, Five Gaps," in *Thinking About Global Governance: Why People and Ideas Matter*, Ramesh Thakur and Thomas G. Weiss, Copyright © 2011 Taylor & Francis. Reproduced by permission of Taylor & Francis Books UK.

Chapter 3
The Oxford Handbook of Political Ideologies edited by Freeden, Sargent, and Stears (2013). Chp. "Political Ideologies in the Age of Globalization" pages 214–231. By permission of Oxford University Press.

Chapter 4
Jackie Smith, et al., "Globalization and the Emergence of World Social Forums," in *Global Democracy and the World Social Forums* (Boulder: Paradigm, 2007), pages 1–25, 147. Reprinted by permission of Paradigm Publishers.

Chapter 5
Hans Schattle, "Global Media, Mobilization, and Revolution: The Arab Spring," in *Globalization & Citizenship* (Lanham: Rowman and Littlefield Publishers, 2012), pages 27–51, 54–58, 178–183. Reprinted by permission of Rowman & Littlefield Publishers, Inc.

Chapter 6
The Travels of a T-Shirt in the Global Economy: An Economist Examines the Markets, Power, and Politics of World Trade, Pietra Rivoli. Copyright © 2009 John Wiley & Sons, Inc. Reproduced with permission of John Wiley & Sons, Inc.

Chapter 7

Moghadam, Valentine M. *Globalizing Women: Transnational Feminist Networks,* pages 191–201, 226. © 2005 Johns Hopkins University Press. Reprinted with permission of Johns Hopkins University Press.

Chapter 8

From *The Globalization Paradox: Democracy and the Future of the World Economy* by Dani Rodrik. Copyright © 2011 by Dani Rodrik. Used by permission of W.W. Norton & Company, Inc.

Chapter 9

COMMUNICATION POWER Second Edition by Castells (2009) Chp. "The Global Network Society" pages 24–29. By permission of Oxford University Press.

Chapter 10

The Googlization of Everything: (And Why We Should Worry), by Said Vaidhyanathan, © 2011 by Said Vaidhyanathan. Published by the University of California Press.

Chapter 11

William H. McNeill, "Globalization: Long Term Process or New Era in Human Affairs?" *New Global Studies,* Volume 2, Issue 1, pages 1–9 (2008). Reprinted by permission of Walter de Gruyter GmbH.

Chapter 12

Nayan Chanda, "Slaves, Germs, and Trojan Horses," in *Bound Together: How Traders, Preachers, Adventurers, and Warriors Shaped Globalization* (New Haven: Yale University Press, 2007); pages 209–243, 360–64. Reprinted by permission of Yale University Press.

Chapter 13

Reproduced by permission of SAGE Publications, London, Los Angeles, New Delhi and Singapore, from Richard Giulianotti and Roland Robertson, *Globalization and Football,* Copyright © SAGE Publications, 2009.

Chapter 14

Lane Crothers, "The American Global Cultural Brand," in *Globalization and American Popular Culture 3rd Edition* (Lanham: Rowman & Littlefield, 2012), pages 133–161, 176–178. Reprinted by permission of Rowman & Littlefield Publishers, Inc.

Chapter 15

Olivier Roy, "The Religion Market" in *Holy Ignorance* (London: C. Hurst & Co. Publishers Ltd, 2010), pages 159–85, 247–50. Reprinted by permission of C. Hurst & Co. Publishers Ltd.

Chapter 16

Mike Davis, "The Urban Climacteric," in *Planet of Slums* (London: Verso, 2006), pages 1–19. Reprinted by permission of Verso Books.

Chapter 17

From *Welcome to the Urban Revolution: How Cities Are Changing the World* by Jeb Brugmann. Copyright © Jeb Brugmann, 2009. Reprinted by permission of Penguin Canada Books Inc. © Jeb Brugmann, 2009, *Welcome to the Urban Revolution*, Bloomsbury Publishing Inc.

Chapter 18

Copyright © 2010 Luis Cabrera. Reprinted with the permission of Cambridge University Press.

Chapter 19

Peter Christoff and Robyn Eckersley, "An Overheated Planet," in *Globalization & the Environment* (Lanham: Rowman & Littlefield Publishers, 2013), pages 71–110, 217–225. Reprinted by permission of Rowman & Littlefield Publishers, Inc.

Chapter 20

© Paul Gilding, 2011, *The Great Disruption*, Bloomsbury Publishing Inc.

Index

Note: page numbers followed by *f* and *t* refer to figures and tables respectively; those followed by n refer to notes, with note number.